the Commissionaires

AN ORGANIZATION WITH A PROUD HISTORY

1925 - 1998

Edited by
JOHN GARDAM, OMM, MSM, CD, BA

Foreword
Patron
His Excellency The Right Honourable
ROMÉO LEBLANC, PC, CC, CMM, CD
Governor General of Canada

Published by

GENERAL STORE PUBLISHING HOUSE

1 Main Street Burnstown, Ontario, Canada K0J 1G0
Telephone (613) 432-7697 or 1-800-465-6072

ISBN 1-896182-88-7
Printed and bound in Canada

Layout and cover design by Derek McEwen

General Store Publishing House
Burnstown, Ontario, Canada

No part of this book may be reproduced, stored in a retrieval system or transmitted in any form or by any means, without the prior written permission of the publisher or, in case of photocopying or other reprographic copying, a licence from CANCOPY (Canadian Copyright Licensing Agency), 6 Adelaide Street East, Suite 900, Toronto, Ontario, M5C 1H6.

Canadian Cataloguing in Publication Data

Main entry under title:
    The Commissionaires : an organization with a proud history

ISBN 1-896182-88-7

    1. Canadian Corps of Commissionaires – History
    2. Veterans – Canada – Anecdotes. I. Gardam, John, 1931 -

UB359.C2C65 1998   331.5'2'06071   C98-900389-2

First Printing 1998

Foreword

RIDEAU HALL
OTTAWA

LE GOUVERNEUR GENERAL
THE GOVERNOR GENERAL

As Patron of the Canadian Corps of Commissionaires, it gives me great pleasure to contribute to their first official history.

At Rideau Hall, I am honoured to have members of the Ottawa Division fulfil the function of security guards. I see them at work on a daily basis and admire their dedication and skill.

The picture of Canada's tenth Governor General, the **Duke of Connaught (1911-1916)** has been included on this page. In 1915, the **Duke of Connaught** wrote to the President of the Military Hospital Commission suggesting that "the formation of an organization similar to the Corps of Commissionaires of Great Britain should be considered." Although it was ten years later that a Canadian Corps was organized, I take pride in thinking that the Duke of Connaught had vision to make that first proposal.

This book is truly a story that touches all of Canada, for the Corps has detachments on duty from Cape Spear, Newfoundland to Vancouver Island in British Columbia. The eighteen chapters, which tell the story of every Division, large or small, cover the entire nation.

I congratulate John Gardam, who has put a human face on the Corps. The tales and the achievements of the men and women who are part of the Commissionaires have been recorded at last. Governors who have freely given of their time and, in certain cases, money to create the Corps have not been forgotten. This is indeed a chronicle deserving of the nation's respect and admiration.

The Corps has every reason to be proud of its history. Its services throughout Canada are exemplary and I know it will continue to contribute to our society for many years to come.

Roméo LeBlanc

Their Excellencies with Members of the Ottawa Division.

Editor's Preface

In this preface I will explain the subject and scope of the history of the Canadian Corps of Commissionaires.

The Corps has been in existence in Canada since 1925, seventy-three years spanning the Second World War, the Korean War and countless peacekeeping operations. These military events produced over a million Canadians with wartime experience and hundreds of thousands with postwar experience. It is these people, who have joined the Corps. This book is all about the men and women who served or are still serving in the Corps.

My first contact with the Corps was through my late father who joined the Victoria and Vancouver Island Division as a night watchman at the harbour. The Corps provided him with a sense of purpose, some cash and most important, despite his First World War wounds, he was able to do the job. My experience with the Corps has convinced me that from sea to sea across Canada, the Corps continues to provide that same vital need for our members in so many capacities.

When René Gutknecht, the Executive Secretary (from 1991 to 1997) asked if I would consider writing the history in June 1996, my first thought was negative, for I was busy writing another book on oral history of Canadians at War.

As I travelled all ten provinces, I found that the two hurdles to be mastered were firstly, getting non-historians with poor archives, and in some cases none at all, to become writers. Secondly, getting people to think about the past when their every moment was being spent looking at the future. As the reader will see, the book does do justice to all eighteen divisional stories. Paramount in each division is the struggle to get started. The task of finding work for veterans, the surge of Second World War veterans in 1945, but above all else, devotion to duty on behalf of the men and women who put on the Corps uniform is an ongoing saga.

Governors from across the land worked so hard to keep the spirit of the Corps alive, to keep Commissionaires working in a myriad of jobs. Some lives were lost whilst on duty, but the spirit gained in war or next to war rose to every occasion in the workplace. The Commissionaires put "service before self" as he, or she, had been taught whilst in a service or RCMP uniform. The chapters which follow show ample examples of "where training and devotion to duty conquers all."

The Canadian Corps of Commissionaires jealously guard their heritage. Their past and present performance is confirmed on every page of this book. They have every reason to be proud, for their standard is second to none in the whole business of providing a service that is unbeatable in Canada.

Who are Commissionaires?

Have you ever stopped to think about or maybe say a prayer,
For those who wear black uniforms and are called "Commissionaire?"
You'll find them at "historic sites" or maybe in a bank,
Collecting tolls out on some bridge or in some place damp and dank.
Or maybe in some theatre gag, where light and life abounds,
Or punching a clock all through the night as they make appointed "rounds."

Who are these people? From where did they come? What are they doing there?
How come they seldom have a name but are called "Commissionaire?"
Short days ago, we have heard it said, when they were fair and young,
They served in Canada's Forces when the battle hymns were sung.
But now they are a little older and perhaps some can't find a place,
In the "outside world of commerce" known now as "the old rat race."

It may have been in the Navy, the Army or in the Air,
In which they earned the medals for the tunics that they wear.
But now that's all behind them; Old rivalries are gone,
For in the "Corps of Commissionaires" all "Elements" are one.
Oh, They may have been an "Officer," a "Soldier" or a "Man,"
But now that doesn't mean a thing, each does the best he can.

So now when you see black uniforms, perhaps you'll understand
They're not some foreign Forces, nor the members of some band.
But honest, hard working Canadians who are trying to help themselves,
Instead of just shining medals which they have put away on the shelves.
Now if you get to Heaven and Saint Peter isn't there,
Don't be surprised if at the gate you find a "Commissionaire."

Written by W.H. Smith
Nova Scotia Division

Contents

Foreword	– Patron, His Excellency Romeo Leblanc, Governor General of Canada	iii
Editor's Preface	– John Gardam	v
Poem	– Who Are Commissionaires?	vii
Chapter One	– Humble Beginning to Nationwide Success: John Gardam	1
	– The Chairmen 1936-1998: Sean Heatley	9
Chapter Two	– Montreal Division	11
Chapter Three	– Toronto & Region Division	43
Chapter Four	– British Columbia Corps	71
Chapter Five	– Hamilton Division	95
Chapter Six	– Windsor Division	101
Chapter Seven	– Southern Alberta Division	113
Chapter Eight	– Victoria & Vancouver Island Division	129
Chapter Nine	– London Division	149
Chapter Ten	– Manitoba Division	185
Chapter Eleven	– Nova Scotia Division	203
Chapter Twelve	– Northern Alberta Division	221
Chapter Thirteen	– Ottawa Division	233
Chapter Fourteen	– New Brunswick & P.E.I. Division	247
Chapter Fifteen	– Quebec Division	261
Chapter Sixteen	– South Saskatchewan Division	273
Chapter Seventeen	– Kingston & Region Division	283
Chapter Eighteen	– North Saskatchewan Division	299
Chapter Nineteen	– Newfoundland Division	323
Chapter Twenty	– Vision for the Future	
	– René Gutknecht and Clive Addy	339
Epilogue	– National Chairman – Maj Tom Bauld	343
After Word	– The Honourable Fred Mifflin, CD	344
The Last Word	– John Gardam – (the Editor)	345

Chapter I

HUMBLE BEGINNING TO NATIONWIDE SUCCESS

WRITING HISTORY is not the reproduction of countless pages of historical data plus an endless list of dates and names. That would be an incomplete portrayal of the Corps, since it is made up of almost twelve thousand who serve, on a daily basis, doing a myriad of jobs throughout Canada. Today's men and women carry on in the same tradition as their predecessors. Veterans of any stripe have learned to put "job before self" and they have a built-in desire to achieve at all costs. This book is about such people. The 18 unique Divisions are where the true history of the Corps resides and their stories have been written from within each Division.

The beginnings of The Canadian Corps of Commissionaires/Le Corps Canadien des Commissionnaires (CC of C) go back to 1925 when the government of the day tried to provide employment for the thousands of First World War veterans who had returned home to find their country had changed in a major way. The Corps began as an employment agency.

The early minutes of the National Corps Headquarters, located in Montreal, portray an organization struggling to get established. Meetings were cancelled for lack of quorum; it lost its first organizer to sickness when MGen King had to return to England; and there was the ever-present battle to obtain jobs for the veterans. [These comments came from various files in HQ, Ottawa. There was no way to check their factual accuracy.]

In researching boxes of files in Ottawa to collate this history, one has to regret that in the past, keeping records was not a high priority. The day-to-day urgency to keep the spirit and purpose of the Corps alive and functioning seemed to have prevailed over historical record keeping. While there are lists of names of governors and descriptions of annual parades, plus financial records, there is no "human face" in those boxes of files. Although many aspects such as the dedication of the governors, trustees, administrators and the Commissionaires are clear, there is a lack of personal accounts of the dedication, courage and loyalty of the "rank and file." In the 48 years the editor has spent with the Department of National Defence and the veterans in war he has written about, the very spirit of the Corps of Commissionaires becomes clear; for almost three-quarters of a century those same type of veterans never wavered. The story of Canada and the Corps between the great wars and since 1953 when the war ended in Korea will unfold in the 18 divisional accounts, which follow in the next chapters.

Women had entered the job market during the First World War and jobs had been protected for "returned" men, but a vast number had nothing to turn to. In *The Corps Chronicle*, written by Rory Balfour in the 1970s, it is explained that in 1915 no one less than the Governor General of Canada, HRH the Duke of Connaught, wrote to the president of the Military Hospital Commission (MHC) suggesting that the formation of an organization similar to the Corps of Commissionaires of Great Britain should be considered. The British Corps had been formed in 1859 after the veterans of the Crimean War were left to fend for themselves. Captain Edward Walter, the founder of the British Corps relied on the known fact that veterans had a proven standard of conduct, coupled with discipline and loyalty, which could be exploited to find them jobs in the civilian sector, a practice still followed today wherever Commissionaires are found.

As the depression of the 1930s deepened, the contracts for Commissionaires grew fewer and fewer. Only the Divisions in Toronto and Vancouver were providing jobs for veterans. Montreal Division had all but ceased to function. The War Veterans Allowance would not fill the void and many of the older veterans still wanted or had to continue working to retain their pride as useful members of the community. In 1936, the Department of Pensions and National Health pressured for the re-activation of the 1925 charter of the early Commissionaires. It did not take long to action the urgent request and by December 1936, negotiations were complete and the following month, the Veterans Assistance Commission gained approval from the Privy Council for the formation of a country wide Corps of Commissionaires. Major General King saw to it that directors were named to the Board of the Corps. The Veterans Assistance Committee pledged to support the Corps with the ideal being a Division in every Canadian city of 40,000 or over. In June 1937, the Governor General became the first Patron in Chief and the Provincial Lieutenant Governors were asked to become patrons. In less than two years, Canada was at war again, creating yet another family of veterans.

During the Second World War, two events unfolded of major impact to the Corps. Many of the Commissionaires were recalled to the Armed Forces and others joined the Veterans Guard of Canada to provide security at prisoner of war camps and vital points. Still others joined the Royal Canadian Navy, Canadian Army, the Royal Canadian Air Force and the Merchant Navy. Here again there is a paucity of information concerning this period of history.

When the war ended in 1945, there was a large contingent of Commissionaires required as security guards for War Assets as they started to dispose of airfields, buildings, vehicles and stores. As War Assets completed their work, there were lay-offs and few new contracts. In March 1945, representation was made by the Corps Headquarters to the Secretary of the Treasury Board to maintain contracts for the Commissionaires. The landmark decision from the Board was as follows: *The Board considers that there is work in the Public Service of Canada that could, with advantage, be performed by personnel obtained through the Canadian Corps of Commissionaires and requests that all Departments, Boards and Commissions give consideration to the employment in positions exempted from the positions of the Civil Service Act.* This **first right of refusal** came at a time when, once again, thousands of returning men and women were trying to re-establish themselves in civilian life. As recently as 1982 and again in 1996, Treasury Board reaffirmed their 1945 decision. The Corps is a major private provider of services to the federal government in the amount of almost $150,000,000 dollars in 1996 out of a total of over $200,000,000 worth of business. The strength report effective as at March 31st 1997 showed that 27.6% of Commissionaires were under 50 years of age and 10.1% were over 70 out of a total of 11,194. In that the Corps aim is to provide employment for former service personnel and RCMP who are trying to re-establish themselves in civilian life, this right must not be allowed to fade.

Although the numbers of Canada's Second World War and Korean War veterans are decreasing, former members of the Canadian Armed Forces and the RCMP are available to carry on the traditions of their predecessors. The statement made in *Legion Magazine* in November 1973, *The aim of the Corps is to find work for persons who need it and when the day comes where there are no longer any veterans who qualify for enrollment then their job is done*, was not only incorrect but, in fact, the Corps serves on. Figures in 1982 show that of the 9,883 active Commissionaires serving, some 25% were not war veterans but rather former Canadian Armed Forces and RCMP members, many with peacekeeping experience. As the editor travelled from Newfoundland to Vancouver Island in 1997, there were still vestiges of the old adage when the last veteran retires, turn out the lights. This is positively not the feeling of the governors or those responsible for the day-to-day operation of the Corps.

Just how large was the task facing the Government in 1946? In looking at the older veteran, Walter Woods in **Rehabilitation (A Combined Operation)** (1953) recorded that there were:

- 10,000 veterans of The World War registered with the National Employment Service and unplaced;

- 2,000 veterans who served in both wars registered and unplaced;

- 3,500 dual war veterans about to be released from the Veterans Guard of Canada, the great majority of whom were faced with unemployment.

When one realizes that a vast number of Second War veterans had no job to return to, the enormity of the challenge must have been daunting. A number decided to become farmers and the Veterans Land Act made this possible. Many made the adjustment to the land but some proved unable to make the transition. The provision of an alternative career for this proud group of unemployed Canadians became paramount and the Corps did its utmost to fill the need.

This history of the Corps will, for the most part, be the story of the 18 Member Corps (now Divisions) who serve from "sea to sea." It is in the Divisions where the day-to-day function is performed by almost 12,000 men and women. It must be clearly understood that the Corps is NOT an agency of the federal or provincial governments but is a private, non-profit, self supporting organization whose sole purpose is to provide services of many kinds using former members of the Canadian Armed Forces and from the Royal Canadian Mounted Police and certain other former military members. The Corps provides Commissionaires to perform a myriad of duties such as:

> Airport security; bridge toll collection; by-law enforcement; casino security; chauffeur, claims investigation; clerical service; condominium security; console operator; custodial duties; elevator operator; fingerprinting service; golf course monitoring; guard; matrons; hospital security & patient assistance; house sitting; identification card service; inventory control; lost and found; mail room; messenger; office management; parking enforcement; parking meter collection; permit issue; photo radar; police emergency despatch; radio control; range control; receptionist; service of documents; shuttle operator; special events security; summons server; switchboard operator, urine analysis collection; vehicle dispatcher; vehicle impound control; Visa applications; watch person; Young Native Training; and Young Offender Training.

Of great interest is the very "Canadian" way in which the structure of the Corps itself has and continues to evolve.

Ian Douglas, CM, QC, of Toronto had a great deal to do with the re-organization of the Corps and he wrote in 1997:

> It is interesting to note that the 1936/37 re-organization was of The Canadian Corps of Commissionaires (to which I will refer as Dominion Headquarters). Toronto and Vancouver continued on their independent ways. Dominion Headquarters, DVA did well because their efforts resulted in sixteen Divisions owned and governed by Dominion Headquarters. It is to be noted that the Divisions were true Divisions – emanations of a single body if you like – and were not legal entities. I believe that this was an important factor in driving the Divisions to seek the re-organization which resulted in the structure we have today. There was widespread discontent among the Divisions for several reasons. The Divisions felt that the Dominion Headquarters was too autocratic; they felt that the money which they had earned and put aside and the property and assets which they had acquired belonged to them and not to Headquarters (which was the legal owner, since the Divisions were just that), and certainly some of them felt that in some ways regional matters of importance were not being recognized. I believe that they developed a strong feeling that they no longer wished to be owned or controlled or commanded by a headquarters in central Canada. It was also felt that with the increase in the dollar value of each Division's business and of the assets, incorporation would be a sensible way of gaining the protections provided by the corporate form. The present structure came out of these feelings. The sixteen Divisions became corporations and therefore separate legal entities and they, together with the Vancouver and Toronto Corps, joined in a federation which is more like our own country in structure, with a national board and headquarters to discuss and settle matters of common interest.

At the outset, once the Dominion Headquarters staff, then located in Montreal, had toured Canada, held meetings and worked with the Department of Veterans Affairs, new Divisions started to evolve. Toronto and Vancouver remained separate entities, growing and prospering.

In 1937, five Divisions commenced operations in Hamilton, Windsor and London in Ontario. Calgary and Victoria joined (separate entity) the Montreal Division under the general supervision of Dominion Headquarters. The next year saw Manitoba (Winnipeg) and Nova Scotia (Halifax) joining. After a two-year break, Edmonton and Ottawa began operations. With the start of the Second World War, one month after Ottawa began recruiting, the problem of retaining members who wanted to join the forces and the Veterans Guard of Canada became a challenge with more jobs to fill than available Commissionaires. In 1946, Victoria & Vancouver Island joined the National Organization and Saint John, New Brunswick (plus P.E.I.) joined as did Quebec City and South Saskatchewan (Regina). One year later only one new Division was formed–Kingston, Ontario. In 1948, there was enough support in Saskatoon to form the North Saskatchewan Division. St. John's, Newfoundland joined in January 1950. At last the Corps was "sea to sea."

At the 1966 Annual Meeting held in Victoria, BC, Mr Lajoie of the Department of Defence Production explained that the Glasco Commission Report had recommended that all government contracts be handled by one department. Defence Production had been named to be that department. Later it was agreed that the Division forecasts be submitted to National Headquarters in Montreal. This one national change in government contract procedures was to have far reaching changes within the Corps. The current procedure for the national contract undertaken by National Headquarters with the Department of Supply and Services (DSS) is an offshoot from that 1966 decision. At the same meeting, Colonel Syd Oland suggested that National Headquarters be moved to Ottawa. This was formally executed at the 1967 Annual Meeting.

In 1969, the matter of the restructuring of the Corps, both National Headquarters and all Divisions, began in earnest. As the Corps became larger and more complex, something had to be done. By 1969, the Corps' strength had gone to over 7,000 members and total billings risen to over $26,000,000. Victoria & Vancouver Island raised a negative vote and Toronto wished to negotiate their own contract. It was time for consolidation but things this complex would take time, understanding and cooperation. One has to realize that this was no sudden change in policy, but one which began in 1937 when formal recognition was made of The Canadian Corps of Commissionaires. The National Headquarters moved to Ottawa in 1967, but it was not until 1972 that Toronto joined the newly configured Corps. The British Columbia Corps joined the national body in 1973 but still retains its own distinctive cap badge.

The years from 1972 to 1978 under the Chairmanship of Capt (N) R.P. White and LCol Ian Douglas saw the bulk of the changes mentioned above come to fruition. The 1974 By-laws became law and form the modus operandi in use today. As Ian Douglas pointed out:

> *The restructuring resulted in each of the former Divisions becoming a corporation, and thus a separate entity. The Member Corps, together with the B.C. and Toronto Corps which also became Member Corps, then voluntarily came together under the national umbrella organization.*

The Corps set out certain principles when it conducted the major reorganization in 1972 and these have not changed through the years. They were enunciated in the 1982 study into the relationship between the Corps and the Federal Security Guard Services as follows:

> *Each Member Corps runs its own operation, while co-ordination is effected through a National Board of Governors consisting of one governor from each unit and four headquarters governors. From this group, all of whom provide their service and expertise without remuneration, a small executive committee is appointed. There is also a small headquarters staff in Ottawa, which carries out day-to-day liaison and co-ordination. Membership in the Corps of Commissionaires is drawn from veterans of wars, ex-service persons, [eligible] reservists plus ex-members of the RCMP. Both men and women are eligible for membership, which is not allowed to exceed the numbers that can be employed in the geographic area covered by the Members Corps.*

In the 1982 study mentioned earlier, there can be no doubt that the prime purpose of the Corps was to provide security in the work place. The study mentioned in part:

> *Commissionaires, through their military background, have qualities of discipline, loyalty, maturity and reliability; as well, their previous experience developed a security awareness which allows them to be easily trained in specific guard duties. In addition to these inherent qualifications, the Corps has always provided a modest form of training which usually consisted of at least a period of indoctrination followed by on-the-job instruction. As a result of the re-orientation which took place in 1974 and in compliance with Government requests, a formal training program for Commissionaires was established. There is a basic course which covers Access Control, Corps History, Crowd Control, Emergency Measures, Fire Safety, Introduction to Protective Security, Manning Instructions, Note Taking and Report or Return Writing, Patrolling and Surveillance, Physical Security, Pilferage, Theft, Vandalism, Powers of a Commissionaire, Responsibilities of a Commissionaire, the Threat, Traffic Control and Work Accident Prevention.*

In 1974, the FLQ Crisis caused the federal government to review the requirement for the physical security of buildings and information. A most important meeting was held in May 1974 when LGen (retired) Mike Dare and Colonel (retired) Robin Bourne (both now deceased), met with the National Chairman of the Corps, Captain(N) (retired) R.P. White. The topic was the essential service provided by the Corps continuing but at an increased tempo.

It is interesting to note that two years later, in June 1976, R.P. White was made a member of the Order of Canada for the work he did with the Corps when it became a truly national organization.

Training had to be improved and recruitment enhanced in the National Capital Region. The RCMP wrote the new specifications for guards, or more properly, watchmen. There was no doubt that the Corps challenge was to meet the needs of what had become a "growth industry." It was at this point that there was a change in Corps philosophy–the Corps would NOT cease to exist once the war veterans had gone.

The impetus of 1974 and thereafter has not changed. The Corps grew larger, took on greater responsibility and continued to provide men and women to give a standard of service not equalled by other companies of similar aims.

As Ian Douglas explained:

> *One of the prime factors in the restructuring was the creation by the federal government of the Department of Supply and Services (DSS) to do the contracting for each and every government department. The Department of Veteran Affairs handed over all responsibility in the area of contracting to DSS. DSS sensibly decided that it would contract with one Corps organization only, namely, National Headquarters. This had the salubrious effect of ensuring that National Headquarters was an important part of the Corps structure and also that the B.C. and Toronto Corps would come into the fold as Member Corps.*

History is an ongoing fact of life, things change as society and the workplace change. In *Our Sergeant* by Peter Reese, *The Story of the Corps of Commissionaires*, he writes about the United Kingdom Corps by recording:

> *In 1982, the Canadian Corps exceeded 10,000 men, virtually double the strength of its parent. This second offspring [the other being Victoria, Australia] far surpasses the strength of its progenitor.*

Size alone is but a measure of success. What makes the Corps so different is its measure against other similar organizations which operate for a profit with far less stringent rules for membership. A dream created after two world wars and Korea is alive and well, serving a nation, which has every reason to be proud. The Corps has adapted to both the needs of the Commissionaires and the requirements of the customer.

No opening chapter about the history of the Corps would be complete if reference was not made to the Governors who have guided the 18 Divisions since their inception. Those men and women have provided guidance and, in the early years, personal financial assistance. In reading the 72 years' worth of Annual Meetings, a picture evolved of years of dedicated service. One Division has had three generations serve as Governors. Within the Table of Contents in Chapter 1, is included the listing to show how the National Chairman has been chosen from the geographical limits of the Corps–Atlantic to Pacific.

The Corps is here to stay and, as Col Spankie of the B.C. Corps wrote over 50 years ago – CARRY ON THE CORPS!

HISTORY OF CHAIRMEN OF THE CANADIAN CORPS OF COMMISSIONAIRES
LE CORPS CANADIEN DES COMMISSIONNAIRES

NAME	YEARS IN OFFICE	RESIDENCE AT TIME ELECTED CHAIRMAN
Prior to 1972 (reorganization)		
BGen G.E. McCuaig, GMG, DSO,	1936 - 1938	Montreal
LCol H. DesRosiers, DSO, VD	1938 - 1941	Ottawa
LCol E.G. Hanson, DSO, ED	1941 - 1954	Montreal
Brig A.E.D. Tremain, CBE, ED	1954 - 1963	Montreal
Brig W.C. Leggat, DSO, ED, QC	1963 - 1967	Montreal
LCdr A. Marcil, OC	1967 - 1971	Montreal
Capt (N) R.P. White, OBE, CM, VRD,	1971 - 1972	Ottawa
After 1972		
Capt (N) R.P. White, OBE, CM, VRD	1972 - 1975	Ottawa
LCol Ian Douglas, CM, CD, QC	1975 - 1978	Toronto
Maj A.E. Bruce	1978 - 1981	Saint John
BGen R. Normandeau, CD	1981 - 1983	Quebec
Maj K.J. McRae, CD	1983 - 1985	Vancouver
BGen H. Comack, CMM, CD	1985 - 1987	Winnipeg
LCol J.C. Stewart, CD	1987 - 1989	Kingston
Col J.H. Turnbull, OMM, CD	1989 - 1991	Saint John
L Gen G.A. Turcot, CMM, CD	1991 - 1993	Montreal
L Gen W.A. Milroy, DSO, CD	1993 - 1995	Ottawa
L Col R.G. Smellie, CD, QC	1995 - 1997	Winnipeg
Maj T.W. Bauld, CD	1997 -	Halifax

Chapter II

HISTORY OF THE MONTREAL DIVISION

Commandant's Introduction – *By Louis Joron*

THE INITIAL phase of the Montreal Division is really the history of The Canadian Corps of Commissionaires in Canada. The Canadian Corps of Commissionaires was incorporated on July 25, 1925 by virtue of a Federal Charter; its main office was in Montreal, Quebec. The Petitioners for the 1925 Charter were John MacNaughton, Albert Isidore Goodstone, Joseph Horace Michaud, Philip Meyerovitch, Max Bernfield, all lawyers, in the city of Montreal.

The Corporation lay dormant for a number of years. The activities of the Founders appear to have been limited to the drafting of the By-Laws. From 1925 to 1937 there are no records of the operations of the Corps.

At the request of MGen W.B.M. King, CMG, DSO, VD, Chairman of the Veterans' Assistance Commission, the 1925 Charter was revived in February 1937 by a group under the leadership of BGen G. Eric McCuaig, CMG, DSO. Therefore, it can be said that the main office of the reactivated Corporation of February 15, 1937, in Montreal, was also the beginning of the unit of the Corps in that city. BGen G. Eric McCuaig, CMG, DSO, was elected the first Chairman of the Board of Governors of the reactivated Corporation.

The period from 1937 to 1946 was one of sustained growth from the high demand of Commissionaires to act as guards to protect public property and defence plants from sabotage during the war years.

In 1948, the Montreal Division was incorporated under Part Three of the Quebec Companies' Act and granted a Provincial Charter constituting a corporation for objects of national, patriotic, religious, philanthropic, charitable, scientific, artistic, social, professional, or sporting character, or the like, but without pecuniary gain. As of today, 1997, the Montreal Division is still operating under the same Charter.

The years which followed the end of the Second World War were marked by the decrease of the number of Commissionaires and the consolidation of their strength which lasted until the mid-fifties. There was a great period of expansion and construction towards the end of the 1950s: This construction boom lasted until the end of the World Exhibition (Expo '67) held in Montreal in 1967.

Although there was a lull in the activities of the Corps following Expo '67, the city of Montreal became the object of terrorist activities which had begun with the placement of bombs in mail boxes in the city of Westmount, one of such bombs having exploded and maimed Sergeant Major Walter Leja while in the process of neutralizing it.

From 1948 to the present, the Montreal Division provided the services of Commissionaires to Canadian government departments and agencies and to a number of important industrial, commercial and business organizations.

The Montreal Division has seen many changes over the years, but has always maintained a fine reputation for the quality of its services, integrity and customer satisfaction, supported by the high calibre of our Governors, Officers and Commissionaires, past and present.

Sincere thanks are extended to our Board of Governors for supporting the Corps history project, initiated by MGen Roland A. Reid, Immediate Past Chairman. Colonel C. Pierre Richard, Chairman, and Capt John G. Chamberland, Vice-Chairman, are to be commended for their research and development.

THE FIRST DECADE (1937-1946)

The Beginning

The actual beginning of the Montreal Division took place on September 22, 1937 when BGen G. Eric McCuaig, CMG, DSO, was elected Chairman of the Board of Governors. Thus was established the unit which became known as National Headquarters in the city of Montreal and which also became the first operational unit of the reactivated Corps. (Toronto and B.C. Corps were already in operation.)

First Meeting of the Board of Governors (1938)

The first meeting of the Board of Governors, for which minutes are available, was held on September 26, 1938 at the Officers' Mess of the Victoria Rifles Armoury on Cathcart Street, now the home of the Régiment de Maisonneuve.

The Board of Governors was made up of the leaders of the business, banking, finance, legal, and professional community of Montreal at the time. The Governors present at the first meeting were the following: BGen G. Eric McCuaig, CMG, DSO, Chairman; Col Jackson Dodds, OBE; Mr Justice C. Gordon MacKinnon, OBE; BGen E. deB. Panet-Raymond, CMG, DSO; Col J.T. Stell, VD; Taggart Smyth, Esq.; Col Robert Starke, VD; Maj G.C. Burbridge, MC, Commandant.

The first item on the agenda concerned the minutes of the last meeting. The Commandant, Major G.C. Burbridge, MC, reported that ". . . certain of the records were found to be missing on his taking over, amongst these being the Minutes of the previous meetings of the Governors." Under the circumstances, the Chairman, Brigadier General G. Eric McCuaig, CMG, DSO, "ruled that, inasmuch as he had been closely in touch with what had been undertaken with regard to the Montreal Division, the lack of minutes was not important and that the meeting should proceed."

The statement of Major Burbridge explains why there are no records to be found regarding the earlier operations of the Corps. This situation may very well be explained by reason of a move to newer premises which had just taken place. The minutes mention that "The Chairman also advised the meeting that it had been considered more advantageous to transfer the Headquarters of the Montreal Division to 45 Ann Street. This he had instructed to be done, the cost of alterations necessary to accommodate the Montreal Division to be charge against the said Division." The move to new premises was unanimously approved.

The Eaton Parking Station

The T. Eaton Company (Montreal) Limited was the first major client of the Corps in Montreal.

The second item on the Meeting Agenda of September 26, 1938 dealt with the evening and night service at the Eaton parking station. It was agreed that the management of the T. Eaton Company (Montreal) Limited be approached with a view of increasing the percentage of the share of earnings from the operation of the Eaton's parking station at nights and on holidays. This question was resolved favourably in favour of the Corps inasmuch as the Chairman, Brigadier General McCuaig, reported at the following meeting held on January 25, 1939 that, "The previous split had been 60% to the Corps and 40% to the Company. The new share of earnings effective February 1, 1939, would be 80% to the Corps and 20% to the Company."

Community Commissionaire Service

Evening and night patrols, better known as its Community Commissionaire Service, constituted an important part of the Corps' business in its early years.

The final item on the Meeting Agenda of September 26, 1938 concerned the matter of Night Patrols in the city of Westmount. The Community Commissionaire Service had on duty thirteen men in the residential district of Westmount and Montreal and in the business district of Montreal. There were 497 subscribers. The monthly income of the Community Commissionaire Service amounted to $1,378.50, with monthly expenses of $1,182.75. It took but a few months to catch up the organization costs incurred in establishing this worthwhile undertaking.

The satisfactory operation of the Community Commissionaire Service was accomplished with a great deal of extra work on the part of those actually handling the Division, besides the necessity for the closest supervision of the men on duty.

The general manager of the city of Westmount, P.E. Jarman, authorized the commencement of the Community Commissionaire Service in the following way:

> *Your application for permission to establish a Night Patrol of your organisation in the city of Westmount was approved by the General Committee at their meeting held on September 19th.*
>
> *Your men must be in uniform and will be subject to the approval of the Chief of Police; also he will require references and finger prints. If you will communicate with the Acting Chief Gough he will go in to the completing of the arrangements with you.*

The necessary authority for commencement would certainly appear to be definite. However, members of the Westmount Council had received a few complaints to the effect that the Community Commissionaire Service was overlapping the police department's work. At the request of a member of the council, the officers of the Corps discontinued contacting residents of Westmount with a view to having them become subscribers. The question of the Community Commissionaire Service was again taken up at the Westmount council, which resulted in the following letter being sent by the general manager, P.E. Jarman, to the Officers of the Corps:

> *The question of services which may be given by members of the Corps to citizens of Westmount was again considered by the General Committee at their meeting on October 24th, when it was decided that the city of Westmount, whilst it has no objections to the Corps entering into private agreements with its citizens, yet cannot authorise that body doing patrol work or exercising other services which are the sole domain of the police force of the city.*

It was known, however, that the police authorities of Westmount would pick up Commissionaires where they were found contacting residents, even for the purpose of making "private agreements" with residents.

Although the Division had not exceeded the authority given it by the city of Westmount, the situation remained to be clarified especially in view of numerous requests to enlarge the Community Commissionaire Service in that municipality.

The chairman, BGen G. Eric McCuaig, reported at the meeting of January 25, 1939 that the Westmount situation was still under negotiations and no official action had been taken at the time. Nonetheless, relations with the city of Westmount remained cordial. When the mayor of Westmount died, a voluntary parade was called for a detachment to attend his funeral.

Much valuable information as to the early days of the operations of the Corps in Montreal is contained in the Report of the Chairman, BGen G. Eric McCuaig, to the Board of Governors on January 25, 1939:

> *The numerical strength of employed Commissionaires, permanent, semi-permanent and casual, has reached a total of fifty. Of this number, thirty-seven are permanently employed, seven semi-permanently and six casually. The six causal are obtaining a good value of work and are ready to be absorbed in semi-permanent or permanent employment. Further enlistments are being undertaken.*

The most notable placement at the beginning of 1939 was the employment of five Commissionaires by the east end plant of the Canada Cement Company. While these Commissionaires were paid directly by the company mentioned, one Commissionaire, who was found to be lacking in the proper Corps spirit, was suspended and replaced by the officers of the Corps. This suspension and replacement saved company officials embarrassment and engendered a greater confidence in the Corps and in the manner in which its affairs were conducted.

At the meeting of January 25, 1939, "A letter written by J.A.R. Shuter, Esquire, was read regarding the satisfactory services rendered by Commissionaire Webster while in his employ as a temporary chauffeur." At the same meeting, the Chairman asked the Commandant to communicate to Brigadier R.O. Alexander, DSO, the sincere thanks of the Board of Governors for having acted with them during the tenure of his office as District Officer Commanding, Military District.

For some unknown reason, the Second World War is always referred to as the 'hostilities' in the minutes of the meetings of the Governors held from May 16, 1940 to the end of the war. Also at the meeting of May 16, 1940, mention is made of the Montreal Division, as opposed simply to the Corps of Commissionaires.

There was exceptional growth in the activity of the Montreal Division during the Second World War. In 1940, the Division was operating under three classifications: uniformed Commissionaires, guardsmen and personnel for the RCMP for duty as guards on the harbour.

From its inception to 1940, the Corps paid upwards of $150,000 in wages direct from the office of the Division in Montreal; this amount is exclusive of the amount which was paid directly to Commissionaires employed throughout the city by individual concerns.

At the beginning of 1940, the strength of the Division was estimated at 219 all ranks. Uniformed Commissionaires were carrying out the ordinary duties assigned to them which included night patrol, Eaton's parking station and the various other duties which came the way of the Division prior to the outbreak of the hostilities.

However, the situation soon changed as Commissionaires were supplied to private organizations requiring guards for anti-sabotage work.

The Division also took over the supplying of personnel to the RCMP for duty of the harbour or other places of importance for which the RCMP was responsible for protecting.

The greatly increased strength of the Division was absorbed without any material increase in Headquarters' personnel. All the necessary work and supervision was carried out by the Commandant, Major G.C. Burbridge, the Adjutant, Capt. D. Thompson, D.C.M., the Divisional Sergeant Major D. Parker and one orderly room clerk, for day duty, and another for night duty. The officers of the Division did not allow the rapid expansion in the strength of the Division to carry them away and make for the appointment of a large H.Q. staff which would have been expensive to maintain.

For the fiscal year April 30, 1939 to March 30, 1940, the total net operating cost of the Division was the small sum of $585.67 which represented the cost of employing anywhere from 170 to 240 men and providing for a proper living wage.

The Commandant reported to the Governors meeting held on May 16, 1940 that:

> *Prior to the outbreak of the hostilities, the Montreal division of the Corps was making satisfactory progress and had increased its enlisted uniformed strength to 76 Commissionaires. At the outbreak of the hostilities the officers of your Division were prepared and had organised to take care of any eventualities and were prepared, also, for an immediate and prompt increase in the strength of the Division in order to supply personnel for any duties which the Division might be called upon to perform.*

Upon the outbreak of the hostilities, the Division was called upon for a large number of men to act as guards for private corporations requiring such services against possible sabotage. The largest commitment in connection with guards was for the Montreal Light, Heat and Power. The mobilization for this duty was carried out smoothly and effectively and the ML&P spoke in the highest terms of the services rendered by the Division on their behalf.

Numerous calls were received from other organizations; men were supplied without any delay whatsoever and the efficiency of the Division was well demonstrated.

The first Commandant, Major G.C. Burbridge died on November 22, 1940. On January 2, 1941, the directors of the Canadian Corps of Commissionaires and Workshops Limited (another enterprise being operated for the benefit of ex-service men) recorded their sorrow at the death of Major Burbridge in a resolution stating in part:

> *Major Burbridge had been actively connected with this organisation since its inception in 1937. He gave untiringly of his efforts to further the interests of the returned soldier for whose benefit the closing years*

of his life were devoted. He understood the difficult problems connected with the rehabilitation of the veteran for whom he always displayed a sympathetic understanding.

This was a most fitting tribute to a person who worked to find remunerative employment for veterans.

On February 26, 1941 the Governors appointed Colonel DesRosiers *". . . for the supervising of the affairs of the Corps as regards Headquarters and the Montreal Division in connection with similar duties to be performed in, and concerning Workshops Limited."*

At the meeting of the Governors held on February 26, 1941 there was raised *". . . a question as to the possibility of Montreal Division being able to continue to operate without Federal financial assistance . . ."*

In August 1941 one of two cars owned by the Corps was sold when it became apparent that a shortage of gas would exist in Canada. It was felt that too much use was made of the two cars and many inspections were then made by streetcar and by walking.

The real danger of sabotage to the Montreal harbour, ammunition, chemical and manufacturing plants, and public utilities and defence installations contributed to the rapid increase of the strength of the Corps during the early years of the Second World War.

By August 14, 1941 the number of men employed had risen from 245 to 377. The increase resulted from the employment of guards at the Montreal harbour, but principally by the contract Defence Industries Limited (DIL) at Ste. Thérèse where 140 men were on the payroll. The men were also employed with Bell Telephone Co. (at 56 points in Quebec and 18 points in Ontario), Montreal Light, Heat & Power, Commercial Alcohol, Consumers Glass Co., Ministry of War Transport, Montreal Coke, C.I.L. Montreal, Ste-Anne's Military Hospital, Dorval Airport, Lachute Mills, Canadian Marconi, St. Lawrence Flour, Dominion Coal, Imperial Tobacco, S/S Fleuris, and United Shipworks.

The placing of guards on ships in the Montreal harbour was beginning during the summer of 1941 and the Corps supplied all the men required for this service. At least 30 men were in more or less continuous employment in this work. A contract had just been concluded with the United Shipworks which employed 43 NCOs and men as guards. The Division also had been asked to take over the guarding of another munitions plant. Activity also extended to many parts of the province well beyond the Montreal area. All this additional work meant the steady employment of at least 600 men during 1942.

The chairman, Col Royal L.H. Ewing reported that during the period ended March 31, 1942 he and the vice chairman had visited the guards at various plants including DIL plants at Verdun, Bouchard and Brownsburg.

The managers of the plants have been called during the course of each visit as it is felt that by maintaining close contact with the various plant managements good relations between the plants and the Corps are helped.

Col Ewing added that:

> There are indications that as time goes on it will probably become increasingly difficult to secure the type of man suitable for admission as Commissionaires. Already it is found that men of the First World War are becoming scarcer. While a certain number present themselves as having been honourably discharged from the present war, the fact remains that until casualties from overseas begin to reach us we shall probably find it increasingly hard to secure the type that we require for guard duties.

The continuation of the hostilities placed much stress on the operations of the Corps. Night patrols were continuing with the same staff and operated at a loss. The night patrols' service was nonetheless maintained so that, at the end of the war, there would be a solid foundation from which to extend. It was felt that this loss, which could be easily absorbed, was well worthwhile.

For the fiscal year ended March 31, 1942, the payrolls for guard services amounted to $590,000. The last five months of the fiscal year the payrolls averaged $60,000 per month. On the basis of further contracts, the payrolls for the services of guards from April 1, 1942 to March 31, 1943 were expected to exceed $800,000. In fact, the wages paid to Commissionaires for the fiscal year ended March 31, 1943 amounted to $1,175,589.31.

The Corps fulfilled its functions in an efficient manner and many ex-servicemen were being assisted who probably would have found it hard to fit themselves into the wartime milieu. At the same time, the Governors felt that the work performed by the men was an important help to the country in its war work.

During the spring of 1942, the Corps placed an order with the Workman Company for 300 light summer uniforms to equip the guards at Bouchard and Brownsburg plants at a cost, including light summer cap with visor, of $23.75 per man. Each man was measured by a Workman's representative who visited the plants. The cloth was Air Force blue, similar to that supplied to officers of that service. This purchase was intended to smarten the appearance of the men, as well as to add to their comfort during the hot summer. The men paid for these summer uniforms by weekly deductions from their pay cheques.

However, in early 1943 the wearing of the summer uniforms introduced during the summer of 1942 was discontinued. The men wore the regular Commissionaires' uniforms but discarded their tunics for the summer. They wore light blue shirts with black ties, the blue trousers and the sun helmets purchased the previous year. The cost of these uniforms was deducted from the men's pay in fortnightly installments.

During 1943, the Corps continued its work of guarding both civilian and military installations against sabotage. The principal plants were the

DIL at Bouchard, Ste-Thérèse and Villeray, the United Shipyards at Bickerdike Pier and the Canadian Ordnance Corps at Longue Pointe, as well as those plants which had been taken over at the start of the hostilities, Montreal Light, Heat & Power and the Bell Telephone Company and several other details.

New premises were rented at 1834 Ste-Catherine Street West where the Division occupied the whole floor with a heated garage for one car and plenty of space for the accounting staff, the orderly room, and adequate room for stores.

The Commissionaires guarded a total of 28 plants at the beginning of 1944. In February and March 1944 the difficulty of securing men for work had become fairly acute, this being caused by the payment of much larger wages by plants which were operating their own guards. The Corps kept going under these restrictions; it was hoped that the additional men returning from overseas would make it possible to keep the number of guards up to strength. Inspections were carried out at various plants and the management of these plants expressed their satisfaction with the work and discipline of the Commissionaires. At March 31, 1944, the total number of men employed by the Division stood at 930 and the wages paid to Commissionaires amounted to $1,410,000.

The chairman, Col R.L.H. Ewing, expressed his concern over the effect of the end of the war in Europe in his report on May 29, 1945, as follows: "The end of the hostilities in Europe and the consequent certainty of a reduction in the number of men required for guarding munitions plants, etc., makes this a suitable time to review our position for the past four years."

The reduction was occasioned by the cessation of work in several small plants and by reductions in the Bell Telephone Company and other organizations. It was difficult to predict the future employment of these guards, but the process of "laying off" these guards was expected to be slow and it was felt that a number of plants would be kept going for some considerable time.

The problem of securing men during the last three years of the hostilities had been at times very difficult. Plants, which had private guards on their properties, were paying very high wages, giving free uniforms and, in some cases, free boots. Many Commissionaires were lured away but it was surprising how many of them returned to the Corps. They seemed to find that they were happier with an organization which was reserved for ex-servicemen.

Nonetheless the Corps had found permanent employment for many of the men and a considerable number secured permanent employment positions for themselves, which the Division had naturally encouraged.

Various companies had used the services of the Corps. The men had always maintained uniformly high standards. The general security officer of DIL stated that the most satisfactory guards they had in all plants across

Canada were the Canadian Corps of Commissionaires and this applied particularly to the Montreal Division.

The Montreal Division looked to War Assets Crown Disposal Corporation in order to find work for the Commissionaires after the end of the war. It was felt that some efforts should be made to secure the continuity of the guarding service which the Commissionaires had done so well during the war years.

Col R.L.H. Ewing and Col Jackson Dodds met with Mr Woods, the Deputy Minister of Veterans Affairs. Col Ewing proposed to Mr Woods that the guarding of all government plants, especially those which had been guarded by the Montreal Division during the war, be given to the Commissionaires when these plants became vacant and under the control of the Crown Corporation. The chairman, members of the executive committee, and Col Hanson, the president of the Corps, met in Ottawa with the Deputy Minister of Munitions and the Secretary of the Treasury Board to pursue this matter. The efforts of this delegation were rewarded and, as plants were declared to be "surplus" and came under the control of War Assets, the guarding thereof was assumed by the Division.

Worthy of mention is the fact that the Commissionaires in Montreal had subscribed to the War Bonds to the amount of $118,200.00. Wages paid to Commissionaires for the period ended March 31, 1946 amounted to $1,162,272.

In June 1947, War Assets employed 161 men, Royal Canadian Ordnance Corps and government departments, 397, and miscellaneous including headquarters staff and patrols, 101 men, for a total of 659. The rates of pay amounted to $0.60 per hour.

The demobilizations after the end of the hostilities and the reduction of the requirements for the services of Commissionaires were causes for concern for the Montreal Division. During the spring of 1947, the headquarters president of the Corps, Col Hanson, and the vice chairman, J.C. Stewart, visited Ottawa and had long interviews with the Minister and the Deputy Minister of Veterans Affairs, the Minister and the Deputy Minister of Defence, and the three officials, Navy, Army and Air Force, in charge of civilian personnel. It was felt that, if the Corps and its mission were not kept constantly in front of the government, the Corps might not receive the support which it deserved. (This action was beneficial to the Corps Canada wide.)

During the hostilities several posts in the Maritimes and Ontario had been administered by the Montreal Division but these posts were gradually taken over by the Toronto Division, the Halifax Division and a new Division formed at Saint John, New Brunswick. The chairman, Col Hanson, mentioned that the Department of Veterans Affairs was doing all in its power to extend and enlarge the scope of the Corps and it was expected that the strength of the Corps all over Canada would be increased by the Dominion Government handing over to the

Corps a great number of jobs that were done by the Mounted Police and other personnel outside the civil service.

The expression, "Headquarters President" came into use in 1946 so as to differ from the President of the Montreal Division, but as yet no formal distinction had been made or recorded.

On May 28, 1947, the Corps was inspected by the Minister of Veterans Affairs, the Hon. Ian McKenzie, on the Champ-de-Mars in Montreal. A detachment numbering 249 men was on parade and the minister expressed his great satisfaction both with the men's appearance and with the splendid work that the Corps was performing.

On November 19, 1947, Captain E.A. Underhay was appointed as liaison officer between the Corps and industry generally to secure employment for members of the Corps. A salary of $200 per month was authorized as well as the expenditure of $600 for advertising in the press.

In November 1947, it was becoming evident that the office of the Corps was becoming inadequate. The landlord had offered the Corps a five-year lease at $4,500 per annum which was declined by the Corps. The vice chairman suggested that a house at 3433 Peel Street would be suitable for the Headquarters. The house was inspected and found satisfactory.

On March 30, 1948, the Governors authorized the purchase of the building at 3433 Peel Street from Percival A. Wood for the price of $22,000. Possession of the building was obtained in June 1948 and the second and third floors were remodelled into three flats for rental.

The meeting of the Executive Committee held on November 19, 1947 was the last meeting held for the corporation named "The Canadian Corps of Commissionaires, Inc."

The duplication of responsibilities between the National Headquarters and the Montreal Division as well as the possibilities of conflicts made it desirable to incorporate a new corporation to carry on the affairs of the Montreal Division.

Letters Patent incorporating the Canadian Corps of Commissionaires (Montreal Division) was granted on March 12, 1948. The petitioners for the new corporation were Allan A. Magee, CBE, DSO, KC, Advocate; T. Taggart Smyth, Banker; John Christie Stewart, MC, Insurance Broker; Jackson Dodds, CBE, Banker; and James Munn Bales, MC, Stock Broker.

The principal objects of the new corporation were:

- *to provide employment for all worthy ex-servicemen, in conformity with the laws of this Province and of the Country;*
- *to better present positions of ex-servicemen;*
- *in perpetuation a whole-hearted allegiance to His Majesty the King and to Canada;*

- *to assist in making this Canada of ours that nature intended it to be, viz.: the best and happiest country in the world;*
- *to create as genuine spirit of comradeship, mutual respect and assistance among its members;*
- *to practice in its fullest sense the principles of the Corps, viz.: SERVICE AND EFFICIENCY, etc.*

The petitioners and other persons promoting the incorporation of the Montreal Division had served Canada under the Red Ensign and were proud, patriotic and true Canadians. They had seen the ravages of wars and they believed that Canada was truly "the best and happiest country in the world." Their military service had taught them "the genuine spirit of comradeship, mutual respect and assistance" to one another. They wished the members of the Corps to carry on such spirit in the performance of their duties and the discharge of their responsibilities.

The first meeting of the directors of Canadian Corps of Commissionaires (Montreal Division) was held at the Division's office at 1834 Ste-Catherine Street West, Montreal, on March 18, 1948. A number of prominent citizens from the business, financial and legal community of Montreal were appointed the first directors and members of the Montreal Division. The great majority of these people had been decorated for their past military service.

Decrease and Consolidation of Strength

On June 9, 1948, the chairman, Col Jackson Dodds, who was also the chairman of the Bank of Montreal, became concerned with the decrease of the strength of the Commissionaires in the Montreal Division. He mentioned that:

Colonel Jackson Dodds speaking to his Commissionaires.

> *During the past twelve months there has been a shrinking in number of men employed. This is mainly due to a decrease on War Assets guards and guards at the Ordnance Depot. At March 1947 our members were 619. As at March 1948 we numbered 512. Today, May 31st, 454 are on strength.*

In order to stimulate the employment of Commissionaires, an advertising campaign was commenced in the newspapers at a cost of $50 per month. This advertising programme resulted in the securing of 53 jobs and was continued for a number of years thereafter.

The government also carried out a campaign to secure work for older veterans through radio and newspaper advertising. The Corps appointed a Campaign Committee under the chairmanship of Col Jackson Dodds, who personally called on many prominent industrialists asking for their help. Considerable success was obtained and the liaison officer found many doors open to him which had been closed before.

Night patrols showed an overall deficit of over $700 during 1948. Captain J.C. Stewart suggested that night patrols be discontinued. Letters were sent to the clients pointing out the position and the necessity of cancelling the service if sufficient subscribers could not be obtained; the deadline was set at October 1, 1948. Total wages paid to the Commissionaires for the year ended March 31, 1948 amounted to $1,006,832.55

The reduction of government installations during the years 1948 and 1949 continued to take its toll on the strength of the Corps. This situation was best expressed by Col Jackson Dodds as follows:

> *At the Annual Meeting last year (1948) the total strength of the Division was 512 men; today our numbers are 444. The closing of War Assets Depots accounted for 35 of the loss while a reduction in the number of guards at the Ordnance Depot reduced us by a further 50 men.*

He continued:

> *... it may be fairly assumed that unless a great period of civil unemployment develops, our present strength may be considered fairly permanent. Through the efforts of some of our Directors, and with the assistance of a number of local citizens, anxious to assist the older veterans by keeping them gainfully employed instead of having to eke out a bare subsistence on the Government 'burnt out' allowance, our service has been brought to the attention of a large number of manufacturing and business concerns, and is becoming better and more favourably known to the public at large. The high standard of character and reliability on which we insist, and the pride of the men in the Corps have no doubt been largely responsible for the good results which have been obtained.*

At the inspection of June 9, 1948 six of the Division's men received ten year service and good conduct medals and 36 received badges for five

Colonel Dodds presents Medals at Parade of Montreal Division.

years service with good conduct at the hands of Brigadier Honourable Milton W. Gregg, VC, (Gregg was the Minister of Veterans' Affairs in the Liberal government headed by the Honourable Louis St.Laurent).

The office night staff, which had carried on during the war, was discontinued during 1948 as it was felt that in peace time this was not really necessary. Any call after six p.m. was made to the residence of the Divisional Sergeant Major.

In 1948, the men received 65 cents per hour in place of 60 cents, and the Corps seven cents per hour for administration instead of five cents. The government department also increased the administration charge paid to the Corps from five cents to six-and-a-half cents per man hour. This extra payment was made to Headquarters of the Corps and was to be allocated as fairly as possible to Divisions which found it hard to carry on. The total payroll for 1948-49 amounted to $878,645.67, a drop of nearly 20% from the previous year.

The period from 1960 onwards was one of prosperity for the city of Montreal. Large office buildings were built and a number of Commissionaires carried out guard duty on several construction sites. There were also preparations for Expo '67.

During 1959, a commission headed by the Superintendent of Civilian Personnel had been making surveys of all National Defence establishments. The commission had estimated the number of Commissionaires that should be employed at each place for security purposes. The commission made recommendations without any consultation with the Commandant and, in some instances, the commission had no proper understanding of the existing agreements and how these recommendations would affect certain situations.

The chairman, Col Jackson Dodds, reacted strongly in a letter dated January 14, 1960 addressed to the Hon. Col A.J. Brooks, Minister of Veterans Affairs, regarding the reduction of personnel at 25 Central Ordnance Depot, Ste-Anne-des-Plaines and Bouchard and the work of the commission which reduced the hours of work of Commissionaires. This letter was a strong endorsement at army bases instead of using enlisted men to do the work which Commissionaires did better and at a lower cost to taxpayers.

Col Dodds mentioned in his letter that:

> *It will be appreciated that we do not contest the Department's right to make any reduction in the Corps of Commissionaires services that they deem fit.*

He continued:

> *We would point out that it is extremely difficult to obtain suitable veterans in this district and asking the remaining personnel to agree, which for the time being we have persuaded them to do, to less hours than they previously obtained, will not be conducive to the best results.*
>
> *You are familiar with the aims and objects of setting up this Corps and the reputation they have earned. Also that without the Corps a large majority of the older veterans could not find employment. These reductions, to a greater extent, will mean those affected will start on unemployment insurance and eventually apply for soldiers allowance, which by reason of their age they are qualified.*
>
> *We suggest that this will result in a much larger cost to the Country with no return, whereas, keeping them employed at the lowest possible cost will help maintain their morale and so keep them from joining those subversive organizations which thrive on unemployment.*

Col Dodds concluded:

> *May I point out that the whole purpose of the formation of the Corps can easily be undermined by the changes to which I have referred.*

The Minister of Veterans Affairs promptly acknowledged the letter of Col Dodds and agreed to look into the matter very thoroughly.

During the period of 1960 onwards, new legislation, which contemplated major economic or social questions, was either introduced for the first time or rewritten entirely by various levels of government. As the result of such new legislation, the Montreal Division had to abandon certain programs and to adopt new programs for the Commissionaires even if, in some cases as pensions, the earlier schemes were more advantageous to Commissionaires. The Commandant spent time in meetings with civil servants in order to understand and apply such new legislation.

There were lengthy discussions with civil servants as to the application to the Corps of the Quebec Security Agencies Act (the Act) introduced in the Quebec legislature in 1962. The Corps did not exercise the functions of police forces nor those of a "detective agency" which investigated offences or gathered evidence or supplied information on the character and behaviour of others. In the end the Corps was subjected to the Act.

The Act required the Corps to replace the former blue uniforms with a new type and colour to be approved by provincial authorities. This would involve an expenditure of at least $75,000 of which less than half could be recovered. However, by careful planning and an extension of the period for the change over from blue to grey uniforms, the cost to the Division was about $6,000. For some unknown reasons, the provincial government later, by 1968, accepted the use of blue uniforms and it took about eighteen months to convert from the grey uniforms back to the blue uniforms.

The Act required all security guards to obtain an annual permit at a cost of $5 per annum. At first, the cost of the permits was borne by the Division but, due to heavy turnover of newly enrolled personnel, all new Commissionaires were required to pay for their initial annual permit while annual renewals were paid by the Division.

It was estimated at the time that approximately 200 Commissionaires joined the Corps for periods of less than 12 months each year and that the Division often had to pay a five-dollar fee for a Commissionaire who might work from one week to one month. Since April 1969, Commissionaires have been required to pay for both the initial and annual renewal of permits.

Colonel Jackson Dodds inspecting his Commissionaires on November 11, 1954.

In June 1964, the chairman, BGen J.A. deLalanne, reminded the Governors that it was a matter of policy decided in March 1949 that there should be close liaison between the local Divisions and the local offices of the Department of Veterans Affairs and that there should be in each Division a member of the Board of Governors who is the regional or local administrator of Veterans Affairs. The then Regional Administrator of Veterans Affairs submitted his resignation as a Governor in his letter of June 1, 1964.

During 1966, the Corps had at one time some 20 Commissionaires working as security guards with Expo '67. They were authorized to use motorcycles in order to perform their work and they were covered for workman's compensation in the event of accidents. Due to difficulties experienced with the local unions, such as working hours, holidays, and recruiting problems, these Commissionaires had to be withdrawn and they did not play part in the maintenance of security at Expo '67.

While the strength of the Montreal Division had increased during 1964 and 1965, the turnover and recruiting of Commissionaires became a matter of great concern because a large number of work opportunities were created during this period. The Commandant, LCol W.H. Draper, reported in June 1965 that the Division continued to have a demand for younger men for replacements from present employers, also for new accounts. Applications to join the Corps were falling off to a considerable extent. Employers requirements, apart from age, included more education, ability to write reports and to record telephone messages, and bilingualism to a greater extent than previously. Firms were reluctant to train men of the older group due to the uncertainty of the length of time they may be able to continue working. There was a requirement for changing qualifications for the Commissionaires of the Division. There was also call to the Commissionaires for better service to clientele in order to keep and attract business.

In 1971, National Headquarters alleged the change in the requirements of the customers and the need to reduce the turnover of personnel in order to propose the categorization of Commissionaires on the basis of their functions and age, namely those under 60 years of age and those over 60 years of age. The chairman, BGen J.A. deLalanne objected strongly to any such proposal on the ground that the 60-year limit would exclude 30% of the strength of the Montreal Division and would adversely affect worthy ex-servicemen. The categorization of Commissionaires was therefore left to be handled by the Divisions. BGen deLalanne also did not believe that there was much hope of achieving a national rate of pay for Commissionaires.

The city of Westmount was always favourable to the hiring of Commissionaires to do work which did not require the assignment of police officers. However, the Quebec Department of Justice did not agree with the work that Commissionaires carried in the city of Westmount. In

November 1966, the Quebec Department of Justice sent the Division a letter questioning the legality of Commissionaires being employed by the city of Westmount for the issuing of parking tickets for parking offences. The use of Commissionaires to issue tickets for parking infractions was eventually discontinued, but the Commissionaires doing this work were hired on a permanent basis by the city of Westmount.

The Montreal Division held annual inspections of the Commissionaires at various armouries, the McGill University campus, or the Longue Pointe Army Base (RCOC School). These inspections were carried out as formal military parades with the inspection, review and march past of the Commissionaires on the parade square or the gym in the event of inclement weather. The chairman, BGen J.A. deLalanne, reminded the Commissionaires at the Annual Inspection held on June 16, 1965 that "the demands we receive for your services depend, in large part, on the smartness of your appearance and your behaviour on and off duty and on the manner in which you carry out your particular assignment." He commended the Commissionaires for the manner in which they maintained the high reputation of the Division. He emphasized that "the men themselves by their apparent pride in the Corps and by their deportment are aiding greatly in presenting a good image to present and prospective employers of their services." The strengthening of the division's administrative staff, both numerically and qualitatively, permitted more contact with employers and with the Commissionaires in the field.

During April 1969, letters of commendation were received from the Department of National Defence and McGill University "for the excellent work done by Commissionaires during recent bombing incidents and demonstrations."

In May 1969, the Commandant, Col R.M. Bourgeois, recommended that future annual parades be limited to a brief inspection of the Commissionaires, followed by a dinner served to the Governors, members of the staff and Commissionaires and the presentation of awards and bonuses. This was the format for the annual inspection of the Montreal Division on June 11, 1969. All Commissionaires were very pleased with the changes. Future annual inspections were to be of the same nature. In May 1971, the Commandant recommended that the annual parade for 1971 be cancelled for reasons of economy and lack of interest on the part of Commissionaires. There were no annual parades held thereafter.

The chairman, BGen J.A. deLalanne, attended the Annual Meeting of the Corps held in Calgary in September 1968. BGen deLalanne, who was a very successful chartered accountant and business man, realized the importance of good communications and the sharing of information between the Commandants. He suggested that the Division Commandants should meet during the month of March of each year to discuss mutual problems. This suggestion was unanimously approved. This initiative gave rise to the Annual Meetings of the Commandants which enabled the Division Commandants to discuss all matters pertinent to their duties and to communicate on the initiatives of each Division.

The Montreal Division is likely the most bilingual Division of all Divisions. The Commandant, Col R.M. Bourgeois noted in his Annual Report for 1968-69 that "Bilingualism has become a very important factor in the placement of Commissionaires, most of our customers request the services of bilingual veterans and, unfortunately it has become more and more difficult to find employment for our unilingual (French or English) members." However, no applicant was turned down for this reason and jobs were found for all.

The Official Languages Act, which was passed by the House of Commons on July 7, 1969, was not detrimental to the Montreal Division because a sufficient number of bilingual Commissionaires was available to meet any and all requirements of federal government offices served by the Montreal Division. In fact, approximately 80% of the Division's Commissionaires were fully bilingual and could speak the two official languages adequately.

The French version of the corporate name of the Montreal Division was adopted on November 20, 1979 to comply with the requirements of the Charte de la langue française.

First World War Veterans

In October 1969, Commissionaire David Simard, DCM, MM, a veteran of the First World War and one of the oldest members retired at the age of 75 years, after 27 years of faithful service with the Corps.

In 1976, there were still 13 World War One veterans in the ranks of the Montreal Division, two of whom were approaching 85 years of age and "all of whom are said to be still rendering exemplary service to respective employers." An official of McGill University wrote a letter of commendation with regards to the services rendered by one 85-year-old Commissionaire.

As a result of deaths and voluntary retirements, by May 1979 there were no longer any Commissionaire who had active service during the First World War. Corporal Henry Hewson, who was the oldest serving Commissionaire at the age of 87 years, died in February 1979. Commissionaire David Roussel, who was the last Commissionaire to have had active service in the First World War, retired in February 1979.

The employment of veterans, young and old, is one of the fraternal objectives of the Corps. An effort is always made to place older veterans in functions that they are physically capable to carry out. Nonetheless, it was becoming difficult to find employment for older veterans and every effort was made to help this deserving group of veterans. It was felt that special jobs should be reserved for older men who needed employment and who were willing to work, but could not be expected to accomplish as much as younger veterans.

The Commandant, Col R.M. Bourgeois, reported in December 1970 that Corps Headquarters had asked the views of the Division concerning the arming of Commissionaires should employers request it. After much discussion, the Governors unanimously decided that the Montreal Division's Commissionaires would not be armed and Corps Headquarters was advised accordingly. The matter of the October Crisis was still fresh in everyone's memory. The Governors wisely thought that it was inappropriate to arm the Commissionaires since they were not authorized to do the work of the police forces nor of the armed forces.

The Chairman, BGen J.A. deLalanne, mentioned in his Report for 1969-70 that:

> *The austerity programme of the Federal Government and the closing of Armouries and other military establishments has reduced considerably the requirement under the Government Contract . . . but the closer contact between our Administrative Staff and Employers and the more aggressive policy I outlined to you last year has produced additional business to offset the losses.*

The Commandant, Col R.M. Bourgeois, mentioned in June 1970 that the recent reorganization of the Militia had caused six armouries to be closed since January 1970 and that three more armouries would be closed by September 30, 1970. The Commandant added that there would also be further reductions by reason of the closing of the LaSalle Naval Supply depot and the Bouchard depot.

The Chairman, BGen J.A. deLalanne.

The training of Commissionaire has always been important to the Montreal Division. The need not only for training, but for keeping up-to-date with the latest methods and techniques has long been recognized and emphasized. First aid and fire prevention courses were given to Commissionaires.

The Commandant, Col R.M. Bourgeois, reported in June 1970 that the Division Commandants, at their annual meeting, had considered the training or indoctrination of newly-enrolled Commissionaires to be a definite requirement. However, due to the difference in jobs requiring different types of training, it was unlikely that any standard training could be developed on a national basis. Training or indoctrination of Commissionaires would therefore remain a Division responsibility and would take the form of brief lectures on duties, responsibilities, dress and deportment in job training and first aid and fire fighting courses.

Department of Defence Production

On April 1, 1966, the Corps began operations under a new uniform agreement between Corps Headquarters and the Department of Defence

Production for services provided to departments of the federal government.

The preamble to the agreement stated that:

> Her Majesty recognizes that the Corps is providing and has provided valuable services to Canada, and Her Majesty wishes to continue Her support to the Corps by purchasing from it the services of Commissionaires.

The new agreement and guidelines caused the Montreal Division to review its procedures and to adapt new ones as the agreement was re-negotiated from time to time.

> The lack of representatives of the Division in the negotiations of such contract caused the chairman, BGen deLalanne, to mention in his report for 1967-68 that:

> We have tactfully suggested that, in any future discussions which envisage drastic changes in procedures, there should be consultations between Headquarters and representatives of Divisions who are familiar with current operations before any financial commitment is made by Headquarters or any material changes agreed to.

In November 1968, the chairman reported that:

> the Comptroller had reviewed the adoption of "Cost Centres" by the Corps at the request of DDP, "in order to ensure a uniform accounting system throughout the Corps and to spell out expenses which are acceptable in the case of Government Contracts." DDP submitted a list of non-allowable operating and administrative costs for Government contracts.

In May 1969, the chairman, BGen deLalanne, reported that:

> While normal contact with the Department of Defence Production is effected through Corps Headquarters in Ottawa, we have had several direct approaches by representatives of the Department and we have found them to be most cooperative and understanding of our Division's distinctive character and requirements.

The financial statements were drawn up to comply with the form and code of accounts prescribed by the Department of Defence Production as a uniform basis for all Divisions.

In 1970, the name of the Department of Defence Production was changed to that of the Department of Supply and Services.

The chairman, BGen J.A. deLalanne, reported in November 1970 that:

> ... a contract had been signed by the QPP requesting the services of some 25 Commissionaires. This was the first contract with the Province and it was anticipated that others would follow.

Unfortunately, this was never the case; at the time of writing (1997) the Montreal Division has no contract with the Quebec government.

The Last Twenty Years (1977-1997)

The period from 1977 to 1997 covers a number of matters which overlap during those years. These matters are sometimes complex and are better treated as separate subjects.

The face of downtown Montreal had changed considerably since the acquisition of the building at 3433 Peel Street in 1948. The Queen Elizabeth Hotel opened in 1958. Place Ville Marie and the Imperial Bank of Commerce Plaza were inaugurated during 1962. A construction boom in downtown Montreal preceded Expo '67.

As early as 1960, there were no convenient parking facilities for Commissionaires visiting Division Headquarters. Rigid parking restrictions were enforced on the Peel Street and Commissionaires were frequently assessed fines.

The Montreal Division occupied all the space in the building after the death of the last tenant, but the building no longer met the needs of the Division Headquarters and a search for new premises was underway. The building was sold on March 16, 1981 for the price of $122,700 which was received in full at the time of sale. The actual move from the Peel Street building took place on March 2, 1981.

Division Headquarters Premises (1981 - 1997)

Following the sale of the Peel Street building, the Division Headquarters rented office space at 5115 de Gaspé, Montreal. This building, which is situated at the intersection of De Gaspé and Laurier Avenue, is readily accessible by bus, metro or automobile. There is a large parking area next to the building to which the staff of Division Headquarters has access.

On May 12, 1981, the chairman, BGen J.A. deLalanne, reported that visitors to the new Division headquarters had commented favourably on the new premises; he also reported an increase in the efficiency of the work of the staff.

At first Division Headquarters occupied Suite 200 of the building at 5115 de Gaspé but, as more space was needed, later moved to larger premises at Suite 100.

The Division Headquarters moved to its new offices at Suite 400 on March 4, 1994. Although the new premises contained more space than the previous location, the cost was much lower in view of the difficult economic conditions prevailing at the time of negotiations. A new conference room makes it possible to train new recruits on-site since they must take the complete Commissionaires qualifying course prior to their employment.

The chairman, BGen J.A. deLalanne, reported on the address given on June 18, 1982 by BGen Raymond Normandeau, of Quebec city, to the Annual Meeting of the Corps held in Calgary in June 1982. BGen Normandeau said that one of the biggest problems the Commissionaires face is perpetuating their diminishing numbers. "If you only keep veterans in the Corps, we can't keep going on because of age." He added that, "the Corps not only provides a valuable service to the public at large, it also provides employment for aging veterans." The comments of BGen Normandeau are still relevant today.

The Commandant, Col J.J.M. Ste-Marie, in his report for 1977-78 expressed his concern regarding competition from other security agencies. He said "We may be on the verge of pricing ourselves out of the market as on some contracts that were lost, we have become the highest bidders." He warned that the Division had to remain at all times vigilant as to costs of operations. There was some further concern in 1978 regarding the effects of the Anti-Inflation Board's requirements with respect to the contracts of the Montreal Division.

In 1975, the Montreal Division joined the "Conseil des Agences de Sécurité et d'Investigation du Québec Inc.," which is better known as CASIQ. This association, which regroups all major security and investigation agencies in the province of Quebec, negotiates the provincial collective agreements for security agencies. The Montreal Division has participated and contributed actively to CASIQ since 1975.

In February 1979, the Commandant, Col J.J.M. Ste-Marie, was appointed to the Executive Committee of CASIQ. He participated in the negotiations with provincial government representatives in the 1979 re-writing of the Quebec Security Agencies Act. Col Ste-Marie was elected president of CASIQ in June 1984. The current Commandant, Col Louis J. Joron, was appointed a director of CASIQ and a director of the Comité Paritaire du Québec on July 1, 1991. Col Joron has served as president of CASIQ since September 1994.

Union Matters and Collective Agreements

In December 1984, a majority of Commissionaires joined a union and negotiations for a first contract started on February 22, 1985. A first collective agreement was signed on May 8, 1985 between the Union des Agents de Sécurité du Quebec, Local 8922, and the Montreal Division; this collective agreement terminated on October 5, 1985. The first collective agreement was subsequently re-negotiated to reflect the provisions of a provincial decree governing security agencies.

A second collective agreement was signed February 6, 1986 in order to coincide with and reflect the provincial decree. The terms of the collective agreement were the same as in the provincial decree, with the addition of a group insurance plan. The provincial decree provided for four salary increases commencing on the first of January of 1986, 1987, 1988 and December 31, 1988.

Because unionized employees had a group insurance plan under their collective agreement, the non-unionized employees and staff were provided with a group insurance plan as of April 1, 1986.

A new provincial decree became effective on January 26, 1990, together with a new collective agreement for the Montreal Division, both of which would remain in force until December 31, 1992. The provincial decree then in force was extended until an agreement could be reached for a new provincial decree. The Montreal Division sought a freeze in wages due to the economic recession and the directives given by Supply and Services Canada. The provincial decree came into force on October 1, 1993 and provided for a wage freeze until June 1, 1994 in view of the economic conditions prevailing at the time.

The Montreal Division and the Quebec Division joined to negotiate the collective agreement instead of doing so separately as in the past years. The collective agreement was identical to the provincial decree except that the two Divisions provided for a group insurance plan for the unionized Commissionaires.

In November 1988, a manual of procedures was being prepared in order to include all regulations and policies of the Corps and the Montreal Division. This project would take as long as two years to complete since all previous records would have to be reviewed.

In view of the reduction in the number of qualified veterans to join the Montreal Division, the chairman, Major Robert Hainault, raised the possibility of allowing ex-members of the Reserve Force to be allowed to work as Commissionaires. The Montreal Division recommended to the National Board of Governors that anyone with 12 years of service in the Reserve Forces should be eligible to join the Corps. In 1989, the National Board of Governors approved the recruiting of candidates with five years of service in the Reserve Forces. (Once again this change became a Canada-wide agreement.)

Training was becoming more important to ensure quality of services and satisfaction of customers. Some 150 Commissionaires passed the correspondence basic security course during 1990. Other courses given to Commissionaires of the Montreal Division included the national advanced training supervisor course, first aid course, and cardiovascular resuscitation.

In November 1995, a complete survey of the Division's current clients was made to find out their needs for the future. The main conclusion was that computers were more and more used by the Division's clients and that the training of Commissionaires on computers was becoming essential in order to improve chances of keeping and renewing current contracts. For example, Commissionaires working at the Canadian Broadcasting Corporation must use computers in the ordinary course of their work.

Governors

Since its establishment in Montreal in 1925, the Corps and subsequently the Division was directed by men with vision and with a sense of social responsibility towards former servicemen. All Governors were prominent citizens, most of them veterans of the First World War. They were very much implicated in the well-being of veterans and their fellow citizens.

The founding Governors, who were all lawyers, devoted their time to the writing of By-Laws to comply with the legal requirements for non-profit organizations.

From 1937 to 1947, the Board was enlarged and the new Governors, mostly senior military officers, became very involved in seeking employment for fellow servicemen. The first customers were merchants such as the T. Eaton Company and municipalities such as the city of Westmount.

During the Second World War, the Corps became very involved in providing personnel to guard defence industrial plants and military installations.

In his report for 1968-69 the chairman, BGen J.A. deLalanne, endeavoured to keep the Governors better informed on current operations and trends. As a result, the Montreal Division circulates an excellent monthly letter to all Governors and Commissionaires.

At the time of his appointment as Commandant of the Montreal Division, Col Louis J. Joron emphasized the need for the Governors to become more involved and added that, from time to time, he would be looking to them for advice.

In June 1992, the Governors unanimously approved the formation of a New Business Development Committee under the chairmanship of Col Pierre Richard. In December 1992, the Governors unanimously approved the creation of a new committee to be known as the National Communications Review under the chairmanship of Major General Roland Reid, with the Commandant and two Governors as members of the Committee. This committee is responsible to study all written reports submitted by national Corps Headquarters and to make the necessary recommendations. In November 1995, the Chairman of the Nominating Committee, Col T.E. Price, invited all Governors to volunteer for service on current and future committees.

In December 1994, the chairman, Major General Roland A. Reid, noted the passing of Col H.M. Hague who had served in both the First and Second World Wars. Col Hague had celebrated his ninety-fifth birthday just a few months before he passed away. He had completed 45 years of devoted service as a member of the Board of Governors which he had joined in 1949.

In 1996, the Governors authorized a donation of $2,500 to the Last Post Fund as a contribution to the new monument in the Peace Sector of the Field of Honour Cemetery in Pointe Claire/Beaconsfield. The Governors also contributed towards the welfare of veterans at the Ste-Anne de Bellevue Military Hospital. In 1996, the Governors authorized the purchase of a television set for the palliative care ward of the hospital.

Computerization and National Computer Committee

In 1965, the Montreal Division purchased an "accounting machine." This was approved and considered to be a great leap forward in terms of technology. The word "computer" was not yet used by the Montreal Division.

The accounting machine, a Burroughs payroll machine, was delivered on January 2, 1966, and proved to be most satisfactory. The chairman reported on June 15, 1966, that there was yet "a more advanced and better type of accounting machine which, in addition to the preparation of payrolls, can pick up the compilations at the computing stage and eliminate some of the present manual calculations." An order was placed for the better machine, against the cost of which Burroughs Company allowed a 100% credit on the machine which had been in use since January 1966. The new accounting machine was delivered in September 1966.

This new accounting machine made it necessary to introduce administrative changes in the pay procedures of the Division. In November 1968, it was decided to acquire a "mechanical cheque signing device" to affix the signatures of duly authorized officers to cheques issued by the Montreal Division. The Montreal Division was issuing at the time as many as 2,000 cheques each month.

In March 1985, the Commandant, Col Louis Joron, recommended the purchase of a word processor for the Division. He also proposed a number of reforms regarding the accounting software and computer equipment to be used by the Montreal Division. Necessary steps were taken to "back-up" on a regular basis, all data stored in computer programs and files. In January 1988, Major Christian Valet was appointed as EDP manager to cope with the increasing use of computers in the Division.

At the Commandants' Annual Meeting held in Edmonton in October 1987, Col Joron recommended the creation of a National Computer Committee. All Commandants accepted this recommendation and Col Joron was appointed its first chairman. The accounting package already in use by the Montreal Division was offered to the other Divisions; in time it became known as the 'Montreal accounting package.' At the Commandants' Meeting of June 1988, Col Joron was re-appointed chairman of the National Computer Committee, a post which he is still holding at the time of writing. The mandate of the National Computer Committee is to improve the effective management of the Corps resources in terms of automation. The Commandants agreed to establish a standardized system throughout the Corps using UNIX and Business Basic Extended Language.

The National Computer Committee developed a computer course which Major Christian Valet first gave in April 1989 to nine candidates of Kingston. Col Joron, who was still serving as chairman of the National Computer Committee, reported in June 1990 the formation of the National Accounting Procedures Committee to study the standardization of all accounting procedures within the Corps.

Supply and Services Canada recognized the efforts of Col Joron and members of the National Accounting Procedures Committee. At the Commandants' Meeting of October 1990, Pierre Paquette, Chief, Security and Outreach Services, Section GA, Professional Services Branch, commended Col Joron and the members of his committee in the following terms:

> *Supply and Services Canada will continue to work closely with the Corps' Computer and Finance Committees and encourage the Corps to automate their financial systems and other data through implementation of computerized information systems.*

Major Christian Valet became responsible for the implementation of the computer standardization programme among the Divisions of the Corps participating in this programme. At the end of 1992, 13 Divisions were operating fully with the Montreal accounting package. The Montreal Division has received a number of thank-you letters for the efforts of Col Joron and Maj Valet.

Organization of the Montreal Division Headquarters

During the 1967-68, the Headquarters of the Montreal Division was reorganized into two distinct departments: the finance department and the personnel and administration department. The finance department was charged with all pay matters, accounts payable and receivable, purchases, building and equipment maintenance, control of stores, equipment and clothing. The personnel and administration department was made responsible for enrolment, postings, transfers, discipline, inspection, dress, vacations, maintenance of records and other administrative duties.

Subsequent changes in the administration functions at Division Headquarters reflected the administrative and operational requirements of the Division. In September 1991, Captain Loyer became the Chief Inspector, and Captain Waite the Recruiting Officer. During 1992, Capt J.P. Thériault became the Human Resources Officer and Warrant Officer First Class D. Thibault became responsible for the Division's archives and filing systems.

In December 1994, Major J. Goulet, one of the Governors, pointed out the need to provide more support for the Commandant in the form of a Deputy-Commandant. In June 1995, following a study of the staff requirements, Col Pierre Richard, also a Governor, called for the creation of the position of Deputy-Commandant in order to assist the Commandant in his functions, to manage the marketing and customer service functions, and to oversee the operations department. In November 1995, LCol Robert Dion was appointed the Deputy-Commandant.

In February 1995, Capt Roger Béliveau, who had previously worked with the Montreal Division during 1991 and 1992, joined the Division Headquarters as Chief Instructor.

COMMISSIONAIRES EXTRA-ORDINAIRES

Commissionaire S. Smith (1896-1962)

On February 24, 1962 a violent snowstorm raged in the city of Montreal making winter transportation very difficult as only Montrealers are aware.

At 6:52 on the morning of February 24, 1962 Commissionaire Smith reported for duty at the Canada Customs building in Montreal. He reported to his superior, Commissionaire J.W. Dawson, that he had had a tough time getting to work bucking the storm. Commissionaire Dawson left for four minutes to attend to other duties; when he returned at 6:56 he found Commissionaire Smith lying on the floor with his head and shoulders propped in a semi-upright position against the wall. Commissionaire Dawson had been within a few yards of Commissionaire Smith during the four minutes but he never heard any sound. Commissionaire Dawson went to him and, on looking, "there was no doubt in my mind that he was dead."

The sense of duty and responsibility of Commissionaire Smith motivated him to report to his post notwithstanding the stormy weather and he had walked a good part of the way to his place of work.

Sergeant Major Gabriel I. Verdun (1895-1968)

Sergeant Major Verdun served the Montreal Division faithfully for over 23 years. Born an American citizen in 1895, he served overseas during the First World War with the 116th United States Engineer Regiment. In 1922, he took employment in St. Jérôme, Quebec, and in 1940 he volunteered for service with the Canadian Army, serving from 1940 to 1946. He joined the Montreal Division on December 13, 1946 and served until September 30, 1967 when he was given leave of absence due to illness. He died in February 1967.

George Carstairs, Quartermaster (1900-1979)

George Carstairs had been the Quartermaster of the Montreal Division for $34^{1}/_{2}$ years at the time that he passed away on February 15, 1979.

A good Scot, he first found employment in a local distillery as office boy and junior clerk. He enlisted in the 4th Battalion Seaforth Highlanders at the age of 18 and served with the Army of Occupation in Germany with the 52nd Gordon Highlanders until April 1920. He moved to Montreal in 1922 where he worked with an insurance company and later with a stock brokerage firm.

Mr Carstairs joined the Corps in December 1940 and was appointed Quartermaster in 1941. The Quartermaster is responsible for the procurement, classification, inventory, and issue and returns of clothing, and the maintenance of stores at the required level to meet the requirements of personnel. In 1969, Mr Carstairs handled approximately $50,000 worth of stores over a one-year period. For 1969, the discrepancy in inventory amounted to less than $50. Mr Carstairs' excellent accounting proved that he was indeed a Scot.

Commissionaire Armand-Moïse Robert (1920-1990)

At about 2:45 in the early morning of Monday, December 18, 1990 Commissionaire Armand-Moîse Robert was found murdered while on duty at the Canadian Forces Armoury at Saint-Jérôme, Québec.

Born on February 23, 1920 at Hearst, Ontario, he had volunteered to join the Royal Canadian Air Force on December 30, 1940. He was demobilized on September 19, 1945. The shocking news heard on a local radio station by Mrs Aline Robert was the official word she received of her husband's death, which divulged his name before Mrs Robert and the family were informed of his death.

The funeral of Commissionaire Robert was held on December 22, 1990 in Saint-Lucien Parish Church in Saint-Jérôme where a number of soldiers formed a Guard of Honour to receive the coffin covered with the Canadian flag and carried by six Commissionaires. The 4th Battalions of the Royal 22nd Regiment, the Canadian Legion, the Corps of Commissionaires, Army Cadets and veterans were represented at the funeral. The parish priest, the Rev. Gérald Thiboutot, deplored the explosion of violence in our society during his homily.

Major Claude Gauthier, the Director of Operations, praised the exemplary conduct and services of Commissionaire Robert in these terms: "He was a very good person, an excellent employee." The coroner, Dr. Linda Talbot, concluded that the death of Commissionaire Robert was of a violent nature.

Commissionaire Robert had last reported by telephone to his immediate superior, Corporal Jean-Paul Leblanc at 1:58 in the morning. At about 2:30, four officers of the St. Jérôme municipal police force went to the Armoury after having been informed of the release of the alarm system at about 2:20 in the morning. The four officers entered by a door situated at the rear of the Armoury and discovered the body of Commissionaire Robert. He had been tied up; his head was covered with a plastic bag. In view of the seriousness of the situation, the Sûreté du Québec was called upon to carry out the investigation.

The murderers were not satisfied with the killing of an unarmed man of 70 years of age. They broke down the door of a vault containing weapons in order to steal some 20 C-7 automatic assault rifles and six semi-automatic pistols. The stolen weapons could not be used because the breechblocks had been kept separately in a secure place.

The suspects fled the Armoury in a military jeep which was on the premises of the Armoury and was found the next day in a ditch on a secondary road nearby.

In the *Journal de Montréal* of December 27, 1990, journalist Normand Maltais raised the following question: "This theft of weapons of a very special type, weapons of war, would it be the work of the René Lévesque Battalion of the Armée du Québec, which, ironically, would be training in secret in the neighbouring region of Sainte-Hippolyte? This is to be followed!" (Translation)

On July 10, 1991 the Sûreté du Québec arrested four young men and seized a number of weapons following a seven-month investigation of the murder and robbery. Three of the men arrested, one aged 20 and two aged 21, were charged with first-degree murder and a fourth, aged 17 was charged as an accomplice to theft. All stolen weapons were eventually found. Two of the men arrested were soldiers. Police had suspected that the theft was an inside job. Keys to the army jeep were stolen, probably after the death of Commissionaire Robert, and the vehicle was used to smash down a door where some 100 weapons were stored.

Police learned that three of the four suspects had been wearing military uniforms when they appeared at the door of the Armoury on December 18, 1990. It is believed that, upon seeing these three persons wearing military uniforms, Commissionaire Robert would have recognized one of the suspects and then opened the door without hesitation, which cost him his life.

Sergeant André Daoust

Commissionaire André Daoust was born in Montreal on March 8, 1938. He served with the Royal 22nd Regiment in Canada and Continental Europe from April 4, 1954 until February 8, 1958. While serving in Germany, André Daoust was the victim of an accident which severed both his legs (one leg six inches below the knee and the other above the ankle). Following this accident, he was honourably discharged from the Canadian Army in view of his physical condition.

André Daoust applied to join the Corps on November 17, 1969. Despite his physical handicap, Mr Daoust had much to offer in terms of his personaility, politeness, refinement and dress. Mr Daoust was fluently bilingual. The Interviewing Officer never doubted that the Corps would be able to place Mr Daoust.

Mr Daoust had been fitted with two artificial legs in order to cope with his physical handicap. Because of his efforts and determination to overcome and live with his physical handicap, Commissionaire Daoust's comportment was such that no one could tell that he had artificial legs. He managed to live a normal life despite his physical condition. He even learned to ski.

Sergeant Daoust served in several locations while he worked as a Commissionaire including McGill University, the Air Canada Base at Dorval Airport, and the RCMP at Mirabel Airport. Sergeant Daoust was awarded the Meritorious and Long Service Award on June 15, 1989. The recommendation for such award states that although "he is physically handicapped of both his legs, he is a continuous example to younger Commissionaires who have the full use of theirs." Sergeant Daoust was awarded the Long Service Medal before he retired from the Corps in 1996.

Commissionaire Francine Baril

Commissionaire Francine Baril was born in Gatineau, Quebec, on May 3, 1938. While in the Canadian Armed Forces, she served at CFB Shearwater, Halifax, from 1975 until 1979. She first joined the Corps in June 1985 and remained with the Corps until November 1986 when she left to look after her young children. She rejoined the Corps in November 1996.

On March 27, 1997 Commissionaire Baril was on duty at Ste. Anne's Veterans Hospital in Ste. Anne de Bellevue. The great majority of patients do not generally cause any disturbance at the hospital, but some circumstances require Commissionaires to show a great deal of calm and to exercise presence of mind.

A former patient returned for a periodic follow-up visit. The security detachment and the hospital staff knew that this particular patient could become very aggressive towards people who contradicted him when he neglected to take his prescribed medicine.

When the former patient showed up on March 27 at the access gate and entered the grounds of the hospital, the security staff acted quickly and efficiently by warning the medical staff and the police of the presence of the former patient. As soon as the patient entered the hospital building, Commissionaire Baril was asked to escort the patient to the office of the Chief of Security and to keep him there until the arrival of the police.

The delicate situation was well managed by reason of the calmness and human approach used by Commissionaire Baril. She talked with the patient and discussed various matters during more than 30 minutes and thus gained his confidence. She remained calm and mastered the situation until the arrival of the police who then brought the patient to the police station very discreetly and without creating an incident.

Mr Jacques Morel, the Director of Administrative Services for the hospital, thanked Commissionaire Baril in the name of the patients, the employees and the management for her professionalism in the exercise of her functions. Mr Morel concluded that Commissionaire Baril was definitely an asset to the Corps.

Lieutenant Henri Latour

Lieutenant Henri Latour was born on May 18, 1931. He joined the Corps on September 19, 1989 and was assigned to the Veterans Hospital at Ste. Anne de Bellevue.

While he was on his annual holidays and not on duty, Lieutenant Latour was walking on the main street of Ste. Anne de Bellevue on April 9, 1997, at about 14:40. Lieutenant Latour recognized one of the patients of Ste. Anne's Veterans Hospital who was getting off bus No. 211 in front of the Bank of Montreal.

As he left the bus, the patient tripped and fell to the ground and hurt his forehead on the cement; he was in a state of shock. Lieutenant Latour immediately came to the help of the patient who was bleeding profusely. Lieutenant Latour asked the bus driver to look after the patient while he went to get his parked car. Lieutenant Latour took the patient back to the hospital for the treatment of his injuries and remained with him until he was well taken care of by the hospital staff.

Ms. Rachel Corneille-Gravel, the Director General of the hospital, wrote to praise Lieutenant Latour for the civic spirit that he showed toward a patient in distress, even though he was not on duty at the time. Ms. Corneille-Gravel stated that the hospital, and the family of the patient, had very much appreciated his gesture. She thanked him in the name of all the patients and mentioned how proud she was that he could be relied upon to ensure the security of the patients.

Chapter III

HISTORY OF THE TORONTO & REGION DIVISION

Commandant's Introduction – *By Marv Rich*

*T*ORONTO IS one of the three founding divisions of the Corps and has the distinction of having the longest continuing service in the Corps.

When the original six Commissionaires started in 1927, all had prior wartime service. This was the general criteria for the next 25 or so years until members who had served in Canada's Armed Forces, but had not served outside the country, also sought membership. From that time, the mix of veterans and those with regular force service worked side by side to make the Toronto and Region Corps a strong organization. The numbers continued to grow following the Second World War and Korea up to the 1980s, but age had taken its toll on our veterans who now represent only 17% of our strength.

During those early post-war years, the Toronto Corps owned its own building and provided a club for its members on the premises. Since most Commissionaires worked in the downtown area, and bars in Toronto in the 50s and 60s were rare, games rooms and a club atmosphere were provided. As jobs moved from the city centre, the club was not used but remained until 1978 when the Headquarters required more space. At that time the Toronto Association was started for Commissionaires who had left the Division but wanted to stay in touch with their colleagues and friends. This group is self-directed with some financial help and meets in the Headquarters building about six times per year including a Christmas luncheon. I am very proud of the success of this venture and the smiling faces of old friends at their meetings.

The changes, which have taken place during my 20 years of service, reflect the technological innovations which have hit business everywhere. Our annual budget, previously prepared by hand and carefully typed is now generated by the use of computers with a capability which has permitted us to establish a variety of scenarios. But even computers have changed dramatically in speed and options available during the past ten years. How could we operate without the photocopiers, fax machines and computers? They make one realize the changes and advancements which have taken place in our approach to business.

Technology has enabled us to travel beyond the security guard role that was our sole business 25 years ago. We now provide a federally endorsed self supporting fingerprint and certified business; are involved in fraud investigations; embarking on a computerized first aid training business for the whole of Canada; provide extensive concierge services to condominium. All these opportunities provide exciting challenges for the technically trained younger Commissionaires who now serve the Division.

The success of this Division can be determined by the quality of Governors who have selflessly given us their time and expertise. This has been true since the day the Toronto Division was formed until today. Two past Chairmen deserve special mention in this regard.

Lieutenant Colonel Ian Douglas was the Chairman of the Board from 1970 to 1972 and became the National Chairman from 1975 to 1978. It was he who brought Toronto into the national organization as a member Corps. He has worked tirelessly ever since and served as our Honourary Solicitor until 1993. He is now a Life Governor.

Colonel Richard Dillon's impressive resume included Dean of Engineering at University of Western Ontario followed by Deputy Minister positions in the provincial government. He was instrumental in the formation of the Association of Ontario Divisions and he was the power behind its success. As Chairman of the Board, he established board committees to encourage more involvement by the Governors for the advancement of Commissionaire benefits. His work at the divisional and national levels on the National Development Committee is still felt today even though this group has been terminated.

These two are representative of our Governors who tirelessly serve on behalf of our Commissionaires who provide services to our clients. It is through the foresight of all Governors that Toronto has an outstanding benefits programme which gives the Commissionaires a degree of security in this very insecure world in which we live and work.

During my service with the Toronto Corps of Commissionaires as Commandant, I have had numbers of dedicated staff who have brought a work ethic of which any business could be proud. They provide that essential base support which enables our men and women to meet the daily demands of service at all posts, but particularly the higher profile and more visible locations. A special mention of MWO Ron McAnespie is required because it was he who was instrumental in researching and writing the history of this Division. This was a demanding job and his tireless efforts and talents deserve the highest recognition.

Our Early Beginnings

An article in the August 10, 1920 edition of the *Evening Telegram* revealed how the people of Toronto and city officials were becoming alarmed at the number of beggars who were "lining the streets." Most of the pan-handlers were vagrants and immigrants, but a growing number were veterans of the Great War.

United States President Woodrow Wilson had promised that the 1914-18 conflict would be "the war to end all wars," and that "good times were just around the corner." But by 1924, conditions had not improved and a Mr C.G. Robertson, a veteran himself, became concerned over the hardships that his former comrades were suffering. Robertson was a member the Canadian Legion of the British Empire Service League, (now the Royal Canadian Legion), and it was here that he first thought of forming an association of uniformed ex-servicemen modelled after the British Corps of Commissionaires with a view to putting these men to work. He tried to promote interest in this idea and even applied for a sub-charter to organize a Corps through the Legion. There is evidence that a few members shared his concern as an item in the *Evening Telegram* (sometime in 1926), read "ORIGINALS FORM SERVICE CORPS." A photograph also appears of three Legionnaires dressed in a uniform similar to our present day Corps uniform. The plan was quickly shelved as these men did little to foster an image of military efficiency and reliability or demonstrate a willingness to work. For them, stepping back into uniform was simply a lark and few had hoped that a corps of unemployed ex-servicemen would be more than a passing fancy.

A Corps of Commissionaires had been established in Montreal in 1925 (No.#1 Company), and Robertson wrote to the Commandant, Colonel W.C. Fellows, to enquire about forming a branch of the Corps in Toronto. Shortly thereafter, Sergeant John Connor of the Montreal Corps arrived in Toronto claiming that he'd been given the authority to organize a Corps here. Robertson and Sgt Connor met several times during 1926 and discussed the problems that they would face; funding, uniforms, badges, etc., and finding a suitable meeting place.

The first official meeting took place at the Central Veterans' Clubhouse, 41 Isabella Street on March 27, 1927. Present were Robertson, Sgt Connor, nine Legionnaires and a Captain W.F. Finney, OBE, (retired). At this meeting, it was unanimously agreed that Captain Finney, would become President and Commandant, and that Legionnaire Mr F.W. Baill would act as Secretary-Treasurer.

A Board of Governors was also appointed. These included retired officers Major J. Basher, LCol LeGrand Reed, Captain (Reverend) E.J. MacLean (Chaplain), and prominent Toronto businessman, Victor A.S. Williams. Mr Williams would later become Major-General Williams, a long-serving member of the Board of Governors.

The Board acted in a purely honourary and advisory capacity during this early stage of our development, but its importance cannot be over-

No. 2 Company's first Commandant, Captain W.F. Finney.

emphasized. These men were all successful in business and their influence was vital to our growth and survival.

By-Laws and Regulations were then drawn up and Captain Finney suggested that only ex-servicemen with at least six years of active military service would qualify for membership in the Corps. Veterans must also be of exemplary character upon discharge and be able to provide references.

Captain Finney drafted a letter describing the services that these deserving men could perform. The letter was published in the *Evening Telegram* and copies were distributed to businesses throughout Toronto.

THE EMPLOYMENT OF THE DESERVING EX-SERVICEMAN

The ever present question of the satisfactory employment of the ex-serviceman is one which should receive attention from all who are in a position to give any kind of employment, and yet we find that the question receives very little consideration when compared with the great sacrifices made by many of these men. True it is that many cases have occurred where the man has been placed and has proved unsatisfactory and this has rather hindered the cause of the really deserving man.

There are in the city of Toronto a great many men who served many years in either the army or navy; men who entered the service young and who have given the best years of their lives in service to the Empire, for which they in many cases receive a pension which, however, is not sufficient to meet all their needs and which they must supplement with money earned. The years spent in service have handicapped them for many types of employment and yet there are positions which they, on account of the years spent under discipline and training, are well able to fill with satisfaction to the employer.

In 1859 there was founded in England the Corps of Commissionaires. The founder, Sir Edward Walters, KCB, started with eight wounded men, and by personal canvas of employers he placed these men and as time went he organized what has now become in Great Britain the best known ex-serviceman's organization in existence. Next to the police and postal services, the most frequently seen uniform on the streets of London is that of the Corps of Commissionaires. They supply practically all the bank messenger staff, hotel and theatre doormen, attendants in museums, special messengers and numerous other temporary positions which call for the service of a reliable, neat and courteous man. There is no better man for this type of employment than the pick of the long service, ex-servicemen. There is no place for the man in the organization, no matter how long his service, if his record is not clean. At the annual parade in London of the Corps there were on parade over 4,500 men; these men all earning and enjoying a living, and all giving satisfactory service to upwards of 3,000 employers.

There is in Montreal and Toronto a similar organization, just now in the early stages of the struggle to become known to businessmen and to all who may at any time need a man for work. A few of these men have been employed in temporary positions and in every case the employer has been satisfied with the man and the work alone.

These men do not ask or want something for nothing. They supply themselves with uniforms believing there is a need for the uniformed man. They want, and can fill, positions as elevator men, doormen, messengers, janitors, attendants at entertainments or at any time when uniformed men would be acceptable.

Many are able and willing to furnish bond when the nature of employment calls for it.

Should you wish for the services of a man at any time or wish to know anything further about the Corps we would like to able to supply you with same.

There are also a number of men who are suitable for employment as handy men around the house or place of business, men to polish floors, attend to furnaces, wash the car or attend a garden; men whose reliability and honesty we will vouch for.

If you have, or know of, any occasion where one of the men could be used, be it even only for one hour, please assist by phoning either the Secretary or President at the phone numbers given.

Your kind cooperation will be greatly appreciated by these worthy ex-servicemen.

Yours faithfully,
W.J. FINNEY, President

On Monday, April 13, 1927, Toronto radio station CFRB, went on the air; Al Jolson appeared in Hollywood's first 'talkie,' "The Jazz Singer;" construction began on the Empire State building, and Number 2 Company of the Canadian Corps of Commissionaires was born.

A meeting took place at the Central Veterans' Clubhouse with Sgt Connor acting as Chairman and without fanfare or ceremony, Captain Finney administered the oath to six dues-paying veterans. C.G. Robertson became Commissionaire #1, W.F. Payne, #2; A. Stephenson, #3; C.H. Tapp, #4; G.M. Walsh, #5 and F.F. Price, #6. Secretary-Treasurer F.W. Baill became Commissionaire #7.

By the end of the year, the staff had grown to 25 but employment opportunities were few. Some found work as bank guards, doormen, elevator operators and night watchmen, while others accepted temporary

The "ORIGINAL SIX" members who were taken on strength, April 13th 1927. Commissionaire #1, C.G. 'Gordie' Robertson stands second from the left in the back row. (Photo taken in 1948 at the annual awards dinner.)

assignments as attendants, office assistants, stock room clerks, and messengers (on foot and bicycle). In each case, favourable reports were received.

To arouse public interest and to gain the confidence of prospective clients, members of #2 Company took part in Warriors' Day, Remembrance Day and church parades. From time to time, articles about the Corps appeared in newspapers and gradually Toronto became aware of our existence. By 1930 our reputation had grown and several out-of-work ex-servicemen had applied for membership.

Major Benjamin Handley-Geary, VC joined #2 Company as Adjutant, (Administration Officer). This distinguished gentleman had been awarded the Victoria Cross (the British Commonwealth's most coveted decoration). His influence among businessmen in Toronto opened several doors and our list of clients began to grow.

THE CORPS BEGINS TO GROW

Advertisement of the day

> The Canadian Corps of Commissionaires has been organized in Toronto and invite you to avail yourself of their services and assure you always of their cooperation at whatever task assigned to them.
>
> Here are some of the firms who have employed members of the Corps and who invite your enquiries regarding their services:
>
> CANADIAN MILITARY INSTITUTE, TORONTO SKATING CLUB, ROYAL WINTER FAIR, TORONTO FLYING CLUB, LTD., I.O.D.E., COLES, LIMITED, CANADIAN NATIONAL EXHIBITION, CANADIAN NATIONAL CLUB, ROYAL YORK HOTEL, CANADIAN GENERAL FINANCE, RETAIL

MERCHANTS ASSOCIATION, SAVARIN RESTAURANTS, LTD., FAIRWEATHERS, LTD., NAT. AUTOMOBILE SHOWS, INC.

Extracts from letters expressing thanks and paying tribute to the efficiency of our Commissionaires:

RYRIE-ELLIS-BIRKS, LTD.:
The Commissionaires employed by us for several years past we have found to be very diplomatic and thorough in doing what was required of them. They were most valuable in the manner in which they controlled the traffic in the vicinity of our premises. The men employed in the store during the Christmas season were very satisfactory.

WALLACE & TIERNAN, LTD.:
We reported a loss we had sustained at a recent exhibit to the Commissionaire who was doorman. We are pleased to report he has recovered part of the stolen material. In this man we believe you have a man who keenly assumes his obligations.

CANADIAN CASUALTY UNDERWRITERS:
The Commissionaire employed by this Association has been found to be a great acquisition to our staff. His integrity is beyond reproach. His personal appearance and willingness to undertake any kind of work has been very much appreciated by us.

BRITISH EMPIRE MARKETING BOARD:
The 30 Commissionaires on duty have acquitted themselves admirably. The fact that we had no loss, and no damage has been done to the exhibits is a striking testimony to the excellent supervision of your men. They are living up to the standard set by the Corps in London who are commended by thousands of firms who employ them.

GEORGE COLES, LIMITED:
We are glad to inform you that the Commissionaires who have been employed by us on many occasions during the past five years have been entirely satisfactory. We have found them ready to cooperate with our customers in whatever duties they were asked to perform: they are smart in appearance, quiet in manner, thoroughly trustworthy and punctual.

CANADIAN INSTITUTE OF MINING AND METALLURGY:
At the Annual Meeting of this Institute, held in the Royal York Hotel, April 4th, 5th and 6th, your Corps had charge of the display of valuable Radium minerals and Radium products. I take this occasion to congratulate you on the efficiency and promptness of the men detailed for this work. They were attentive and proved entirely satisfactory. Their uniforms were favourably commented upon, inasmuch as this feature gave your guards the authority necessary on such occasions. We feel therefore, that your men can be faithfully recommended for such work.

TORONTO FLYING CLUB, LTD.:
In connection with the employment of Commissionaires, please be assured that the Canadian Corps of Commissionaires will receive first consideration in the event of the Toronto Flying Club requiring the services of Commissionaires.

NATIONAL AUTOMOBILE SHOWS, INC.:
Referring to the services of the Commissionaires in connection with the national Motor Show of Canada, January 14th to 21st, we would like to say that the services rendered were satisfactory in every respect.

TORONTO HOSPITAL FOR INCURABLES:
On the occasions on which we employed members of the Canadian Corps of Commissionaires in the capacity of taking care of the parking of cars, answering the door, etc., at certain functions at our hospital, we wish to say that the Commissionaires added greatly to the occasions, especially is this true in the instance of Their Excellencies' visit to the above institution, when they not only took care of the attendance, but announced the Members of the Board of Management, and others who were formally presented to Their Excellencies.

DEPT. OF AGRICULTURE (Royal Winter Fair):
This is an appreciation of the contingent of the Canadian Corps of Commissionaires, arranged at our request, for service at the Royal Winter Fair.

The appearance, bearing and general efficiency of these men is to be commended. They were prompt on appointment, attentive to their work and, all in all, everything one might desire.

GEO. A. TOUCHE & CO.:
We have continuously employed a member of the Corps of Commissionaires and wish to advise you that his services have been eminently satisfactory. Knowing something of the excellent work of the Corps in London, England, we have always felt that it would be an excellent idea to have one here.

AMERICAN HOSPITAL ASSOCIATION:
I wish to express my appreciation of the fine service which the Members of No. 2 Company of the Commissionaires rendered the American Hospital Association and its guests during the convention, and after. These men were neat in appearance, orderly in the discharge of their duties and courteous to the people with whom they came in contact.

RETAIL MERCHANTS ASSN. OF CANADA:
We would like to take this opportunity of expressing to you our appreciation of the courteous and efficient service rendered to this Association by your Commissionaires.

We have used their services at every convention sponsored by the Association during the past few years and we have found that they performed their duties to our entire satisfaction, and we shall use them again whenever occasion arises.

Our first business office located at 11 Wellington Street East above a bakery on the second floor. (Courtesy of Bulloch Tailors)

Weekly meetings were still being held at the Legion, the Central Veterans' Clubhouse or the Occidental Hall at Queen and Bathurst Streets. The day-to-day business of the Corps was largely carried out at Secretary-Treasurer Baill's home. But as money became available, #2 Company was able to rent office space at 11 Wellington Street East (September 17, 1931).

On May 28, 1933, the first annual inspection of No.#2 Company was held. His Honour, the Lieutenant Governor of Ontario, Herbert Bruce took the salute. On parade were Captain Finney and 53 uniformed Commissionaires. Seven Governors also attended.

At this time, important decisions and matters of policy and finance were subject to a membership vote which often resulted in conflict. Another solution had to be found, and by a majority vote, the members agreed to hand over complete control of the administration of #2 Company to a Board of Governors. In the latter part of 1935, Colonel A.E. Kirkpatrick, VD was elected first Chairman of the Board and Major Handley-Geary also became a member.

#2 Company reorganized in 1936 under a new Dominion of Canada charter and on April 22, we became known as the Canadian Corps of Commissionaires (Eastern Canada).

First Annual Inspection Canadian Corps of Commissionaires, #2 Coy, Toronto, May 28, 1933.
O.C. Captain W.J. Finney, OBE

Throughout the 1930s, #2 Company enjoyed slow but steady growth. In the midst of the Great Depression, the list of employers was impressive some of whom have remained clients to this day.

THE DUTIES PERFORMED

The nature of the service regularly rendered by members of the Canadian Corps of Commissionaires is shown below. Ex-servicemen of this type are intelligent and accustomed to strict discipline and permanent or temporary work–a few suggestions are shown below.

PERMANENT:
ENQUIRY DESK - MESSENGERS - DOORMEN - GUARDS - WATCHMEN - ELEVATOR MEN

TEMPORARY:
BALLS - DANCES - RECEPTIONS - WEDDINGS - CONVENTIONS - OPEN AIR FETES - EXHIBITIONS - ATTENDANTS

RATES
*Temporary – 50¢ per hour; - minimum $2.00.
Permanent – According to service required.*

TELEPHONE YOUR REQUIREMENTS
Intending employers requiring men in any of the foregoing capacities are requested to telephone the Adjutant, Lieut. W.G. Davis, at Waverley 4066 or call Headquarters, 680 Bay Street.

In 1939, as the nation was recovering from the paralysing effects of the Depression, war was declared in Europe and many of Toronto's Commissionaires were called back into active service. Those that remained found work as guards and watchmen at the Canadian Aluminum Company (later ALCAN), the Dunlop Tire and Rubber Company, National Cash Register, Canadian Industries, Ltd., the Gooderham & Worts Distillery and The Evening Telegram. Some became doormen at Massey Hall and the Royal Alexandra theatre while others took on casual assignments as attendants at weddings, receptions and other social functions.

MrJulian Mott, son of the late Commissionaire Jeremy D. 'Jerry' Mott (#161, who served with the Corps from 1939 to 1946), remembers that his father had been called to stand sentry duty during 1943-44 at Toronto's famous landmark, Casa Loma. MrMott recalls that the assignment seemed rather mysterious at the time as his father, a normally talkative man, would only say that his work was "a big secret."

Casa Loma had been designed and built in 1914 by Toronto millionaire, Sir Henry Mill Pellat, Commanding Officer of the Queen's Own Rifles of Canada. By 1923, Sir Henry had fallen upon hard times and could no longer pay his taxes or maintain the castle. Furniture, antiques and other possessions were auctioned off and the administration of the property was taken over by the city of Toronto. Following several attempts at restoring it, Casa Loma fell into disrepair.

With information that has recently come to light, it was learned that during the Second World War, Casa Loma's sub-basement, wine cellar and carriage house were used for Defence Department munitions work, a secret that was well kept from the citizens of Toronto.

One night during a patrol, Commissionaire Mott discovered a gaping hole in one of the second-storey gables through which pigeons would fly to nest amongst the oak beams in the Great Hall. He decided to patch the hole with a makeshift screen or net to prevent more pigeons from fouling the few remaining treasures and artifacts that hadn't been placed in storage. Mott fetched a ladder, climbed to the outside gable and tacked the net up over the hole. Commissionaire Mott was an amputee and he accomplished this feat with only one arm.

The building which is now our headquarters at 80 Church street was once home to a doctor and a number of financial institutions: The Bank of Toronto, The Home Savings & Loan Company and the Imperial Bank of Canada. It was built on the site of the York Volunteer Fire Brigade hall which was destroyed by fire in 1849. The cornerstone for the new building was laid in 1850.

The building has walk-in vaults on three of its four floors and spacious meeting rooms on the top floor which once served as the bank president's chambers. The Corps purchased the property in 1943 and it is now on the inventory list of the Toronto Heritage Society.

80 Church Street, circa 1879, and; Toronto & Region Headquarters as it looks today.

In 1945, Toronto celebrated the end of the war by welcoming home its heroes with spectacular victory parades and lavish public ceremonies. But the effects of wartime rationing were still being felt. Drivers lined up for their daily allowance of gasoline; Spam was often the main course at evening meals, and jobs were scarce.

Thousands of demobilized soldiers, sailors and airmen flooded Toronto's Union Station daily. Facing an uncertain future, many turned to the Corps for help. But finding suitable employment for these men became a challenge.

On March 6, 1945, a committee of senior Corps officials appealed to the Secretary of the Treasury Board in Ottawa. The committee felt that certain positions within the Civil Service could be satisfactorily performed by our members and asked that "consideration be given to men who had spent the best years of their lives in the service of their country."

That same year, the Liberal government under the newly elected Louis St. Laurent (who had served as a Governor with the Quebec division), and his brilliant Minister of Munitions and Supply, C.D. Howe, granted the Canadian Corps of Commissionaires an almost exclusive right to provide security (and other services as required), at government-run facilities across Canada.

This "right of first refusal" gave the Toronto Corps many opportunities for employment at federal establishments, DND installations, the Canadian Broadcasting Corporation, Malton Airport (later Toronto International Airport, now Lester B. Pearson International Airport), and at post offices throughout the city.

The Ontario provincial government followed suit and our members soon found themselves on duty at Queen's Park, provincial courthouses and the Ontario Hydro-Electric Commission.

The years following the Second World War were the most productive and prosperous for the Toronto Division. Membership had grown to over 400 and for the first time in our brief history, the demand for our services exceeded the supply.

Prior to this period, Commissionaires relied solely upon their military training for guidance in deportment and discipline. But in a peacetime environment, employers wanted men who were less regimental and people who could offer a variety of skills. Changes were rapidly taking place and our men were being advised to adapt.

The time had come for an organized training program to be developed. Beginning in January, 1946, new members were required to attend a basic qualification course and take instruction in security, fire prevention and public relations. Safety in the workplace and emergency first aid procedures were added to the course later.

Individual records of Commissionaires who served throughout the post-war years have disappeared. But copies of Corps Routine Orders do exist and examination reveals a clear picture of the Division during this period, including our strength, and who our principal employers were.

> It is interesting to note that disciplinary measures; suspensions, dismissals, reprimands for misconduct, (along with the individual's name and a description of the infraction), were published in these orders; a practice that would undoubtedly bring a lawsuit today. (Failure to remit one's dues or maintain contact with the Orderly Room would also be cause for disgrace and being struck off strength).

Sunnybrook Veterans' Hospital, the Department of Inland Revenue, the Department of Public Works and the War Assets Corporation, (later Crown Assets), all employed Toronto Commissionaires in large numbers.

The War Assets Corporation, Post #29 was built on the grounds of DeHavilland Aircraft Industries (which would become RCAF Station Downsview, and later, CFB Toronto). In 1952 the building grew to become No.1 Supply Depot. So vast was its floor space (over one million square feet or roughly, the size of 19 and one-half football fields), that Commissionaires rode bicycles from station to station.

Throughout the 1950s, the post office also employed large detachments of Commissionaires. Many were dispatched to the main sorting station at Bay Street and Lakeshore Boulevard (now the home of the Toronto Raptors basketball team). Our members didn't actually sort mail, but they did distribute parcels and containers which led to complaints at having to walk several miles a day (half days on Saturdays).

One bright Commissionaire decided to reduce the wear and tear on his feet by bringing in his roller skates. The idea was enthusiastically approved by HQ and the post office, but because of the many accidents and injuries, it was mercifully short-lived. For a brief period in 1952 however, Commissionaires actually reported for duty with roller skates.

In the 1960s and 70s, Toronto became the entertainment capital of Canada; "Hollywood North," some called it. Many large-scale motion pictures, documentaries and TV programs were produced here and a few of our members have had their share of the lime-light.

Here, pictured with the comedy team of Wayne & Shuster is former Spitfire pilot, Commissionaire Norm Phibbs. Phibbs stood by for many

Spitfire pilot, Norm Phibbs, is pictured here with two other famous World War II vets he met while on duty at 90 Sumach.

years at his post in the wings of CBC Studio IV during live telecasts of the network's longest running panel show, Front Page Challenge. A last minute mystery guest was necessary in case the scheduled celebrity failed to appear.

While Commissionaire Phibbs never did appear on Front Page Challenge, his story was aired on the CBC program, "Take One" on March 12, 1975. Phibbs was the first Canadian to land in Paris after D-Day, carrying with him important communiques for General Eisenhower.

Commissionaires were also featured prominently on CBC-TV's award winning series, Street Legal. But the actors union would not allow actual Corps members to appear on camera. Only experienced actors who "looked the part" (veterans with erect posture, white moustaches, a chest full of ribbons, etc.), could appear in the role.

In the "life imitates art" department, actor and Second World War veteran, Ken Fralick had appeared in several episodes of Street Legal. Mr Fralick was approaching 65 when the series began, and calls for his services were becoming fewer and fewer. One day, he enquired about joining the Corps, and the on-duty Commissionaire explained that all he needed was military experience and a desire for this type of work.

Ken Fralick applied the next day and after completing the basic qualification course, he became #6456 Commissionaire Kenneth W. Fralick. Commissionaire Fralick served with the Toronto Division for many years.

At the Headquarters annual meeting in 1972 following a Royal Commission on the Status of Women, it was agreed that women who had served in the Armed Forces and had met the minimum service time requirements would qualify for membership.

Shortly after, the Honourable Pauline McGibbon was installed as the Twenty-Second Lieutenant Governor of Ontario and in 1976, she was invited to become a Patron of the Toronto Corps. She graciously accepted our invitation and in 1983, became the first woman member of the Corporation. Colonel The Honorable Pauline McGibbon served with the Board of Governors for seven years and was named Life Governor in 1992.

Many men and women have served the Toronto Division with distinction. But on occasion a Commissionaire "extraordinaire" brings credit to the Corps through an act of bravery, distinguished service or performance above and beyond the call of his or her duty.

Commissionaire Rufino Mosquera

#5187 Commissionaire Rufino "Ruf" Mosquera has served in every conceivable NCO position in the Corps; from Commissionaire to WO I, and from night watchman to Chief Inspector. In the twelve years that he has been with the Toronto Division Mosquera has worked at an unbelievable 52 detachments; often at the request of clients.

Commissionaire 'extraordinaire' Rufino 'Ruf' Mosquera.

Mosquera served with the Royal Air Force Air/Sea Rescue team between 1939 and 1945. Following the Second World War he returned home to Jamaica to accept a position as Port Secretary and Chief of Security at Ocho Rios, a job that lasted five years. The Jamaica Constabulary recognized Mosquera's negotiating and investigative skills and asked him to join the force in 1951. He accepted the invitation and was immediately promoted to the rank of Detective.

Commissionaire Mosquera is a multi-talented individual. He is a gifted writer, an artist, he once played bass for the Salvation Army and he is a past president of Toastmasters International.

His paintings decorate the living rooms, dens and bedrooms of a hundred or more Commissionaires, friends and relatives. Ruf thoroughly enjoys his hobby and cheerfully gives his works of art away to people he likes. He exhibits the most admirable qualities of a Commissionaire; honesty, integrity, loyalty and dependability. He is understandably well liked for the warmth and courtesy he extends to everyone he meets. His personal file bulges with commendations and letters of appreciation.

He has also been instrumental in preserving a number of our contracts through his good humour and natural flair for diplomacy. This earned Ruf a Commendable Service award in 1987.

To show their appreciation for his many years of outstanding service and dedication, on July 6, 1995, the Board of Governors presented Commissionaire Rufino Mosquera with a special Exemplary Performance award; the Toronto Division's equivalent to the Order of Canada.

Commissionaire Twistleton Bertrand

#3516 Commissionaire Twistleton St. Rose 'Twist' Bertrand would undoubtedly have become Prime Minister of Domenica had he remained in his island paradise and thrown his hat in the ring. But he cast aside any political aspirations so that his children could be raised and educated in Canada.

Bertrand served during the Second World War with the South Caribbean Defence Forces where he was awarded the 1939-45 Star, the Defence Medal and the British War Medal.

He was taken on strength in Toronto on March 3, 1978 and appears to hold the

Major 'Twist' Bertrand, Honorary Aide-de-Camp to three Ontario Lieutenant Governors, and the Division's first Inspector.

record for the greatest number of promotions in the shortest period of time.

Following the basic qualification course, 'Twist' was promoted to Corporal and appointed Assistant Training Officer. He also became the Toronto Division's first Inspecting Officer. A month later he was promoted to Sergeant and in April 1980, to Staff-Sergeant.

Always ready to accept a challenge, Bertrand took over the Dispatcher's chair in July of that year and was promoted to WO II. Taking on the added responsibilities of Regimental Sergeant Major earned him another promotion to WO I in January of 1983.

Warrant Officer Bertrand became Lieutenant Bertrand in October of 1985 when the Honourable Lincoln Alexander, Lieutenant Governor of Ontario, asked him to become his Aide-de-Camp. His acceptance led to yet another promotion; this time to Captain.

In addition to his duties at Queen's Park, Captain Bertrand acted as our Special Events Officer, and in 1991, was the first member to be awarded the Corps' Distinguished Service Medal.

Today, Major Bertrand is retired from the Corps but continues in his role at Queen's Park. He was recently invited to serve another term as Aide-de-Camp to the Honorable Hilary Weston, the newly appointed Lieutenant Governor of Ontario.

Major Wilfred Ellis

Major Wilfred Dancy 'Dick' Ellis, CD joined the Toronto Division in 1964 as Corps Paymaster after a 49-year career in banking and investment counselling with the Bank of Commerce.

Major Ellis was the last surviving member of the 1,000-strong Canadian Corps of Cyclists Battalion that fought during the First World War as part of the Canadian Expeditionary Force.

He began working for the Corps in his 69th year and retired 12 years later at the age of 81. Not one to sit and watch the world go by, Dick then began taking courses in Philosophy and English at the University of Toronto.

The last photograph of Major W.D. 'Dick' Ellis, taken shortly after his one-hundredth birthday.

Major Ellis became a Member of the Corporation in 1968 and was elected to the Board of Governors when he retired in 1976. In 1982, Major Ellis was named a Life Governor of the Royal Canadian Military Institute. In 1995, the Chairman of the Board announced his appointment as Life Governor.

On November 6, 1995, a few months after his 100th birthday, Major Ellis rose from his wheelchair at the head table during our annual awards dinner and toasted the Corps. The applause was deafening.

He died on August 14 1996, just 34 days shy of his 101st birthday.

Commissionaire Bob Orlinski

A team of Hollywood screenwriters could not have scripted a more colourful, action-packed life than the one led by #2416 Commissionaire Boleslaw 'Bob' Orlinski. Born in Poland, Orlinski served as a cavalryman in the Russian Imperial Army. In 1915, during a cavalry charge near the Polish-Russian border, the 17-year-old Orlinski bravely took command of his squadron of lancers when the officer in charge was killed. But sabres and thundering hooves were no match for enemy cannon or machine-gun fire and Orlinski was wounded. When he recovered he was promoted to 2nd Lieutenant and awarded the Order of St. George and the Silver Cross.

Lenin and Trotsky had strange ideas in 1916-17 about Russia's future and communism. Military officers were routinely rounded up and shot as enemies of the people. By disguising himself as a Private, Orlinski made his way through hostile territory back to Poland where he joined the Polish Army, only to find that they were fighting his former Russian comrades on one front, and Germans on the other.

Sgt. Boleslaw 'Bob' Orlinski decorated eighteen times by five countries.

Thousands of lives were lost but Orlinski miraculously survived, and when the war was over he enlisted in the Polish Air Force. In 1921 he completed his his pilot training and was promoted to Lieutenant. Throughout his 27-year flying career, Orlinski flew over 100 different types of aircraft, often as a test pilot.

In 1926, Orlinski flew from Warsaw to Tokyo and back, a record-setting flight of 14,000 miles. The event was front page news–more than a year before Charles Lindberg made his famous crossing of the Atlantic. Captain Orlinski received the golden medal of the Japanese Imperial Aeronautical Society and the Order of the Rising Sun. France and Poland conferred similar awards.

At the outbreak of the Second World War, Orlinski joined the RAF as a flying instructor with the rank of Flight Lieutenant and in 1943, he flew back into action. He was wounded by shrapnel many times and three of his planes crash-landed in enemy territory. Incredibly, Orlinski made it back to England each time only to pilot another aircraft into aerial combat.

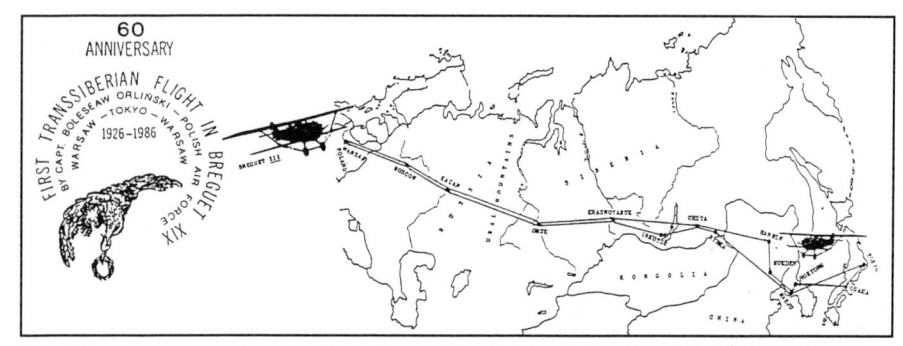

Special commemorative envelope issued in 1986 celebrating the 60th anniversary of Orlinski's 14,000 mile flight.

In 1986, a special commemorative envelope was issued celebrating the 60th anniversary of the Orlinski flight.

He was promoted to Squadron Leader in 1944 and to Wing Commander the following year. Orlinski was awarded England's Distinguished Flying Cross in 1945 and the end of the war had decorated him 18 times by five countries.

Following a brief period in South Africa, Orlinsky came to Canada in 1953 and worked for the DeHavilland Aircraft Company. Retiring from DeHavilland in 1967, Bob joined the Toronto Division and worked at Corps Headquarters for many years. Sergeant Boleslaw 'Bob' Orlinski retired in 1980 at the age of 81.

Captain Allan Griffith

At the Toronto & Region Division's annual awards dinner on November 6, 1996, Training Officer, Captain Allan Griffith, CD was presented with the Commissionaires' Distinguished Service Medal; the highest honour the Corps can bestow.

Captain Griffith was honoured for his loyalty and dedication to the Corps, and was recognized for his superior training skills and continued efforts in promoting the employment of our members.

Griffith served with the 1st Canadian Highland Batallion in the 48th Highlanders Company, the Royal Canadian Regiment and the Black Watch, and at the age of 21, was the youngest Sergeant in the NATO armed forces.

He began instructing at the School of Infantry at Camp Borden where he taught officers from every branch of the military. He also taught Military Law at Gagetown, N.B.

At Borden, he took parachute training and shortly after, joined the Canadian Airborne regiment. Sergeant Griffith was also a Commando attached to the American Forces in Germany.

St. John Ambulance had been made aware of Griffith's instructing ability and in 1978, asked him to become their Toronto District

Administration Officer – an offer he couldn't refuse.

While with St. John, Griffith became familiar with every aspect of first aid and acquired valuable marketing skills. But the supervision of hundreds of volunteer emergency first aid workers and over 200 instructors made his life anything but peaceful, and in 1980 he retired.

Griffith soon grew restless however, and one day he responded to a newspaper advertisement about the Corps.

21-year-old Allan Griffith, the youngest Sergeant in the NATO armed forces.

#4597 Commissionaire Allan Griffith joined the Toronto Division on August 19, 1983 and proceeded to work his way through the ranks in record time.

In 1985, after being posted to a number of high-profile detachments, Sergeant Griffith was appointed Training Officer, and this is where his instructing experience and marketing skills paid off. In addition to training new members, Griffith developed our condominium program. The Toronto Division has over 50 members employed as concierges in this rapidly growing part of the security industry.

Griffith also became the Division's recruitment officer and, in association with Metro Police, established our municipal law enforcement officer program. He also selects candidates for the Corps' supervisors and instructors courses.

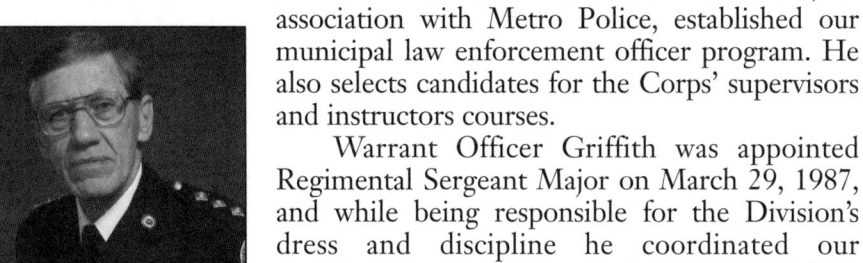

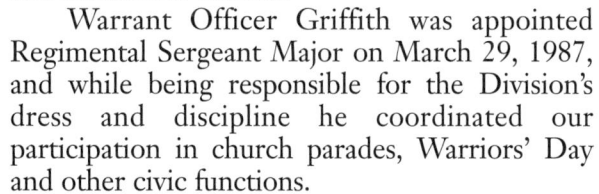

Warrant Officer Griffith was appointed Regimental Sergeant Major on March 29, 1987, and while being responsible for the Division's dress and discipline he coordinated our participation in church parades, Warriors' Day and other civic functions.

In appreciation of his many years of splendid work on behalf of St. John Ambulance, Captain Allan Griffith was summoned to Ottawa on October 1, 1996 where he was made a Serving Brother of the Order of St. John.

Training Officer Captain Allan Griffith, the Toronto division's last R.S.M.

Commissionaire John Leprich

Toward the end of the Second World War, #4615 Commissionaire John O. Leprich served as the mid-upper turret gunner aboard an AVRO Lancaster heavy bomber with the 429th Bomber Squadron of the Royal Canadian Air Force.

Reconnaissance photos taken in 1943 by the RAF revealed that Nazi Germany had designed, built and tested the world's first jet propelled fighter; the Messerschmidt ME-262. This extremely agile and manoeuvrable twin-engine flying machine could reach speeds of over 540 mph . . . unheard of for a propeller driven aircraft.

On March 31, 1945 Flight Sergeant Leprich's seven-man crew came under attack in enemy territory by an ME-262. The Lancaster's Browning twin-barrelled machine-gun had been damaged in a previous encounter and Leprich was forced to hold the broken breech block together with one hand to keep it from jamming. With the other he fired a burst of .303 bullets at the diving ME-262 and down it went in a trail of black smoke.

Commissionaire John 'Ace' Leprich, awarded the D.F.M. in 1945.

"For great gallantry in the performance of his duty," Flight Sergeant 'Ace' Leprich was awarded the RCAF Distinguished Flying Medal and was the first man to be credited with shooting down an ME-262.

Leprich was born in Romania but spent his youth in Hanover, Ontario practising the trumpet and entertaining family and friends with his impressions of Harry James, Ray Anthony and other trumpet greats of the big band era, a pastime he still enjoys.

Before retiring from his post at the Oakville Parkade in August of 1997, Commissionaire John O. Leprich, DFM, had received no less than six commendations for his outstanding performance as a Commissionaire.

Commissionaire Pat Stewart Leil

#3805 Commissionaire Pat Stewart joined the Toronto Division as Assistant Paymaster on October 30, 1978, and has worked at Corps Headquarters since then.

No stranger to hard work, Pat still regularly puts in 12-hour and 14-hour days, and never asks for time off in lieu. When a glitch occurs with our computerized payroll system, Pat thinks nothing of unravelling a sleeping bag and camping out on the second floor of Corps Headquarters until the problem has been solved.

Commissionaire Stewart served as Chief Clerk with the Toronto Service Battalion for 19 years. In 1972, she was posted to Toronto District Headquarters and for many of those

Chief Warrant Officer Pat Leil, Assistant Finance Officer.

years, Pat worked for the Corps during the day and did double-duty as Chief Clerk and Recruiting Officer for the Regiment several evenings a week.

While acting as Chief Clerk with the 48th Highlanders at Moss Park Armouries in 1989, Warrant Officer Stewart met a kilted drummer with a roguish smile named William 'Sandy' Leil. The two struck up an instant friendship that resulted in their being married that same year. In 1994, Sandy became #6903 Commissionaire W.A. Leil.

Today, Chief Warrant Officer Pat Leil serves as the Toronto Division's Assistant Finance Officer. She is a tireless worker and no one is more dedicated to the welfare of our Commissionaires.

Commissionaire Randhir Singh Rana

The Toronto Division has its own Olympic gold medal winner. #5314 Commissionaire Randhir Singh Rana gained world acclaim for his skill in field hockey at the 1956 Olympic games in Melbourne, Australia. His team finished with a gold medal and Rana also distinguished himself at basketball and tennis.

Commissionaire Rana was born in Sansarpur, Punjab and comes from a family where military life is a proud tradition. His father and grandfather both served with the world famous Gurkha regiment and two elder brothers were killed in action during the Second World War while serving with Sikh regiments attached to the Allied Forces.

Rana joined the Indian Army when he was 19 and served in Vietnam during 1967-68 with the International Supervisory Control Commission, a peacekeeping unit made up of members from the Indian, Polish and Canadian Armed Forces. In 1968 Rana received the United Nations Peacekeeping medal.

Commissionaire Randhir Singh Rana, Olympic gold medal winner in 1956.

After a glorious 38-year military career Commissionaire Randhir Singh Rana retired as a Lieutenant Colonel with the Indian Army Ordnance Corps. He joined the Toronto Division in 1986 and today at the age of 73, he serves at Lester B. Pearson International Airport.

This brings an end to those selected for their outstanding service.

While these personal profiles are glowing and praiseworthy, our public image hasn't always been as rosy.

An incident at Toronto's Osgoode Hall did little to improve our reputation. One afternoon, a huge painting of John Graves Simcoe that had been painstakingly restored was being returned to its place of honour near the main entrance. The movers had carefully laid the painting on the floor while wall measurements and levels were taken. A Commissionaire who was on duty nearby decided to step outside for a quick puff and without looking, he marched blindly through a doorway and directly onto the painting. The media had a field-day and the incident placed the entire Division in a bad light.

Throughout the 1970s, the Toronto Division enjoyed only modest success. Our standing order with the Government of Canada provided steady employment but there was little growth.

The mess at 80 Church Street with its billiard and ping-pong tables opened daily at 1100 hrs and members seemed more concerned with cribbage tournaments, monthly dances and stag nights than their increasingly lacklustre performance and declining reputation. Participation in parades and civic ceremonies had dwindled and few men volunteered for any activity that would bring credit to the Corps.

Colonel M.E. 'Marv' Rich, C.D., became Commandant on January 1, 1978, and the Toronto Division's image underwent an immediate and dramatic change.

After a distinguished 26-year career in the Royal Canadian Artillery, Colonel Rich, a graduate of Upper Canada College and Royal Military College, took a no-nonsense approach to his new role and was determined to re-establish a favourable relationship with our clients and the people of Toronto. His first move was an unpopular one. He closed down the mess. Colonel Rich reasoned that regardless of our right of first refusal, it was wrong to send a man to any location with liquor on his breath.

Colonel M.E. 'Marv' Rich, CD, Commandant of the Toronto division since 1978. Rich once hosted his own Jazz radio program at RMC.

Then through a series of interviews, he began weeding out members whom he felt were too old or failed to meet Corps requirements. Colonel Rich would not tolerate appearance or behavior that disgraced the Corps.

He also assembled a team of inspectors (now called Liaison Officers). These men were selected from a handful of experienced Commissionaires with proven leadership ability and other skills. Their job was to inspect each detachment on a regular basis, maintain contact with clients and report irregularities directly to the Commandant, a policy that exists to this day.

Colonel Rich also felt that Commissionaires who performed heroic deeds or distinguished themselves beyond the call of duty should be honoured and given special recognition. Beginning in 1980, Commendable, Exemplary and Meritorious service awards were presented to deserving members at annual awards dinners by a Governor or other dignitary.

These measures soon achieved positive results as members of the Toronto Division began taking pride in their appearance and job performance. This also commanded the respect and admiration of our employers and the public.

In 1984, Mayor Art Eggleton presented the Toronto Division with a certificate of appreciation for the part we played during the Queen's Royal Visit when Toronto celebrated its sesquicentennial year.

CITY OF TORONTO

An Appreciation

Canadian Corps of Commissionaires

The visit by Her Majesty the Queen and His Royal Highness the Duke of Edinburgh was a memorable event for the City of Toronto in our Sesquicentennial year. The enthusiasm of the people who attended the civic celebrations and lined the streets of the royal procession routes gave evidence of the loyalty, affection and esteem our community holds for Her Majesty and His Royal Highness. This warm welcome, together with the dedication and diligence of those who contributed to the arrangements, resulted in an outstanding royal visit.

His Worship Mayor Eggleton and the members of City Council wish you to accept this testimonial in appreciation of the notable part you played in making the royal visit enjoyable for Her Majesty and His Royal Highness. The Royal Visit was indeed an event of which the City of Toronto can be justifiably proud.

Since 1946, only three Commandants have led the Toronto Division through both prosperous and troubled times. These men were noted for their outstanding leadership ability, and not surprisingly, each was a graduate of Canada's Royal Military College.

Colonel Morris H.A. 'Boy' Drury, OBE, CD, was nearing completion of his military studies when war broke out in 1914. At the age of 19, he was granted a commission with the Royal Canadian Dragoons. This earned him the nickname 'Boy' and it stayed with him the rest of his life.

The Dragoons were promptly shipped off to France where they served as cavalry in the dismounted role. After the war Boy Drury was promoted to Major and became the regiment's Intelligence Officer.

An accomplished horseman, Drury formed the Canadian Army Equestrian Jumping Team which entertained audiences throughout Canada and the U.S. during the Great Depression.

He was chosen to represent the Canadian Army at the funeral of King George V in 1939 and also trained an escort squadron for the visit of His Majesty King George VI and Queen Elizabeth the same year. In 1941 he was made an Officer of the Order of the British Empire.

Drury was then appointed Deputy Assistant Adjutant General of Military District No.2, the largest military district in Canada. After a brief period of service in England he became Senior Administrative Staff Officer; an appointment he held until the end of the war.

Colonel M.H.A. Drury, became a Captain at the age of 19, earning him the nickname 'Boy.'

In 1946, less than two weeks after retiring from the military, Major Drury became Commandant of the Toronto Division and served until 1968. During his 22-year command, the Division's strength more than doubled.

At a testimonial dinner in 1968, Colonel M.H.A. 'Boy' Drury was named Life Governor of the Corps. He died in 1977.

After the Second World War veterans of the Royal Canadian Mounted Police qualified for membership in the Corps.

Colonel John F. 'Jack' Thrasher graduated from the Royal Military College in 1928 and joined the RCMP as a 1st Class Constable. In 1932 he was posted to the Winnipeg detachment and during this period, Thrasher earned an LLB degree from Manitoba Law School and received a commission.

Superintendent Thrasher was appointed Assistant Adjutant at RCMP Headquarters in Ottawa in 1944 and served as Adjutant of the force from 1945 to 1951.

Thrasher commanded "O" Division in Toronto until 1956, and after several successful years in private business he decided to step back into uniform.

R.C.M.P. Superintendent J.F. (Jack) Thrasher, Commandant of the Toronto Division 1968-77.

Superintendent Thrasher joined the Toronto Division as Deputy Commandant in 1963 and was appointed Commandant in 1968. He served until 1977.

Thrasher was awarded the 1952 Coronation medal, the RCMP Long Service medal and the Queen Elizabeth II Silver Jubilee medal. Following his retirement, Colonel Thrasher was elected a Governor of the Corps and became a Life Governor in 1978. He died in 1990.

THE CORPS ASSOCIATION (Toronto & Region)

The formation of the Corps Association in 1979 is especially noteworthy. The brainchild of Colonel M.E. Rich, Toronto & Region is the only Division with such a fraternity.

Former members of the Division with at least five years' service are encouraged to join the Association and continue the spirit of comradeship that they enjoyed during their service with the Corps.

Members meet for lunch several times a year at 80 Church Street where they are entertained, kept informed of important changes, Corps activities and other items of interest.

Association members are also invited to Divisional functions from time to time where they can meet new Commissionaires and keep in touch with former co-workers and shift-mates.

The most celebrated member of the Corps Association, #0036 Warrant Officer Miles Harrison, joined #2 Company in 1936. When he retired in 1979 he became a charter member of the Association, and at 95 years of age, Harrison still regularly attends meetings, a remarkable 61-year affiliation with the Toronto Division.

Superintendent Colonel J.F. Thrasher served as first Chairman of the Association which today has over 60 members.

Commissionaires have been a part of the Toronto scene for 70 years. We've survived a world war, a crippling Depression, several recessions and a number of political regimes. Today, although growing competition, budget cuts, downsizing, restructuring and technology threaten our survival, the Corps is still big business in Toronto. In 1996 our revenues exceeded six million and our books have never shown a deficit.

As we at 80 Church Street celebrate our 70th anniversary, there is good reason to be as optimistic as we were in 1927. We have a strength of almost 800 men and women (and growing), a state-of-the-art computer on each desk, our own web site on the Internet and there are plans for on-line video conferencing. We also enjoy a benefits package that is equal to any in the private sector and the Corps is now recognized as an ISO 9000 company.

The Commissionaires in Canada were formed with a life expectancy of 50 years. Record keeping has therefore never been a priority and most of our early files have either been discarded or were destroyed by fire in 1941.

Little is known today of the original six members. The records we do have show that Commissionaire #1, Charles George 'Geordie' Robertson was promoted to WO II in 1949 and was still employed as a Commissionaire in Toronto as late as 1960.

Sgt John Connor returned to Montreal shortly after #2 Company became operational. Although he didn't become a member of the Toronto

Corps, he maintained a keen interest in our progress for many years. He died at Sunnybrook Hospital in November, 1954. His son, Gordon John Connor did join in 1937 and became Commissionaire #128. He was promoted to Staff Sergeant in July, 1960.

Secretary-Treasurer, Commissionaire #7, Frederick William 'Bill' Baill served with the Toronto Division until 1960. He died on June 28th after more than 33 years of faithful and loyal service. His son, Charles Leslie Baill, #R-1640, a reservist joined the Toronto Division on July 31, 1958.

Our first Commandant, Captain W.J. Finney, resigned in 1933 owing to the pressures of his civilian interests and handed over the office of Commandant to Lieutenant Colonel S.B. Pepler. Captain Finney remained a member of the Corporation until his death in 1973.

Colonel A.E. Kirkpatrick, the first appointed Chairman of the Board of Governors, served in that role only throughout 1936 but remained a member of the Board until 1951.

In addition to our first office at 11 Wellington East and the building we now occupy at 80 Church Street, we have rented space at 680 Bay Street (1936); 22 Leader Lane (1939); and 117 Wellington Street East (1941), where most of our early files were destroyed by fire. The writer located Mr Julian Mott, son of the late Commissionaire Jeremy Mott at the North York Extendicare in February 1997. Mr Mott related the Casa Loma story among others that were neither flattering to his father nor complimentary to the Corps. Mr Mott, 76, was lucid and I have no reason to doubt his version of the event especially in light of the information that was uncovered about the ASDIC (Anti-Submarine Detection) sonic device (Sonar), that was being assembled below ground at the castle during Commissionaire Mott's time with the Corps. He lost his left arm (at the elbow) at Vimy Ridge in 1917.

COMMANDANTS - (1927-1997)

1927-1933	LCol W.J. Finney, OBE
1933-1936	LCol S.B. Pepler, MBE, MC
1936-1936	Col G. Godson-Godson, DSO, DCM
1936-1937	LCol R.J.S. Langford
1937-1940	Maj T.D. McManus, VD
1940-1946	Capt Palmer Wright
1946-1968	LCol M.H.A. Drury, OBE, CD
1968-1977	Supt. J.F. Thrasher, RCMP
1977-	Col M.E. Rich, CD

ACKNOWLEDGEMENTS

I would like to thank the following for their assistance.

Toronto historian, Mike Filey, who provided copies of early documents and old newspaper files which were thought to have been lost or destroyed; Ms Julie Kirsh of the *Toronto Sun* for allowing me access to the microfilmed records of the *Evening Telegram;* Paul and Shelly Lau of Beauty Print Photo Lab for their fine work in reproducing (and in some cases, restoring) old photographs; and MrJulian Mott, son of the late Commissionaire Jeremy Mott.

I would also like to thank Chief Clerk, Master Warrant Officer Joe MacDonald for providing dates, times and obscure but important details and the many Commissionaires in the Toronto Division (former and active), for their tips, suggestions and recollections.

Master Warrant Officer R. McAnespie

Chapter IV

HISTORY OF THE BRITISH COLUMBIA CORPS OF COMMISSIONAIRES

B.C. Corps of Commissionaires

Commandant's Introduction – *By Graham Jenkins*.

The First 70 Years

*I*N 1997, the British Columbia Corps of Commissionaires celebrated its 70th Anniversary. It was a time to pause, not just to remember the past but also to look at where we are today, and to plan for the future. Until recently, the primary purpose of the Corps was to serve the needs of former servicemen and women caught up in major events: First World War, Second World War and Korea. Each of these events provided a specific recruiting base for the Corps based on those who served in war. Now, for the first time in the history of the Corps, we are recruiting from a generation who have been part of an ongoing series of commitments, NATO, peacekeeping and other activities primarily associated with a Regular Force. Our clients have been similarly affected; many of them too were veterans of war. This is the first generation of Commissionaires to provide services to clients who have had no association with the military. The feeling of affiliation and tolerance based on shared experiences and hardships has given way to a more demanding operating environment that can only be satisfied with higher standards of training and performance.

Each generation has had to deal with the problems of its own time, and has done so successfully, bringing the Corps to where it is today. That requirement still exists, but another dimension has been added, that of planning for the future in an operating environment characterized by rapid change. In this short history, mention is made of just a few who have shaped the Corps in the past. We who serve today acknowledge their contribution, accept responsibility for the present and the challenge of the future. "Carry on the Corps."

Early Days and Hard Times

The first settlers on the site that was to become Vancouver built their homes in 1862. In 1886, the bill incorporating the city of Vancouver was passed by the Provincial Legislature. In 1927, Vancouver was only 41 years old and was enjoying a resource industry based boom that was to come to an abrupt end with the stock market crash of 1929. The Depression that followed continued until the Second World War. It was in these challenging times that the B.C. Corps of Commissionaires was born and struggled for its existence.

As with the British Corps, the B.C. Corps had its origin with disabled veterans who, despite the boom, were unable to find steady employment. Three men: Percy Lawrence, A. Farthing and C.B. Strickland formed the Disabled Veterans Association. After some initial success, they approached LCol. A. Leslie Coote, VD, a well-known pre-war officer, for guidance and support. With his assistance, they decided to form a unit of Commissionaires, and extended membership to include any unemployed veteran. Whether handicapped or physically fit, jobs were difficult to find for the returned veteran.

During this same period, the Canadian Corps of Commissionaires was being organized in Montreal and Toronto. While there was probably an awareness of this in Vancouver at the time, there is no record of contact until after formation of the B.C. Corps. On the 26th of October 1927, the British Columbia Corps of Commissionaires was formally incorporated under the Society Act of British Columbia. The first General Meeting was held on the 10th of November at the offices of the Disabled Veterans Association loaned for the occasion by the Department of Veterans Affairs (DVA). The first problem, understandably, was one of finances. It was agreed that Life Members and Patrons be admitted on payment of a membership fee of $25. The next question was one of eligibility. It was decided that disabled veterans already in the Disabled Veterans Association be given first preference followed by other veterans. Fees for membership were set at $5. It is recorded that at the conclusion of the meeting, Percy Lawrence and James Lee tendered their membership fees thus providing the first capital of the Corps. At a meeting held on the 15th of December, it was also agreed that a limited number of persons be admitted to Honorary Membership on payment of a fee of $10. A unique feature of the B.C. Corps was that the Commissionaires were members of the Society rather than the Governors (Trustees) as was the case in every other Division in Canada, a distinction that was to remain until 1996.

The Canadian Corps

By December 1927, the Canadian Corps had made contact with the national body and in February of the following year the Corps accepted the offer to join them as No. 3 Company, Canadian Corps of

Canadian Corps of Commissionaires – No. 3 Company, Vancouver, B.C. – March 18, 1928.

Commissionaires. On July 2, 1931, the name change to Canadian Corps of Commissionaires (No. 3 Company) was made official. In March of 1928, Lt. Col. Coote, in his capacity as Officer Commanding, visited Ottawa and made contact with Capt. Finney, who at that time was both President and Secretary of the Toronto Company who brought him up to date on the Corps in Eastern Canada. He saw the heads of various government departments and received many offers of assistance; however, there was a reluctance to be obligated to the government. He was entertained at lunch by Col. Ralston, Minister of Militia and afterwards addressed 30 Members of Parliament on the work of the Corps. In an interview with the Rt. Hon Mackenzie King he was promised all assistance. Instructions were given that all positions in British Columbia that could be filled by returned men should be given to the Corps. After his talk with Capt. Finney it was decided to make the Corps Canada-wide. As a first step, on his return journey to Vancouver, he stopped in Winnipeg to promote the idea of a Corps there. Very clearly Lt. Col. Coote believed in the Corps and approached the organization with missionary zeal.

March 30, 1928 saw receipt of a letter from the Army and Navy Veterans of Victoria with reference to formation of a Corps on Vancouver Island. This was followed by another enquiry in 1937 from the "Imperial Veterans Association" on the same subject. At the same time, a letter was received from the Veterans Assistance Commission in Calgary requesting advice in setting up a Corps there. By April 1937, the Corps was established in Calgary; the Victoria and Vancouver Island Division was authorized and on August 4, 1937, the B.C. Corps gave authority for its formation under the B.C. Corps Charter where it remained until 1946. In reporting on this affiliation, it should be noted that relations between the two organizations were of a supporting nature rather than that of command. A similar relationship existed between the B.C. Corps and other Western Divisions as they got their start, although without the legal attachment.

The relationship of the B.C. Corps to the national organization was cordial but at the same time retained a level of independence that was not altogether surprising. In the early '30s some 70% of the population of Vancouver was of British origin and almost 50% of the B.C. Corps were British veterans with a strong feeling for the British Corps of Commissionaires. Corps archives show regular correspondence between the two organizations. At the same time, the national organization was sorting out its Headquarters' structure, By-laws and Rules and Regulations.

Individual Divisions were focusing increasingly on their own struggle for survival in a country locked in the grip of the Depression. Finally, December 18, 1941, No. 3 Company was dissolved and the Corps reverted to its original identity as the British Columbia Corps of Commissionaires deemed "to have continued in existence as if it had not previously been struck off." It would be easy to refer to this move as a severing of relations with the national body but this was not the case. While there were concerns with the proposed national by-laws, the primary reason was that the Corps was receiving $1,200 a year from the Vancouver Welfare Federation (Community Chest), which it felt would be jeopardized by a formal association and the required contribution of financial support to the national body. The Corps continued to send a representative to national meetings and assured the Canadian Corps of continued cooperation. The grants from the Welfare Federation were subsequently repaid in full once the Corps became self-supporting. Another debt that was repaid in 1929 was the twenty dollars given by The Disabled Veterans Association in 1926 "to start the Corps of Commissionaires."

Depression Years

Vancouver, 1929, saw the unemployed raiding the city relief office and parading the streets demanding work. By August 1930, Vancouver had 7,000 unemployed. By 1932, as many as 34,000 needed relief in Vancouver and 15,000 hunger marchers paraded the streets. By 1935, demonstrations sparked by desperation reached the point where the Riot Act was read in Victory Square. The population of Vancouver at that time was in the neighbourhood of 250,000 with almost a quarter of that number out of work or needing relief. Many of those seeking work were veterans. The Corps was able to find work for some, but very few. For veterans without employment, the Corps set up a depot in a vacant building in Vancouver's Gastown, donated by Maj JG Fordham, a local businessman and Patron of the Corps. Trustees of the Corps called upon the business community and were successful in obtaining donations of food, blankets and clothing. Sleeping accommodation and meals were provided for about 60 veterans at a time provided they were prepared to abide by the strict rules established by the Corps. With the continuing support of local businessmen this was continued until the outbreak of the Second World War when employment improved and the need declined. Neville Chamberlain's name is forever associated with appeasement, but to veterans who had experienced the horror of trench warfare in the First World War "peace in our time" had an undeniable appeal. At a General Meeting of the Corps, September 30, 1938, following the Munich Conference, it was unanimously agreed that a letter be sent to Neville Chamberlain expressing "the loyal support of the B.C. Corps of Commissionaires at this time of crisis." His reply, on file in the Corps archives expresses, "very warm thanks for your kind message." Subsequent correspondence from Commissionaires reflects the disillusionment that followed when Hitler invaded Poland the following year. As the Depression came to an end, the Corps received a request from Trans Canada Airlines to provide traffic and security services at Vancouver Airport. This was the beginning of a long association that has continued until the present day. It was also in that year that the first transcontinental air service was launched between Vancouver and Montreal.

The Second World War

The advent of war was a great stimulus to the economy and the demand for Commissionaires to fill the jobs available increased dramatically. The strength of the Corps soon grew to 315 with most being steadily employed. There are no records to indicate how many Corps members returned to the services. It is of interest to note however, that several trustees attained high rank during the war. Major General V.W. Odlum was promoted to that rank to command 2 Canadian Infantry Division and later served with the diplomatic service as High Commissioner to Australia followed by service as Ambassador to Turkey and China. LCol. J.P. MacKenzie returned to serve with the Royal Canadian Engineers, later to become Quartermaster General with the rank of Major General. Col. W.W. Foster, DSO, VD, Chief Constable of Vancouver and a former national president of the Royal Canadian Legion was also to reach the rank of Major General, assigned to coordinated Auxiliary Services overseas. He took with him Major Victor MacLean, who up to that time had been Commanding Officer of the Corps, to serve on his staff. LCol. W.C. Woodward, an early Patron of the Corps, served as the Lieutenant Governor of the province for most of the war.

Among those who joined the Corps after the war was Victor Louie. Victor was born in Victoria and had his first experience fighting the Japanese in China from 1931 to 1938 where he led a band of guerilllas. Returning to Canada at the outbreak of the Second World War, he joined the Special Operations Executive (SOE), parachuting into Malaya on Operation Tideway Green to work with the Malayan Peoples Anti-Japanese Army, acting as an interpreter for other members of the team. After operating in the jungle, at times suffering from hunger and disease, he still remembers the thrill of receiving the Japanese Adjutant's sword during the surrender. He worked for Eaton's after the war and, on his retirement took up gardening, winning many prizes for his beautiful flowers. If you saw him handing out suckers to children whose parents were in the welfare day line-up, you would never think of him operating behind enemy lines.

Victor at the Toll Booth.

David Birch, born in China of missionary parents was a student in a British boarding school in Shandong at the time of Pearl Harbour. He spent his boyhood in Weihsien Concentration Camp in Japanese-held North China and did not see his parents until after the war.

Bob Rogers who served the Corps well for 17 years both on the job and as a member of the Membership Committee was a member of 419 Squadron in the United Kingdom. On the 29th of December 1944, he was on a bombing mission over Germany when the aircraft in which he was rear gunner was struck in the bomb bay, causing the entire bomb load to explode. The entire plane disintegrated throwing him clear. He descended by parachute, landing in Essen. He was the only one of a crew of seven to survive. With burns, injuries from flak and a sprained ankle he was unable to escape and was made prisoner. Conditions in the camps and his experiences as a prisoner of war were nothing less than atrocious until he was liberated in 1945 in Munich. Bob had an integrity and loyalty to the Corps that earned respect wherever he went.

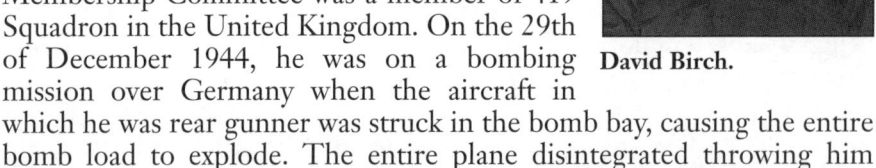

David Birch.

Corps RSM for many years, Bert Grant joined the Canadian Scottish in 1929 and when war broke out was assigned as a machine-gunner to Yorke Island, a 120-acre islet with

AVM Stevenson presents a medal to RSM Grant. Cec. Merritt, VC, holds the list.

two 4.7-inch guns guarding the channel about 150 miles north-west of Vancouver. Such was its isolation and living conditions that it was referred to as "Little Alcatraz." Subsequently, Bert Grant landed in France on D-Day and was discharged with the rank of WOII. When he joined the Corps in 1945, he was assigned as an armed guard at the *Daily Province* newspaper's cashiers cage. While in the Corps he was also employed at the University of British Columbia Fire Department from whence he retired with the rank of Captain in 1973.

Commissionaire Charlie Brown at the time of writing is the longest serving member of the Corps, having joined in 1959. His wartime service was in minesweepers off Canada's East Coast. D-Day saw him aboard *HMCS Caraquet*, one of an all Canadian flotilla clearing approaches to "Omaha" beach for the Americans. After a brief taste of civvy-street following his discharge, in 1953 he joined the RCAF serving for three years at radar stations on the East and West Coasts. He served for many years as a member of the Corps Advisory Committee and has been anchorman at *HMCS Discovery* for some 21 years and is still serving.

Charlie Brown.

He has written his history of Discovery and was awarded the B.C. Corps Meritorious Service Medal in 1988, among other things, his service with *HMCS Discovery*.

His dedication has become almost legendary.

Librarian – The Dawson Free Public Library

One of the more interesting characters in the Corps history is Ferdinand Enevoldsen, a veteran of the First World War, who joined the Corps in 1928 at 68 years of age and was Sergeant by 1933. The volume of correspondence between Enevoldsen and the Corps is a fascinating commentary on the times and covers the period 1929 to 1954. One of his narratives tells the story of his being wrecked in a full rigged sailing ship on an island off the Malabar Coast of India. In fact, his experiences were such that he wrote two books himself.

The Corps was somewhat taken aback when he requested that the Vancouver office select and order books for the Dawson Library on his behalf. Most appear to have been ordered from the Times Book Club in England

Enevoldsen.

although some were purchased locally. In those days a book sold for anywhere from one dollar to two-fifty.

In 1943, as a Captain in the Pacific Coast Rangers, he was energetically and successfully recruiting for the Rangers in the North. At this point he was over 80 years of age. However, once he had Yukon Rangers Unit No. 135 established he recognized the need for a younger person to take command and stepped down the same year.

Enevoldsen was also a prospector and his letters are full of his activities in this field. Always enthusiastic, and always an optimist despite hardships and setbacks, his letters give a real sense of what it was like to head out into the wilderness looking for the "big strike." It was also interesting that some of the Corps Headquarters staff were grubstaking him in his endeavors. His last letter, written at 94 years of age, was still full of reports on his prospecting and activities of mining companies in the North. To read his letters is to gain a real appreciation for what is meant by "leading a full life."

Coleopy Park Developments

Following the Second World War, once the Corps finances began to improve, Stephen Coleopy, the Executive Secretary at the time, gave some thought to finding a way to provide affordable housing for retired elderly members of the Corps. Unfortunately, although he completed much of the groundwork he passed away before the project was completed. It was left to Air Commodore A.D. Bell-Irving who was Commandant of the Corps, to see the project to completion with the assistance of the Corps Trustees and office staff. The project,

Stephen Colepy.

comprising 36 units of low cost housing, at a cost of $200,000 was named after Stephen Coleopy. Financing was arranged through the Central Mortgage and Housing Corporation. The first tenants moved in May 1, 1959. It is interesting to note that none of the original tenants were Corps members although all were veterans or widows of veterans.

With the completion of the project, it became necessary to set up a separate Society, "Coleopy Park Developments," but the Directors continued to be the Trustees of the Corps and the office staff oversaw the operation, working with a local building management company. The Corps RSM, Bert Grant, took a personal interest in the project, continuing to provide caretaker and maintenance services until it was torn down.

In 1989, it was recognized that the buildings no longer met modern standards and the land it occupied was under-utilized. Plans were made to redevelop the site with the leadership of BGen D.J. Anderson, CD.

Merrithew and Anderson.

BGen Anderson with Gerald Merrithew, (VAC) and Alderman Bellamy.

Additional information on BGen Anderson appears later in this narrative. The new development, which was opened in March 1991, consists of a Seniors Complex of 36 units and Families Complex of 22 units, including handicapped units. While there is no longer an implicit obligation for B.C. Corps Trustees to serve on the Board of Coleopy Park Directors, the current Board are still Corps members. It is also gratifying that there are more Commissionaires or their widows currently living in Coleopy Park than at any time in the past.

Command and Control/Care and Responsibility

The Corps has prospered because of the strong personal commitment of those charged with its care. Each generation has shaped the Corps to meet the demands of the times and, following military practice, provided that essential firm base required to continue to the next. It is fair to say that, in the early days, the Corps was managed more like a society than a business, with heavy reliance on volunteers to conduct its business. The assistance provided by the Welfare Foundation was tacit acknowledgment of the social service provided by the Corps. All who were involved demonstrated a strong personal commitment to the well being of its members. Without that commitment, the Corps would not have survived.

Patrons – In the thirties and forties, most prominent businessmen had served in the First and Second World Wars so it is not surprising that the list of Patrons and Trustees sounded like a "Who's Who" of Vancouver.

Early Patrons included the Mayor of Vancouver, Gerry McGeer, Col W.C. Woodward, founder of Woodwards Stores Ltd., who also served as Lieutenant Governor of British Columbia through the Second World War, LCol Victor Spencer, whose large department store used to sponsor the Santa Claus Parade in Vancouver until taken over by Eatons, Col H.S. Tobin, DSO, VD, ADC, former Commanding Officer of "Tobin's Tigers," the 29th Infantry Battalion and Capt, later BGen

Aeneas Bell-Irving who began his family's long association with the Corps, to mention just a few. Although not established as such, some Patrons approached the role of Trustee by virtue of their interest and the degree of support provided.

Management and Responsibility – The early records of the Corps show Percy Lawrence, Esq., as President and A. Farthing, Esq., as Secretary. LCol Coote was initially listed as an "Advisor," then Commanding Officer. At this time, every Commissionaire was a member of the Society. Not all were seeking employment. Some joined to support the organization, or for the fraternal association. In 1931, on recommendation from LCol Coote, they decided to form a Board of Directors, to be known as Trustees. While there had been a Secretary in the original organization, it was at this time that the position of Executive Secretary was established to carry on the day-to-day business of the Corps. Until that time, the secretarial function had been performed on a volunteer basis, as in fact was that of the Trustees and Commanding Officer. In 1933, at the suggestion of the Commanding Officer, a standing committee known as the General Purpose Advisory Committee was formed. This committee, initially comprising ten Commissionaires, provided advice and information to the Commanding Officer as well as assisting with the administration of the Corps. This committee too operated on a volunteer basis. They were involved in the discipline of Corps members, recruiting, canvassing for employment, arranging Corps meetings and social events, dealing with members delinquent in payment of Corps dues, and visiting the sick. "Just a minute," you say, "Corps dues?" Yes, in 1985, they were $2 per month and a Commissionaire could be released for non-payment. The Committee not only set the level of dues but also recommended the disciplinary action. For a brief period in the early days, when the Corps was small, and had a set establishment of non-commissioned ranks, they also functioned as a promotion committee. In later years, the Advisory Committee become known as the Membership Committee and in 1996 reverted to the title, "Advisory Committee."

Gentlemen of the Board – Following are brief sketches on some Board Members, primarily those who served as chairmen. They are by no means complete. In reading about them one cannot help but be struck how fortunate the Corps was to have men of such stature take an interest in the Corps.

Col James P. Fell was the first Chairman. Originally, he had served in the Royal Artillery, reaching the rank of Captain. In 1911 he organized the 60th Company, Canadian Engineers, in North Vancouver and took half the Company with the original Canadian Division to France in 1914. He did much to put the Corps on a firm financial footing from which the Corps could continue to build. He also maintained an ongoing liaison with the British Corps, exchanging ideas and always searching to improve. His term as Chairman extended for 23 years (1931-1954). It was during his term that Mr W.G. Murrin, Esq., a senior executive of the British Columbia Electric Railway Co Ltd. (later B.C. Hydro), served on the Board (1931-1960) providing much valuable support.

Air Commodore Duncan Bell-Irving served as Commanding Officer 1957 to 1959, joined the Board and served as Chairman from 1959 until his retirement in 1965. A/C Bell-Irving went to war as a Seaforth in the 16th Battalion (Canadian-Scottish) in the First World War and was commissioned in the 3rd Gordon Highlanders. After serving in the trenches, he transferred to the Royal Flying Corps in 1915. Initially, he was an observer/gunner. On December 14, 1915 while returning to base, a Fokker E III piloted by the German ace Max Immelman attacked them. Bell-Irving was shot down and seriously injured. On returning to duty in 1916, he learned to fly and was the first Canadian-born airman to achieve "ace" status. He received an MC and bar for his exploits. Between wars he developed and commanded the first RCAF auxiliary squadron to fly. He also organized the first Air Cadet Squadron in Canada and talked Squadron Leader Nick Carter, a former Royal Naval Air Service Officer who later became a Corps Trustee, into leading it. He returned to active service in the Second World War, finally completing a most distinguished and adventuresome career with the rank of Air Commodore. While he contributed much to the continued success of the Corps, he will perhaps be most remembered for his work in the planning and setting up of Coleopy Park Developments. For more information on the career and times of this remarkable man, "Gentleman Air Ace," the Duncan Bell Irving Story by Elizabeth O'Kiely is well worth a read.

Squadron Leader A.W. (Nick) Carter, OBE, MBE, served as a Trustee from 1945 to 1977. In 1912, he was head rider at the Calgary Stampede. In 1916, he went overseas and joined the Royal Naval Air Service. Posted to a squadron attached to the French he took part in daylight bombing raids. He rose to the rank of Captain, and was awarded the Distinguished Flying Cross for conspicuous courage – twice shooting down German aircraft when outnumbered, on one occasion five to one. On returning to Canada, he was appointed to the newly formed Canadian Air Board. He left the civil service in 1923 and founded A.W. Carter Ltd., Hudson automobile dealership in Victoria, expanding to Vancouver in 1933. He told of having to teach potential customers how to drive before he could sell a car. Nick Carter was a quiet man, providing solid support to the Corps. It was he who set up the first bookkeeping system to meet the requirements of an expanding organization.

Air Vice Marshal Stevenson, CB. Legion of Merit (USA) was another who won his Commission on the battlefield in 1916, later transferring to the Royal Flying Corps and receiving his wings in 1918. In 1921, he joined the Canadian Air Force rising steadily in rank and responsibility. In 1944, he was appointed Senior Canadian Officer on the staff of Lord Mountbatten, Allied Commander South East Asia. After a distinguished career, AVM Stevenson retired in 1945. He served as a Trustee for 20 years and held the position of Chairman from 1965 to 1967, retiring from the Board ten years later.

LCol C.C.I. Merritt, VC, ED, QC, served as Commanding Officer (1959-1967), Trustee (1959-1984) and Chairman (1967-1969). He served on the Committee (1962) set up to establish a pension plan for the Corps office staff. It was interesting to note that during this period the Corps payroll was in excess of $510,000. It was on his recommendation to the Board that the Corps auditors, Touche Ross & Co., were consulted and a new accounting system established using the services of a payroll service company.

Cec Merritt, VC.

Group Captain Alf Watts, AFC, ED, QC served the Board from 1961 to 1987 and as Chairman from 1969-1971. With a genuine concern for the lot of the veteran, he was the first Second World War veteran to be elected National President of the Royal Canadian Legion. It was in his time as Chairman that negotiations were begun leading to the B.C. Corps of Commissionaires re-joining the national organization.

The realization of that initiative fell to Col D.F. Spankie, OBE, CM, ED, Chairman 1971 to 1975, a long serving member of the Irish Fusiliers of Canada (The Vancouver Regiment) who had served in a number of staff appointments overseas, returning with the rank of Colonel. In addition to his association with the investment firm of Pitfield, Mackay, Ross which made him a natural choice for Financial Advisor, he was an internationally respected military historian. Col Spankie wrote the first history of the B.C. Corps entitled "Carry On," which he dedicated to Air Commodore Duncan Bell-Irving. He retired in 1989 after 23 years service to the Corps.

Spankie was followed by Air Vice Marshal Walter Orr, CBE, CD and in turn Major K.J. McRae, CD who served with both the British Columbia Dragoons and the British Columbia Regiment, NPAM 1939-40, Active Service 1940-1946 and Militia from 1947 to 1957 with the "Dukes." He was Advertising Director for the *Vancouver Sun* newspaper. He became a Trustee in 1977 and served as Chairman 1977 to 1981. Maj. McRae was also the first member of the B.C. Board to serve as National

Chairman, a post he held with distinction from 1983 to 1985 after which he was appointed an Honorary Governor. At the time of writing, he is the longest serving member of the B.C. Board, having served from 1971 to the present. He was awarded the Commissionaire Distinguished Service Medal in 1996.

Next in the Chair was Wing Commander Gordon Bell-Irving, CD. Gordon was attached to the RAF during the Second World War, completing 50 low-level sorties over Germany flying Mosquito fighter-bombers and became a career officer at war's end. As the son of AVM Duncan Bell-Irving, he felt a sincere family obligation to follow his father's lead in the Corps. A project close to his heart was Coleopy Park Developments and he was very active in the planning aspects of its re-development in 1990 and 1991. Unfortunately, he died and was unable to see the project come to fruition.

Wing Commander Don Bain was a young Flying Officer piloting a Halifax bomber heading for Aachen in the summer of 1943 when he was badly shot up by night-fighters five minutes before reaching the target. He pressed on, only to find that his hydraulics and bomb doors would not operate. On his return to England, he out-maneuvered two other enemy fighters. Unable to crash land because of his bomb load, he ordered his crew to bail out. He then directed the plane to a safe area where it crashed into a hill and exploded and bailed out himself, breaking both ankles badly on landing. Subsequently, he was awarded the DFC and went on to a distinguished career in the RCAF. He served the Corps as a Trustee, for 17 years until his death in 1993 following a brief illness. It was Wing Commander Bain and BGen Anderson who formed the Selection Committee to select the Corps' first Commandant in 1984. He also provided a great deal of much appreciated guidance and support in the early days of his term.

Col W.J. (Jack) Aird, CD, served as a Governor from 1977 to 1997 and Chairman 1987 to 1990. A former Commanding Officer of the British Columbia Regiment, District Commander, he was also a past President of the Armoured Corps Association and Chair of the Conference of Defence Associations. He also served on the National Executive and was made an Honorary Governor of the National Board. In his civilian career, he was a senior executive with Fraser Valley Dairies. Col Aird cared deeply about Canada, the Canadian Forces and the Commissionaires. More than that, he played an active part and made major contributions to all three.

BGen D.J. (Doug) Anderson, CD, served as a Trustee from 1981 to 1996 and Chairman from 1990 to 1992. In addition, he was President of Coleopy Park Developments during its re-development. At that time, it was the accepted practice that the Vice Chair of the Corps would be also President of Coleopy Park. BGen Anderson was a former Commanding Officer of the Seaforths. He commanded Pacific Militia Area and also served as Senior Reserve Advisor to the Commander Mobile Command until his retirement in 1976. He was a Commanding Officer of the Corps, Provincial Commissioner for St. John Ambulance in BC, Past President of the Last Post Fund, Past Chairman of the Conference of Defence Associations, Past Vice President (West) of the Army Cadet League of Canada and, Past Chairman of the Canadian Infantry Association. Somehow, while participating in all these activities, he also managed to operate successfully his own printing business. Unfortunately, he passed away in 1996. If one could summarize his life in one word, it would be "service." He was a major contributor to all the organizations to which he gave his time and talents.

Commander D.M. Johnston, CD, has been a Trustee since 1979 and served as Chairman from 1992 to 1995. He is a former Commanding Officer of *HMCS Discovery*, is currently Chancellor of the Priory of Canada, St. John Ambulance, Past President of the Last Post Fund and has served as Honorary Consul of Malaysia and as an Executive Member, Canadian Forces Military College Advisory Board. In civilian life, he is a lawyer with a prominent Vancouver law firm.

Col Ron Webster, CD has been a Governor since 1985 and Chairman since 1995. His service began in 1944 with the U.S. Merchant Marine, which was followed by aircrew training in 1944 and a transfer to the Infantry in 1945. He spent 44 years with Richardson Greenshields of Canada Limited retiring as Vice President. He also served as Honorary Consul of Bolivia and plays an active leadership role in the community. He has had a long association with the Artillery in Vancouver and served as Honorary Colonel of 15th Field Regiment (RCA). His presence in this history represents the passing of an era in that he will be the last Second World War veteran to chair the Board. It was during his term that the B.C. Corps made a major structural change whereby the Commis-

The B.C. Board of Governors – March 1994.

sionaires voluntarily relinquished their position as the voting members of the Society, ceding that responsibility to the Trustees, who with that change assumed the title "Governors." This move brought the B.C. organization into line with that used by other Divisions of the Corps.

Commanding Officers – There have been 12 Commanding Officers since the inception of the Corps. Each served on a voluntary basis giving as much time as their personal careers and activities allowed. LCol Coote, mentioned earlier was the first. Maj Barker-Benfield who served for one year only followed him.

Major Victor MacLean, MC, served from 1931 to 1940 when he left for service overseas. At that time, he was associated with Kelly-Douglas & Co. Ltd. Later, he joined the brokerage firm of Ross, Whittal Ltd. Maj MacLean had served in the First World War with the 16th Canadian Scottish in 1914. He was wounded and taken prisoner at Festubert after which he spent three years in a German prison camp. In the words of Sergeant Tommy Slater, who also worked at Kelly Douglas, despite the excellent work done by LCol Coot there were problems in the Corps and there was concern for its future. He approached Maj MacLean and when asked, told him he could do the job provided he had a good secretary. It was then that Stephen Coleopy came into the picture. They formed an excellent team. He got the Corps involved with the Community Chest, which gave them an office and the money to pay Coleopy as a full-time Secretary. They were able to get groceries donated to help Corps members and set up and operated the barracks for out of work veterans. It was also noted that when the men asked if they could have a smoker, he went to a friend who was also a patron of the Corps, Col Tobin, who managed Brewers & Distillers of Vancouver Limited and asked him to provide the beer. He gave them all the beer they wanted provided they took the bottles back. The party was held at the Seaman's' Institute on Hastings Street. From all events, a good time was had by all. During his term, the Corps held its first Church Parade, marching to Christ Church Cathedral. While LCol Coote had planted the seed, it was the partnership of Maj MacLean and Stephen Coleopy that made sure those early beginnings brought forth fruit.

LCol J.S. Tait, CBE, VD, assumed command in 1940, serving until 1948. He had commanded the Seaforths in the Second World War. The records show he was very successful in finding employment for Corps members and worked well with Stephen Coleopy, the Executive Secretary. He was followed by BGen J.C. Stewart, CBE, DSO, CD from 1948 to 1957. BGen Stewart was a retired Permanent Force Artillery Officer and veteran of two world wars. It was during Brigadier Stewart's time that the Corps set up what was then called the Corps "Endowment Fund" which later was more accurately referred to as the "operating capital" of the Corps. He was followed by Air Commodors Bell-Irving and LCol Merritt who are referred to earlier in this narrative.

Next was Brig The Honorable H.P. (Budge) Bell-Irving, OC, DSO, OBE, ED, CD. Brig Bell-Irving went overseas in 1939 with the first contingent of Seaforth Highlanders and commanded a company of the battalion in Sicily, Italy and northwest Europe before succeeding to the command of 10th Infantry Brigade. He was awarded the DSO and bar, the OBE and was twice mentioned in dispatches. He stepped down as Commanding Officer on accepting the honour of being appointed Lieutenant Governor of British Columbia (1978 to 1983). As Commanding Officer he made a point of getting to know the Commissionaires, he initiated the B.C. Corps system of medals, and presented the first Colours to the Corps. There had always been a strong Seaforth presence in the Corps and the Bell-Irving family played a prominent part. He cared deeply about Canada and had a strong commitment to his regiment, the community and the Corps.

BGen H.P. Bell-Irving and O.K. Kennedy.

Brig Bell-Irving was followed by Supt. J.J. Atherton (1971-1976), a retired RCMP officer who made a major contribution towards improving training standards in the Corps. He went on to serve on the Board until 1982.

Major E.S. Thorne served from 1976 to 1978. During his term he also served as legal council for the Corps and made necessary revisions to the Corps By-laws. It was Maj Thorne who first identified the need for a full time Commandant. He also joined the Board, serving with distinction until 1989.

BGen D.J. Anderson followed Capt (N) J.M. Thornton, OMM, CD followed in 1981, serving until 1985 and as a Trustee until 1987. Capt "Jack" as he was affectionately known by the Commissionaires was an ex-Regular and former Commanding Officer of *HMCS Discovery*. It was during his term that the Corps hosted its first National Annual General Meeting. He also fulfilled a long-felt need with the introduction of the Commandant's Commendation. It fell his lot to be the last volunteer Commanding Officer of the B.C. Corps, a post that he filled in the best traditions of the service.

Executive Secretaries – Secretaries and Executive Secretaries of the Corps seldom had a high profile, nor did they seek one. They carried on the day-to-day business of the Corps and provided the stable environment and support that allowed the Commanding Officers and Trustees to play their part.

The first Secretary, E.A. Paige was a well known retired newspaperman. Serving from to 1927 to 1930 he was responsible for much of the early publicity and donated a bolt of cloth for the first uniforms.

Capt A. Morlidge, DSO, served from 1932 to 1934 until returning to England to become a Chelsea Pensioner. He had served in the 15th "The Kings Royal" Hussars and the 23rd Northumberland Fusiliers in 1918 when he was awarded the DSO.

Stephen Coleopy was the first full time, paid Executive Secretary. He was a veteran of the regular British Army with 18 years' service with the Middlesex Regiment and wartime services with the Royal Flying Corps. He managed the Corps office from 1934 until his death in 1957, a record 23 years. His service, starting in the middle of the Depression, through the Second World War and well into the post-war period provided much needed stability through three challenging and radically different periods in the history of the Corps. If there was one person deserving the title "Commissionaire Extraordinaire" which has been used elsewhere in this book it was Stephen Coleopy. He ran the Corps in his day, with the full support and cooperation of the Trustees, Commanding Officers and the Advisory Committee, which he chaired. His name is perpetuated in the Corps' housing project, Coleopy Park.

The next Executive Secretary (1957 to 1968) was O.K. Kennedy, who had been a member of the office staff since 1941. It is said that he was a hard-nosed disciplinarian of the old school who ran the Corps with an iron hand. Nonetheless, he earned the respect of the Corps and was made an Honorary Commanding Officer on his retirement.

Following O.K. Kennedy was Capt Fred Gray (1968-1978) whose military service was with the British Military Police. In an interview for the Corps newsletter he observed, "It was not until my first posting as a 'Redcap' that I first realized my illegitimacy." Instead of being referred to as Military Police or Redcap, he found they were referred to as "Redcap Bastards." Such was their reputation that on his entering a pub one evening, every soldier walked out. Being a bastard had some merit, he noted.

Charlie Brown, Graham Jenkins, Bert Grant, Fred Gray and Sid Paget – 1984.

One could get a beer without being jostled. He was subsequently transferred to the Indian Army, transferring to the Intelligence Corps from which he retired with the rank of Captain. It was in Fred Gray's time that the Corps took its first step in the use of computers by having the payroll processed by a Payroll Service Company.

It was Sid Paget's lot to be the last Executive Secretary, serving from 1978 to 1985, in all 25 years service, most of which was in the Corps office. His administrative ability provided the necessary stability for the Corps to build on the accomplishments of his predecessors.

The Passing Parade

To this point the narrative has been much on personalities, many of them in the senior ranks of the Corps, simply because we have more information on them. It is appropriate now to pause and review the passing parade, a progression of people and events that shaped the Corps over the years.

In 1930, the Governor General, Lord Willingdon inspected the Corps. In June 1941, the Rt. Hon W.L. MacKenzie did the honours and in 1946, His Excellency Field Marshal H.R.L. Alexander honoured the Corps with his participation.

March 29, 1930, Mr E.W. Beatty, President of Canadian Pacific Railways, presented the Corps with a flag. In 1982, the Lieutenant Governor of British Columbia, Brig H.P. Bell-Irving presented the Corps with its colours.

His Excellency Governor General Viscount Willingdon inspects, April, 1930.

Sgt Tommy Slater, who is mentioned earlier, came from Lancashire. He was being interviewed by the curator of the art gallery who was rather disturbed by Tommy's accent and decided to see if he could get someone whose speech would be more pleasing to the patrons. On approaching the Corps Secretary he was told, "he could supply a taller man, a shorter man, a fatter man or a thinner one, he could supply a man with any sort of accent but he could not supply a better man!" Tommy got the job.

At the 10th Anniversary Banquet it was noted that the B.C. Corps was the second largest in the Empire, the London Corps in England being the largest.

In July of 1947, Harry Knight, DCM, aged 70, an ex-RSM of the Royal Warwickshires and RSM of the Corps was preparing to sail around the world in his 28-ft. schooner.

The Birch brothers, Charles and George served the Corps for 41 and 45 years respectively. Both became sergeant majors and served on

Bill Bunnet, Senior. **Dave Bunnet.** **Bill Bunnet.**

the Advisory Committee. Other family compacts were the Bunnetts – Bill senior, now retired and sons Bill and Dave who are currently serving; Les Cairney and his daughter, Leslie Wilkins; Hilda Campbell and her son Colin; and Ev Clausen, now retired and her daughter Diana B a world class martial arts student currently working in the Corps office.

Mike Miko who served 1946 to 1990 was the last Commissionaire to bear arms in the B.C. Corps. In the discussion on carrying arms, both the *Province* newspaper and Loomis noted that the Corps at that time functioned as an employment agency. They considered Commissionaires and their employees had to accept the potential liability if they were armed.

In 1974, Lila Cunningham was enrolled as the first female Commissionaire and assigned to the Westcoast Transmission Building. Betty Easton, who served at Shaughnessy Hospital and the Airport Cashiers thought to be the first female to qualify for the ten-year Long Service Medal. Deanna Weir was the first to join the office staff, first as

Les Cairney and his daughter Leslie Wilkins.

receptionist and later as Administrative Assistant. She received the Commissionaire Distinguished Service Medal in 1997.

January of 1974 the Department of Supply and Services conducted their first security-training course in Vancouver. This had now evolved into a professional, much more demanding course to Canadian General Standards Board and Provincial Standards.

Sgt Lee Dunn, late of the Queen's West Kent Regiment (1938-1946) who served in the Corps 1968-1981 was the first editor of the "Corpsman." After he retired in 1981, there was a hiatus until Commissionaire Les Warnock agreed to accept the task. Once started John Bromley and then Emil Lautard carried on conscientiously until finally, because of practical problems of coordination, it was taken over by the office staff in 1989.

Cpl George Massie served Granville Island and the Corps well although he was only there for seven years. When he retired, he was presented with a model tow truck with an inscription to remind him of his nickname and his highest one-day towing record. "CAPTAIN HOOK B 21." His smiling face also graced the front of the Corps information brochure for many years.

George Massie.

Social activity has always been an important part of Corps life. In the early days, the Advisory Committee organized smoker, dinner dances, picnics and Christmas parties for the children. Today there is an Annual Governors and Supervisors Dinner, a dinner dance or dinner cruise in the spring and the Awards Dinner in the fall. In addition, the Annual Golf Tournament has become a popular event despite the water hazards. But then of course, there's always the 19th hole.

Looking at the present, the Corps is seeking registration under ISO 9002 quality standards. Once again, we look to the future. Only the Commissionaires can secure that future and it is the responsibility of the Corps to support them and give them every opportunity to succeed.

Change, Change and More Change

In the early eighties, competition was increasing and whatever advantage may have existed with the presence of war veterans was fast disappearing. For over 50 years, the Corps had depended on voluntary efforts freely given by members of the Board, Commanding Officer and the Membership Committee to manage the affairs of the Corps. However, they too had business and personal responsibilities limiting their time. Further new legislation, changing financial requirements and above all, the imperatives for change could no longer be adequately dealt with by volunteers, no matter how willing or enthusiastic. The Corps required a full time Manager. It was decided to combine the functions of Commanding Officer and Executive Secretary into one position, that of Commandant.

On February 1, 1985, Col Graham Jenkins, CD, was installed as the first Commandant. His military career encompassed 29 years Regular Force, Royal Canadian Corps of Signals/Communications Electronics Engineering Branch from which he retired as a Lieutenant Colonel in 1980; ten years in the Reserves, four before he joined the Regular Force and six after; reaching retirement age as Deputy Commander, Pacific Militia Area. On leaving the Service he was employed for a short period with the University of British Columbia and four years with Consultec Canada Limited, a premier telecommunications consulting firm where he gained valuable experience in marketing and client support. Col Jenkins was awarded the Commissionaire Distinguished Service Medal in 1997.

The challenge was to transform an organization that had operated successfully for many years more like a society than a business into an organization that could compete in the '90s and beyond. There was no instant solution and it was difficult for some to accept the need for change. It was necessary to focus more on being operations and client driven. The pace of change continued to increase and the Corps was pressed to keep up. The collecting of membership dues and Caution Money (the security deposit on uniforms and Identification Card were canceled since they were no longer legal). The Corps made its first step into the computer age with the purchase of two Radio Shack computers – no hard drives in those days. The office staff were taught to use them by "The Baron," Commissionaire Les Warnock who bullied and coerced them until they became proficient. The Corps purchased its first car.

Capt Frank Peterson, a Second World War veteran and retired Inspector of the Vancouver Police, was recruited and assigned to Vancouver International Airport to work with WO1 Bert West who had been responsible for the detachment for many years. Bert is well remembered for his public relations skills as well as his dedication to the site. A high point in Frank Peterson's career was when he was put in charge of Commissionaires for the Asian Development Bank Conference in 1991. In peak shift, he had 109 Commissionaires. His morning inspections are firm in Commissionaires memories.

Bert West.

The pension plan, which no longer suited the demographics of the Corps, was changed to a Group RRSP. The Annual Parade was cancelled in favour of an Awards Dinner, held every fall. With that, Commissionaires were no longer fined for missing the parade. The Corps Office, which had been in the Province Building for many years, was no longer suitable due to deteriorating conditions in the neighbourhood. For the first time, the Corps moved out of the general area of Victory Square into new offices in the centre of town. 1995 and 1996 were critical years for the Corps as an organization. To protect the non-profit status of the Corps it was necessary to change the structure so that the Trustees would be the voting members of the Society and Commissionaires, employees. This could not be done without passing a special resolution at a General Meeting of the Corps. It was also decided to take the opportunity to rewrite the By-laws and Rules and Regulations to reflect the needs of the current operating environment. A Committee chaired by LCdr Chris Haines, a Trustee and Lawyer, comprising four Commissionaires, the Commandant and four Trustees worked for two years to develop the necessary changes. Finally, in 1996 a mail-in vote was held so that every Commissionaire could make his or her wishes known. 381 votes were cast. 371 for, 10 against. The B.C. Corps now had the same structure as all other Divisions of the Corps and the name "Trustees" was changed to "Governors" to conform to national usage.

The Corps continued to grow. In 1985, although the nominal strength was 368 in fact approximately 100 Commissionaires were not working. This arose from two factors. From early days, some belonged for the association and to help where they could. The other factor is that if a Commissionaire resigned he was not allowed to rejoin, so quite a few

Commissionaires at the Asian Development Bank Conference in 1991.

were actually employed outside the Corps retaining their membership against future need. With the change in structure these factors no longer applied. The Corps continued to expand on the lower mainland and new contracts were opened up in the interior in Prince George, Castlegar and many other communities. WO II Bob Stephenson, CD, former Station Chief Warrant Officer at Baldy Hughes radar site has played a major role in the Corps success in Prince George, and before him Sgt Lou Blackburn provided loyal service for many years. Sgt George Turcotte in Vernon, Sgt Keith Smith in Penticton, Cpl Brian Hill in Prince Rupert and Cpl Gene Croken in Castlegar also deserve mention. WO II Bob Slaney, OMM, CD, in Kelowna with 37 years of distinguished military service was awarded the Commissionaire Distinguished Service Medal in 1997. These are the area representatives who make things work in the interior. New opportunities were also sought to diversify into areas other than security to provide more interesting and lucrative employment for those with the necessary skills. To give an indication of progress made, following are the financial statistics for the period.

Annual Report 31 March 1985   Gross $ 6,856,656
                                Wages $ 5,500,028

Annual Report 31 March 1997   Gross $16,698,004
                                Wages $13,094,425

Administration costs throughout this period have been 5% or less.

In June of 1997, the B.C. Corps had the privilege of hosting the Annual Meeting of Divisions of the Canadian Corps of Commissionaires. The previous year, Toronto had used as its theme, "The Challenge of Change." In 1997, the B.C. Corps selected "Making Things Happen." It was evident that there was a momentum developing that could only assist the Corps in its efforts. Ideas that would have been rank heresy only a year ago were being seriously discussed as options for the future. Much progress was made and useful ideas exchanged. It is true that change has always been with us. The challenge is to anticipate change rather than to react to it.

In this narrative, we have mentioned just a few of those associated with the Corps. In so doing we recognize that there are many more who deserve recognition but space and lack of information has of necessity limited our efforts. We are, however, deeply conscious of the fact that none of the achievements mentioned were the work of one person alone. The support, encouragement and entire participation of all those who have helped make the Corps what it is today is acknowledged and appreciated. The changes that have been mentioned are significant, but we cannot just look back. We are proud of our history but the challenge of the future remains. With the dedication of the Board and the staff of the Corps office, the genuine concern and constructive support received by the Corps Advisory Committee and quality of the Commissionaires, we have nothing but optimism for the future of the B.C. Corps. What started over 70 years ago has now become a magnificent Division of the Canadian Corps of Commissionaires.

Chapter V

HISTORY OF THE HAMILTON DIVISION

Introduction by – *Capt D.R. Begin, CD - Board of Governors and Jack Evanoff – Commandant*

THE COMPILATION of a history of the Hamilton Division in any detail was almost impossible but thankfully our main source comes from the memories of the "old timers" who are still with us.

On the night of March 29, 1997, the top floor office in the Imperial Building suffered from an explosion and fire caused by arson in an adjoining office. This happened to be the location of the Hamilton Division offices. It was exactly two months to the day later on May 29, 1997, that the Commandant and his Adjutant Lt Cliff Degner were allowed to enter the building only to find that basically everything had been destroyed. The filing cabinets were subjected to high temperatures

Damage done on March 29, 1997. Almost the end.

and the walk-in safe had a hole drilled into the side so the firemen could fill it with water. What was not burned or cooked was drowned. Our occupancy ended with a bang. With this problem came the request for our Division's history. The timing could not have been worse.

With luck the telephone lines had been turned over to the paging company which allowed both the clients and the Commissionaires to be in touch with the office staff 24 hours a day. Full operation continued with the outstanding cooperation of the Commandant and office staff. With the use of personal computers, cell phones and five home-based offices, the staff were able to carry on daily business until the new office at 3385 Harvester Road in Burlington was available for occupancy on May 1, 1997.

The Beginning

The Hamilton Division was first established in April 1937. LCol Inch, MC, VD, was appointed Chairman and Capt A.H. Frame, DCM, MM, MSM, as Commandant/Board member. There were originally ten governors appointed in April with a further eight added later the same year.

During the Second World War, Hamilton had 40 to 50 men employed as Commissionaires. These men consisted of First World War veterans and demobilized members of the Veterans' Guard of Canada.

In 1946, a letter over the signature of LCol F.P. Healey, VD, the Board Chairman at the time, was widely circulated to potential employers. The results were rewarding and an office was opened in downtown Hamilton in the Lister Building at 42 James St. N. Two Sergeant Majors and two clerks ran the office. Board members took on the executive duties. In May 1982, with a need for larger quarters, the offices were moved to the Imperial Building on Hughson Street South.

Recent Years

In 1971, Flying Officer Bert Norton, a Board Member who was Chief Financial Officer at the Civic Hospital, was acting as Secretary/Treasurer and realized the administration problems of this arrangement. He approached the Board who accepted his recommendation to appoint a Commandant of officer rank, to be the Office Manager. This move was also beneficial to Hamilton since other Divisions had officer Commandants, and it gave us more clout with employers.

The first full time non-Board member Commandant was Flight Lieutenant Alex Gillespie who took command on 1 October 1971. He had just retired from the Civil Service and brought many considerable skills to this position. Flight Lieutenant Gillespie held this position until 27 June 1978 when he became a member of the Board of Governors and served until 30 June 1988. He became an Honorary Life Member on

1 July 1988 and is still attending the Annual Division Meeting when possible.

On his retirement from the Civic Hospital, Flying Officer Bert Norton relinquished his position of the Board of Governors and became the next Commandant. He served as Commandant from 27 June 1978 until 1 July 1984 at which time he returned as a member of the Board of Governors and served until 30 June 1991. On 1 July 1991, Flying Officer Norton became an Honorary Life Member and is still active in this capacity.

LCol Hal Wilcox, CD, joined the Hamilton Division in May 1974 after serving 23 years with the Royal Canadian Air Force. He was the Chief of Operations until July 1976 then became Adjutant, a position he held until July 1984 when he was promoted to Commandant. LCol Wilcox held the position of Commandant until his retirement on December 31, 1995 giving him 21 years of service with the Hamilton Division. During his 11 years as Commandant LCol Wilcox helped set the standards that have made Hamilton a strong and well-respected Division. He became a member of the Board of Governors on January 1, 1996, but unfortunately because of a health problem decided to relinquish this position. He is now an Honorary Life Member.

LCol Jack Evanoff joined the Hamilton Division in April 1994 after 32 years of service with Stelco Steel Inc. He served as Deputy Commandant until the retirement of LCol Hal Wilcox at which time he

Hamilton Division Original Members - 1937
W. Tourtel; W. O'Dell; T. Middleton, DCM; A. Landin; A. Greenhalgh; A. Stubbs;
J. Hopkins, DCM; W. Robertson; A. McArthur; J. Baylis; H. Culver; W. Weston, MSM;
H. Ireson; H. Sweeting; W. Walmsley; Lt Col George Inch, MC, VD (Vice Chairman);
R. Thompson (Adjutant); Capt A.H. Frame, DCM, MM, MSM (Commandant).

was promoted to Commandant and still serves in this position for the Hamilton Division.

LCol Evanoff joined the Canadian Army Pay Corps in January 1956 just after his seventeenth birthday and served for three years. On his release he joined the Argyll and Sutherland Highlanders of Canada (Princess Louise's) and served for two years. He is still an active member of the Regimental Association whose main purpose is the preservation of both Militia and the Regimental Traditions.

It is unfortunate that photographs of the previous Commandants were lost in the fire. Only the picture of the original 1937 members was found and a new negative made. This allowed us to redevelop and reframe the picture. It now hangs once again in the new office for all to see.

Commissionaire Extraordinaire
Warrant Officer Allan Rathborne (ret'd)

Allan Rathborne enlisted in the Canadian Army on June 30, 1940 as a private. He served with the Argyll and Sutherland Highlanders (Princess Louise's) in Jamaica, United Kingdom and Europe. He was discharged in November 1945 having attained the rank of Captain.

Allan Rathborne joined the Corps on November 25, 1982 and was posted to Canada Centre for Inland Waters (CCIW) as a security guard. On July 27, 1983 he left the Corps to attend to personal commitments.

On December 5, 1983, Rathborne returned to the Corps and was assigned as a By-Law Enforcement Officer for the city of Burlington. During his 12 years as By-Law Enforcement Officer, Commissionaire Rathborne was promoted to Corporal in February 1987, Sergeant in December 1987 and then in July 1988 became the Detachment Commander attaining the rank of Staff-Sergeant (now changed to Warrant Officer).

Over the 12 years with the city of Burlington, WO Rathborne has received commendations from both the Halton Regional Police Service and the city for his assistance in helping to recover stolen vehicles or observing suspects as he did in June 1990 until police arrived to make an arrest. The one commendation that is really special is the one given to WO Rathborne in December 1995 when with the assistance of his By-Law Officers over the years he recovered his 120th stolen vehicle. This definitely is a "Commissionaire" who went above and beyond the call of duty.

WO Allan Rathborne retired from the Corps on 25 July 1996, having served the Commissionaires with distinction.

Cpl Ivan T. Cooper

Cpl Ivan Thomas Cooper joined the Hamilton Division on 5 May 1992. His first and only assignment has been that of a Mobile By-Law Enforcement Officer for the city of Burlington.

During the Second World War, Cpl Cooper was with the 1st Canadian Parachute Battalion and served in Canada, the United Kingdom and Continental Europe.

On May 1, 1997, Cpl Cooper while on mobile patrol, listened to a police broadcast about two suspects that had tendered a counterfeit bill at a local restaurant. The description of the vehicle and licence plate were mentioned during the broadcast. Cpl Cooper observed the vehicle, provided information and offered assistance to the police which led to the arrest of the suspects without incident.

Letters of appreciation from both the Halton Regional Police and the city of Burlington have been placed on the personnel file of Cpl Ivan Cooper.

Cpl Cooper still serves with the Commissionaires as a By-Law Enforcement Officer for the city of Burlington, and is always willing to give that extra effort.

These are just two of the many stories that have taken place over the years in which Commissionaires have shown that they are willing to safeguard both the client and the community.

Operations and Business

The geographical area that the Hamilton Division covers has no permanent military installations and very few federal government operations. Therefore, we have always had a limit to the number of recruits available to us, especially female members. Our optimum size over the years has remained at 250 to 300 Commissionaires.

Unlike most other Divisions, a very small portion (17%) of our business comes from federal contracts. Most of our contracts are with municipalities, private businesses and educational institutions. Although the bulk of our job sites are security related, we do supply 65 full and part time Provincial By-Law Enforcement Officers to eight different municipalities within our Division. Some of our oldest clients are municipalities that use our Commissionaires in by-law enforcement.

Governors and Philosophies

From the start of the Hamilton Division in April 1937, the members of the Board of Governors have brought with them their diversified knowledge to share with the Corps. With backgrounds in law, accounting, education, human resources, policing and management as well as good military training, they have been able to offer their expertise when it is called upon.

Looking into the background of some Board Members, we find the stories of two gentlemen who served with the Royal Hamilton Light Infantry during the raid on Dieppe in August 1942.

Lieutenant John Gartshore from Dundas, Ontario was taken back from Dieppe bleeding heavily from an arm wound. He was one of only three from his platoon of 37 who came back from the beach that day. Capt J.B. Gartshore, MC, joined the Hamilton Board of Governors in December 1976 and served until March 1989. He is now an Honorary Life Member.

Corporal John Williamson was 19 years old when he landed on the beach of Dieppe. He had barely made the seawall when he was hit with shell fragments. Before the war ended he would be wounded three times. By the fall of 1944, he had become an Officer. Colonel John Williamson joined the Board of Governors in December 1986, served as Chairman from June 1992 and is still an active Member of the Board.

The legacy of the original Board of Governors was to provide honourable employment for our ex-Military personnel. In later years it was expanded to include ex-RCMP Officers. This philosophy was the reason for the founding of the Corps and has been followed strictly by the Hamilton Division. On the present Board, members are all of Officer Rank and hold the CD.

The Board of Governors for the Hamilton Division along with the Commandant and his staff have dedicated themselves to new initiatives that will carry them into the new millennium.

Chapter VI

HISTORY OF THE WINDSOR DIVISION

Commandant's Introduction – *by Dennis DeJager*

*T*HE WINDSOR DIVISION, although by far the smallest Division within The Canadian Corps of Commissionaires, has continually demonstrated its resolve to survive in the face of financial difficulties, manpower shortages and economic downturns. Over our 60-year history the Windsor Division has also been blessed by a number of unique characters and noteworthy events.

The Windsor Division was started on June 4, 1934 under the diligent auspices of Colonel George H. Wilkinson, VD, H.O. Comrie-Palmer, Esq., Colonel John W. Warden, DSO, OBE, VD, and Major H.C. McMordie, MC and a $500 grant from the National Headquarters. The first Headquarters was located in the office of the Honourary Local Veterans Assistance Committee in Room 608, Dominion Public Building, Ouellette Avenue, Windsor, Ontario

The initial few months proved to be most trying and within a month the Board of Governors had grown to include Colonel E.S. Wigle, Mr Cyril Cooper, Esq., Mr Howard Smale, Esq., Mr G.M. Duck, Esq., and Mr S.G. Bull, last of whom was soon appointed the Division's first Sergeant-Major.

The initial pool of applicants numbered 18 and the files of all were forwarded to the local office of the Department of Pensions and National Health, the local Pension Adjustment Officer of the Canadian Legion and to the Civic Welfare Department for confidential character reports. Of the original 18, nine were rejected. The remaining nine individuals were interviewed by the Board on September 22, 1937. From this group came Windsor Division's first five Commissionaires: Mr Alex Scott, Mr Jas Washer, Mr H.B. Parker, Mr Arthur Eyre, and Mr Victor G. Bays.

Parallelling the hiring of Commissionaires came the ordering of uniforms, all of which were being manufactured at Workshops Limited,

Montreal, PQ. Initially, uniforms were not an issue item and were paid for by the Commissionaire through payroll deduction. Since work was very limited in those early years, most Commissionaires did not have their uniform accounts paid off prior to their retirement.

Work for the Commissionaires in the Windsor Division during the first six months centred on their appointment as Special Constables. They conducted night patrols of the downtown area and acted as the doorman for the Norton-Palmer Hotel. Most jobs were procured at the companies or businesses owned by the Board Members.

Those Early Years

During the day, those Commissionaires not working remained in the Assembly Room beside the Division Office. This approach, although appearing harsh by today's standards, permitted parcelling out of Commissionaires for work assignments from a central location. Remember that in 1937, communications were limited and few residents save the wealthy had phones.

To provide a perspective of the period, in November 1937 the Windsor Division was approached by the Essex County Humane Society to employ the services of a single Commissionaire at a weekly wage of $20 for 56 hours of work. This job and the use of Commissionaires as tour guides at Hiram Walker and Sons Limited, resulted in the hiring of an additional five Commissionaires on November 29, 1937. The roll was increased with the inclusion of Mr J. Challen, Mr R. Gracie, Mr Wm.M. Swanson and Mr C.A. Thompson.

By the end of 1937 the number of applicants awaiting interview had grown to 30. A most fortuitous situation, because in March 1938, all of Windsor's nine original Commissionaires were being interviewed about an incident of disgraceful conduct while on duty as Special Constables on night patrol. Although the records do not clearly state the particulars of the occurrence, comments in the minutes of the meetings indicate that "drunk and disorderly" was the suspected source of the problem. The interviews were conducted by the Board at a Special Meeting on 29 March 1938. Following the interviews four of the Commissionaires were suspended for 30 days. Three of these individuals tendered their resignations and the other was terminated when he failed to report for work after his suspension. These losses and some additional part-time employment forced the hiring of eight new Commissionaires. This brought the Division strength to 14 at the end of the first year.

Time changes little especially in the area of marketing. In 1938 the Division decided to expand its operation by placing Commissionaires at the tunnel and bridges to Detroit with the purpose of handing out tourist information. This worked well as long as it was done for gratis. We also decided to look into "Residential Night Patrols." This was done by having the Commissionaires canvas the residents door to door soliciting support. Again, it was a great idea until someone mentioned money and that ended that.

The direction of the fledgling Division changed abruptly with the outbreak of the Second World War. Save for the original Divisions of Toronto and Montreal, the other Divisions like Windsor suffered. We were just starting to get permanent employment at several work sites when the call to arms significantly altered our recruitment base. Although the records are incomplete, it would appear that by 1940 the Division was employing about 35 Commissionaires in the immediate Windsor area.

The early war years caused turbulence and rapid change in the appearance and structure of all the Divisions within the Corps. Able-bodied Commissionaires who could re-enlist did so, while other relinquished their appointments for better-paying jobs with the military industrial base which sprang up at major cities across Canada. In parallel, the demand for Commissionaires to provide anti-sabotage security at various military, industrial and commercially important facilities rose exponentially. In February 1941, Windsor Division had a strength of 47; 14 months later it stood at 75 and by June 1944 had reached 82.

This period of exceptional growth also highlighted an unresolvable problem for most Divisions–the availability of suitable persons to perform guard duties. By mid 1944 the lack of suitable candidates for the Corps prevented it from taking on any more work. However, six months later the availability of persons to perform Commissionaire duties became a mute point. The cessation of hostilities provided an unlimited source of veterans but it also ended the demand for anti-sabotage protection and placed the jobs of the older First World War veterans in jeopardy.

The activities of Windsor Division during the Second World War were limited to commercial and industrial protection (i.e. Bell Telephone) and tunnel and bridge custodial work. However, the demands were of a significant nature and as such Windsor Division along with Montreal, Winnipeg and Calgary were the Divisions which saw the greatest growth during the war years. But, since Windsor had no federal institutions, it also suffered substantial losses in the immediate post war period.

The war years also marked the commencement of the military career of one LCol. Kenneth S. Kersey, CD. An officer of distinction, who would over the next five decades serve his country, his province and the Canadian Corps of Commissionaires.

On July 15, 1940 LCol. Kersey received a commission with the 2nd Battalion of Essex Scottish Regiment. Over the following years he rose through the ranks to ultimately command the unit in 1956. LCol Kersey took an active role in the Windsor Branch of St. John's Ambulance

Association. A member of the Board of Directors of the Windsor Branch, he rose to the rank of Commander in the Order of St. John.

Parallelling these activities, LCol Kersey was made a member of the Board of Governors, Canadian Corps of Commissionaires (Windsor). He served in many capacities on the Board, providing leadership during the Division's lean years.

The Post-war Years

The post-war period resulted in a long hiatus for Windsor Division. Our strength dropped to 47 Commissionaires in 1946 and a year later sank to 32 Commissionaires. This general reduction in Division strength was accompanied by a loss in revenue. In 1948, Windsor Division levied $2,500 in fees and dues on its Commissionaires to keep from going into arrears. This practice continued for the next three years until sufficient work was procured to cover administrative costs. At the same time the Windsor Division Headquarters was being staffed on a part-time basis by one Mr S.G. Bull, Esq., whose individual efforts were the only thing which kept the Division from folding in the years immediately after the war. Mr S.G. Bull, Esq. was one of the more unique characters to enter the realm of the Windsor Division. Born at sea on a British Ship of Registry in 1875, Mr Bull's career commenced as an apprentice seaman on several ships and included sailing around the Horn on a three-masted schooner. After a number of years at sea Mr Bull returned to England and enlisted in The Life Guards. He served in India and South Africa being taken prisoner in the latter during the Boer War.

On the outbreak of the First World War, Mr Bull enlisted in the 99th Battalion and saw action in England, France and Belgium, before returning to Canada in 1918. From then until just prior to the commencement of hostilities in 1939 he worked for an American firm in Detroit. When the firm received contracts for secret work, Mr Bull was asked to swear allegiance to the U.S.A. This he refused to do and returned to Windsor to assume the duties of Adjutant and Paymaster Windsor Division, a job he held for the next 23 years.

Post-war trials and tribulations were certainly not limited to Windsor and as a result the Corps was forced to consider reallocation of

LCol. Kenneth S. Kersey, CD, being presented his 15 year Long Service Award by Colonel W, Rae Martin, CD, ADC. LCol. Kersey went on to serve another 12 years before retiring in July 1997.

Divisions in 1950. However, the independent nature of all the Divisions stymied any attempts at amalgamation or re-alignment. Throughout the remainder of the 1950s, very little changed in the Windsor Division. Growth was extremely slow and limited by low pay and the Corps' continued resolve to maintain its policy of hiring older veterans. Windsor Division was further hampered by the heavy reliance of the Corps on government jobs. The city of Windsor had minimal federal infrastructure which placed the Division in constant competition for local commercial business.

The post-war years were also marked by a lack of record keeping. In fact outside of two brief references to Windsor Division in minutes of Annual General Meetings, we have no accounts of strength, revenues or clients from 1949 to 1960.

The Years Prior to Corps Reorganization - 1960-1972

This period continued the slow steady growth of the Corps. In the Windsor area, we commenced work at the Cleary Auditorium, handling both security and bookkeeping functions. We also undertook jobs at the Cedar Springs Regional Hospital, Point Pelee National Park, numerous construction companies and last but not least the Dresden Race Track. This job lasted but one season. It was rumoured that the Commandant acted as the site supervisor and his twice-weekly visits did not always prove profitable. At the same time the Corps was being offered most federal and provincial jobs because hiring Commissionaires meant that the Department of Veteran Affairs did not have to pay disability benefits including full medical coverage.

There was always sufficient demand to find employment for those veterans who truly needed work and could not find employment in industry. However, in Windsor and the surrounding area the problem was a shortage of suitable candidates. We had our share of veterans but few needed the Corps for employment. Industrial expansion and large automotive plants in the "Automobile Capital of Canada" provided lots of work for those who had fought in the war. Few veterans wanted to work for the Corps unless they had reached retirement age and wanted something to do to keep busy. As such Windsor's strength had difficulty reaching more than 75 and those on the waiting list usually ran around 10 to 15.

A significant change in Windsor's workload was the invention of the "guard dog." In the early sixties, Commissionaires in Windsor were used by most construction and lumber companies in the area. However, when the clients found they could use dogs who ate less and who worked for about the same pay with no legislated benefits, we lost a substantial number of long-term clients. Had there not been an upturn in the government work to parallel the loss in commercial business, there is a strong possibility that Windsor would have had difficulty surviving into the seventies.

Reorganization, Incorporation and Revision of the Veteran Content Rules

The seventies saw the injection of new pressures on the Corps in Windsor and across Canada. There was a great surge of interest by the federal government to use Corps services; however, this interest was stymied by the general lack of resources to fill the requirement. There was also a growing interest in security services and a general belief that the demand for security had unlimited potential. These factors and a rapid rise in private security services made the government lobby for a general federal contract for security services from a single provider. This combined with the fact that by employing Commissionaires reduced the government's requirement to pay veteran benefits made possible the development of the National Standing Offer which is still in existence today.

Existing Corps By-laws mandated the composition of each Corps and guaranteed that at least ninety percent of their strength would be veterans. In addition existing legislation also limited the amount of money a veteran could earn before affecting his/her veteran benefits. These two limitations directly contributed to the size of any Division and the amount of work a Division could undertake. What occurred was a great disparity in the individual Divisions to recruit sufficient personnel to conduct Corps work. In 1972 and 1973 most large Divisions were unable to recruit sufficient personnel to support federal generated requirement. This problem was further exacerbated by the requirement to provide security support for the 1976 Olympics.

All of these factors, plus the fact that the existing veteran population was aging rapidly and there was much talk of the government's introduction of social security which would further reduce the number of veterans who would seek employment after the age of 65, forced the National Executive to rethink how the Corps of Commissionaires should be reorganized and what new if any eligibility requirements should be introduced. Most of these long-term problems were identified in 1971, when at the Annual General Meeting it was stated "that as far as the (National) Board was concerned we do not believe that the duty of the Corps is to perpetuate itself and if the day arrives where there is not a single veteran looking for work, our job is finished." The question now came down to two choices: slowly devolve and basically cease to exist by the year 2,000 or reorient, restructure and realign. Needless to say the latter course was chosen.

During this period Windsor Division was in a rather fortunate position compared to most other Divisions. We had a limited number of federal contracts and more than adequate strength to handle the jobs at hand. In fact from 1973 to 1976 we were one of the three Divisions which had a manpower surplus and were able to provided limited support to our sister Division in Sarnia. This period also marked the arrival of Brigadier General W.W. Bradley on the Board of Governors. A man with an

Brigadier General W.W. Bradley, CD, Chairman of the Board of Governors from 1976-1992, presenting a Ten-Year Service Award to Commissionaire F. Van Boven.

illustrious military career and numerous civic appointments, he would serve on the Board from 1972 to 1994 and be its Chairman for some 16 years.

Born and raised in Windsor, Ontario, Brigadier General Warren W. Bradley's military career began as a Trooper in 1937. He was commissioned the following year and went overseas with the Ontario Regiment in 1941. He saw duty in England, Sicily, Italy and Northwest Europe. Following the war, Brigadier General Bradley joined the Windsor Regiment and served the militia in numerous capacities over the next 20 years. He was appointed Honorary Aide-de-Camp to the Governor General in 1967 and Honorary Colonel of the Windsor Regiment in 1982.

Following his tour with the militia, Brigadier General Bradley served as the Sheriff of Essex County from 1971 to 1983. At the same time he held numerous civic appointments including Chairman of the Windsor Chapter of the Ontario Heart and Stroke Foundation, President of Canterbury College, Vice-Chairman Board of Governors University of Windsor, President of the Windsor Club, and Member and Director of the Military Institute.

Besides his other activities, Brigadier General Bradley also found time to serve on the Board of Governors of the Canadian Corps of Commissionaires (Windsor Division). Appointed to the Board in 1972, he assumed the Chairmanship in 1976 and retained the position until his retirement from it in 1992. He continued as a Member of the Board until his demise in 1994. From 1982 until 1988, he served as a Member of the National Executive Committee. The longest serving Chairman in the Division history, Brigadier General Bradley led us through our worst and best of times.

This move to the east established new areas of interest and employment. A recruiting program started in Wallaceburg, Blenheim, Dresden, Ridgetown, and Chatham. This initial thrust proved extremely positive as we commenced work at the Southwestern Regional Hospital, the Ridgetown Agricultural College, Point Pelee National Park, Fort Malden and Navistar International. These jobs and the transition of Airport Security from the RCMP to the Corps allowed the strength of the Windsor Division to steadily grow from 1970 to 1984 when it peaked at 134 Commissionaires.

The general presence of the Windsor Division in all areas of southwestern Ontario also resurrected some old boundary disputes. The original Division boundaries as established in the 1940s made Sarnia part of Windsor Division responsibilities; however, it was ignored for many years and taken over by London because of its proximity to their Headquarters. Since our inception, Windsor had historically had difficulty in recruiting veterans to the Corps and it was not until our Letters Patent were amended in the late 1970s that we could now find enough people to seek work in areas outside of Windsor proper. With our success in Chatham, we were now anxious to reclaim jurisdiction over the now lucrative petrochemical industrial market which was rapidly developing in the Sarnia area. Although the Windsor Board lobbied diligently, our pleas fell on deaf ears and to this day Sarnia remains an enclave of the London Division.

In 1982, the Division hired Colonel John A. Baxter, CD, as the Commandant. In concert with Brigadier General W.W. Bradley, CD, Chairman of the Board of Governors, and in particular, Colonel Leonard N. Baldock, CD, CGA, Treasurer of the Board, they moved the Division into new territories and work areas. These individuals, and other members of the Board built the Division up to a strength of over 130, obtained new contracts, and streamlined operations. They also laid the groundwork in the late 1980s for the Annual General Meeting of 1993, held in Windsor.

Colonel Leonard N. Baldock, KStJ, CD, CA, CGA, being promoted to a Knight of Grace in the Most Venerable order of the Hospital of St. John of Jerusalem.

Colonel J.A. (Jack) Baxter, CD spent most of his adult life in uniform be it militia, active duty, reserves or the Corps of Commissionaires. A corporal in the 2nd Battalion of the Essex

From left to right: Colonel Walter L. McGregor, CD, QC; Lieutenant Colonel Kenneth S. Kersey, CD; Brigadier General W.W. Bradley, CD; Colonel Leonard N. Baldock, CD, CA, CGA; Lieutenant Colonel A.H. Tupper, CD; Colonel J.A. Baxter, CD (the Windsor Division Board of Governors in 1984).

Scottish Regiment at the outbreak of the Second World War, Colonel Baxter left Windsor in 1941 to join the active force as an officer cadet. After receiving his commission he went overseas in May 1941, joining the Essex Scottish Regiment at Middleton-on-Sea, England the day after the disastrous raid at Dieppe. Following a stint of action in Northwest Europe, he was captured by German forces, and spent the remainder of the war as a POW. He commanded the reorganized Essex-Kent Scottish from 1960 to 1965 and the Windsor Militia District from 1970 to 1972.

Always willing to undertake new challenges, Colonel Baxter at the age of 62 was appointed Commandant for the Windsor Division in the summer of 1982 and held the position until 1989. Under his tenure, the Division grew by 50% and the revenues doubled.

Colonel Jack A, Baxter, CD, the Windsor Division Commandant from 1982 to 1989.

Sergeant John Hogan displays some of the weapons seized by "Hogan's Heroes" while employed on Courthouse Security.

The eighties were also a time when the Windsor Division had some of its most enjoyable and most publicized jobs. We provided security for the federal Forestry Service at Point Pelee National Park and Fort Malden. This included monitoring the annual smelting run off the shores of Lake Erie. Windsor Division also took part in a two-year pilot program of Court Security. A team of nine Commissionaires was formed and they roamed the various court houses in Windsor screening all persons entering the courts. The team was headed by Staff Sergeant John Hogan and quickly was named "Hogan's Heroes" after the famous television series. Although they remained in operation for only a short time, some 20 months, the members of the team gained significant notoriety and lots of press. During their brief tenure they intercepted more than 130 dangerous weapons and had charges laid against a dozen individuals.

Staff Sergeant Hogan and fellow Commissionaires Watson Dunlop and John Dunbar were also credited with saving the life of a heart attack victim who collapsed after suffering a massive heart attack in the County Courthouse lobby. Staff Sergeant Hogan discovered the victim, commenced loosening his tie and shirt and summoned assistance. Commissionaires Dunlop and Dunbar administered cardio-pulmonary resuscitation until the ambulance crew arrived. The hospital staff stated that the timely efforts of the three individuals certainly saved the man's life.

It was the character of Commissionaires like Staff Sergeant John Hogan who typified the diligence and dedication of the members of the Windsor Division. They reinforced the strong reputation of the men and women who made up this smallest yet successful Division. They established the benchmarks against which future Commissionaires in Windsor and southwestern Ontario would be measured.

The Nineties

In the nineties the watch word has been financial restraint at the federal, provincial and commercial level. Many clients, especially provincial, have been deleting or severely curtailing their spending on security services. In concert with this reduced demand is the increased prevalence of technology and computer in the security services industry. These two factors have resulted in a decline in the demand for Commissionaires and a parallel decline in the strength of the Windsor Division. From the heydays of the early and mid-eighties when Windsor had a peak strength of 130, we have in recent years stabilized at 80. However the work being done now is in most cases much more challenging, with greater responsibilities, and relies significantly on previously gleaned qualifications. This is most evident in our work at Navistar Corporation Canada in Chatham, Ontario. Twenty-seven highly trained Commissionaires not only provide Loss Prevention services at this truck assembly facility but they also issue all new trucks, conduct confined space work, and do statistical reporting. To date their diligence has saved the company thousands of dollars in downtime and resulted in the presentation of the 1995 special recognition award to Commissionaire Alan Christian. As stated by Mr John R. Harne, President and Chief Executive Officer, Navistar International Corporation, Chicago, Illinois: "Commissionaire Christian's actions saved the pumps and saved Navistar a substantial amount of money. This award is Navistar's way of showing its appreciation for outstanding employee performance."

Commissionaire Yvon Boivin as perceived by his fellow workers at the Windsor Airport.

In 1993, the smallest Division hosted the Annual General Meeting of the Corps in Windsor, for the first time. Over 300 attended and the event marked the expansion of the Windsor Board to accommodate the taskings of the many committees required to organize and operate a programme of this magnitude. Five years of planning and coordination were spent on this project, as well as the day-to-day operations of the Division. Colonel Ralph D. West, CD, the Chairman of the Board, also assumed chairmanship of the AGM Committee, in the final weeks before the event. The Annual General Meeting was pronounced successful, and many innovative social functions were enjoyed by all. The result was worth the work and effort.

The nineties are also marked by a new type of Commissionaire. The new candidates are not only young, with broad academic qualifications, but they also have very broad experience levels. As with all parts of society people who decide to become Commissionaires have had numerous and varied career changes. They are more full of life. They seek job satisfaction as a primary goal. This new type of Commissionaire is best typified by the late Sergeant Yvon Boivin.

Sergeant Yvon Joseph Boivin joined the Royal Canadian Air Force in 1953 as a transport pilot serving in Canada, Germany and Egypt. Released in 1961 he went on to get an aeronautical engineering degree and received an Honorary Doctor of Science Degree from the University of Rome. Always a free spirit, in the next year Yvon held a myriad of jobs in various vocations including instructor pilot, airport manager, logging camp cook, bush pilot, lodge owner, and aircraft maintenance manager. In 1977 he joined the Victoria and Vancouver Island Division of the Corps and in 1980 transferred to Windsor Division. His previous aeronautical experience made Yvon an ideal candidate to work at the Windsor Airport. His talent and knowledge quickly came to the fore and he was promoted to Sergeant and made systems manager for the airport's computer system, a position he held for the next nine years until stricken with cancer. Always dedicated to his military roots, Sergeant Boivin was a life member of the Royal Canadian Air Force Association and the Warbirds Society of the Royal Air Force.

A most interesting individual, Sergeant Yvon Boivin typified what the Corps is all about and what everyone should envision when describing a Commissionaire.

To this writer Sergeant Boivin personifies the spirit of the Windsor Division of the Corps when it started some 60 years ago. Windsor Division may be small but we have certainly had an illustrious and colourful history.

The current executive of the Windsor Division consists of:

Supt J. Trainor Fraser	Chairman
LCdr William C. Bear, CD	Vice Chairman
Col Ralph D. West, CD	Past Chairman
LCol Jack A. Lambe, CD	Treasurer
Capt Alison M. Martine, CD	Secretary
Lt John E. Lyster	Member
LCol C. Ward Yorke, CD	Member
LCol Dennis G. DeJager, CD	Commandant

In addition, Past Chairman, Colonel Ralph D. West was elected as a member of the National Executive in 1997.

Chapter VII

HISTORY OF THE SOUTHERN ALBERTA DIVISION

Commandant's Introduction – *by Dick Dossett*

IN ITS over sixty years of service the Southern Alberta "Calgary" Division has evolved from an initial strength of seven Commissionaires in 1937 to today's (1997) slightly over 1,000 employees. The growth of the Division and its expanded client base have in fact kept pace with the vibrant economic climate of Calgary and Southern Alberta.

Not only has the Division changed its approach to business and operational procedures, but also the face of the Board of Governors and the management team certainly reflect the changing years. From a Board made up of mostly First World War veterans, through the years when mostly Second World War veterans sat on the Board, to today when only four of the 18 Governors and four Honorary Life Members can claim Second World War service. The Division office staff which into the 1980s consisted solely of Second World War veterans now has only one, the current Commandant.

From the days of checking residence doors, at so much per door, this Division with less than 25% federal business has become an organization that means many different things to many different clients. These changes did not occur overnight nor were they unforeseen. One example can be seen in the handling of parking tickets which Commissionaires have been writing throughout Southern Alberta for many years. These were handwritten and processed through a manual, labour-intensive system. Today, in at least one Alberta city, the by-law infraction information is entered in a hand-held computer by the Commissionaire, a ticket is generated and the information from the hand-held devices is processed electronically by a dedicated computer system. Commissionaires, who for years only wrote the tickets, are now involved in every step of the process, including the data entry and electronic processing.

Uniforms have also changed. From the military style tunic of wool worsted with brass buttons which had to be dry-cleaned, Commissionaires now are issued with wash and wear, work-dress style uniforms. Suitable work friendly items are also the norm, such as coveralls, safety helmets and patrol jackets. Additionally, there are more and more clients asking for the non-military appearance which has created the "Soft Look" of blazer and flannels with white shirt and Corps tie (at many work sites).

Training has also gone through an evolution. In the early days training, if any, consisted of a few hours of on-the-job training with heavy reliance on the past military or RCMP experience of the individual. This changed over the years to short one- or two-day, or part day, courses (no exams) where instructors stood in front of a class and read from the short available precis on any given subject. Not only is today's Commissionaire required to successfully complete a comprehensive qualifying course, he or she must also obtain emergency first aid and basic CPR qualification.

The change in this Division over the years is perhaps best illustrated by the changing profile of the most important element of any Division: the Commissionaire. The membership, which over the years consisted mainly of the veteran who needed work; the individual who served many years ago then went on to a post-service civilian job; and the long-service Canadian Forces or RCMP member just retired, has been changing at a fairly rapid pace. The new generation of Commissionaire is on average younger, better educated and has more useable skills. The chances are that the new Commissionaire is computer literate, is more physically fit and has the flexibility to accept a wider variety of job assignments.

There is no doubt the history of the "Calgary Division" is in many respects similar to that of other Divisions. The uniqueness of this Division may be that over the years the philosophy has been that of placing more emphasis on seeking out more commercial business and ensuring that its members understand that our clients are number one. "If you don't look after your clients, someone else will."

THE HISTORY

The initial organizational meeting of the Calgary Division of the Canadian Corps of Commissionaires was held in the Calgary Board of Trade building on May 27, 1937. Seventeen individuals attended of which 12 had former military service, and the remaining five were businessmen. It is interesting to note that eight of the military members had been decorated including: 2 MCs, 3 DSOs, 2 CMGs, 1 MBE, and 1 KC.

The Division was activated on June 29, 1937. The federal government provided office space at no expense to the Corps and a $500 loan from Headquarters enabled the Division to proceed. Officers elected as founding members were:

Honorary President	– Col G.E. Sanders, CMG DSO
Chairman of the Board	– Mr John Burns
Commandant	– LCol J.W. Littlejohn
Adjutant	– Maj F. Graham

The Calgary Division commenced operations in October with an initial strength of seven Commissionaires. One year later it had grown to a very healthy 57. Further, by the spring of 1939, the minutes of the Annual General Meeting record, "The Calgary Division is considered to be the best in Canada, and a model for other Divisions."

The work of the Division in the pre-war years consisted primarily of security patrols of local businesses and private residences, with a payroll as follows: Permanent Positions – 15; Semi Permanent – 2; Night Patrol – 37; Office – 2; Casual – 4.

At the outbreak of war, many members of the Division left to rejoin the Forces, and many others became members of the Veterans Guard.

During the war years the employment of Commissionaires gradually changed from routine patrol work to providing permanent guards for factories, office buildings, and government facilities and installations. Great difficulty was experienced in maintaining the strength of the Division as the war progressed, due to the plentiful and more lucrative positions being offered by industry. The strength of the Division on the cessation of hostilities was 65.

In the postwar years the mix of services offered by the Division continued to change. Whereas the greatest single area of employment had been to patrol work, this diminished and by the mid-1950s had been almost eliminated. In 1953, the Division commenced supplying Commissionaires to the city of Calgary to perform ticketing for parking meter violations.

In the late 1950s the areas of employment were as follows: Federal Government – 40; Provincial Government – 4; Full Time – 112; Patrolmen – 3; City Parking – 25; Office – 6; Part Time – 67; Total – 257

By the mid-1960s the services offered by the Division changed geographically from being exclusive to the city of Calgary to include the military installations at Penhold and Suffield, as well as municipal services at Red Deer and Lethbridge.

The strength increased correspondingly and by 1965 was 357, involving the following areas of employment: Federal Government – 56; Provincial Government – 14; Municipal Government – 49; Industrial/Commercial – 176.

The name of the Calgary Division was changed to the Southern Alberta Division early in 1972, and on August 17, 1972 it was incorporated as a non-profit company under Part 9 of the Companies Act of Alberta as the Canadian Corps of Commissionaires (Southern Alberta).

In 1972 a decision was made to discontinue offering night foot patrol services, as by this time only one Commissionaire was so employed, and he had been subjected to some physical abuse by some rowdies.

Due to the economic climate, the Division experienced difficulty during the 1970s in attracting sufficient qualified recruits to fill positions offered. Areas of employment included: Federal Government – 65; Provincial Government – 73; Municipal Government – 50; Industrial/Commercial – 189.

During the 1980s the Division continued its efforts in identifying positions that could be filled by ex-service personnel. While unfortunately there are no statistics on the breakdown of employment, total staff continued to increase by approximately 20% per year.

As there were gradual changes in the type of employment performed by the Commissionaires, there were also over the years changes in the Board of Governors. Originally the Board included a significant percentage of civilians (normally prominent businessmen), but the 1960s made up membership exclusively of former members of the forces. Whereas there traditionally had been a shortage of Commissionaires to meet offers of temporary/permanent employment, currently as well as in the past few years, Southern Alberta has been in a position to immediately respond to requests for Commissionaires. Of interest is the fact that we have recently filled requests for secretarial assistance and in another case, catering management.

In short, while the original role of the Southern Alberta Division was to find employment for former members of the forces primarily in the role of uniformed security, or other police related functions, Calgary now devotes a great deal of its efforts in the broader role of a former service personnel employment agency.

This progressive change resulted in a requirement for a more aggressive approach to marketing the skills and experience of former soldiers, sailors and airmen, with emphasis on their inherent loyalty, dedication and discipline.

This is reflected in the current strength of the Division as of June 10, 1997.

	Male	Female	Totals
Commissionaires	697	37	734
Guards/Matrons	176	130	306
Civilians (Admin/Clerk)	27	6	33
Totals	**900**	**173**	**1073**

Contracted Personnel

Federal Government	96	9%
Provincial Government	52	5%
Municipal Government	105	10%
Calgary Parking Authority	75	7%
Calgary Airport Authority	98	9%
Commercial	308	30%
RCMP	306	30%

It is obvious that during the history of this Division, it enjoyed the participation of a great many outstanding personalities. To name them all would require several sizable volumes, and to name just a few may be an injustice to the many. However, there are a few who are quite unique, and should be at least mentioned in any history of the Corps.

THE COMMISSIONAIRES

Mary Dover, MBE

In 1952, LCol. Dover was elected to the Board of Governors of the Southern Alberta Division, the first female to serve on a Board in Canada. Dover served in the CWAC during the Second World War. She was the daughter of Mr A.E. Cross, one of the founding members of the Calgary Stampede and a granddaughter of Col. MacLeod, founder of Calgary and for whom the city of Fort MacLeod is named.

Helen Kozicky

In February 1974, Helen Kozicky became the first female to become a member of the Southern Alberta Division. Helen served in the CWAC from 1941 to 1945 in Canada and the United Kingdom. In the post-war years, Helen remained active in the Calgary Military community. In recognition of her many contributions, she was made the Honorary Commander of the Lord Strathcona's Horse (Royal Canadians) Mounted Troop in 1987, and in 1990, Patron of the Regiment. Dame Helen continues to attend all parades and functions of her regiment.

Helen Kozicky.

Allan T. (Pony) Love

Pony Love joined the RCNVR as a seaman in 1941 and was commissioned as Sub-Lt in 1942. He served in a number of ships in the Atlantic and at war's end, joined the RCN as a Lieutenant. He served in a number of sea going appointments and shore establishments, until his discharge as a LCdr. in November 1967. Pony was enrolled in the Corps of Commissionaires as the Southern Alberta Division Adjutant in 1968. He became Commandant in 1975 and at the time of his retirement from the Corps in 1991, he was the longest serving Commandant of the Southern Alberta Division.

Harold Pallin

Harold Pallin enrolled in this Division in April of 1972, serving in various positions in the Red Deer area until his appointment as Detachment Commander in January 1974. Resigning from the Corps in 1988, he returned to work as a Commissionaire in March 1989 and eventually retired in 1996. Bo enlisted in the RCNVR in July 1940 at the age of 17 and served until March of 1946. His wartime service with the Navy resulted in his being seriously wounded, which probably saved his life. He was serving on *HMCS Athabaskan* when it was struck by a missile from a German aircraft in August 1943. As a result of this attack, five men were killed and 12 wounded. To quote Able Seaman Pallin, "I was blasted off my feet – the blast tore my pants and shoes off. I still had my socks and shorts on, so I don't suppose I could have been done for indecent exposure." Pallin was seriously injured with shrapnel wounds to his head and his left thigh and these wounds ironically, probably saved his life. He spent many months in the hospital after the stricken Athabaskan limped home to a British Port. He was not with the ship when she sailed from Plymouth on her last voyage. On April 29, 1944, the Athabaskan was hit by two torpedoes in the Bay of Biscay and went down stern first in three minutes, taking 127 of the ship's company with her.

Harold (BO) Pallin.

Dick Dossett

Dick Dossett, the current Commandant of the Southern Alberta Division, enlisted in the NPAM 4th Div Sigs in Montreal in 1943 as a Boy Soldier. Transferring to the RCAF later that year as an aircrew trainee, he served for over 33 years in the Canadian Forces retiring in 1977.

After working for over five years as a civilian with NATO HQ in Brussels he returned to Canada and enrolled in the Southern Alberta Division of the Corps in January 1983. His first job as a Commissionaire, working the graveyard

Dick Dossett.

shift at the General Hospital, was followed by a stint as the corporal supervisor of detail at the Shell Research Centre. Transferred to the Corps office in August of 1983 as the Administration Staff Sergeant, he filled various office positions including that of Operations Officer for five years and was appointed Commandant of the Division in June 1991. It is believed that he is the only Commandant in the history of the Corps to have enlisted and served as a Commissionaire.

John William Begg, DSO, ED

After service with the Canadian Army during the First World War John joined the 1st Battalion of the Calgary Regiment on December 7, 1920 and rose quickly to Sergeant by July 1921 and Lieutenant by February 1922. In July 1922 he attended the Royal School of Infantry in Esquimalt. He was promoted to Captain in 1930, and to Major in 1936 of what by then had become the Calgary Regiment (Tank). On September 6, 1939 he was called to active service and went overseas in June 1941. He was second in command of the 14th Army Tank Battalion (Calgary Regiment)(Tank) on the Dieppe Raid in August 1942 and assumed command of the Regiment at Dieppe when the CO was killed. John returned to Britain following the Dieppe Raid, was awarded the DSO and promoted to Lieutenant Colonel. In 1943 he returned to Canada where he commanded a tank training centre and completed his military career.

John became a Governor of the Calgary Division on 21 October 1947. At the Annual Meeting on 19 May 1949 he was elected Vice-Chairman and became the Chairman at the Annual Meeting on 28 June 1951, succeeding Lt Col W.T. Colclough, VD. During his term as Chairman (1951-1964) several new contracts were obtained in Red Deer, Lethbridge, Medicine Hat, Suffield, Penhold and Calgary, and the strength of the Division increased from 99 to 357. In 1964 John became the Commandant, which post he held until his resignation on 1 October 1975. John was a tower of strength in his support of the Canadian Corps of Commissionaires nationally and of our Division. He was a stickler for detail and was always concerned about the welfare of his Commissionaires.

Reginald (Reg) Jackson, OBE, VRD

Reg Jackson joined the RCNVR as an Ordinary Seaman when the Calgary Half Company was formed in 1923. He received his commission as a Sub Lieutenant in 1931; was appointed the Commanding Officer of the Calgary Division in 1934 in the rank of

Reginald (Reg) Jackson OBE, VRD.

Lieutenant, and served in this position until 1939. He was called to active service in 1940 and served in various ships in the Atlantic. He commanded the corvette *HMCS Orillia* in 1943 and the Algerine mine sweeper *HMCS Sault Ste. Marie* from 1943 to 1944. He was awarded the OBE in June 1945 and was demobilized in the rank of Commander in 1946. Reg commanded Calgary's Naval Reserve Division *HMCS Tecumseh* from 1946 to 1952, retiring in the rank of Captain.

In 1951 Reg was elected a Governor of this Division and became its Vice-Chairman at the Annual Meeting on 18 May 1961. At the Annual Meeting on 23 May 1964 he was elected Chairman and served as Chairman until he died on 21 November 1978. John Begg and Reg Jackson worked very effectively as a team for over 25 years, promoting the interests of this Division and particularly the interests and welfare of the Commissionaires serving in Southern Alberta.

Joseph Norman (Joe) Jackson

Joe Jackson joined the Southern Alberta Regiment in Medicine Hat in 1936 and transferred to the Calgary Highlanders at the outbreak of war. He served in Canada and Europe with the Highlanders and later with the Canadian Provost Corps and the Royal Canadian Artillery. Following demobilization in 1946, he remained active with the Militia and was employed by several companies including 15 years as a constable with the Canadian Pacific Investigation Branch.

Joe enrolled in the Corps of Commissionaires in February 1967, and because of his background was placed in charge of the Commissionaires assigned to the provincial building security, the court house, night patrol and customer relations. He served with the Corps for over 19 years and in January 1982, was appointed Honorary RSM, a position he occupied until 1987. Joe Jackson was one of the most popular and highly respected members of the Division in recent history.

Joseph Norman (Joe) Jackson.

ABOVE AND BEYOND

Unfortunately over the years no Division historical record was maintained listing significant events or outstanding Commissionaires and their achievements. In December 1991, the Division introduced a Commissionaire Of The Month (COTM) award. The aim of this program is to identify those Commissionaires whose overall performance or specific act "above and beyond," receives recognition. Recommendations for the award, received from clients, supervisors or the general public, are reviewed by a committee and the name of the recipients(s), (there can be more than one in a month) and those other nominees worthy of honourable mention, are published in the Division's bi-monthly newsletter. The award recipients also receive a modest cash bonus. The list of recipients since the onset of the program and their individual citations would cover many pages, therefore only a brief chronicle of relevant events is included in this history. Regrettably, there are no photographs of those whose names are mentioned.

The first recipient in January 1992, was Sergeant Brian Kelly of CFB Suffield. During the early morning hours of October 24, 1991, an impaired driver failed to stop for the Military Police. Kelly calmly managed to coordinate simultaneous communications, using two open telephones and a radio link between the Military Police, Medicine Hat Police and the RCMP. He was instrumental in bringing a speedy end to the event. Kelly was cited again in May 1993, for personally apprehending an individual who had committed a break and enter offence.

Commissionaires Brian Sheppard and Ron Carrick, both employed at CFB Calgary, were nominated for COTM during 1992 for separate but similar attention to detail. Brian spotted a person who was "most wanted" by Military Police and assisted them in arresting the individual. Ron on duty at Harvey Barracks noticed three individuals who had been listed as armed and dangerous by the Calgary Police Service. He immediately reported their location and kept them under observation until the police arrived.

During his first tour of duty during April 1992, as a night patrol supervisor, Commissionaire Donald Pike noticed a broken window at one of the buildings he was checking. On closer examination he heard noises from within the building, where much valuable equipment was kept. He immediately summoned the police who apprehended the individuals while they were still in the building. A month later Commissionaire Gordon Sanderson on duty at the City Electric facility was in a similar situation of observing two intruders in the process of stealing property. He immediately radioed for assistance, resulting in the arrest of the two culprits.

Two further nominations in 1992 were for Commissionaires Harold Pallin and Fraser MacDonnel of the O & Y detail both instrumental in the arrest of individuals being sought by the police. Harold, on duty at the Red Deer Museum, chased and detained two juveniles who had stolen a wallet and Fraser identified and reported a person loitering around his work site who was wanted by the police. In August of 1992, a female visitor to the Calgary Zoo complained to the Security Office that a male person had exposed himself to her. She identified the individual who was leaving the zoo to Commissionaire Stanley Besse. Besse followed the individual to a nearby apartment building, maintaining radio contact with Corporal Mike Melnik who had called the police. Following Besse's relayed directions, the police arrested the suspect who was later charged and convicted of the offense.

Commissionaire Douglas Norton-Westwood was cited twice during 1992. The first incident involved preventing major water damage to a building at CFB Suffield where a pipe had burst and Douglas immediately took action to find the shut-off valve before summoning help. No sooner had that been accomplished when a second water pipe burst and he was again able to locate the shut-off valve and prevent further damage. Later in the year Norton-Westwood was commended for outstanding performance and attention to detail during a NATO meeting held at Defence Research Establishment, Suffield.

Other COTM awards during 1992 were not for specific actions or events but were as a result of recommendations received from clients citing individual Commissionaires for outstanding professionalism and public relations skills in dealing with the client, the client's employees and the general public. These included Commissionaires Mary Petrie, Red Deer detachment; Elsie Craig, city of Calgary Public Building; Sergeant Andy Dufour, Olds College; Sergeant Bill Egberts, Mewata Armoury; and Les Ramsey, Shell Research Centre.

In March of 1993, Commissionaire Doug Hamilton waiting in his patrol vehicle for the light to change heard a crash and what sounded like broken glass falling. As he got out of his vehicle he noticed a crowd gathering and a body lying on the roadway in front of an office building. Evidently, the man had jumped or fallen from the 45th storey of the building. After determining that the man had no pulse, Hamilton, who had radioed for the police, questioned some of the bystanders and asked them to remain on the scene to assist the police who showed up within minutes of Hamilton's call. Hamilton assisted police in rounding up the witnesses and keeping the crowd of onlookers under control. Hamilton was subsequently highly commended by the police service for the maturity, good judgement and the assistance he provided to the police throughout the incident.

In February 1993, Commissionaire Rick Sletten on duty at the Municipal Complex responded to a complaint that a male person was behaving in a threatening manner towards an employee. Rick caused the offender to be moved from the immediate area and stayed with him until the police arrived.

When the police constable was being overpowered by the suspect, at her request Sletten intervened and physically restrained the suspect. Rick was commended by both the police service and the building management for his promptness in responding to the incident and exercising due care and minimum physical control in assisting in the arrest.

Other incidents during the year resulted in awards. Commissionaire John Cryer's quick action prevented a potentially serious accident to a small child using the escalator at the Calgary Airport. Commissionaires Ernie Lay and Bob Dassett of Red Deer College detected a gas leak and with quick action cleared the area, turned off the power and summoned an emergency crew, preventing a potentially dangerous situation.

Commissionaire Vern Amero on duty at the Museum of the Regiments was advised that a visitor to the museum had collapsed in the washroom. Vern immediately responded and used his CPR skills until the ambulance arrived. Commissionaire John Stoppard of CFB Suffield discovered a fellow Commissionaire unconscious because of a candy stuck in his throat. John immediately used the Heimlich maneuver and dislodged the obstruction.

On the night of the 6th of August 1993, Commissionaires Jim Belmont and Kent Fisher were on duty at television station CFCN. One of them noticed that an individual was climbing the station's antennae mast. Their first action was to shut off all power to the building and mast and then summon city police.

Other COTM awards for 1993 as recommended by clients were for professionalism and dedication to duty in dealing with clients and the general public. The nominees were as follows: Commissionaire Jack Manson, Village Square Leisure Centre; Sergeant John Friedt and Commissionaire Kelsie Howatt, McDougal Centre Premier's Office; Staff Sergeant Bob Hoad, Imperial Oil; Commissionaire Henry Labadie, Calgary Zoo; Commissionaire Doug Hamilton , City of Calgary detail; Chief Warrant Officer Al McLaughlin, CFB Suffield; Sergeant Art Holm, Corporal Luc McCabe, Commissionaires John Cryer, Don Artindale, Norm Davis and Betty Crowther, all Calgary Airport; and Commissionaire Ingrid Hamel, Calgary Public building.

Early in January 1994, Commissionaire Ron Simmons, on duty at the Municipal Complex, noticed what appeared to be a person covered with snow lying on the outside steps of the building. With the temperature at −25°C, Simmons decided to investigate. Simmons went outside but failed in his attempt to rouse the person. Calling for assistance he managed to drag the individual into the building and summon the Emergency Medical Service. The individual, clearly under the influence of some substance, would have perished if left out in the extremely cold weather.

The Municipal Complex was again the scene of an incident in April of 1994. Commissionaire Scotty Tillott responded to a report of a hold-up in the building washroom. The victim was calmed down and questioned and Tillott then observed a trio of miscreants fitting the descriptions leaving the building. As one of them was reported to be carrying a firearm, Tillott followed them at a safe distance, meanwhile relaying his location to the police through the building operations centre. He subsequently assisted the police in the arrest of the three suspects.

Commissionaire Rick Ostrowski, on duty at a Petro Canada station one late evening in July was held up at gun point. He obviously remained calm and in control of the situation because he was able to give the police an accurate description of the individual, his car and the licence number. He then further assisted the police by positively identifying the individual they had arrested with the help of his accurate information.

Several incidents during the year reinforced the positive image of the Corps and its members. Commissionaire Chester Miller, AMOCO Centre, noticed a young man in apparent distress outside the building. He discovered that the young man had hitch-hiked from B.C. to find his father who lived in Calgary. The young man had been robbed of his wallet and did not know where his father lived in the city. Miller with much perseverance and several telephone calls was able to reunite that boy and his father who were extremely grateful for the action voluntarily performed by Miller. Commissionaire Ian Christie on night patrol came across a woman who had fallen down a river bank and broken her arm. Christie immediately summoned EMS and stayed with the woman until they arrived. Commissionaire Len Leblanc on duty during the annual Stampede parade noticed one of the costumed parade mascots slumped over in a chair outside of the building. Len quickly assisted the individual into the building and provided some water for the person who was on the verge of heat exhaustion. Commissionaire Mike Crabbe, off duty but visiting his work site to pick up his cheque, discovered a man with a serious head wound. Mike immediately rendered first aid to contain the bleeding, then used his own vehicle to transport the victim to the hospital.

Other Commissionaires cited during 1994 for performance worthy of recognition included Don Birch, City Electric Yards, for assisting police in the arrest of two individuals stealing copper wire from the yards; and Raymond Fouquet, CFB Suffield, Mike Gagnon and Ed Hurley, both CFCN Television, each involved in separate incidents where they were able to prevent major damage to a client's property by their quick reaction to a potential disaster.

Early in 1995, Commissionaire John Hudon, on duty at the Southern Alberta Institute of Technology (SAIT), came upon a vehicle with the motor running and a hose running from the exhaust pipe into the car. He immediately disconnected the hose, removed a person from the vehicle and summoned medical assistance. John undoubtedly saved this person's life.

Commissionaire Ray Chaput of the Parking Control Detail, while on patrol noticed an explosion from under the hood of parked vehicle and the start of a fire. A five-year-old girl was in the vehicle with her seat belt on and the door locked. Ray, acting with calmness and authority, convinced the young girl to unlock the car door. He unfastened the seat belt and removed her to safety. His cool action under fire averted a possible tragedy.

Also in January 1995, Commissionaire Doug Jennings, on duty at the city police, Arrest Processing Unit, scanning his surveillance monitors noted a female prisoner with her head completely immersed in the toilet bowl. Doug's immediate reaction was to run to the cell, reach through the bars and yank her head out of the toilet while his on-duty partner, Constable Steed, unlocked the cell door. The prisoner was checked by the paramedics and transported to the hospital.

Commissionaire Bill Kennedy, Calgary Parking Authority, while conducting a routine investigation of a stolen licence plate remembered that he had written several tickets against that particular plate and that it was on a vehicle parked in a city parking lot. Bill confirmed the location of the vehicle and summoned the city police. While waiting for them to arrive he observed three females enter the vehicle and drive away. Bill reported the status by radio and Commissionaire Dick Elliot followed the vehicle and kept reporting its location until the police arrived to make the arrests.

On the 5th of April 1995, Commissionaire Rick Adams, on duty at the Municipal Complex, was alerted by the building operations centre to be on the lookout for a female armed with a butcher knife. Adams immediately responded saying he already had the person under observation in the Plus 15 overpass. Commissionaires John Parris and Roy Spencer also responded to assist and the three Commissionaires took up positions isolating the distraught woman and keeping the general public away from the area until the police arrived. The citation by the building manager states that these three Commissionaires responded to a dangerous situation without hesitation and that they had demonstrated personal conduct that calmed the woman and prevented an escalation of her anxiety into an act of violence.

Other Commissionaires received the COTM award during the year. Ian Christie on night patrol came upon two persons in a semi-conscious state and alerted EMS. Tony Dossett, Manufactures Life building, observed a firearm on the back seat of a car and reported his observations. The driver was subsequently fined. Bill Grant and Ernie Lang of Red Deer College whose quick action to alert the RCMP, assist in the arrest and provide suspect identification, was instrumental in the prevention of a serious loss of equipment from the college. Doug Hamilton prevented a potentially serious accident on a very busy road by his clear thinking and quick action to rescue four individuals from their stalled vehicle and have it towed away in a matter of minutes. In October, Commissionaire Andre Bernier was alerted that his neighbour was choking and had fainted. Andre rushed over, assessed the situation and using a plastic drinking straw helped his neighbour to breathe, until EMS arrived.

On the 14th of December at 2215 hours, Commissionaire Dave Stensrud doing a regular mobile patrol of Hansen's car storage lot discovered one of the transport drivers lying on the ground in a pool of blood. Using his cellular telephone to summon EMS, with the help of another driver Dave managed to revive the injured person and help him to a nearby washroom. Paramedics arrived within 15 minutes and transported the injured person to a hospital.

During the year several other Commissionaires were cited for their exemplary conduct and dedication at various work sites. Commissionaire Pat Middlebrook assisted a woman who suspected that she was being stalked. Chief Warrant Officer John Johnson, Commissionaire Dave Drummond and several other Commissionaires at ESSO Plaza were on duty when a murder was committed in the parking garage. Their quick reaction to seal off the area and protect the crime scene were of great assistance to the police in their investigation.

On the 14th of February 1996, Commissionaire Adrian Duhault was on duty at the Arrest Processing Unit when an individual who was found sleeping on a light rail transit car was brought into the unit. During the mandatory search of the individual three prescription pill bottles were discovered. Duhault immediately summoned the EMS who determined that the detainee did in fact require immediate medical attention. Duhault's prompt action may well have saved the individual from serious medical complications.

Commissionaire Dave Stensrud was cited again in early 1996 for quick action to prevent major damage to a client's property. Likewise Commissionaire Howie Firth who as a result of his alertness and attention to detail during one of his rounds of a valuable historic building, discovered a fire in the making and was able to prevent it from spreading and causing damage.

During the month of September 1996, Commissionaires Bill Stuart and Ken Johnston of Olds College responded to a reported assault of a female student. Both Commissionaires were in turn assaulted and slightly injured by the suspect who subsequently assaulted an RCMP officer. The two Commissionaires along with the RCMP member were finally able to restrain and arrest the suspect who was eventually charged and convicted of eight separate offenses.

During the year a number of letters were received from clients recommending Commissionaires for the COTM award, not for specific actions or events but because the individuals had demonstrated that they are dedicated professionals who go out of their way to serve the client and the general public. Commissionaire Glen Nagy used his initiative and perseverance in tracking down a client's employee, out of town on business, and relaying some vital information to him. Commissionaire Henry Aldrich was cited for his dedication in improving the service to the client and enhancing the client's business. Commissionaire Henry Labadie not only did his job in an exemplary manner at the zoo but spent many extra hours of his own time at the zoo as a volunteer. Commissionaire Don Merritt of the Drumheller Institute, through his knowledge and experience in a prison environment and his outgoing personality was able to provide service to the client far above what is required.

The months of January and February 1997 were very busy ones for Commissionaires in their ongoing duty to protect clients and their property. Commissionaire Ken Manning on duty at the Harry Hays federal building noted on his CCTV monitor that someone was breaking into a government car. He dispatched Commissionaire Bob Neale to the scene, meanwhile calling the city police. Although the suspect escaped, Bob's quick appearance on the scene resulted in the recovery of some very valuable equipment taken from the vehicle. During February, Commissionaires Ray Thomas and Frank Latocki on duty at the Municipal Complex were responding to an intrusion alarm and observed a person crawling out through a broken window. They pursued the suspect for several blocks and were able to report his location during the pursuit and assist police in making the arrest.

In March of 1997, Commissionaire George Easton, patrolling the Olds College parking lot, noticed damage to several vehicles and observed two individuals prowling the lot. Acting quickly, he was able to catch one of them and turn him over to the RCMP who shortly thereafter caught the second individual and recovered a large amount of stolen property. Commissionaire Darren Strand, on duty in the Municipal Complex during the month of April 1997, interrupted three persons committing an act of vandalism to city property. He pursued them until the police arrived and arrested them for causing wilful damage.

In May of the same year, Commissionaire Lois Grace, on duty at the Calgary Airport, saw a two-year-old getting on an escalator without an adult. The girl's coat was open and she had fallen. Without hesitation Lois quickly ran down the up escalator and lifted the child to safety. At the same work site, the Calgary Airport, Commissionaire Colin Birt noticed that a taxiing jet aircraft had ingested a plastic bag. Birt immediately informed the control tower who in turn informed the pilot. The aircraft returned to the ramp. Colin's action may well have prevented a serious accident.

To round out 1997 on a high note, Commissionaire Andy Bernier, on duty at the Peter Lougheed Hospital, approached a vehicle parked at the main hospital entrance and was met by a very excited man who said that his wife was in labour in the back seat of the car. While Andy went for a wheelchair and alerted the hospital staff, the baby decided to make his appearance in this world. When Andy returned to the vehicle he had to calm both mother and father and make mother and baby comfortable until the emergency response team showed up, too late to assist in the delivery.

Chapter VIII

VICTORIA AND VANCOUVER ISLAND

Commandant's Introduction – *By Bob Kadonoff*

DEVELOPMENTS WITHIN the Victoria and Vancouver Island Division over the years have been characterized by a gradual reduction in the reliance on federal and other government taskings, efforts to find more employment opportunities with commercial clients and a desire to expand the scope of services to more than just security. Candidates for membership in the Corps are now younger, highly motivated and well-trained in a variety of disciplines marketable outside the security field. This wealth of available talent results from reductions in the Canadian Forces and the state of the economy. This allows the Corps to respond to a desire by institutions to reduce expenses through the employment of cost-efficient Commissionaires. The net result of these developments has been an opportunity for the broadening of our activities.

The unique geographical location of the Division, while ideal from a living standard perspective, presents challenges in transportation to outlying islands, towns and villages which, in many cases, are served by infrequent ferry service or unimproved roads. Nevertheless, the Commissionaire family is undaunted and provides excellent service to such far flung locations as the Queen Charlottes, the Gulf Islands and the west coast shores of Vancouver Island.

Security, and its associated tasks, continues to be the focus of our work. Stationary guards and foot patrols for Government House, Royal Roads University, Victoria Airport, the Royal British Columbia Museum and Canadian Forces bases at Esquimalt and Comox still employ a large portion of our Commissionaires. By-law enforcement is also a key function of our services to most communities on the island. The city of Victoria is provided with a modern automated parking enforcement system and the Division is currently the largest process serving company in its area of responsibility because of an association with the provincial photo radar program.

A desire to properly position the Division in a competitive business environment has resulted in a number of initiatives. Marketing has taken on a new dimension with proactive programs designed to inform prospective clients of the value of Commissionaires. As with many other Divisions, we have achieved ISO 9002 registration as a commitment to provide quality management to our clients. The Division has also formed a for-profit subsidiary which will allow the provision of services not normally available through the Corps.

Training has always been the hallmark of Commissionaires and a major reason for our success in supplying quality service. We continue to emphasize this aspect of our operation and now have Commissionaires qualified to the new British Columbia standards for security guards. As well, our training facility is accredited by the Post Secondary Education Commission and the Justice Institute of British Columbia to provide security guard training commercially.

Dealing with change in a positive manner will ensure the viability and continued success of the Corps. That we in the Division have shown flexibility and dedication since 1937 is a testament to our ability to fulfill our important mandate of providing meaningful and dignified employment for those who have served the country well.

This chapter was written by Colonel (retired) Bob Peacock, PPCLI, one of the Board of Governors. This Division is in his debt for his excellent work.

The Early Days

In November 1936 during the height of the Great Depression a group of concerned naval and military officers in Victoria came together to see if there was any way that a Company of Commissionaires could be formed on Vancouver Island to provide some employment assistance for war veterans. A Company had been formed in Vancouver in 1927 and had been highly successful. After many consultations with officials of the Commissionaires in the United Kingdom, Ottawa, Montreal and Vancouver it was decided to go ahead. The Vancouver Company was duly incorporated under the Societies Act of British Columbia and, to get started without too much delay, the Victoria Company was formed as an offshoot of the Vancouver Company. On August 4, 1937 the new Lieutenant Governor of British Columbia, the Honourable Mr Hamber, presented the Victoria Company with its charter.

In July 1937, in anticipation of receiving their charter, the founding group appointed the first Commandant, Brigadier General Sir Charles Delme-Radcliffe, and the first Adjutant, Lieutenant Colonel H.H.B. Cunningham. Sadly, Sir Charles Delme-Radcliffe died suddenly in December 1937 and was replaced as Commandant by Colonel J.S. Dennis, CMG, DSO. The founding Corps Council included Colonel J.S. Dennis as Chairman, with Lieutenant General Percy Lake, KCB, KCMG, Mr

G.C.L. Howell, Esq., Captain Hobart Molson, MC, and Mr Hew Patterson, Esq. as members. There were also four Life Governors appointed from concerned citizens Mr J.A. Wattie, Mr D.J. Angus, Mrs W.C. Nichol and Captain Hobart Molson, MC. These Life Governors were active workers in the organization.

By December of 1937 there were already seven Commissionaires in permanent employment with a total of 16 in uniform and available for work. Very quickly the first small office at 2382 Rose Street proved inadequate and new quarters were occupied in the Metropolitan Building on Courtney Street by the end of 1937. Money problems were a burden to the organization from the outset. This venture was seen as a method of providing some relief for the high levels of unemployment as well as supplementing the income of deserving veterans. With this purpose in mind, it was decided to seek financial assistance from the Community Chest of Victoria, the Corps Headquarters in Montreal, the Veterans Assistance Committee or the United Services Institute to help in the daily operation of the Victoria Company. The Community Chest, with regret, turned down the request for funds as the limited funds available for distribution had already been allocated for the year. It was decided to canvass the general public and a number of concerned citizens to raise $1,500 operating funds for the Company. This was successful and brought in sufficient donations to keep the organization afloat until an operating loan could be received from the National Headquarters. This loan enabled the Victoria Company to get on its feet and operate on a sound, but weak, financial basis. Finances were a continuing problem in spite of the loan and Mrs W.C. Nicoll, one of the Life Governors, formed a Women's Auxiliary to help raise funds to support the administration and operation of the Company through 1938. The Victoria Company was well and truly established and held its first Annual Inspection and Church Parade in Victoria on Sunday, September 11, 1938.

The service of some of the original members of the Victoria Company reads like a history of the British Empire armed forces from the battles in the Kyber Pass, the campaign in the Sudan in the late 1800s, through the South African War and the First World War 1914-15. Staff Sergeant E.H. "Pops" McDonald held medals from the India Campaign 1895-98, and the Boer War 1899-1902 where he was in the force that relieved the besieged garrisons at Ladysmith and Maefkinq. He also held the General Service and Victory Medals from the First World War, where he served from the Retreat from Mons through the First Battle of Ypres in 1915. Other combinations were the King George V Jubilee, Long Service and Good Conduct, and the Indian Frontier Medal held by Staff Sergeant A.L. Marchant. These were not uncommon and reflected the years of dedicated service these veterans had given to their country and would continue to give to the community through their service in the Commissionaires.

LCol H.W. Laws, CMG, DSO; LGen Sir Percey Lake, KCB, KCMG; Cmdr C.T. Beard; Hon Commandant Sgt Major E.H. McDonald and QMS Brinkley, July 1939.

War clouds were gathering once again in Europe and the Far East as the Victoria Company gradually increased its strength. On March 6, 1939 Commissionaires commenced patrolling at night in downtown Victoria. These were unsettled times as members of the Council were recalled to active duty and a number of others succumbed to the ravages of age. Others in government and the civilian world had their personal responsibilities increased to the point where they no longer had the time available to give the Corps. Fortunately there were others who had some time and the willingness to come onto the Council to assist. The turnover was steady but the quality of work remained high. By the middle of July 1940 the Victoria Company had a strength of 17, of whom four were on Victoria City Night Patrol, nine others were permanently employed and there were two casuals. The war brought an increase in the work done by the local police who were faced with decreasing manpower resources because of enlistment of their personnel in the armed forces. Negotiations were concluded to swear in 12 members of the Corps of Commissionaires as special constables with the same powers as regular constables of the city police department. These men were selected because of their past experience in police work in their military service. The first nine were sworn before Magistrate Henry C. Hall in late June 1941. This arrangement proved very satisfactory to both organizations and continued until the end of the Second World War. Their authority as special constables was restricted to the city of Victoria and County.

February 1979 –
Government House
From Left to Right –
CWO L.S. Kennedy,
Comm B. Leclair,
The Honourable
Henry P. Bell-Irving,
DSO, OBE, CD,
Lt Governor of B.C.
Comm John Laurie,
MBE, and Comm
J.N. Gauley.

Other employment opportunities were being sought at every turn. There were notices of escort services available for conducted tours, fishing, shopping, motoring and sightseeing. Golf courses, small and large retail stores, the HMC Dockyard, and the Rocky Point Ammunition Depot all are listed in the employment schedules. A sign of the intemperate times and old attitudes is noted in a letter from Mr Cecil French, the Honorary Commandant, on July 8, 1941, to the Chairman of the British Columbia Coast Vegetable Marketing Board. Mr French was seeking employment for Commissionaires to help the board deal with the problems of "bootlegging Orientals" who were suspected of disposing of their wares on the waterfront streets near Victoria's Chinatown. The Chairman of the B.C. Board respectfully declined the offer. The old picture of a Chinatown filled with crime and intrigue would die hard in Victoria.

The Victoria Company continued to operate at a modest level until it was decided in 1946 to amalgamate with the national body of the Canadian Corps of Commissionaires, which had its Headquarters in Montreal. This was a fortuitous move by the local Company as the National Headquarters were aggressively seeking contracts for Commissionaires to guard Department of National Defence camps and properties taken over for disposal by the War Assets Corporation. The success of these first ventures brought other contracts with the Department of National Defence and other government departments. Everyone did not greet this amalgamation with the national body with enthusiasm. At one preliminary organizational meeting two members of the Board of Governors of the British Columbia Corps of Commissionaires, Lieutenant Colonel J.P. Fell, OBE, and Lieutenant Colonel J.S. Tait, CBE, were present and voiced their strong objection to the Victoria Company's plans to join the national body. Their objections were heard and considered seriously but it was agreed that amalgamation was the proper course of action to take if the Victoria and Vancouver Island Company were to prosper and survive. It would appear that a $2,000 loan from the National Headquarters in Montreal might have had some influence on the Board of Governors in making their decision. In any case the loan was paid off in full by June of 1947.

Not everyone in Victoria was pleased when the Commissionaires received the contract for guarding government property. The Civilian Security Guards affiliated with the Canadian Congress of Labour launched a strong protest against the Corps of Commissionaires claiming that veterans who were drawing union pay were being forced out by the Commissionaires with their lower wage rates. The President of the Security Guard Union, Mr R.B. Hilton, stated that the Commissionaires were not a democratic organization. He said that he had no objection to his guards taking employment with the Commissionaires if union wages were paid, other personally restrictive regulations were dropped, and the Commissionaires ceased negotiating for jobs now held by his security guards. Mr Culhane of the Canadian Congress of Labour stated that the Commissionaires were offering white-collar jobs to men and informing them how easy they were to perform, thereby doing union men out of union scale wage jobs. Meanwhile, Colonel E.G. Hanson of the National Headquarters pressed ahead with a recruiting drive for sufficient men to take over all the Department of National Defence guard jobs across Canada, which were currently being filled by civilian guards. As a solution

Her Majesty Queen Elizabeth II and Sergeant Sir Alexander George Anthony Allan Mackenzie, Bt CD NCO i/c Duncan Detachment.

the existing guards were given the opportunity to join the Corps and continue their employment or be discharged. This type of problem and confrontation would be a recurring one in later years and has left some bad feelings toward the Corps in labour organizations. Regardless, the additional contracts enabled the Victoria Company to modestly prosper, create more employment for veterans and expand the reputation of the Corps as the provider of good reliable security service. To its credit the Corps has never accepted work where its members could be considered as strike-breakers.

For many Canadians in the late 1940s the sight of a Commissionaire was not a common one. This was understandable, as there was not a general exposure to the Corps of Commissionaires in every part of the country. Those cadets, who attended the military college at Royal Roads from 1947, came from every province and territory and fondly remember the elderly and decorated Hall Porters in the small room by the main staircase in the castle fully in charge of the public address system. Most had strong and varied British accents and were for the most part naval veterans of the RN or RCN. They are not as fondly remembered for their 0630 morning "wakee, wakee!" calls and broadcast of notices with true naval flavour, using the bosun's pipe, over the public address system. The dreaded call for some cadet to appear at the Commandant's or the Officer Commanding the Cadet Wing's offices gave the Commissionaire the aura of the bearer of mostly bad tidings. "Belay last pipe!" was one of the welcome calls cadets remember. The Commissionaires were a familiar

The Commissionaires on Remembrance Day Parade, November 11, 1949. (Victoria, B.C.)

sight to the cadets as they did their rounds of Hatley Castle during the evening hours. They often stopped to talk and share their stories with the young officer aspirants who should have been studying. They overlooked, or chose not to see, the many illegal coffee makers which second-year cadets secreted in hiding places in their study positions.

By June 24, 1947 the Victoria Company ceased its existence and became the Victoria and Vancouver Island Division of the Canadian Corps of Commissionaires. Members of the Board were constantly changing as members moved away from Victoria, died or felt they could not continue to contribute fully as working members of the Board. New blood on the Board in 1947 included Major General G.R. Pearkes, VC, CB, DSO, MC; Mr F.E. Winslow OBE; and Captain D.J. Proudfoot. The quality and enthusiasm of the Board members for the Corps was always high and typified the sense of civic duty and responsibility for others which has characterized the Board of Governors of the Corps from the outset. To single out any one individual as being better than the others in this regard would be grossly unfair but, as an example of this type of public service, Captain Hobart Molson, MC is one of many like him in Victoria at that time. He was a veteran of the First World War with the Black Watch of Montreal winning a Military Cross. Captain Molson was actively involved in the original organization of the Victoria and Vancouver Island Company, was a Life Governor and Honorary Commandant. After military service in the RCAF in the Second World War, he returned to take up duties with the Victoria Company as acting Commandant. At this time he was instrumental in proceeding with the amalgamation of the Victoria and Vancouver Island Division with the national body. He was active in the city supporting hockey teams and other sports, the Red Cross and the RCAF Rehabilitation Centre at Colwood, B.C. At his death he was the senior aide de camp at Government House where he had served seven Lieutenant Governors. Captain Molson often used his extensive business and government connections to advance the interests of the Corps. When he died suddenly in November of 1951 at the young age of 63, the Victoria and Vancouver island Division lost a great supporter, hard worker and close friend. This example of community and public service profile was typical for the members of the Board and the Victoria and Vancouver Island Division owes them a great debt for the sound professional, organizational and fiscal foundation that it enjoys today.

During the late 1940s and early 1950s the make up of the Board and the body of the Commissionaires as a whole was changing gradually, reflecting the influx of younger veterans of the Second World War. The strength of the Victoria Division reached 280 by May 1954 and for the first time Long Service Commissionaire medals and badges were presented to eligible Commissionaires. This Investiture was done at Government House under the kind sponsorship of the Lieutenant Governor of British Columbia. In September 1956 the Board of Governors felt the Victoria and

Comm W.E. Major, Cpl J.T. Jenner, Comm J.W. Roach, Comm H.W. Leacock accompanied by Lt Governor C.A. Banks, CMG and Mrs Banks.

Vancouver Island Division was well enough established to host the National Annual Meeting of the Corps of Commissionaires. This meeting, which was attended by delegates from across the country, was held at the Empress Hotel. The Victoria and Vancouver Island Division had come of age.

After the untimely death of Captain W. Hobart Molson in 1951, the position he had held from 1943 passed to Major William C. Merston MC, DCM, who guided the affairs of the Victoria and Vancouver Island Division for the next 11 years through a period of building, consolidation and change. Continuity was vested in Captain V.E. Hadland, who served the Corps as Adjutant from March 1947 to December 1974. Every effort was made to enlarge the area of work available to Commissionaires. In the 1950s the city of Victoria turned over the job of patrolling the city's 1,750 parking meters to the Corps. This was done in spite of the protests of the Victoria District Trades and Labour Council (AFL) whose members had been accustomed to parking all day in the same spot to avoid paying for more expensive off-street parking. The nasty word "scab" was heard at labour council meetings but the efficiency and savings to the city of the new arrangement proved the city of Victoria had taken the correct approach. Mayor Claude Harrison and the City Council were able to show a profit of nearly $11,000 for the year as well as providing employment for five Commissionaires. Another type of employment, duly reported in the newspapers, involved Commissionaire Arthur Tongue who was tasked to provide protection for a display of $64,000 in the display window of MacDonald's Furniture Store in Victoria. This was back when $64,000 meant something.

March 1956 – Comm Arthur Tongue guarding $64,000 as part of a sales promotion at MacDonald's Furniture Store in Victoria.

A name which appears often in correspondence with HMC Dockyard in Esquimalt is that of Commander Alfred Wurtele. He was very demanding in the standards he would accept from everyone in Dockyard including the Commissionaires on contract. Commander Wurtele was a Canadian, born in Kingston and became a cadet at the RCN College in Halifax in 1913. He was commissioned in 1918 on his graduation. Alfred Wurtele was a sea veteran of both world wars and was an avid sportsman throughout his long career in the Navy. On his retirement from the RCN in 1945 he became active in local politics. A quote he gave to the *Victoria Times Colonist* published on June 9, 1997 outlined his direct approach to his civic duties "We never regarded municipal affairs as politics . . . We didn't like politics interfering with municipal affairs." He spent 20 years as Reeve and Councillor in Esquimalt and in 1987 he became the first person to receive the Freedom of Esquimalt. (During the busy period of his retirement he was the Commandant of the Victoria and Vancouver Island Division where he gave yeoman service for five years from 1962 to 1967 in difficult times.)

Commander A.C. Wuretle, Rear Admiral J.B. Caldwell, MBE, CD and Major-General G.R. Pearkes, VC, CB, DSO, MC.

At the time of writing (June 1997) Commander Wurtele has reached his 100th birthday and has been honoured by CFB Esquimalt by naming the new sports arena complex on the base after him. He remains as feisty and interested in life as ever.

From the end of the Second World War the Division has had a series of unfortunate incidents with local labour groups where the Victoria and Vancouver Island Division has been cast as anti-union. From the early contracts to guard war surplus materials and the later principle of the right of first refusal in federal government contracts, local labour groups have expressed their dislike of any special treatment for the Corps of Commissionaires. These situations surface periodically and have been dealt with on an individual basis.

One such situation was the creation of an organization composed of "disgruntled" Commissionaires and other veterans to compete for security business. This organization developed a constitution for its prospective members and an advertising campaign to lure current clients of the Division away, by offering lower rates than the Corps could offer. The new group called itself "The Three Cees Veterans Security Service" and was actively recruiting Commissionaires from within the Division. This action could have created severe problems within the Division and possibly affected discipline. The situation could not be tolerated and immediate action was taken by the acting Commandant, Commander A.C. Wurtele, to require each Commissionaire to state in writing where they stood. The response was overwhelming and all but two Commissionaires stated their full support for the Corps. The continuing support of the clients of the Division and the overwhelming support of the rank and file Commissionaires spelt the end of the challenge.

The Secretary of the "The Three Cees Veterans Security Service," Mr Donald Sykes, went on to form the "B.C. Veterans Security Service" to try to do the same thing. Mr Sykes and the two organizations subsequently became embroiled in internal financial problems that ended in a series of acrimonious lawsuits between their members. Mr Sykes, in press reports, pictured this action as intimidation and a violation of Commissionaires' rights under the new Canadian Bill of Rights. Commander Wurtele countered by saying there cannot be two governing boards in the Corps and the members had to make a choice of which organization they wished to follow. The Board of Governors asked a respected local lawyer, Mr E.E. Perlman, to do an independent review of the internal procedures of the Division and the way complaints were handled as well as allegations of unfair disciplinary practices. In a 28-page report, Mr Perlman stated that the internal affairs of the Division were handled fairly and then went on to make a series of recommendations to the Board for changes to some of the internal operating procedures of the Division. The personnel problems, which had caused a few Commissionaires to be upset, could be identified with a few poor supervisors.

The new Commandant, Rear Admiral J.B. Caldwell, and his Adjutant, Captain V.E. Hadland, quickly addressed these problems.

The challenges to the Division were not over. In April 1971, the city of Victoria decided to cancel its security contract for Beacon Hill Park and give it instead to the Victoria Police Department. This came about as the result of an intervention by a competitor to the Corps. A security firm called Metropolitan Security Services Ltd. sent a letter to the Victoria City Council in April 1971. In this letter they stated that their company "is forced to pay out fabulous amounts of monies for licences etc., whilst the Corps (of Commissionaires) are operating as a supposedly non-profit sharing organization under the British Columbia Societies Act and by using this as a screen is not accorded the same financial responsibilities." The Victoria City Council did not wish to get involved in the intergroup conflict and, in any case, the problems in the park were more and more of the type requiring police intervention.

This whole series of confrontations had sounded a warning bell for the Division. On the basis that where there is smoke there is fire, an in-depth review of the method of handling of complaints and a review of leadership and management styles was undertaken. Where there were mistakes made, these were corrected with improved training. Changes were also made to procedures to try to avoid any recurrence of the problems. There is now a continuing internal review to ensure that our Commissionaires are well trained, professionally supervised and treated with dignity and respect. This also reinforces to everyone in the Division that the individual Commissionaire is our most valuable resource and should be treated as such. On the commercial side there had to be a more aggressive approach to securing contracts, broadening the client base, and improving the image of the Corps with the general public. In May 1978 Commissionaire Shirley Semple was the first woman recruited into the Division. A further 135 women followed her over the years. Their service has been exemplary and they have received a number of awards for excellence in performance of their duties. The addition of women has given the Division a more balanced image in the public eye.

From the earliest days of the Victoria and Vancouver Island Division, concern for the welfare of individual members was foremost in the way the Division operated. In 1966, the Division established a Members Charitable Trust "to be used for the benefit, welfare and useful employment of members." Revenues for the fund came from interest generated on assets deposited with a financial institution. Expenditures were made from the fund to subsidize annual dinner dances, clothing purchases and to provide modest cash incentives for Commissionaires who received Long Service Awards. In 1974, the Board of Governors approved a pension plan for all Commissionaires to be run by Royal Trust Company. The plan was known as the Security Fund Plan and $151,594 in start-up money was provided from the Members Charitable Trust Fund. A pro-rata share of the start-up money was placed in each qualified member's Security Fund Plan. Contributions to the plan could only be made by the employer and were based on the member's gross wages. The purpose of the plan was to provide each qualified Commissionaire with a gratuity on leaving the Corps. In 1995 the provincial government enacted legislation which restricted the cash-out option of the Security Fund Plan and a move was made to establish a Registered Retirement Savings Plan with Royal Trust as a replacement plan. The purpose of the plan remains the same and the Division contributes a percentage of gross wages to the plan in the name of each Commissionaire.

In addition to the financial support offered to members there is a Division Chief Warrant Officer whose duties include acting as an official ombudsman for members. The purpose is to eliminate personnel and disciplinary issues before they escalate into major problems. The Commandant also has an advisor, on women's issues, who has the responsibility to bring relevant items to his direct attention. During the 1990s a group of chaplain services has been made available to members. These services include advice on availability of support services from the community, support for emotional, health and welfare, and financial problems. In 60 years the Division has come a long way from its start as a quasi-charitable organization to having established internally financed programs and services to support its members.

While most of the Victoria and Vancouver Island Divisions action was in the Victoria and Esquimalt area there were a number of detachments "Up Island." As early as 1948 there were Commissionaires at the Comox Airport and the Nanaimo Pulp Mill. Later additions were in the Nanaimo

Detachment at COMOX – 1948 Lt. Grant, A.B. Scottant, and R.A. Hye.

area as the "Cold War" increased in intensity throughout the 1950s. Commissionaires were employed at the Provincial Warning Centre bunker at Nanaimo and at the centre's remote transmitter site at Nanoose Bay. Later during the 1980s the test range at Nanoose Bay was beset by groups of protesters. Fortunately these were non-violent protestors and restricted their activities to stringing rolls of toilet tissue across the road to dissuade entry. The Commissionaires on duty placed barricades across the road and informed the protestors that they should not pass the barricade. The protestors accepted the Commissionaires' word and the protests continued peacefully without disrupting work at the test range.

Other increases were at the early warning radar sites at RCAF Stations Holberg and Tofino on the North and West Coasts of the Island. In 1969 CF Station Masset, in the Queen Charlotte Islands, was added to the list of work for Commissionaires. The 1950s and 1960s saw a continuing increase in the use of Commissionaires by a mix of government and commercial enterprises. From 1966 the Commissionaires assumed responsibility for the security of the aboveground facilities in the Nanaimo Camp when those installations were transferred from National Defence to the Department of Indian Affairs. It became necessary to organize three Districts to supervise the increase in work "Up Island." These were in Port Alberni, Duncan and Nanaimo.

From the outset the Victoria and Vancouver Island Division has enjoyed the support of the successive Lieutenant Governors of British Columbia. The Commissionaires assigned to Government House are carefully selected and trained and tend to stay there for long periods. Over the years of this happy association there have been many compliments

Governor General Viscount Alexander and Lady Alexander inspect the Guard of the Corps of Commissionaires – May 1948.

received by the Division for the courtesy and professionalism of this small group of Commissionaires. The Division has been honoured to provide a series of Aides to the Lieutenant Governor starting with Captain Hobart Molson in 1938 to the present incumbent, Colonel Alistair MacIsaac.

In 1981 a retired RAF officer and little known Canadian legend joined the Division after a stint as a bush pilot in Australia. Vernon Woodward, a Victoria native, was a fighter pilot in Egypt, Libya and Middle East during the early part of the Second World War and was second only to "Buzz" Beurling in his score of victories. Like Beurling, he had joined the RAF in 1938 and was in Egypt at the outbreak of war flying obsolete Gloster Gladiators biplanes and later Hawker Hurricanes. Woodward went with the abortive British expedition to save Greece from the Italian invasion in 1940 and withdrew through Crete and Cyprus when the Germans launched a full scale offensive to save the Italians from disaster. After a further period of successful air action in the Libyan Desert, Woodward was taken off operations and sent to Rhodesia to train fighter pilots. He continued in the RAF in the post-war years until his retirement in 1963. He had earned two DFCs for his skill and bravery in the desert and Greek campaigns. His service with the Victoria and Vancouver Island Division covered the island with isolated service at RCAF Station Holberg, duties on *HMCS Chaudiere* and with the 443 Squadron at Patricia Bay Airport. Woodward's health during his Commissionaire service deteriorated rather quickly. He earned the Five-Year Award and Ten-Year Medal before he was forced to retire from ill health. He asked if the medal could be given in time to be court-mounted as he wished to wear it on Remembrance Day 1991. An ironic twist to his service in the Commissionaires was the request from 443 Squadron that he be removed from duty with them as he was considered a security risk. Apparently the old fighter pilot could not keep away from standing by the door to the pilots' briefing room and eavesdropping on operational briefings. Most pilots, if asked, would be honoured to have him among their number reliving his youth. Sic transit gloria!

Members of the Corps have an enviable reputation for vigilance and service to our clients. In one incident on July 5, 1994 at the British Columbia Systems Corporation, which was responsible for all computer-related functions within the British Columbia Government, Sergeant Warren Brownlee and Commissionaire Carl Ryan discovered and reported a fire which had not been detected by the automatic fire warning system. A fire in this facility could have caused hundreds of millions of dollars in damages and a major disruption of service. In recognition of their diligence, Brownlee and Ryan were each awarded the organization's Employee Recognition Award. Another incident occurred during February 1996 at the Royal British Columbia Museum while extensive renovations were underway. Sergeants Susan Arness and David Fortier detected and reported a fire in the complex. They were credited with saving the exhibit hall from a catastrophic disaster. They performed their duties in textbook fashion, winning the praise of everyone associated with the museum.

The nature of business in the 1990s has brought some fundamental changes in the approach to the types of work the Corps is able and willing to undertake. Most important have been the efforts to change the image of the Corps from a limited old style security service to a modern collection of services backed by the appropriate technology to serve a broader commercial market. These changes in what services can be provided are possible because of the increased technical skills newcomers to the Corps bring with them from the Armed Forces. To survive in the new world of business, where severe and often cut-throat competition is the standard, the Division has had to reassess its business approach. In 1995 the Victoria and Vancouver Island Division took over the custodial duties of the RCMP in the municipal detention centres. This venture brought with it an increase in Commissionaire strength of 201 Guards and Matrons and required that an exception be made to the rules governing enrolment in the Corps. Commissionaires are currently participating in the delivery of speeding violation tickets in support of the provincial photo radar traffic enforcement program. With Commissionaire detachments spread throughout Vancouver Island the rapid delivery of violation tickets to speeders is an efficient venture. The opportunity to deliver similar services for legal firms on Vancouver Island is a logical development and is now being actively developed.

The Victoria and Vancouver Island Division is justifiably proud of its record of training excellence. The first three-day Commissionaire Qualifying Course was held in the spring of 1971 with CWO Leonard (Len) Kennedy as the Chief Instructor. The first four-day Commissionaire Qualifying Course plus Emergency First Aid was held in the spring of 1988 with Chief Warrant Officer Charles (Chuck) Addison as the First Aid Instructor. The training standards and programs have been developed to a high level by successive groups of training staff in the Division. Training is a service that is now offered to non-Corps candidates at commercial rates. The levels of training excellence in this Division are traditionally the highest in Canada in numbers qualified and the standards achieved by individual members.

As part of this leap into the future, the Victoria and Vancouver Island Division has increased its participation in public events where the image of the Corps as a progressive and modern organization can be enhanced by greater visibility in the community. One event, in December 1996, which received excellent public recognition was the participation of the Division in the inaugural "Operation Red Nose" program where assistance was given to drivers of private vehicles who felt they had too much to drink to drive home safely. This first-time effort was modest and raised some $4,800 for charity. Of this the Victoria and Vancouver Island Division's participation raised $1,000. The 36 Commissionaires who volunteered their time and expertise drove ten vehicles and performed telephone and dispatch duties setting a standard that will be hard to beat in following years. The program was so successful the Commissionaires will increase their participation in this worthy cause next year.

One measure of the training, discipline and dedication of the personnel in any organization is their ability and desire to perform when faced with an unexpected and unprecedented emergency. The latest challenge to the Victoria and Vancouver Island Division was a natural disaster that hit Vancouver Island and the Lower Mainland over Christmas 1996 and into the New Year of 1997.

"The Modern Look" – CWO Roy Aylesworth, Comm Barbara MacDonald and Capt Richard Rennie.

"The Blizzard of 96" as it has become known was the worst snowfall in recorded memory for the Victoria area. On the southern part of the island there is a serendipitous view that Victoria is excused from the ravages of winter. The practice of calling one's friends in Eastern Canada and the Prairies and telling them about the sunshine and the flowers occasionally backfires. 1996 was such a year. The snow started just before Christmas and never ceased until after the New Year. In some areas there was over five feet of snow with almost three feet falling in one night. Roads could not be plowed as there was not enough equipment available, power was out for extended periods of time, hospitals were impossible to get to, the airport and the ferry system ceased to function.

Throughout this crisis the members of the Corps performed their duties with ingenuity, dedication, good humour and perseverance. Commissionaires remained at their positions for multiple shifts until replacements could arrive. These replacements had to fight their way through the drifted snow on foot for long distances to get to their places of duty. The many problems that this type of natural disaster raised were tackled head on with enthusiasm at every level.

The Base Commander of CFB Esquimalt gave the entire Commissionaire Detachment the "Base Commanders Commendation" for devotion to duty under extremely difficult conditions. The Royal British Columbia Museum, the Institute of Ocean Sciences, Victoria International Airport, Royal Roads University, and the Ministry of

Transport and Highways were also loud in their praises of the magnificent response of the Corps as a whole but especially of the dedication of individual Commissionaires to their tasks. At Victoria International Airport there was standing room only as travellers waited for flights which were delayed for two days. The Commissionaires on duty worked around the clock.

The "Blizzard of 1996" tested the Corps severely and it was not found wanting. The many telephone calls and letters of commendation praising the work and performance of individual Commissionaires under severe conditions attest to the dedication and training of our members. One client ended his letter, "As usual, the Commissionaires did a wonderful job!" In Victoria and the southern part of Vancouver Island the snow rapidly disappeared in the monsoon-like rains which brought a period of flooding and the problem associated with too much water. In true Victoria style the annual flower count held in February each year and broadcast with glee to the rest of Canada, continued but with fewer blossoms and a more humble tone than in previous years. Mere mortals cannot trifle with Mother Nature.

In 1997 the Victoria and Vancouver Island Division celebrated 60 years of service to the Federal and British Columbia Governments, business organizations and municipalities on Vancouver Island. The Division continues to evolve to meet the challenges and opportunities that are there in abundance in the rapidly changing business environment. High standards of training, service and excellent personnel give the Division the means of taking advantage of newly developing opportunities. This in turn provides continuing diverse and interesting employment for our members and a valuable service to the community. The way ahead is never certain, however the professionalism, hard work and dedication of all ranks over the past 60 years is a sound basis for moving into newer more exciting times. *Success breeds success!*

THE COMMISSIONAIRES   147

From Left to Right and Top to Bottom: D. Barnes, J. Kerr, B. Leclair, S. Weldon, R.S. Virk, G. Brandshaw, A. Robertson, C. Grohs and S. Gaerret.

Chapter IX

HISTORY OF THE LONDON DIVISION

Commandant's Introduction – *by Brian McGrath*

*T*HIS WRITING of our history was limited by a lack of records and the limited number of old timers still around. It would have been great if more tales about individual Commissionaires could have been told. Nevertheless the work depicted here is an accurate reflection of our past, both the good and the not so good. It chronicles the growth of the Division from a few men in the late '30s to a multi-million-dollar company employing over 400 men and women. Throughout there are the constants: integrity, honesty, loyalty and respectable jobs, as well as our ability to attract dedicated and hard working Governors. It is obvious that the Division is not a "run of the mill" security company.

Our history mirrors the changes of our society over the years. It identifies cycles but the trend is always positive. There is certainly a lot we can learn from our 60 years' history if we want to take the time to study it. For instance, not only must we respond to change but if possible anticipate it. Looking for solutions and being innovative will often provide the best answers in the long run. That being said, the military principle of "maintenance of the aim" must be the major consideration for every proposed solution. Our aim has always been and will continue to be "to provide gainful and meaningful employment to ex-service personnel and R.C.M.P."

When the Division was formed in 1937 the people we were trying to serve were First World War veterans and we were in the middle of the Depression.

Their requirements were reasonably straightforward. Today it is far more complicated; Second World War veterans are dwindling in number and Korean veterans, former RCMP and peacekeepers are replacing them. Society has changed, the military has changed and so must the Corps if we are to fulfill our mandate. To accomplish this we must continue to be proactive; this approach has served us well in the past. There is, of course, always an element of risk and there will be resistance to change. Therefore, to increase the probability of making new ideas and concepts work, they must be tackled on a collective basis. This requires a maximum of understanding, participation and commitment from all concerned. The soul of the Corps is the Commissionaire and he/she must continue to be part of any process if we are to be successful in the future. My special thanks to Bob Doyon, Mel Kay and Ron Patrick who did the research into this chapter.

Enjoy this chapter and feel free to read between the lines!

Introduction

The history of the London Corps reflects the twists and turns, the ups and downs, and the joys and miseries created by the various forces which have shaped the whole Canadian society over the past 60 years. The Corps was not formed in isolation; it has not changed, thrived or suffered in isolation. As have gone the elements at work in the nation, so has gone the London Corps.

In the Beginning (1937-1946)

In 1937, Canada was in the eighth year of a depression of unprecedented severity. Hundreds of thousands of Canadian men were out of work. Those who had seen action in the First World War by now in their forties and fifties, and those who had been wounded or otherwise physically incapacitated, were the least likely to find jobs. The situation in London matched that of countless Canadian towns and cities. In December 1939, a small group of retired senior officers, living in London and already serving on the Veterans' Assistance Committee, and at the behest of the Veterans' Assistance Commission (forerunner of today's Veterans Affairs Canada), met to discuss means by which they might assist those men they had led in battle two decades before. Those discussions led to the meeting of December 16, 1937 which formally organized the London Corps of The Canadian Corps of Commissionaires.

London (1997 population: 325,000) has long been thought of as a mid-sized city with a small town outlook. Its course has been orchestrated by a small group of wealthy and influential homegrown families. It would be foolish to deny this. In the late 1930s, London had a population of 72,000, but this figure included 26 millionaires. Many of those had a military background and a sense of noblesse oblige, so it is not surprising that their names are found on the early boards of Governors of the

London Corps. These same people often employed the first Commissionaires to work in the stores they owned, the industries they controlled, the theatres and concert halls they supported, and the offices of the governments they influenced.

While six men were hired in London's 1937 intake, Mr J.K. Lewis is the first Commissionaire named in the London Corps' records. He was in attendance at the Board Meeting of February 17, 1938, probably to model his new uniform (paid by payroll deduction from his 45 cents per hour wage rate – 65 cents if he worked nights).

In June 1938, the Veterans' Assistance Committee of St. Thomas, whose borders today are a mere five kilometres from a much expanded London, saw a need to follow then distant London's lead in forming a Corps. The result was the creation of an outstation of the London HQ but under the guidance of local trustees. St. Thomas hired two men in its first draft. Though growth came quickly, the budget remained lean. A case in point, London's Adjutant R.G. Goldston was asked, "If he would be agreeable to the appointment of another man (E.J. Major) if the uniform made for H. Farr could be altered to fit him." Similarly, the uniform of a suspended Commissionaire was altered to fit newly appointed Commissionaire S. Jones. The original team are shown in this 1938 or 1939 photograph.

The St. Thomas sub-Corps continued to grow, reaching a peak of 19 men in 1942. Its semi-independent status was terminated in April 1942 when it was folded into the London operations. A major employer of the day was the Ontario Hospital (now St. Thomas Psychiatric) which opened in 1938. In December 1939, this sparkling new facility was taken over by the RCAF and used throughout the war years as a technical training school, the only one of its type in Ontario.

Back in London, Board Chairman LCol G.J. Ingram and the Governors were learning that not all their employees were without warts.

Original Executive and Commissionaires 1938 or 1939.

In December 1938, the Board created a Promotions and Disciplines Committee with two serving Commissionaires included as members – to deal with "a certain matter of discipline." Later that same day a Commissionaire was removed from the rolls for " misconduct while on duty at the Hotel London." This was not a wise choice of locations for a Commissionaire to foul up. At the time, the Hotel London, in addition to being the city's major purveyor of beer and spirits, was its number one hostel. It was also the site of the London Corps Board Meetings.

London Governors had been quick to see the need for regularizing their operations. In June 1938, a committee was structured to draft a set of by-laws for the Division. Local judge, Capt Arthur LeBel, and department store owner LCol Gordon Ingram (store sold to Simpsons in 1945, later the Bay) were members. From this exercise came the first set of Rules and Regulations for Conduct, a copy of which was issued to all Commissionaires and Board Members.

LCol Gordon J. Ingram.

1938 also saw the origins of formalized training courses for Commissionaires. In December of that year, less than one year after its formation, the London Division made the St. John's Ambulance First Aid course a requirement for all working members.

Dignity, dedication and tenacity are characteristics common among Commissionaires. Nowhere were these last two more evident than in St. Thomas in 1938. There, two men earned "little over $60 for the year." At 45 cents per hour, that is about 130 hours or about one hour per week per man–perhaps. The secretary of the day, having found afternoon employment, tendered his resignation, but it was refused by the St. Thomas trustees because "the hours at his disposal would be sufficient for the needs of the committee."

By the opening days of 1940, Canada had been at war for four months but, surprisingly, the records of the day make virtually no mention of it. Through 1940 and '41 one must read between the lines of the Board's minutes to see the impact of the Second World War. What seemed more important then was the inspection – during the annual general meeting – of a dozen Commissionaires by the Chairman or his deputy and the realization that the Adjutant had gone unpaid for the whole of 1939. This was quickly put right, and in one of those minor quirks of history, the 3 by 5 inch scrap of paper survives on which the Adjutant, no doubt dizzy with excitement, notes that he has been awarded an honorarium of $250 as payment for his efforts since the formation of the Division more than two years before. Soon after he was awarded a salary of $50 per month.

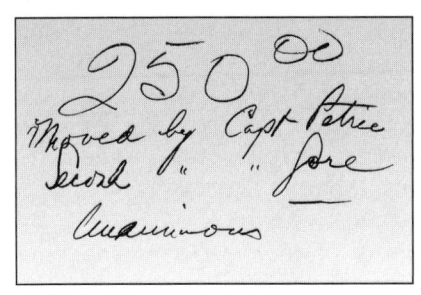

$250.00 "Honorarium."

It is noteworthy too that by this time Commissionaires were serving as pallbearers at the funerals of "indigent war veterans." Herein lay the seed of a service which fully blossomed in the 1960s and '70s (including honorary pallbearers at the 1964 funeral of the father of then Ontario Premier John P. Robarts, by then a long serving member of the Board).

An early visit by Maj G.C. Burbridge, national secretary-treasurer, was the occasion to hear London's position relative to others in Canada. For example, it was learned that Montreal Division employed over 200 men on guard duty alone. London had four, but London provided more casual work, "probably the most of any division in the Dominion." It was also explained that day that all Commissionaires were now covered by insurance and that this should be advertised as a draw to prospective employers. Maj Burbridge also explained how Montreal paid its office expenses. Briefly stated, Montreal hired out Commissionaires on contract with a set hourly rate, then paid the men slightly less, applying the difference to overhead and expenses. Apparently this notion (today's norm) had not occurred to London's Board who until then had relied chiefly on government grants to cover their expenses.

Both casual and permanent contracts increased briskly in late 1939 and early 1940, the direct result of Canada having declared war in September 1939. Bell Telephone employed Commissionaire guards at three of its London facilities. The men were sworn in as special constables and issued with .38 calibre revolvers (bought by the Division). Security was provided 24 hours a day, seven days a week. The war and the threat of fifth column activities were being taken seriously.

The Commonwealth Air Training Programme was started in 1940, and by mid-year Commissionaires were on guard duty at the London Elementary Flying School at Crumlin. Two 12-gauge shotguns and some flashlights were purchased for the guards, but so too were some cheaper uniforms. These were probably issued to the members of the newly created "Special Guard Section," men who were not necessarily Commissionaires because they did not meet the prerequisites for enrollment, but who were paid and administered by the Division for "as long as the job should last." When London created Core II in the mid-1990s, it thought it was being very innovative. It was. But as it turns out, the prototype was established here more than a half-century earlier.

These wartime contracts were being reflected in the financial statement by the end of 1940. Earnings had more than doubled in 1939 from the previous year, and more than trebled in 1940 (to $14,156.70).

By March 1941 the Board was feeling its oats. "The Division was a going concern doing business to over $15,000 annually." The Veterans Assistance was about to be replaced by the Veterans Welfare Division (VWD), under the Department of Pensions and National Health. Now was the time to "demand" support from the VWD for the services the Division provided.

Their demands and requests included a full time secretary, a dedicated telephone line, an office, and an orderly room sergeant.

So convinced were they of the merits of their requirements, the Division executed all of the demands, being prepared to pay for the services should they not be approved by VWD. The estimated cost of maintaining an office per month was: secretary's salary $60; rent $20; postage, printing etc $7; telephone $5.10; hydro and water $1.50; janitor service $4; sundries $6. Total $103.60.

On October 15, '41 the Board increased the commercial billing rate to 60 cents an hour. This allowed for a 55-cent wage. It should be noted that the government was still paying Commissionaires a 45-cent wage. The first Christmas bonus was paid to Commissionaires at a rate of $2 per month of service. This equated to approximately one week's pay for a Commissionaire with 12 months' qualifying service.

The St. Thomas branch of the Division was disbanded in May 1942. It is not clear if it was from lack of interest or if the Veterans Assistance Committee was disbanded as part of the reorganization under the Department of Pensions and National Health. In any case, the branch seldom employed more than three or four Commissionaires.

For the first time the Division decided to pay NCOs a monthly premium; Sgt Maj $2; Sergeant $1.75; Corporal $1.50. Christmas bonuses were increased to $5 per qualifying month.

It should also be noted that while the Division had a payroll of over 200 personnel it would appear that only 16 were classified as Commissionaires. An analysis of the financial statement and vague references made in the minutes to the fact that duration of the work was uncertain and that cheaper uniforms were required would make it reasonable to assume that the Division acted as an employment agency for the federal government providing guards, etc, on a required basis. (Could this be the forerunner of Core II?) The year ended with the founding Chairman, Col Ingram, handing over the chair to Col F.B. Ware.

The London Board of Governors made two significant amendments to their by-laws

a. Members of the armed forces serving in Second World War were made eligible for membership.

b. The Executive Committee was formed to deal with special matters of policy pertaining to the administration of the London Division. It would consist of the officers and three members of the Board. A quorum would be two officers and two members.

On April 12, 1944 Capt Gunn, who had served as a Commandant since the Division's inception, resigned for reasons of ill health. On accepting his resignation the Board appointed Capt Gunn an Honorary Member.

London Division's records for 1945 are scanty in the extreme; only the minutes of the annual meeting survive. They are as interesting for what they omit as for what they say. The meeting was held on May 29 just three weeks after the cessation of hostilities in Europe. No reference is made to this, and only the authorization to purchase a $500 Dominion of Canada War Bond suggests that a war was being waged. Fifty years later the London Corps would play a pivotal role in supporting London's VE Day Plus 50 parade, one of the largest and most successful in the country. The war had swelled the coffers of the Division. At the same May 1945 AGM, the Board authorized the payment of a bonus (to be paid just before Christmas) of $7.50 per month of service that year to each Commissionaire.

By 1946, the Second World War was over, and Canada's fighting forces were coming home. The term "baby boomers" was still to be created, but the return of the troops foreshadowed it. Local industry, limited to war production for six years, could see a potential for huge sales to a population whose purchasing had been drastically reduced over the same period. The public's pent-up demands, once released, led to instant industrial expansion, and London and area got its share. The Kellogg Co. had begun its post-war expansion in December 1945 with a $500,000 warehouse, and countless companies followed suit. New companies arrived, many of them branch plants of U.S. concerns. Years later these would be seen as agents in reducing the influence of London's "Old Boys' Club," including many on our Board, but at the time it meant prosperity for thousands, including the Commissionaires.

By December 1946, London Division had placed 40 men (Commissionaires plus Veterans Guards) into regular jobs with another two dozen or more in part-time work. Expansion into St. Thomas, Woodstock, Sarnia, Chatham, and Stratford, all thriving post-war communities, was being investigated. Most of our Commissionaires were employed as doormen, stewards, janitors, chauffeurs, guards, hall porters, elevator operators, watchmen, store detectives, ticket takers, and pall-bearers. The emphasis was still on placing First World War veterans ("those over 45 years of age") because the veterans of the Second World War were easily finding trades and professional employment never available to survivors of the century's other major conflict. "Younger men should be encouraged to compete in the open labour market and thus are not the primary concern of the Corps." This was the Board's position as expressed by its newly appointed Commandant, Col W.G. Hagarty, DSO.

Meanwhile, back at the Board room, it was learned that the Department of Veterans Affairs was setting a new pay scale for

Commissionaires across Canada: 60 cents per hour plus 5 cents per man hour to cover administrative costs, unemployment insurance, and public liability. Those with regular jobs would be granted one week's holiday per year with pay. DVA's involvement with the Corps was considerable those days. In London, at least, this had even included rent free office space since the Division's inception, but the minutes of the 1946 AGM hint at a possible termination of this happy arrangement: moved and seconded "that Col Emmerton go into the question of rent for the office with the landlord and make the necessary arrangements." Perhaps DVA sensed the Division was thriving. After all, the Board raised the secretary's salary to $30 per week with a further $5 promised "when the anticipated new work starts." In addition, the Commandant was to be paid $20 per month car allowance plus six cents per mile and hotel expenses when on long distance journeys. And, as if this spending spree was not enough, the Chairman of the Board was granted expenses not to exceed $25 in order that he might attend the national AGM in Ottawa.

The Post War Boom (1947-1959)

The centre of power was shifting from the establishment to a nouveau riche, and many aspects of pre-war life were gone forever. For the Commissionaires it meant difficulty in hiring–jobs elsewhere were plentiful–and it meant a shift away from the many traditional types of employment. The new world order had little place for doormen, hall porters, and the other earmarks of a smaller but more pampered group of wealthy citizens.

By June 1947, it was reported at London Corps' annual meeting that our strength was at 38 (only 28 of those were employed full time). This was an increase of a third over 1946, but HQ had a list of 15 men in each of Stratford and St. Thomas for whom no work could be found. Despite this, the office staff was increased with the addition of two part-timers.

By now, the federal government could see the difficulty the older (First World War) veteran was having securing employment, and it began to get involved. The Minister of National Defence, Hon Brooke Claxton, wrote to the commander of Military District No. 1 (London and area) outlining the qualities of older vets and urging him to hire such men for static security on bases and facilities. Within a year, this and similar efforts by DVA had led to a growth in London's strength to 47 (31 full time). Disbursements for the fiscal year totalled $45,000, but the Division found itself with a $1,600 deficit. The hoped for sub-units in Stratford and St. Thomas had still not opened.

Part of London's 1947/48 deficit came about because the Division was now paying rent. When the landlord announced plans to double the rate in 1949, the Corps found an old friend in DVA who offered free space in their offices at 201 King Street. Despite this good fortune, the Board anticipated a further deficit for 1949, according to the minutes of the Annual Meeting. The hourly rate was creeping up – 75 cents for casuals plus 8 cents to Headquarters. The national AGM for 1948 was held in Ottawa. The meeting was planned to last two hours plus a working lunch. Delegates were asked to book sleeper car berths both to and from Ottawa, thus eliminating the cost of hotel rooms.

By 1948, DVA was playing a very active part in helping Commissionaires find work. Newspaper ads were frequent, as were radio commercials and "short human interest" spots. The minister wrote to leading Canadian businessmen urging them to hire Commissionaires and asking them to sing the Corp's praises to their associates. In addition, London HQ ran frequent ads in the *London Free Press* extolling the virtues of the Corps and others seeking the best possible candidates for work.

By mid-1949 the Division's strength had risen to 60 (90 by year-end), with eight employed through a sub-unit in Guelph. It is worthy of note that the uniforms for these men were provided by the Guelph branch of the Royal Canadian Legion. Such generous acts were helping the Division's balance sheet, but a cash flow problem persisted. The minutes of the 1949 annual meeting blamed this largely on the failure of the RCMP to pay the 70 cents per hour it had agreed to (it paid 60 cents and our HQ made up the difference from reserves) for a number of men and for a fairly prolonged period.

The first reference to Long Service Awards is found in 1949. Commissionaire J.K. Higgins received his Ten Year Award (the Division was only 11 years old) while Commmissionaire Haight and Bond received their Five Year. The first two naval officers (retired) were invited to join the Board in 1949, the RCAF having broken the army's stranglehold on Board positions in 1945.

Financial woes were not gone and forgotten by late 1949, but the end, it was felt, was in sight. Wages paid totalled $60,000, there was no rent to pay, and HQ had managed without an Adjutant (and his earnings) for most of 1948 and much of 1949. Within ten months of his being hired, the new Adjutant was seeking a pay raise (to $50 a week) for himself and to $1 per hour for the paymaster.

The successes of the Commissionaires in the late 1940s can be largely explained by a sentence from the minutes of the 1949 annual meeting. "The DVA and the Commissionaires are becoming more closely interwoven day by day." The status of the London Division is best described by the words of the letter which follows.

Once again the story of the Commissionaires in London mirrors those prosperous days. The Division's strength grew to nearly 200 by the end of the decade while wages paid reached $400,000. The birth pangs were behind. This was good for all concerned then. But for today's reader, the minutes of meetings and the records of the day are generally about as

158 London Division

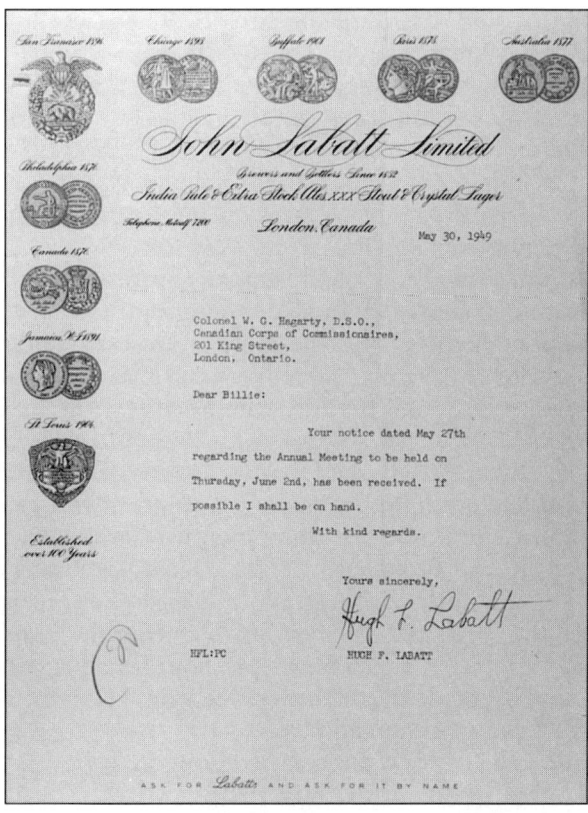

Invitation to John Labatt Limited to attend Annual Meeting with Corps of Commissionaires.

Department of Labour Employment Ad.

Second Ad from Department of Labour.

Canadian Corps of Commissionaires, Guelph
(London Division)

Extend Greetings to the Col. John McCrae Memorial Branch
Canadian Legion
and wish to compliment them on the splendid work they are doing

Captain John Clark — Officer in charge
F/L A. E. Lunn — Executive Officer
Fred J. Clayton — Secretary

Members of the Board of Governors

Personnel:—
Commissionaires
Corporal C. O. Harris
Comm: F. Ayres
R. Bowyer
S. Dickenson
W. Fletcher
J. L. Gray
A. Kennedy
A. Moseley
G. W. Peer
J. C. Peer
B. Perkins
F. W. Southey

"SERVICE AND EFFICIENCY"

★

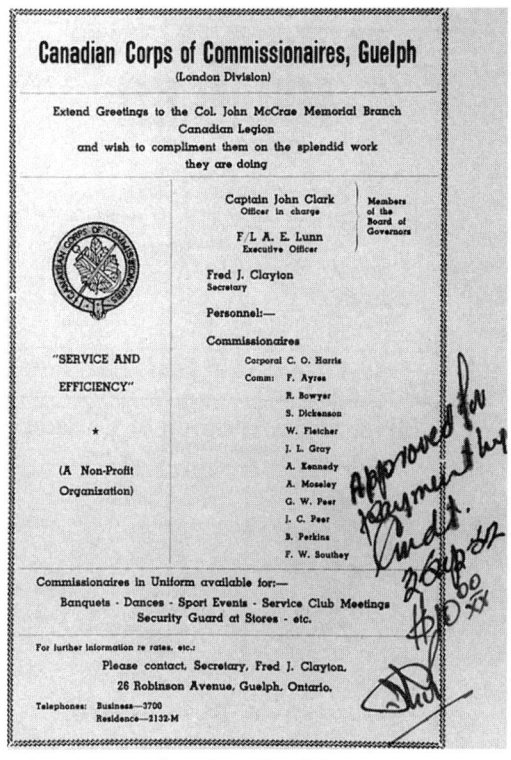

(A Non-Profit Organization)

Commissionaires in Uniform available for:—
Banquets - Dances - Sport Events - Service Club Meetings
Security Guard at Stores - etc.

For further information re rates, etc.:
Please contact, Secretary, Fred J. Clayton,
26 Robinson Avenue, Guelph, Ontario.
Telephones: Business—3700
Residence—2132-M

Advertisement in the "Torch"

exciting as watching paint dry or grass grow. Nonetheless, there are some fascinating tidbits.

Veterans Affairs and the Department of Labour continued to be driving forces behind the Corps' success. Local and national newspaper ads sang the praises of hiring Commissionaires for a variety of roles. National Headquarters encouraged the outlying Corps to trade ads and publicity ideas. The National Secretary Treasurer of the day, who worked alone in the national office, devoted an inordinate amount of his time to corresponding with local Commandants on the matter of publicity.

Local military bases were encouraged to hire Commissionaires, and with an army base, an air force station, and a military area Headquarters in London, hiring was active. Throughout the 1950s the area commanders spoke to our Board of Governors about their ongoing involvement in "selling our product" to other government sites. Disbursements reached $100,000 for the first time and $5,000 was spent on uniforms, according to the report of the 1950 AGM. This figure would be roundly challenged by a serving Commissionaire within days of its publication. No disagreement has been found, though, with the Board's decision to award each Commissionaire with "Christmas poultry" that year. The AGM minutes also reveal that "business had doubled over the previous years" and "the Division is now in a much sounder financial condition as a result," phrases that are repeated with almost monotonous regularity throughout the 1950s. No doubt, ads like those included were helping to make these things happen. The annual report closes with reference to the presentation to the Ten Year Medal to Joseph C. Bond. Commissionaire Bond had come on strength in 1940 when the London Division was two years young.

Documents describing London Corps' activities in 1951 are few. A newspaper article of May 16 notes that Commissionaire Dennis Haight received his Ten Year Medal, five others their Five Year and George

Thorpe his 1914-15 campaign star for the First World War, a decoration he had previously not received.

By 1952, the Guelph section had grown to 12 men and could afford ($10) to take out a full-page advertisement in the "Torch," the annual newsletter of Guelph's Colonel John McRae Memorial Branch of the Canadian Legion.

The choice story of the year centres around the activities of a dog. "Skipper" was a pet of Commissionaire Arthur Whittlesea, a guard at RCAF Station London. A bout of pneumonia had confined "Skipper" to a few days in doggie hospital and had resulted in a bill for $25. Whittlesea and his fellow Commissionaires paid the tab, but when the dog was returned to hospital–this time for 25 days–the vet's bill was nearly $60. This was beyond the wallets of Commissionaires earning less than one dollar an hour, so the Air Force personnel took up a collection and saved "Skipper" from the bailiff.

1953 was apparently another quiet year in the London Corps. Finances had now reached the quarter-million-dollar mark, and the Adjutant had no difficulty in coaxing the *London Free Press* to report this item only one day after the year's annual meeting.

In 1953, Canada had a new monarch, and the Chairman of the Board advised that all London Commissionaires had been administered The Oath of Allegiance to Her Majesty, Queen Elizabeth II.

A year later, two Commissionaires, Maj F.S. Pannell (Adjutant) and Sgt Maj R.T. McDaniel were awarded the Coronation Medal. They had been recommended for this award by Board Chairman Col F.B. Ware just prior to his death, a short time before. He had served as Chairman since 1942.

Long service to the Corps resulted in rewards for one Commissionaire and two Governors in 1954. Commis-

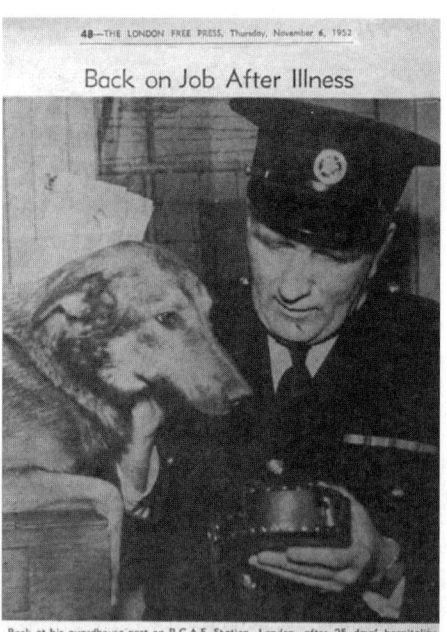

Saving "SKIPPER."

sionaire John K. Higgins, employed by the London Division since its first full year of operation, received his 15 Year Medal. Col Ibbitson Leonard, a Board member since 1940, was chosen as our third Chairman. He would remain in that appointment until 1970, by far the longest term ever as Chairman. Capt George Foote was selected as first vice-Chairman but would not assume the chair for 16 years. When he did finally succeed Col Leonard, he would introduce the two-year term which remains in place to this day.

Fiscal 1954-55 saw a considerable increase in the size of the Corps. A record strength of 179 men was in place, and wages totalled $308,000. The London Corps' increase in strength since 1949 was set at 434%, the greatest in Canada. This was seen as a milestone in a city which that year celebrated its centennial. Longtime Commissionaire Joseph Bond received his 15 year medal, Staff Sgt Edwin Akiens his ten-Year.

Long service with the Corps was becoming the norm by 1956. That year saw the 15 Year Medal awarded to Commissionaire Dennis Haight, while three others – Sgt. Maj. Richard McDaniel, Commissionaire Robert Fraser, and Commissionaire William McMillan, received their Ten Year Medals. McMillan had begun his service to the Crown in 1894 as a drummer boy under Lord Kitchener. His 62 years of service were under five monarchs, from Queen Victoria to Queen Elizabeth II.

Did a 1956 incident involving a London Commissionaire provide Alfred Hitchcock with the plot line for his 1963 movie "The Birds?" (Based on the Dauphne Du Maurier Novel) On a June morning in that year, Commissionaire Ernest West was walking home from his night watchman duties at the army's 27 Central Ordnance Depot when he was attacked by "a strange huge bird." The *London Free Press* account of the attack describes the bird as being all black, with a yellow hooked beak and a wingspan of three or four feet. It may have been attracted by West's bright brass uniform buttons as it first attacked from the front. West ducked but the bird came at him from behind. Again West ducked, and this time he swung at it. When the bird landed on a parked car, West threw a brick at it. This drove the bird away, "emitting a horrible screeching noise." Lest the reader conclude that the offended Commissionaire had been dipping into the antifreeze before leaving work, it should be noted that the newspaper reported that "people in nearby houses witnessed it."

The major event for the London Corps in 1957 was an unfortunate dust-up between London's city fathers and the union representing their employees. A long time city employee, the city hall elevator operator, retired and was immediately replaced by a Commissionaire. The vacancy was not advertised inhouse and the union took strong exception to council's action. They suggested, and some aldermen agreed, that the job might have gone to some recently retired employee. Today, such an arrangement might be labelled double-dipping, but that issue was not raised in 1957. For several weeks this fight raged in the pages of the local newspaper, with the Commissionaires caught in the crossfire. The matter was finally resolved when the council and the city administration apologized and promised never to do such a naughty thing again. Seems they had simply wanted to hire a person who was "presentable, capable, and trained in this type of work." The Commissionaire in question kept his job at city hall. Even elevator operators have their ups and downs.

In other news for 1957, the Division reported disbursements to its employees of $377,000 for the fiscal year, an all-time record. There can be little doubt that the growth experienced during the 1950s, while largely due to the burgeoning economy throughout Canada, is in part the result of the intensive advertising campaign first sponsored by DVA and The Department of Labour but continued by the individual Divisions. By August 1957, the situation in London was judged to be so rosy that the Board instructed Adjutant Pannell to cancel its monthly ads in the *London Free Press*.

December 1957 marked the twentieth anniversary of the London Corps. The occasion was marked with the production of a two-page historical report. It reported much that has been said in this chapter including the fact that the first Commissionaire hired in London was "the late Mr J.K. Lewis," but goes on to say," "whose son, Commissionaire Ronald C. Lewis is presently serving with the Corps in London." This is the first mention of a father/son Commissionaire team in the London Division; there would be more to follow (such as Frank and Roger Holland) as well as other family combinations.

1958 brought two interesting additions to the Board of Governors. One was an ex-Second World War naval lieutenant by the name of Robarts. He had served as an alderman on London's city council and was on his way to the Ontario legislature. John P. Robarts would serve as MLA for London North riding, Minister of Education,. and, finally, Premier of Ontario.

The other new Board Member was London business-

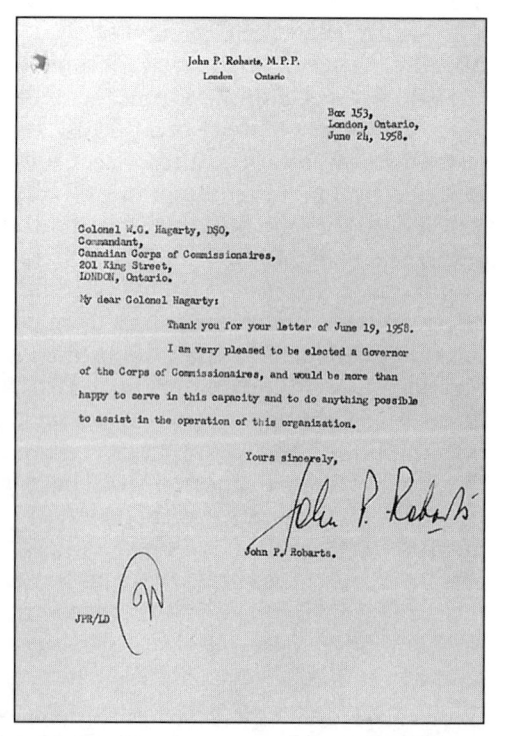

Letter to Col Haggerty, DSO from John P. Roberts, M.P.P.

man Tom Lawson. A company commander (Canadian Fusiliers of London) in the Second World War, his father Raymond served as Ontario's Lieutenant-Governor. In time Tom Lawson served as honorary Chairman (1990/91) but is best known for his appointment as honorary Colonel of The Royal Canadian Regiment. In addition he was known for many gifts and donations to worthy causes, chief among these The University of Western Ontario.

1960s - the First "New Age"

The "Swinging Sixties" are marked by the pop counterculture that swept across North America and most of Europe. Hair was long and skirts were short; people were encouraged to "make love, not war," and free sex, psychedelic drugs, "sit-ins," "love-ins," and "down with the establishment" activities became the norms for the time.

All of this was, of course, anathema to all of the values held so highly by the Corps and its many dedicated members: honour, discipline, and integrity.

Among the many new feelings that became popular at the time was the "rent-a-cop" attitude towards the Corps, the perception held by many that the Commissionaires were not really police, and were not really necessary, and, in fact, were there to prevent people from having a good time.

But the Corps' members dug in and held on. Faced with this revolutionary change in social attitude, the Commissionaires did what they have always done: they maintained their time-honoured outlook, they worked harder, they dug deeper, and they persevered. In fact, they prospered. Numbers of contracts and numbers of hours increased in the face of what was perceived by many as the beginnings of widespread anarchy, and demand for security services increased. In 1961, for instance, the London Division had a complement of 192 Commissionaires, most of whom were employed on a full-time basis: in 1937, only 24 years earlier, the London Division had been formed with only six Commissionaires.

A few noteworthy examples from the sixties stand out to mark the many changes in society and in the London Division. The city of London wanted to annex large quantities of land that surrounded the city, but there was a need for tight security on the actual plans to prevent insiders from using any advance knowledge to make huge profits. Clearly, the plans had to be safeguarded by a group whose integrity was beyond question and, equally clearly, the London Division of the Corps was the best choice for the role. Accordingly, the Corps, in the person of Sergeant Major R.T. McDaniel, was entrusted with the precious documents, and he kept them both safe and secret until they were officially released in 1960.

Lieutenant Colonel H.K. Ingram, VD, was appointed Commandant in 1961, following the previous Commandant, Colonel Hagarty, who retired through ill health. With this appointment, the next generation of the Ingram family took its place at the helm of the London Division. Such was the cachet of the Corps that it was considered a great honour to be associated with its leadership and governance, and the roster of the Board of Governors contained many of the names from the social blue book for the city.

The Corps was still enjoying "most suitable and rent-free quarters" at 201 King Street, as Colonel Leonard, Chairman of the Board of Governors, described them in a letter to Lieutenant Colonel Rider.

Major Pauley, the Adjutant of the London Division at that time, was interviewed as part of CFPL-TV's "Panorama" series. Among his other comments, he spoke of the many advantages of the Corps to be enjoyed by employers and Commissionaires alike, and stated that, in 1961 and again in 1962, the London Division had paid out more than $500,000 in wages and benefits, compared to $6,000 in its first year of operation. This same focus on advertising and public relations was apparent on a national basis. A motion picture was made available by National Headquarters to all Divisions. It stressed the history and purpose of the Corps, described the investigation and swearing-in of recruits, the rules and regulations, and also showed some Commissionaires at work in a number of roles.

Those were certainly days of growth and prosperity for the Division, and contracts were in place in Sarnia, Stratford, Woodstock, St. Thomas, Aylmer, Centralia, Clinton, Goderich, as well as in London.

Records and photographs from 1963 reflect that approximately 30 uniformed and be-medaled Commissionaires turned out on Remembrance Day and marched proudly, together with military groups, from the Dundas Street Armouries to the cenotaph in Victoria Park.

March 1964 marked the death of Mr Herbert Robarts, father of then Ontario Premier John P. Robarts, who was a member of the Corps' Board of Governors. The Corps was honoured by having some of its members serve as pallbearers for the funeral.

London Division on parade, Nov. 11th 1963.

Funeral Service for Mr. Herbert Roberts, father of then Ontario Premier John P. Roberts.

1965 marked the London Division's turn to host the Annual General Meeting of the Canadian Corps of Commissionaires, and no efforts were spared in making this, London's first occasion to host the meeting, a truly memorable occasion. Delegates from all of the Divisions across Canada were in attendance for this three-day meeting which was held at London's finest hotel, the Hotel London. In addition to the many meetings, receptions, and dinners that marked the occasion, there was also a special trip to Stratford for dinner and a performance at the Shakespearian Festival. The three days were a time for both serious work on behalf of the Corps and good fun and relaxation for the many delegates and their ladies. So successful was this Annual Meeting that other Divisions have spent the next 30 years in trying to match it.

The members of the London Board of Governors represented not only the military, but also the social, political, and financial elite of the city, evidence of the status of the London Division. The Governors at that time were: Colonel W.E. Bawden, ED, CD; Brigadier Russell H. Beattie, MC, ED; Lieutenant Colonel J. Innes Carling, OBE; Lieutenant Colonel E.N. Chesham, VD; Lieutenant Colonel H.B. Davies, ED; Lieutenant Colonel R.M. Dillon, MC, ED; Lieutenant Colonel W. Eric Harris, OBE, CD; Colonel Howard L. Hayman, MBE; Brigadier W.H. Hemphill, CD; Lieutenant Colonel E.V. Hession; Captain H. W. Hockin, QC; Squadron Leader John E. Jennings, AFC; Lieutenant Colonel T. Lawson; Hon. Arthur M. LeBel, QC; Lieutenant Colonel S. Lerner, CD; Lieutenant Colonel H.L. Petrie, OBE, MC; Lieutenant Commander W.R. Poole, QC; Lieutenant J.P. Robarts; Squadron Leader W.L. Scrandrett; Major W.T. Shrives; Major C.R. Somerville, MBE; Captain Harry Wooster.

Londoners will certainly recognize many of these names as members of the power structure of the city in the sixties and seventies, and for years to follow.

Alas, not all of London's citizens aspired to high social status, and it became apparent in the same year that there was trouble in the Forest City. Several examples of what the *London Free Press* somewhat quaintly called "hooliganism" occurred at the Fred Landon Branch of the London Public

Library, and at the bookmobile in Ridgeview Heights. Additionally, the *Free Press* reported that "drunks and other unsavoury characters" were making a nuisance of themselves at the Williams Memorial Library on Queens Avenue. Commissionaires were employed to provide additional security, the London police force increased its patrol activity, and the problems were soon solved. Significantly, only the municipal government as a suitable private security force considered the Corps of Commissionaires. The message was clear: if you have a problem, call for the Corps.

1970s – Upwards and Upwards

Inflation! This dirty word became the war cry throughout Canada in the 1970s. Salaries and wages skyrocketed during the decade, often more than doubling along the way. Whether the purchasing power of the dollar and/or the actual wealth of Canadians improved is for the economists to debate, but the take-home pay of the average Canadian worker of 1979 bore little resemblance to the pay packet of 1969.

The inflationary spiral of the '70s is nowhere better seen than in the Canadian Corps of Commissionaires. From an average hourly rate of just under $2, Commissionaires' wages rose to over $4.50 – a 125% increase in a decade. These increases were easily matched by the administrative costs charged to customers, the salary increases of the HQ staff, and the cost and variety of benefits available to all our personnel.

In 1971, Capt George Foote, one of the original Board Members, was Chairman of the Board. His annual report shows that the unit's strength was down six to 215, due largely to deaths and retirements. Only seven were released for cause. The average age of the men was in the high sixties, but nearly 15% were under 50. Pride was expressed in the fact that London's was a non-segregated Corps; it employed one black and one native Indian. But still no women.

Federal government contracts accounted for 50% of jobs, at $2.15 per hour. (Dupont near Sarnia paid the top wage at $4.11.) Revenue reached $870,000, but signs of tougher times ahead could be seen. Integration of the three armed services was moving ahead and base closures were on the horizon. The closing of RCAF Clinton and 27 Ordnance Depot in London cost the London Corps a dozen jobs that year.

At the executive level, Maj Les Pauley retired as Adjutant after 13 years and was succeeded by Maj John O. Howitt. Capt (N) G.A. MacLachlan who came onto the Executive Committee of the Board. "Archie" of the snow white hair and ever present smile had joined the Board in the 1950s and would serve as Chairman in 1989 to '91. He expects to leave the Executive Committee this June (1997) with, after George Foote's, the longest record of service of anyone associated with the London Corps.

In 1972, revenues reached over $925,000, 28 new jobs were found from nine new contracts, and unit strength was at 232. The now familiar white forage caps and lanyards were introduced, and a bi-monthly newsletter (of one page) called PATROL was introduced. HQ staff wages ranged from $6,600 to $8,500 while men's rates ranged from $1.90 to $4.40 per hour. The average of $2.30 was up 15 cents or 7% from 1971. The age brackets of London's Commissionaires remained virtually unchanged but, at 15%, London's over-70 group was the third lowest in Canada.

London Corps incorporated in 1972, providing us with a slightly different name ("Division" was dropped), a release from financial liability for Governors, and the right to retain locally any monetary reserves. Six of our 17 sister Corps had already incorporated; the remainder would soon follow suit although Vancouver would remain an independent Corps for a few more years. Longtime Governor, Col Innes Carling (of the brewing family) died in 1972. George Foote, with 35 years with the Board, retired as Chairman although he would serve 11 more as Honorary Chairman.

Federal government contracts continued to drop, accounting for only 40% of jobs, all with DND and Veterans Affairs.

If revenues were all that mattered – a mighty big IF where the Corps of Commissionaires is concerned – 1973 would be hailed as a banner year. Revenues went over $1 million for the first time as London's income rose 10.5% over 1972. Christmas bonuses of $35 to $45 dollars were paid, and a fledgling gratuity fund was paid out and closed. Over 240 were now on the payroll, and the office staff was swamped with writing pay cheques. Thus the introduction of the McBee One-Write payroll system at a cost of $1,400. It was touted as being faster and easier with no additional staff required. It would last three years.

As a precursor of the 1990s, the Department of Supply and Services announced that it was displeased with the need to sign 18 separate contracts across the nation (and with the $200,000 profit the various Divisions made from federal government contracts).

Our neighbouring Corps in Windsor initiated action in 1973 to bring about boundary changes in south-western Ontario. They wanted to take over the Sarnia area and its lucrative "Chemical Valley." Each Corps was instructed by national HQ to submit a brief outlining its position. London won, and the area remained within our scope: it remains a major employer of Commissionaires. National Headquarters also approved a uniform for females that year although the squabbling went on for a few more months over the style of the headgear. This was purely academic in London as we still employed none of the fair sex.

Inflation was in high gear in 1974. The new federal wage rate was $2.75 per hour and the average was nudging $3.00 (up nearly a $1.00 since 1971). The funerals detachment was averaging over five funerals per week, and each man earned six dollars per time. The provincial government passed the Employment Standards Act which, among other things, legislated double time and a half for work on statutory holidays (and regular rates even if the men did not work). Paid holidays were now mandatory, and a fund amounting to 4% of each man's wages had to be set aside for this. HQ staff salaries were up to the $8,000 to $11,500 range. And to fuel the furnaces of inflation even more, a recommendation was made in November 1974 to increase the men's wages a further 16% and to pay five cents an hour uniform allowance. At that same November meeting, $18,000 was budgeted for training courses for the year. This single expenditure represents over three times the entire revenue of the Corp's first year of operation.

The old guard was passing on. London's longest serving (16 years) Chairman, Col Ibbotson Leonard, died in 1974. In 1975 LCol H.J. Ingram retired after nearly 15 years as Commandant. Maj. J. Howitt, Adjutant since 1971, took over and the appointment of Adjutant was done away with. Before he left, Col Ingram offered his view of the philosophy of the Corps, as part of his annual report. His remarks are worth repeating here:

> *I would like for a few moments to dwell on the changing philosophy of the Corps. At the last annual meeting of the Corps in Quebec City, the old philosophy of the Corps was changed. This was brought about by the continued insistence of the federal government that we provide more and better trained men for security service. Do you realize that we are the only national organization dealing with security that is Canadian owned? The governments are concerned. This does not mean when the last veteran and ex-service person no longer needs our assistance we will not fade away. We will. However, D.V.A. estimates that in the early Eighties there will be an even greater demand, by Second World War and Korean veterans, for the services of the Corps and, of course, we have the responsibility to those currently being discharged from the forces. What the change does mean is that we are to aggressively solicit veterans and ex-service persons to join the Corps. We are not to just sit back and wait for them to come to us. Wages are to be raised. They have been, and any benefits we can offer are to be provided, to attract younger, better types of people into the Corps. The Corps have agreed to provide the government and private sector with men having a basic knowledge of security and an esprit de Corps in the Corps.*

Sources of pride to the Board in 1975 were the 10% increase in wages, increased revenues, the lowest billing rates to customers in the Corps (slightly lower than private security firms), free uniforms, the smallest per capita paid office staff in Canada, and a unit strength of 251, including 104 new men recruited in 1974 and 1975, a $50 Christmas bonus for each Commissionaire, and the prospect of a 21% wage hike for the men working at London's city hall.

In 1976, inflation continued unchecked. Hourly rates rose by nearly 8% to an average of $3.85. HQ staff saw their salaries boosted to a range of $9,900 to $16,200 up over 50% since 1972. At the Annual General Meeting of the Board, greetings from the mayor were brought by Councillor Elaine Hagarty, the daughter-in-law of long time

Commandant Col W.G. Hagarty. There were 225 on strength, a reported increase of 25% in five years. Training courses increased in number, duration, and difficulty, but employers were seeing this as good for their purposes. Revenues were at $1,535,000, a 50% increase (admittedly in inflated dollars) over that of only three years earlier. And 1973's McBee One-Write payroll system, the panacea the year it was adopted, went the way of the bustle and buggy whip. Payroll and cheque preparation was contracted out to the Bank of Montreal.

1977 was a quiet year for the Division. Revenues ($1,700,000 plus) and wages continued to escalate. The most interesting comment in the year's records – and one that could be made only by a not for profit operation like the Commissionaires – comes from the Commandant's report to the annual meeting. "We were unsuccessful in losing as much money as we hoped on the federal government contract. We lost $206 and had tried to lose close to $8,000." Pity!

The age groups of those 223 Commissionaires working in 1980 seemed to follow the rule of 13. The majority (71%) was between 51 and 65, 13% under 50, 13% between 65 and 70, and 13% over 70. Jobs were difficult to find and the London Division, unlike most other Divisions, had more applicants than jobs. The other Divisions also had the advantage of enjoying a significantly higher ratio of federal government work (65% to 95%). London's federal contracts represented approximately 20% of business.

Also the provincial government aggravated the problem. Until recently they had often awarded the Corps contracts in accordance with a Provincial Standing Offer. Now they were tendering and awarding contracts to the lowest bidder. The dilemma faced by the Division was that the provincial fair wages for security guards was considerably less than the $4.45 wage paid Commissionaires. Competing security companies were only paying the fair wage and thus enjoyed a considerable advantage. On the commercial front they paid minimum wage thus making the competition even tougher.

Unlike the competition, the London Division was diligent in ensuring that all of its Commissionaires received a 40-hour basic security course and that the commanders of major detachments attended the supervisor's course conducted by National Headquarters. While this cost added significantly to the overhead the Board of Governors refused to compromise.

All was not bad news though; by far the majority of Commissionaires performed their duties in an exemplary manner. An act that came to public attention was that of Commissionaire Harrington. While working at city hall on the twelfth floor observation deck over the Christmas holidays, he came to the rescue of a young boy who tried licking the frost off the railing and stuck his tongue to it. Commissionaire Harrington's calm and reassuring manner and actions freed the boy and sent him home none the worse for wear but definitely wiser. Ten years later Commissionaire Harrington, by now working at Catholic Central High School, celebrated his seventy-fifth birthday on the golf course while participating in the Division's golf tournament.

Up to now the only non-statutory benefit Commissionaires received, beside free uniforms, was a Christmas bonus and only then when there was a surplus. In April 1984 the Board authorized the purchase of portal to portal insurance for all Commissionaires. This provided accident coverage while travelling between the home and work. While not a frequently used policy, it proved to be a very wise investment over the years.

In an attempt to find more ways of improving the London Division, the Chairman, LCol Burdett, made a liaison visit to the Kingston Division in May. While impressed with their organization, the Chairman's main observation was that unlike London the Kingston Division offered a wide range of pay rates. They based their rates on making sure they were competitive in the tender while aiming for the best wage. This philosophy was applied in London on their next tender, Parkwood Hospital, with the result that the tender was successful; however, the wage rate was less than standard London rate. The experiment was not, however, considered a success. The stigma of being the only detachment being paid less than the regular rate apparently caused a number of Commissionaires to request transfers. Obviously, job satisfaction was adversely affected. It would be four more years before the principle was reintroduced, but this time the first detachment was paid 25 cents an hour more. This was followed by an information campaign outlining the need for versatility and that not all wage adjustments would be down. This, combined with extra attention to other job satisfaction factors, made the policy popular and permanent.

The London Division hosted the 1985 National Board of Governors Annual Meeting. The attendance of 318 delegates and guests was a third higher than in previous years. All agreed the London Division did a first class job and that it was a success in every way. (It should be noted that London will host the meeting in 2003.) In honour of the occasion, Staff Sergeant Rolly Smith, the chief clerk, established a fund to purchase Corps colours for the Division. He, along with a colour party consisting of Commissionaires Torrance and Temple, presented the colours to the Board at the Division's Annual Meeting in May prior to the national meeting. This initiative coming from the ranks

London Division Colours.

brings a special significance to the colours and is an indication of the pride the Commissionaires have in their organization.

Throughout 1984 and 1985 the small office staff was plagued with illness. Maj Howitt was forced to resign as a result of his illness in March 1986. Maj R.R. Doyon was appointed Commandant effective April 1, 1986. The terms of his contract were simple; make the Division more competitive by exploring new areas of work, and double the size of the Division in five years. As of April 1, 1986 the Division strength was 204 all ranks; it had experienced a 25% turnover in personnel the previous year. Half of the Commissionaires were between the ages of 55 and 65, the other half being equally divided as older or younger. Compounding the situation, the competition in the security industry was frenzied and the Division was losing contracts to lower tenders. Major security companies were competing for market share. They paid minimum wage and often took contracts at a loss. On the other hand, the Division's standard wage, which was based on federal contracts, was considerably higher than the minimum wage. Despite all of this the Division broke even for 1985/86 thanks to the efforts of the staff and the executive.

The new Commandant visited all of the Ontario Divisions in May, examining in detail their operations. It was quite apparent that the London Division was unique primarily because of its size, second smallest in Canada and its low percentage of federal work was at 26%. The Division was considerably more vulnerable to market conditions and commercial competition. The solution would lie in the Division's ability to function as a not-for-profit organization while operating in a business mode. An aggressive attitude had to be taken and maintained if the Division was to remain solvent and just as importantly fulfil its mandate to provide jobs for ex-service personnel. The Executive Committee agreed and continued to support this premise.

London Division on parade.

In an effort to make the Division better known, over 200 letters were mailed to the major companies in the area informing them of our services. Existing clients were invited to our awards night dinner in an effort to consolidate the rapport already established by our existing contracts. While the mailing was not a great success, the awards night invitations have become an important and permanent feature.

In an effort to increase office efficiency, a consultant was hired to advise on what type of computer system would be practical for the Division. This resulted in the awarding of a contract to provide a computer and training to the staff for a sum not to exceed $10,000.

To honour the occasion of the Division's fiftieth anniversary in 1987, a badge was designed to be worn on the pocket. It proved too heavy when summer dress came into effect, and on the suggestion of a Commissionaire working at the London Airport it became the hat badge for the rest of the year. In addition to mess dinners and Awards Night, the Division paraded complete with their colours on Remembrance Day. It was the Division's largest ever turnout.

Whenever practical, the Division participated in community activities. Volunteer members of the Division participated in Cell-a-Friend, a fundraising event for Victoria Hospital Building Fund. Commissionaires dressed as Keystone Cops would "arrest" designated businesspersons at work, take them down to the Middlesex County Court House where the Commandant, acting as the prosecutor, would bring the culprit before the judge. It was not only a lot of fun but very successful. In later years Commissionaires volunteered their services for the Jerry Lewis Telethon.

An information booth designed both to attract recruits and business was set up at the Western Fair in September. While it could be termed as modestly successful as far as the aim was concerned, the major contribution was the identification of how little the public was aware of the Corps of Commissionaires. Our recognition factor was less than 5%. This fact was to be a major motivator in the coming years as the London Division played a leading role in public awareness promotions on both provincial and national levels.

In October, the Headquarters staff was increased: Staff Sergeant Matty Matheson became Quartermaster and the dispatcher for casuals. Initially it was to be a part-time position but as the Division grew so did the Quartermaster's responsibilities. Matty became the first detachment commander for the city of London By-Law Detachment the following year.

On the benefits side, a term life insurance policy for $10,000 for all Commissionaires working more than 20 hours per week was purchased. This was provided at no cost to the Commissionaire. In addition, a 5% wage increase for all Commissionaires effective April 1, 1988 was approved.

The fall of 1988 was interesting to say the least. Col Ed Quinn became the Operations Officer, and Gerald Hikele replaced Al Muise as paymaster on his retirement. A second computer was purchased at a cost of $2,895, to be used as a word processor and for administrative files, nominal rolls, etc.

A milestone of sorts was set on Oct 3, 1988 when the London Division conducted its first basic course, at Wolseley Barracks, using the new Corps training manual based on the Canadian Standards Board standards for security guards. A second milestone was established a month later when the Division won a one-year trial by-law contract with the city of London. The original requirement was to provide fire lane and handicapped parking enforcement Monday through Saturday. Under Matty Matheson, six Commissionaires were trained and four Firefly cars were leased. Over a period of six short years the detachment has grown to 18 Commissionaires and 12 cars. As they grew so did their knowledge and expertise, which they documented in the training manuals they produced. The manuals, combined with courses and seminars, serve as a basis for the by-law centre of expertise for which the London Division is responsible.

The National Public Awareness Committee of which Maj Doyon was a member conducted two focus groups in London in November. Paul Costello, a consultant, came from Toronto to facilitate these groups. The first was held at Wolseley Barracks and consisted of armed forces personnel about to retire. The second, downtown at Jock Shield's Driving School, consisted of retired armed forces personnel. The results of these and three other focus groups held in other cities confirmed that even among service personnel serving and retired there was a definite lack of knowledge about all aspects of the Corps of Commissionaires.

In 1989 the economy took a down turn, and with it went the diligence of some of our clients to pay their invoices on time. A cash flow problem quickly presented itself causing a serious overdraft situation. As a result the executive authorized the Commandant to levy a 1.5% per month carrying charge on all delinquent accounts. This action helped reduce the overdraft significantly. 1989 was also the year the Division's office moved from

London's By-Law Detachment.

Baseline Road to the Waterloo Building in Western Counties Wing. It was also the year the new logo "the COMMISSIONAIRES" was introduced. The logo was the result of work done by the Public Awareness Committee with Paul Costello. The final selection for recommendation was made at a meeting in London.

The city of London provided Sgt Collins cause to celebrate the New Year. As the city hall detachment commander he was also Sergeant-at-Arms for the city council. On instructions from the mayor, Sgt Collins was promoted to WOI effective January 1, 1990.

A review of the Division Headquarters staffing sub-committee, chaired by LCol Geddes, recommended, and the executive approved, that the quartermaster's position be a dual one by adding administration and making it full time. A competition to replace Sgt Matheson who had retired prior to the announcement was held in February. Sgt Moran won the competition based on his performance as the by-laws detachment commander and his experience as a town clerk. Accounts receivable became part of his new job description.

In the area of finance, two significant events took place in 1990. The Executive Committee authorized a bereavement leave policy and the provincial government imposed an Employer Health Tax. The tax had the immediate effect of increasing the Division's billing rate by 2%.

1991 got off to a sombre start with the passing of Col Tom Lawson, our much-respected Honorary Chairman. However the signing of the Esso contract in Sarnia did wonders for the Division's spirits. By far the largest single contract to date and boasting a wage scale 35% higher than the Division average, it was considered a major achievement. The contract was enhanced because of its requirement for a level of advanced and specialized training and a wide diversification of tasks. This of course demanded an above average guard force that would be continually challenged. The transition went smoothly with a minimum of serious problems despite the fact the Gulf War called for more guards than were originally planned for. A total of 50 guards were deployed at the refinery at the height of the war. While Esso was looking good, the Division was having problems in London where its base wage was $6.85 an hour. The competition in London was paying only $5.70 an hour. This resulted in the loss of a provincial contract through tender; the job had employed 28 Commissionaires. Ironically the $60,000 tender differential was far less than the wage differential over the two-year period of the contract, and when the fair wage was later increased the cost to the province was considerably greater than the Division's bid. Based on the new fair wage, the Division would have won the contract by a considerable margin and saved the province money.

Notwithstanding the challenges encountered since 1986, the Division strength on April 1, 1991 was 408. The Commandant had met the requirement of doubling the strength of the Division in five years. The increase in staff and additional government requirement caused the workload of the staff to increase significantly.

It was obvious that a more sophisticated computer system was required. A computer committee consisting of Col Newman, Commander Rutherford, Lieutenant Commander Magee, Maj Urquhart and Col Doyon was formed. There were two options within the Corps, the national and Heron systems. After visiting Kingston and Toronto for demonstrations, the committee successfully recommended that the Heron system consisting of both hardware and software along with technical support be purchased at a cost of $45,000.

The next year (1992) got off to another sombre start when WO 11 Dave Moran was killed in an auto accident on his way into work. Dave had become not only a key member but a very popular member of the Headquarters team. He had wrestled the accounts receivable down to a point where overdrafts were a thing of the past while maintaining very efficient QM stores. He accomplished this while retaining his integrity and a wonderful sense of humour. Staff Sergeant Horace Smith was selected to replace Dave. His experience and superior performance as the first full time By-Law Detachment commander and as the detachment commander for Victoria Hospital Parking made Horace the unanimous choice of the selection committee.

Public awareness was an ongoing project. When the national Board of Governors turned down the public awareness committee's recommendation to produce a new video about the Corps, seven Divisions decided to produce it on their own. A professional studio was contracted to produce the film with assistance from the Kingston, Toronto and London Divisions. After the script was prepared, all the camera work was shot in Toronto and London over a period of just three days. Not all the volunteer actors made it to print. A few Commissionaires who were normally never at a loss for words literally froze when cued by the director. The majority, though, did an admirable job and represented their Divisions well. The video came in under budget and, by editing, the studio was able to make a five-minute version of the twelve-minute video for use in sales.

The London Division, like the rest of the Ontario Divisions, enjoyed a very low Worker's Compensation rate. It was only a matter of time before the Division would be caught in a debit position as the injury costs exceeded the annual assessments. London was levied a fine of $26,000, because of the Division's poor previous three-year experience. At a WCB Appeal Board hearing the Commandant was successful in reducing the amount to the minimum fine of $11,000. As a result of this experience the Commandant instituted a series of safety policies and practices which have proven very effective and more importantly provide for a safer work environment. It should also be noted that as a result of a London initiative and by mutual consent the rate was adjusted to more accurately reflect the Corps' working conditions and potential costs.

This was not the only government activity the Division was interested in. The Government of Ontario tabled two pieces of legislation in 1992. Both had the potential of severely curtailing the operation of the Corps. Bill 40 established successor rights for security guards, and Bill 79 proposed employment equity based on regional demographics. Specifically Bill 40 provided that when security contracts changed contractors, the incoming contractor had to retain all existing guards, and if a union was in place the collective agreement was also to remain in force.

Not being able to replace "inherited" guards who did not meet the Commissionaire membership criteria had the effect of preventing the Ontario Divisions from competing for contracts where there was an existing guard force. The London Division was one of the most seriously affected as 75% of their work was based on commercial contracts which were re-tendered on a regular basis. Not being able to gain new business to replace contracts lost in the normal course of business would eventually put the Division out of business. On the other hand, obeying the new law and ignoring the Commissionaire criteria for membership would jeopardize the right of first refusal with the federal government. This loss would be disastrous for a number of other Divisions across Canada where the federal government provided the bulk of their work.

The Association of Ontario Divisions agreed to attempt to obtain exemptions from both acts and hired consultants to help prepare and present the Corps' case. These efforts over the next three years, because of government stalling tactics, were to prove costly, time-consuming and unrewarding.

1993 started off on a high note. The two major contracts, Esso and London by-laws, were renewed for three years. However in the tendering of new contracts, some competitors were undercutting the Division by as much as 5%. This was significant, as it was 12% less than what was considered the break-even point of security companies. On the other hand, the London Division's excess of revenue over expenses for 1992/93 of less than 1% provided very little opportunity to reduce prices without incurring a loss.

The first tangible problem caused by Bill 40 came when the Division tendered a contract worth over $1,000,000 annually and had to include caveats making the client responsible for any additional costs that might arise, legal and otherwise, due to Bill 40. On receipt of the tender the client dropped the Division from the most favoured to the least favoured contractor. On another occasion, where, again the client specifically wanted the Corps, and the annual value of the contract was over $250,000, the result was the same. These experiences served to underline the urgency of the situation for the London Division and the Association of Ontario Divisions as they continued to lobby the Departments of Labour and Citizenship for exemptions. In the trenches, however, the Commissionaires continued to provide stellar service. Two Commissionaires exemplifying this were Cpl Ed Templeton and Commissionaire Gary Owen. At 0025 hours on November 15, 1993, while monitoring the Accuride surveillance system, they noticed two men tampering with the gate of a neighbouring lumber yard. They called the police and continued to report on the criminals' activities until police arrived. The culprits had gained access by cutting through a back fence and had used a front-end loader to load a company truck in the yard with materials. They were attempting to open the front gate for their getaway when they were spotted by the ever-alert Commissionaires. A grateful lumberyard manager treated the two Commissionaires and their wives to a night out.

The Governors were kept busy in 1993. The Division By-Laws were reviewed and rewritten to reflect both the changes to the National By-Laws and the current character of the London Division. The review committee Chairman was LCdr Magee with members, LCol Buchner, LCol Kay, Capt(N) MacLachan and Col Way. The by-laws were approved at the 1994 Annual General Meeting.

At the request of National Headquarters to support the requirement for the right of first refusal, a survey was conducted in early 1994 to establish what percentage of Commissionaires received pensions. In London, 78% responded, and of these, 26% were in receipt of a pension. The average annual value of a pension was $13,900. This was not a surprising result as approximately 25% of the serving Commissionaires were eligible for Canada Pension Plan and Old Age Security. The myth that Commissionaires did not need work could now be put into its proper prospective.

In keeping with the old adage that "all work and no play make Commissionaires dull boys," the inaugural London Division golf tournament was conducted in August 1994. Col Newman and WOI Hardy were the main driving force behind the event, which was so successful it has become an annual event. A great selection of prizes and a BBQ steak dinner rounded off a day of fun and camaraderie. The field is traditionally made up of serving and retired Commissionaires, Governors and clients. In Commissionaire Harrington's eyes it will be remembered not only as a golf tournament but a big surprise party. He was presented with a birthday cake and a rollicking version of Happy Birthday in honour of his seventy-fifth birthday.

The by-law detachment proved during the summer that they were more than a bunch of meter maids. For almost three months, vandals seemed to be enjoying a supplementary source of income at considerable expense to the city of London. On a daily basis meters were found with the casings broken, and the clocks and coins missing. With the blessing of the Traffic Division at city hall, and the cooperation of the London police, the detachment commander, WO 11 Ed Hare, implemented an overnight surveillance team made up of four Commissionaires armed only with hand-held two way radios and a collective wish for a little good luck.

Two weeks of stationary vehicle surveillance in random locations bore no results. A change in tactics was immediately effective. A system of mobile patrols triangulated around an indoor observation point with a video camera was established. The vandals were spotted from the observation point and the patrols were notified. Cpl Rick Hodkinson with Commissionaire Frank Murchland and Commissionaire Tony Cooper had closed in and contained the suspects by the time the police arrived to make the arrests. The physical evidence recovered from their hiding places in the bushes and the video tape enabled the police to encourage the suspects to confess, and the police got speedy convictions. This put an end to the vandalism and significantly enhanced our relationship with the police.

The lack of success with the attempts to gain concessions from the Ontario government caused the London Division Long-Range Planning Committee to become extremely concerned about the potentially detrimental serious effects of Bills 40 and 79. The formation of a subsidiary company was identified as a viable option and a draft paper was prepared outlining the concept and guidelines. It was presented to the Ontario Commandants and to the national executive who were examining the problem of employing non-eligible, for consideration and comment. The London Executive Committee approved the concept and guidelines in principle on September 14, 1994.

On September 16, 1994 a motion by LCdr Magee and seconded by LCol Kay that CORE II be formed in accordance with the approved guidelines was passed by the Executive Committee.

On March 16, 1995 the Executive Committee passed the following motion detailing the operational requirements and protocol for CORE II;

CORE II

14 Moved by Cdr Rutherford, seconded by Maj Ogelsby that,

1. *The Canadian Corps of Commissionaires, London Division (thereafter referred to as the Commissionaires) purchase 1,000 shares of CORE II Security Inc. Common shares at $0.10 per share.*

2. *Thus as shareholder;*

   a) *That the Executive Committee of the Commissionaires be appointed as directors of CORE II and shall represent the Commissionaires Board of Governors and their objectives in the operation of CORE II.*

   b) *That the CEO (Managing Director, Secretary-Treasurer) of CORE II be appointed by the Board of Directors of CORE II , normally the Commandant.*

   c) *That a Director, Officer or Administrator may hold office in both the Commissionaires and CORE II.*

   d) *That the Board of Directors of CORE II appoint a President, 1st and 2nd Vice Presidents whose duties and responsibilities will be the same as those of the Chairman, Chairman Elect and Vice Chairman respectively of the Commissionaires.*

e) *That CORE II will be operated in accordance with the guidelines outlined in "Annex A" so far as it is practical to do so.*

f) *That CORE II retain any profit it might make until sufficient operating capital is realized. When dividends are paid to the Commissionaires, these monies will be used to further the objectives of the Commissionaires.*

g) *That the Chairman of the Commissionaires Board of Governors or in his/her absence, a duly appointed representative, shall represent the shareholders at any CORE II meetings of shareholders.*

h) *That the operation of CORE II will be reported to the Commissionaires Board of Governors.*

i) *That the Commissionaires be authorized to enter an agreement with CORE II to provide administrative support at cost based on the proportional number of hours worked by the two firms.*

j) *That loans be authorized to CORE II for operational purposes. The interest rate for these loans shall be prime plus 1%.*

k) *The fiscal year for CORE II shall be the same as the Commissionaires (eg: 1 April to 31 March).*

CORE II was incorporated in March 1995 as a for profit corporation and a wholly owned subsidiary of the London Division. The officers were Col W.R. Newman, President; Maj B.A. Urquhart, 1st Vice President; Cdr D.C. Rutherford 2nd, Vice President; and Col R.R. Doyon, CEO. With exception of the membership criteria, CORE II was to operate in every way as a mirror image of the London Division. No Headquarters staff was added.

During its first six months of operation, three tenders were successfully contested and 30 personnel were employed in the detachments at the Bluewater Detention Center in Goderich, Robarts School, and Fanshawe College in London. All of these contracts had been held by the Division but lost during the previous tendering process. As a matter of policy, as attrition took place, all replacements were in fact personnel who met the Commissionaire membership criteria and after 18 months over 75% of CORE II met this criteria.

In 1995 the Employment Equity Law (Bill 40), was rescinded, and the Ontario Labour Act was amended deleting the requirement to honour union collective agreements and the mandatory retention of all of the existing guard force. In its place was the requirement to pay termination and severance pay to all guards not retained. All previous service with the outgoing security company was to be counted in calculating these payments. In many cases this amounted to six months' pay, several thousands of dollars per guard. The effect of this requirement was much the same as that of Bill 40 had a few years before and underlined the requirement to have a fallback organization such as CORE II. An example of its value quickly presented itself when Esso requested the Division to extend its Sarnia contract to the Nanticoke Esso refinery. To replace the non-Commissionaire workforce would have cost approximately $50,000, which the client would not entertain and the Division could not afford. As the request was predicated on an Esso policy for national contracts, not to assume the new contract would jeopardize the Sarnia contract which represented about 10% of the London Division hours. Not only did CORE II protect an existing large contract but added eight full time positions with above average wages which over time will be manned by Commissionaires.

The practice of laying-off loyal and dedicated workers, who are capable and willing to meet Corps standards on assuming a contract, is seen by many in today's society as repugnant and immoral. The Corps was founded on grounds of compassion, albeit for veterans. It would seem logical therefore that the Corps would show compassion when dealing with an existing workforce who are often working under stress. It therefore appears that CORE II will remain an essential adjunct to the London Division. In doing so the Corps will be in a significantly better position to execute its mandate to provide meaningful employment to ex-service personnel and be less vulnerable to outside pressure groups who might view the Corps as unfair competition.

On 7 July 1997 the first CORE II/Commissionaire cycle was completed when the CORE II parking contract at Fanshawe College was successfully re-tendered as a Commissionaire contract. This change was made possible due to staff turnover, leaving the detachment 100% "Commissionaire" qualified.

While CORE II was the centre of attention, it was not the only game in town. The Commissionaires set up a downtown public fingerprinting centre. The establishment had the unqualified support of the RCMP and the London City Police. Except for special cases such as criminals all administrative requirements for fingerprinting in London was referred to the Commissionaire centre. This venture served as an excellent example of how the Corps can reduce the workload of the police, and still be less expensive for the client. Sgt Bob Ashby, an ex-bobby and Military Policeman, put his expertise to work in setting up the centre, establishing and maintaining standards second to none.

The Chairman, Major Bruce Urquhart, was typically busy. He took on the Chairmanship of the London Canada Remembers Committee. Naturally the Division would become involved as well. The first act was to purchase and have all Commissionaires wear a commemorative pin on their uniform. A second commitment was to have a float in the June parade. When the parade ran into problems obtaining liability insurance, the Division was able to provide it. The float depicted the peacekeeping aspects of the Canadian military and represented a Cyprus style observation post. It was built by Col Newman, Col Doyon and

Commissionaire Doug Little. The float was escorted by six by-law cars. A side note of interest was that another Governor, LCol Kay, was able to squeeze into his old battle dress uniform to ride in the parade, as parade marshal.

On a matter that had previously been very controversial, the Board of Governors finally agreed to award the Long Service Medal to Governors with ten years' service. However they made an additional prerequisite that the qualification include service on the executive. Nine Governors received their medals and bars at a dinner held at the Wolseley Barracks Officers' Mess in February 1996. The Board also took the opportunity of the occasion to present Col Doyon with the Distinguished Service Medal. It was the first to be awarded to a member of the London Division.

Downsizing, which had significant effects on the Division over the past three years, began to level off in 1996. While Commissionaire positions were reduced in many cases, there also were opportunities for the Division to move into other areas of employment where clients reorganized. While the number of these jobs obtained to date has been limited, the potential is significant, and the Division is working on both the local and national levels to achieve the desired results. Two examples of the new contracts coming on-stream are those with Bank of America and The University of Western Ontario.

The messenger service provided by the Commissionaires to the Bank of America is a more complex service than is normally provided by the Corps. Bank drafts and securities from the Bank of America arrive each morning by courier at the Corps office. Commissionaire Dave Bell delivers these securities, in a vehicle supplied by the Corps, to Bank of America customers in Southwestern Ontario. Dave collects exchange currencies as cheques from the customers and takes them to the customers' bank for certification or bank draft. He deposits these securities in a local bank at the end of each day and faxes a record of these transactions to the Bank of America. This London operation is a branch of the Bank of America and has its own branch number.

Graphic arts sign production is a new service provided to the Parking Service of UWO and attests to the versatility of some of the functions that the Commissionaires are able to provide. This service initially consists of part-time work by Commissionaire Bell setting up the computer and loading sign designs into the program. Eventually, the service will provide vinyl cut signs to replace existing old and deteriorated traffic, safety and parking signs around the UWO campus.

When Col Doyon indicated his desire to retire by December 31, 1996 a selection committee was formed and the position was advertised on a national basis. Over 70 applicants were screened leaving five finalists. Col Brian McGrath who saw the ad in the *Globe and Mail* while serving as military attaché and literally flew around the world for his interview came out on top. The handover too was complicated as Col Quinn, the operations officer, had a hip replacement and was not available for much of the time. The result was on the job training for both the Commandant's job and the operations officer. At the end of the day when it came time to bid Col Doyon good bye the one thing Col McGrath knew for sure, and maybe the only thing he new for sure, was that there were just not enough hours in the day.

Taking on the mantle of Command, Col McGrath quickly reorganized the Headquarters' staff instituting an assistant operations officer position. This addition strained the already cramped Headquarters accommodation. Therefore when the opportunity to lease surplus accommodation on former CFB London presented itself, the Commandant was quick to act and the Division Headquarters moved to Wolseley Barracks on April 12.

1997 also saw a resurgence in the country's economy and a brightening of the employment picture. For the first time in four years the Division advertised for "recruits." Contracts calling for non-traditional skills were obtained as the emphasis for greater diversification is pursued.

In summary, the London Division is a good Division because it has dedicated and loyal personnel. It is a proud team, even in death. Members often choose to be buried in their Commissionaire uniform. No finer tribute can be made to an organization. We will carry on.

COMMISSIONAIRE EXTRAORDINAIRE
Commissionaire Jack Barker

At approximately 0815 hours on 20 October 1996 the only work related fatality in the London Division occurred when Commissionaire Jack Barker fell down a ventilation shaft. It was truly a tragedy; the police have categorized it as a criminal act. Whether it was an act of vandalism or a prank that went wrong does not matter, a decent man lost his life through no fault of his own or his employer or the client. He epitomized what the Corps represented.

Commissionaire Jack Barker 1934-1996.

Cpl John West

On June 15, 1997 Cpl John West was enjoying a relaxing afternoon with friends on a sailboat on the St Clair River. What transpired is best described in the words of the man he rescued, Mr Brendan D'Arcy. The following is an edited excerpt of his letter of July 9, 1997.

> *At approximately 1:00 PM on June 15 1997 we left the Bridgeview Marina on a 35 foot sailboat. On Board were John West, three other adults, my eight-year-old son Ciaran and myself. We sailed pleasantly in the lake until around 3:00 PM then we dropped sail and motored south down the St Clair River. I brought my son forward and we sat*

on the front of the cabin. Ciaran was wearing a life preserver, I was not and I was fully clothed.

The river was quite choppy due to a brisk wind but at no time did we appear to be in danger. We crossed under the bridge and cut diagonally across towards the marina. Ciaran and I were discussing going back to the cockpit when something happened that caused Ciaran and I to be in the water. It happened so quickly, mind could not comprehend it. In an instant Ciaran and I went from being safe and secure on deck to being submerged. I remember being doused with water, losing my spectacles and being submerged. We surfaced very close to each other about fifteen feet behind the boat. The crew on the boat were desperately trying to regain control of the vessel and apparently unaware of us being in the water. An American boat heading north and about ten yards away noticed Ciaran in the water and raised the alarm. Ciaran was crying and clinging onto me and we were both bobbing up and down. I was very concerned that if I got into difficulties and panicked I would pull my son down with me. After a while, I separated myself from Ciaran reassuring him that he would be OK and that they would come and get him in a little while. He was very upset at my letting him go. I then tried to swim for our boat. I managed to swim a bit, but my saturated clothing and shoes weighed me down. Each time I tried to breathe, it seemed another wave crashed on me and prevented me getting air. I swallowed enormous amounts of water. I saw the people in our boat pointing at me and they threw a life preserver towards me but it never reached me. I began to go under. My shoes and clothing felt like lead, I did not feel the cold, and I knew I was losing consciousness. It felt as if the lights were going on and off. I knew I had only a few moments of consciousness left and thought if I put my hands as high as possible above my head it might help them locate me. I knew if they did not get to me I would die and was resigned to this. I was thinking, how ironic, that I was going to die in the way I had feared most all my life, by drowning. I believed my son was safe. I went unconscious.

I regained consciousness in the bottom of the cockpit of a boat at a dockside. A girl named Debbie was holding me upright in a sitting position, crying with relief I was alive. Ciaran was also in the boat and appeared to be OK.

I was taken by ambulance to the hospital. My body temperature was 90 degrees F. My blood pressure low, less then a hundred. And my blood had turned acidic. I was released after 24 hours.

Apparently what happened, two speedboats raced by our boat. The combination wake and wave action slapped our boat broadside on the bow causing the bow to snap upwards for ten or so feet. Ciaran and I went upwards with it. Then the boat kicked sideways and Ciaran and I dropped directly into the water.

Watching me attempt to swim and lose control, John West decided, realizing my difficulties, to rescue me. He dived in still in his tee shirt, *shorts and socks. The water was very choppy from the wind, current and wakes of boats. The water was also very cold, about 50 degrees F. By following my bubbles he found me sinking about five feet under the surface. He grabbed my hair and swam to the American boat. It took about 10 minutes from when he left his boat until we got to the American boat. With great difficulty they got me on Board. I weigh 200 pounds live weight and dry.*

Debbie Sullivan instantly commenced resuscitation. I was not breathing, had no discernable pulse and was a blue-gray colour. All the signs of death were apparently setting in. In a very constrained area, she did mouth to mouth and CPR and revived me.

Without the intervention and determination of both John and Debbie, I would have died. John put his own safety and life at risk to rescue me in very dangerous waters and Debbie gave everything she could to revive me in very difficult conditions. Their determination saved me. I owe my life to these two brave and unselfish people and words will never do justice for the feelings I have in my heart for them.

Cpl John West is the Detachment Commander at the Canadian Coast Guard Regional Headquarters in Sarnia. The Coast Guard has recognized his bravery by awarding him the Commissioners Commendation and an inscribed clock. The London Division awarded John with the Commandants Commendation. In addition the London Division has recommended him for the Medal of Bravery.

Chapter X

HISTORY OF THE MANITOBA DIVISION

Commandant's Introduction – *By Ron Werry*

THE STORY begins at a historic Winnipeg landmark, the Fort Garry Hotel on Broadway Avenue. It was in the sitting room of a visitor, Major General W.B.M. King, the President of the "Corps" in Montreal, on May 10, 1937 that a seed was planted. After a few steering committee meetings, which included some watering during stag lunches, germination occurred and Manitoba Division came to life on January 6, 1938.

As the narrative unfolds, it is apparent the success of the Manitoba Division may be attributed to the ardent interest of its Governors, the dedication and eagerness of its officers and staff, and the courage and hard work of its Commissionaires.

Manitoba Division, probably a misnomer, not only services the geographical area of the province of Manitoba, but also includes Northwestern Ontario. At present, besides the city of Winnipeg, there are major detachments in Brandon/Shilo area, Portage la Prairie, Thompson, and the "Land of the Sleeping Giant" Thunder Bay, Ontario.

Post-Second World War brought the radar stations of the Mid-Canada line to our roster – Canadian Forces Stations Gypsumville and Beausejour in Manitoba, and Sioux Lookout in Ontario. These sites were deactivated in the late 1980s.

As a result of the catastrophic Air India crash in June 1985, Transport Canada's airport security received serious attention and we staffed airports at Churchill, The Pas, Thompson, and Brandon, Manitoba and Dryden, Ontario. Only the Thompson detachment, the transportation hub of Northern Manitoba, remains.

Winnipeg is the centre of activity, with a 1997 strength of 326 Commissionaires. The Division total is 394.

Not to distract from our many valued clients; federal government comprises 60 percent of our business, while provincial, municipal and commercial clients represent 40 percent of our contracts. The Division has a special bond with the city of Winnipeg Police Service and we have provided Commissionaires to assist in by-law enforcement since January 1955. Our detachment numbers 46.

We also have a special connection with "air services" since our first client was Trans Canada Airlines in 1938. Today we still provide security for its successor, Air Canada, at the administrative centre on Portage Avenue. We mentioned the other airports within our boundary, but we have served at various temporary flying schools during the Second World War. Our long relationship with transport Canada's Winnipeg International and Thunder Bay Airports, which includes serving with the RCMP, was always rewarding and mutually satisfying. We now have the privilege of serving different owners, the new Local Airport Authorities of the two cities, and welcome the resulting challenges. We should also mention our past commitment to Air Command Headquarters and now to 1 Canadian Air Division and 17 Wing, Winnipeg.

Like other Divisions, we are experiencing the refreshing challenge of assuming tasks not directly related to security, and will continue to harmonize our resources with the winds of change.

One of our most recent "adaptations" (1995) was to accept the invitation to employ and administer the Guards and Matrons of Manitoba's D Division, RCMP. By doing so, we share with the western Divisions in providing service to a most valued client.

These "winds of change" have been addressed through the conduct of a recent Strategic Planning weekend involving Commissionaires, clients and Governors. We are now poised to prepare specific plans for future operations and to commit ourselves to the Corps mission, our membership and to our clients by providing superlative service.

We also dedicate ourselves anew to supporting the grand "federation" of Divisions and playing our role in Commissionaires Canada.

Special thanks are offered to Colonel Douglas Ludlow, our present Chairman, for his strong input to this capsule of Manitoba Division's history, and to Sergeant Laurilyn Greig-Haines for her editorial assistance.

THE DEBUT

Manitoba, and in particular, the municipalities and cities that comprised the greater Winnipeg area, contributed an incredibly high percentage of its manpower to serve with the Canadian Expeditionary Force during the First World War. The survivors, supplemented by thousands of ex-servicemen who came West to seek a living in those difficult post-war years, along with similar numbers of eligible Commonwealth immigrants also seeking employment, provided fertile ground for creating a Manitoba Division of the Canadian Corps of Commissionaires. The Great Depression, severe drought, and devastating crop losses experienced in the "Dirty Thirties" all contributed to the ranks of the unemployed.

A number of concerned and influential Manitoba businessmen with military backgrounds were aware of the organization, modelled on the British Corps of Commissionaires, which had started up in Montreal in 1925 in order to relieve the seemingly endless unemployment situation facing those who had served King and Country and who now sought the opportunity to maintain their self-respect and obtain meaningful, rewarding work within their own community. This group researched the potential for creating a similar entity initially in Winnipeg, but with a view to expanding eventually into other provincial locations.

The stage was set when, in May of 1937, a meeting was arranged in Winnipeg, between Colonel J.Y. Reid, Chairman, along with several other members of the "Manitoba Steering Committee" and Major-General W.B.M. King, CMG, DSO, president of the newly activated Canadian Corps of Commissionaires, to discuss the feasibility of forming a Division in Manitoba. As a result, and taking into account the lessons learned in the recently re-established Montreal Corps, the Manitoba Division was officially formed on January 6, 1938.

Colonel John A. Gunn, CB, OBE, VD, MD was elected as the first Chairman of the Board Governors and Major A. John Taunton, DSO, was appointed as the Adjutant. These two gentlemen shared the duties of Commandant pending the appointment of same. Using the "Old Boy Network" to seek out opportunities for employment and then identifying deserving ex-servicemen who would be engaged to form the basis of the new Division, it was off to a very good start.

The Early Years 1938-1945

Division Order No.1 was published March 6, 1938 and 15 Commissionaires were approved for enrolment. This list of charter members included Henry S. Bennett. Bennett had been a Company Sergeant Major in the original battalion of the Princess Patricia's Canadian Light Infantry. Obviously a man of great initiative, he obtained a uniform from Montreal Division in 1937 and had been on duty during the winter months at the Dominion Theatre, Winnipeg. In the Spring of 1938, he became the first Commissionaire to work at Trans Canada Air Lines (TCA). He was given the appointment of Honorary Division Sergeant Major on October 13, 1939 and on January 22, 1940, when appointed as Division Sergeant Major, he left the post at TCA and assumed full time duties in his

Henry S. Bennett.

new position. Three years later, in January 1943, he became the first Commissionaire in Canada to be appointed Sergeant-at-Arms of a Provincial Legislature, a position he held for 13 years until his resignation in August 1956. His consistently efficient service to the Manitoba Division for over 20 years was of inestimable value to the Manitoba Division. We consider Mr Bennett a Commissionaire Extraordinaire.

The initiative taken in 1937 proved successful and gradually, as opportunities presented themselves and more men sought the assistance of the Corps, it evolved into a proud and viable organization. Early enrollments were approved by the Executive Committee and three classifications were used to record their decisions; accepted and given priority of placement; accepted; and rejected.

The first inspection of the new Division was held on the grounds of the Provincial Legislature on May 15, 1938. The inspecting officer was His Excellency Lord Tweedsmuir, the Governor General of Canada. For such an auspicious occasion, Major A.J.S. Taunton, DSO, the Division's first Adjutant, was determined the Division should make the best possible impression and turned out every man not acutally on duty. Major Taunton, Sergeant Bennett and nine Commissionaires were on parade, all smartly attired in uniforms provided by Montreal. The number of men employed at the end of 1938 reached a total of 38.

During the "break-in" years 1939-40, records indicate that discipline, including appearance in uniform, was strictly enforced. Order No.12 in 1940 notes that for conduct detrimental to Good Order and Discipline a certain Commissionaire was suspended from duty for one week and also forfeited his day off each week for three months. Smoking in uniform on or off duty was not permitted. This decree was softened later to allow commissionaires "to use discretion when in uniform off duty."

Trans Canada Air Lines (TCA) was the first client of the Division with seven Commissionaires employed under Sergeant Bennett. Wages were paid directly to the men by TCA, with a small administrative charge paid to the Corps for uniforms. Uniforms were purchased from Montreal and a Commissionaire's pay was debited by periodic assessment. TCA provided our first recorded diversification from the security role by requesting the services of a Commissionaire janitor in civilian dress. TCA officials were so impressed by the excellent service that the recommendation to employ Commissionaires in this capacity was made to their other western cities' airports.

Trans Canada Air Lines hanger, 1938.

In June 1940, Major Taunton, on being appointed as a Wing Commander in the Royal Canadian Air Force, resigned his post as Adjutant. Wing Commander Taunton was later promoted to Group Captain and served as a Governor of the Manitoba Division.

Unable to find a replacement for the position of Adjutant, the Executive Committee appointed Mr W. H. Wilson as Acting Secretary. Mr Wilson was a lawyer with the Department of Veterans Affairs and it was arranged that he give some time daily to the work of the Division. He continued in this capacity until February 1941. Conveniently, the Corps office was co-located with the Department of Veterans Affairs, an arrangement that lasted until well into the 1980s.

Following the outbreak of the Second World War, it soon became apparent the war effort was creating abundant employment opportunities for the type of men the Corps attracted – mature, disciplined and reliable ex-servicemen who for a variety of reasons were unable to enlist in the Active Service Force.

One of the earlier recorded wartime requests for the Corps' services was the requirement for a 75-man security force to guard and provide surveillance to the Dominion Industries Ltd. munitions factory in Transcona. Such an opportunity for growth in membership of the Division demanded some reorganization of the staff. To recruit and maintain a guard detail of the size envisaged necessitated the examination and approval of many hundreds of applications. Colonel G.F.C. Poussette, VD, our first Commandant, was working on plans to select, enrol and uniform these 75 Commissionaires when he was stricken and died of a heart attack on February 1, 1941.

An emergency meeting of Governors was called to address this crisis. It was suggested that Lieutenant Gyles and Colonel E.A. Pridham might consider invitations to accept the appointments of Adjutant and Commandant respectively. The Governors agreed and were appointed February 24, 1941. The examination of applicants continued for weeks. Eventually the required number of uniformed Commissionaires was posted under command of Sergeant Major A. Ramsay, formerly of the Royal Canadian Mounted Police. On May 8, the guard had reached a strength of 105, including 7 Sergeants, and the number shortly increased to 120. Some Commissionaires were required to carry 12-gauge, single barrelled shotguns, and to wear bandoliers of ammunition over their shoulders.

Within a few months of operation, the demand for manpower at the plant necessitated the employment of female staff. All employees were required to submit to a search of their clothing when going off duty, and this task was performed by Commissionaires. The presence of female workers highlighted the need to enroll women in the Corps, as it would hardly be appropriate for male Commissionaires to search women who may be attempting to smuggle contraband such as brass or explosives out of the plant area. No other Division had ever encountered this situation. As a result, the Manitoba Division sought out five young women who either had service backgrounds or were wives or daughters of Commissionaires. The Women's Division, uniformed in a style similiar to the Canadian Women's Army Corps, supplemented the men who made up the initial detachment. The detachment was eventually expected to employ up to 150 personnel for the duration of the war.

During 1941, the Division manned security detachments at various temporary flying schools such as Virden and Portage la Prairie and were instrumental in organizing sections at Prince Albert, Saskatchewan and Fort William, Ontario.

Ramsey and the four women.

It was during 1941 that, for the comfort of Commissionaires, pith helmets were purchased along with a "good type" blue shirt with military pockets and epaulettes. These articles would permit the Commissionaires to discard their tunics during the extreme summer heat.

An interesting public relations gesture was attempted during this time. The Adjutant ordered that "on receiving a serious complaint and to avoid unnecessary correspondence, an NCO will take the accused to the house of the complainant in order that the complaint may be fully inquired into and, if possible, settled without delay."

1942 was the year of incorporation of Manitoba Division. Colonel Pridham had previously voiced his deep concern regarding "liability" at Board meetings, and strongly recommended this action. His perseverance and hard work brought about incorporation by provincial ordinance on May 13, 1942. Letters Patent were obtained under the Companies Act of Manitoba for a not-for-profit corporation under the name of "Canadian Corps of Commissionaires (Manitoba Division)."

Colonel Prideham.

At one point, the Commandant was "disturbed" over some shortcomings of the Montreal Headquarters organization in that representatives of Divisions had "no place or say." This was one reason for seeking our own charter. He was elated that a re-organization of Dominion Headquarters was in the offing. These coming changes "will bring a feeling of confidence which should endure to the benefit of the whole movement." It was during this period that Montreal had requested $5 per capita to support the national cause. This was not accepted, but a "token" grant of $50 per year would be made. The Division repaid the $550 advance by Montreal with the appropriate thanks.

In October 1942, at the request of the Department of Transport, Manitoba Division was instrumental in forming the nucleus of a new Division in Regina, Saskatchewan, where the Department wished to form a guard at the Airport. Mr R. Lamont of the Department of Pensions at Regina was appointed the representative of the Manitoba Division. Later, guards were set up by this Division for the War Assets plants at Moose Jaw, Saskatoon, Estevan and Swift Current. Officers of the Manitoba Division, when on business trips in these areas, took time to help organize the units and our Divisional Sergeant Major attended to set up the guards. Trained sergeants were sent out from Winnipeg as Post Commanders.

By the end of this exciting year, the Adjutant reported a strength of 288 Commissionaires. 240 were paid by the Division, and 48 were paid directly by the client.

As early as 1943 the end of the war appeared to be in sight. An ad hoc committee of the board was instructed to prepare for this event by recommending possible courses of action to accommodate the influx of returning combatants. Also, a novel question was posed regarding admission of Second World War applicants whose service was restricted to Canada and islands such as Kiska in the Aleutians. It was found advisable to defer decision on this matter.

Manitoba Division established its first true benefit in instituting a Division Gratuity Fund to provide retirement funds and, in cases of death, to assist widows. A special committee of Governors was tasked to administer the funds. This fund provided $1.75 per month of service and was increased to $2 in 1944, $3 in 1949 and $4 in 1953. The fund was dissolved in 1977 when government social benefits were established.

During the later war years, Division Rules and Regulations were promulgated and a few interesting extracts are worthy of note:

> *Men who grumble or are unwilling to make themselves useful; who try to avoid all work but that of an easy nature or are in the habit of committing petty breaches of the rules will always find themselves at the bottom of the selection roll.*

> *A Commissionaire wearing chevrons will, on conviction of any offense, forfeit the whole of them.*

> *When a Commissionaire, having been deprived of his rank, seeks for restoration to his former position, he will be dealt with as follows:*
>
> *For every chevron forfeited, a Commissionaire must serve 12 months in the Division without any Division entry. Thus a Sergeant will be have to serve 3 years before he can regain his chevrons, but he may wear the chevron of a Lance Corporal.*

After the War 1945-1954

As the war closed, so did the "temporary" clients associated with the massive national effort. It was a time for lay-offs. Colonel Pridham, with regret, reported in 1945 that there was difficulty in maintaining the present rate of pay for Commissionaires employed by the federal government departments and that wages were to be reduced by five cents per hour.

In 1947, at the Annual Meeting held at the Manitoba Club, the Commandant reported that the federal government promised to provide more jobs for Commissionaires but that initiative was evident only in the East.

With the power of the pen and without fanfare, Manitoba Division transferred 21 Commissionaires to the "Regina" Division on January 2, 1947. When that decision was made, approximately $1,000 in administrative expenses were incurred in support of the Commissionaires in Saskatchewan. Manitoba Division absorbed that sum as a gesture of neighbourly support.

After reaching a strength of over 300 in 1945, Manitoba reported only 106 Commissionaires by June 1947. Ten years later, the Division reported to the Annual Meeting in Kingston, Ontario that "with the closing of War Industries, the Air Training Schools and the plants of War Assets Corporation, it was impossible to find employment for all the Commissionaires who had been engaged with these projects and the Division declined in strength." During this period, the policy of frugal administration that had characterized the organization since its inception, proved its value and made it possible for the Division to survive.

By 1950, the support of the Dominion government, through publicity and offers of employment, began to produce results. The Department of Veterans Affairs supplied the impetus and the encouragement given Divisions of the Corps was most opportune. Colonel P.J. Philpott of Veterans Affairs was always available with advice and inspiration in times of difficulty. Appreciation of his services was demonstrated in 1956 when the Division made him an Honorary Governor of the Division. Lieutenant Gyles resigned as Adjutant on August 17, 1950. Lieutenant Colonel R.S. Robertson, MC, ED replaced him, and then served as Commandant from 1971-75. Both of these highly competent officers provided exemplary service to the Division.

Resulting from a need to find jobs for returned veterans and in addition to federal government support to the cause, it was felt that a public relations program should be implemented. This initiative was approved by the Executive and $100 was laid aside for a business card advertisement in the local papers, the *Free Press* and *Tribune*. This was in 1946. During the following year, $300 was approved for advertising. Satisfactory results were reported. Division strength was down to 79 regular, full time Commissionaires by the end of 1949.

During 1950, the rampaging Red River practically brought Winnipeg to its knees and many Commissionaires, their families and friends, together with the population of the city, rallied to defeat the menace. On June 25, 1950, the Board of Governors approved $1,000 to the Manitoba Flood Relief and there was a suggestion that a Disaster Fund be set up for future emergencies. This was not acted upon, however.

In his report of 1954, Colonel Pridham outlined the federal government policy of making the Divisions show that industrial firms using our services pay a higher rate over the current federal rate, to justify our request for a general increase by them.

The Middle Years 1954-1974

It is well in the course of this tale to pause and pay due compliments to a Commissionaire Extraordinaire. The gentleman singled out is our second Commandant, Colonel E.A. Pridham, MBE, MC, ED, who assumed his duties in 1941 until his retirement in 1970. During his tenure, Col Pridham's annual reports to the Division's Board were extremely comprehensive and personal as he guided the fledgling organization toward success and financial security.

Early on, our Commandant, who was also a Division Governor, became disturbed over Manitoba and other western Divisions not have voting representation on the National Board of Directors in Montreal and voiced strong criticism over what he perceived as a dictatorial body. In 1950 he reported that the situation had not changed, "However, I feel that the Politburo cannot hold on much longer." A motion by Col Oland of Halifax placed the Board of Directors on notice to allow more representation, and as a result the suggestion was taken under advisement by "the sacred 6" – the six national directors in the east. In 1954, after the President and Vice President had resigned, Col Oland and Col Pridham were elected to the National Board. He was honoured, but recorded in that year's report that, "I know the artfulness of the Directorate at Montreal and I recognize it (my election) serves a double purpose, as it effectively ends my 14 years of criticism."

To make way for rotational representation in the West, Colonel Pridham resigned from the National directorship in 1970. He was paid the following tribute:

> *His association with the Corps began in 1941 when appointed Commandant of Manitoba Division. He was elected to the National*

Board of Directors in 1954 where his experience and sound advice have been of the greatest value. His almost 30 years of devoted service has contributed greatly to the work of the Corps.

Colonel Pridham retired as Commandant in 1970, receiving a "coloured" television set from his Division colleagues. He remained on the Manitoba Board as Governor until his death in 1973, an extraordinary contributor to the Corps' cause.

On January 1, 1955, a special bond was formed with the city of Winnipeg Police. On that date, the services of 12 members of the Corps were acquired to enforce the Parking Meter By-law. With more than 1,600 meters erected throughout the city, the acquisition of Commissionaires released police officers for other duties. In subsequent years, as the installation of parking meters increased, so did the strength of the Corps assigned to this duty.

It is interesting to note in the book "100 Years of Service", a history of the Winnipeg Police Department published in the late 1970s, a photograph dated 1973 shows 23 Commissionaires attached to the police for traffic duties, and another picture dated the same year shows 3 Commissionaires with their trusty 3-wheeled steeds – members of the motorcycle patrol.

Our "family" relationship continues today with 46 Commissionaires assigned to parking enforcement and delivery of legal documents.

Manitoba has always kept in mind that the policy of the Corps was the re-establishment of the older veteran. It is interesting to note that, in 1958, the average age of Commissionaires in this Division was 63 years. Further, the Division has always maintained a substantial majority of its men in the employ of clients other than the Government of Canada. In 1958, the men of Manitoba Division were employed as follows: with the Dominion government 115; with other employers 187.

Delegates were accommodated at the landmark Hotel Fort Garry when Manitoba hosted the Dominon Annual General Meeting in September, 1955. Saturday, September 10 featured a sojourn by bus to the Motor Country Club at the "Capital of the Canadian West," Lower Fort Garry, where the Governors and their ladies were received and dined.

Until 1964, all Annual Board Meetings of the Division were held at the Manitoba Club adjacent to the Fort Garry Hotel, a 25-

Members of the Motorcycle Patrol.

year association. Since 1964, the Board has met annually at the St. Charles Country Club, but have returned to the Manitoba Club on a few splendid occasions such as the 1970 meeting of the National Body.

It was during the late 1950s that manpower (now called human resources) difficulties arose that continue to plague the Division today. Manitoba, as yet, is not considered a focal point for military retirees and there were consistent reports to the Governors of the day that, "We still face difficulties in getting sufficient men to meet demands." As late as 1973, during the 35th Annual Meeting of the Division, the Commandant reported "the ever present shortage of reliable men kept us constantly pressed to satisfy clients and we still cannot take on new jobs other than of a minor nature."

Another special connection was established in the 1960s with a valued client and a source of eligible candidates for the Corps, the Royal Canadian Mounted Police. In 1962 Chief Superintendent Cruikshank suggested that we contact the Department of Transport (DOT) to have Commissionaires replace some constables at Winnipeg International Airport. This was done, and the partnership continued at the airport for many years. In 1971, the RCMP ("D" Division) requested our Division assume custodial duties for their civilian guards throughout Manitoba. We were in favour of proceeding along the same lines as the Saskatchewan Divisions, i.e., on an administrative basis.

The 1960s brought the advent of government-imposed social benefits to working and non-working citizenry. These added financial burdens to the employer (the Division) generated considerable dismay as initially some government departments and clients balked at the additional billing expense. This was overcome in due course, but the cost of doing business increased dramatically.

The first benefit injection was the introduction of two weeks' vacation pay and the reduction of the work week from 48 to 44 hours, which resulted in an eight-hour day before overtime payout. Workmen's Compensation assumed on-job accident coverage, and in 1966 Unemployment Insurance and the Canada Pension Plan (CPP) completed the social safety net.

All of these encumbrances to our costs greatly helped the cause by improving the well-being of our Commissionaires. Corps administration increased ten-fold. We also increased these complications by bringing in a bi-weekly pay system. The year 1964 brought the surprise of paying rent for our co-habitation with the Department of Veterans Affairs which up to that time was zero. $200 per month was a shock. All of this created a "no pay raise" period of four years as adjustments were made.

As CPP catered to the needs of the Commissionaires under 70, the Division's Gratuity Fund was reduced to cover those aged over-70 only. By the end of 1966, the total sum of $136,079 had been paid out to deserving Commissionaires and by 1970 there were only 20 remaining who were entitled to receive monies from the fund.

During these busy years, the strength of the Division remained stable at 202 (1955), 220 (1960), 249 (1965), and 178 (1974). Over the same period dollars in revenue increased substantially–one-half million was reached in 1956 and the one million mark was attained in 1962. Col Pridham stated in 1962 that those who were involved in the early years of the Division's struggles never dreamed that revenues would reach such lofty plateaus. In fact, the pioneer stock found the situation downright unbelievable. During leaner times, the Governors regularly signed personal notes to the bank in order to meet the monthly payroll.

The Division always stressed quality in the recruit screening process, the needs of the client being uppermost. In 1964, the Corps assured prospective clients that the best man for the job would be provided to them. If any proved unsatisfactory, he would be replaced immediately, "even one who goes stale on the job over the years." One significant comment on our efficiency occurred in 1971 when Lieutenant Governor W.J. (Jack) McKeag, during the Annual Meeting, congratulated the Governors for being members of such an efficient organization. He had received a traffic ticket while attending the previous year's meeting, "so our men were on the job."

To emphasize the requirement to cater to the needs of the client, a negative comment was reported. A total of eight jobs had been lost as the client felt his needs were better served by younger and more vigorous men. This type of reaction generated some apprehension amongst those in office.

A statement of philosophy made during the 1971 National Meeting was fully debated by the Division's Executive Committee and is reported here for its significance:

> *As far as the (National) Board is concerned, we do not believe that the duty of the Corps is to perpetuate itself and if the day arrives where there is not a single veteran looking for work, our job is finished.*

We were divided on this one, and it was allowed to rest until later in this chronology.

In 1973, Divisional monetary awards to accompany national long service recognition were instituted. Awards parades had been conducted at HMCS Chippawa on an annual basis for several years. The monetary awards were one dollar for each year of service, to be paid out at the 10, 15, 20 and 25 year level. Fifteen years' service would therefore garner a $15 award. Later, the awards parades became difficult and the Executive Committee was informed that there was declining willingness amongst the men to give up a spare evening. It was decided to forego the event and have the Commandant make the presentations individually, or during small assemblies at the Divisional office.

An added and welcome benefit was realized in 1974 when uniform items such as tunics, trousers, hats and coats were to be issued without cost to the member. This meant that Divisional staff could demand a higher standard of dress because the Division owned the garments. Until this development, some men were inclined to "make-do," and threadbare uniforms were not uncommon. Later in this history, the Commandant of 1985, Colonel Ron Werry came to realize the importance of this decision. A certain Sergeant had twice been ordered to replace his uniform. Upon his demise, the widow conveyed her husband's wish to be interred in uniform. Approval was quickly given. When the Commandant approached the coffin during visitation, he was dismayed to see the stalwart Sergeant attired in his older uniform, the one (his wife maintained) he had paid for with his own earnings!

A parting story. WO I G.E. Lowe assumed Divisional Sergeant Major duties when Mr Bennett retired in 1968. As a Sergeant in 1945, he arranged to employ his son as a Commissionaire and it was his personal duty to subsequently dismiss the young man for insubordination. He was reinstated in 1975, and remained with Manitoba Division until his death in 1987.

The Current Years 1975-1997

During the decades previously reported, the shortage of recruits was mentioned as a major problem in the affairs of the Division. This condition continues to hamper the current years. In 1975, the deficiency was primarily due to two reasons: the demand for employees in the commercial world and the higher rate of pay; and lack of "suitable" recruits because of our low remuneration.

During 1975, a 28 percent increase in pay for our "other than federal" clients and 23 percent increase for federal agencies was successfully negotiated. The base pay jumped from $2.45 to $3 per hour.

In 1978, it was reported that three out of four applicants failed to meet our standards. In 1986, the Commandant reported that it was still "touch and go." During 1990, it was stated that "we did not aggressively pursue new clients as our problem continues to be in obtaining new, quality members, regardless of concentrated efforts."

Along with those benefits imposed by government legislation for which the Division contributes substantial sums, other assistance is provided by the Division. Free uniforms, including a parka which is essential during prairie winters, were introduced in 1976. In 1980, the blue hat was replaced by the readily identifiable Commissionaire white hat, along with epaulettes to be worn with the shirts. In 1981, we adopted an "expander" uniform produced by a Winnipeg firm, and a modified version of the original design is still being worn today.

A much needed benefit was initiated on June 1, 1988. A Group Life Insurance policy provides $10,000 to beneficiaries on the death of a Commissionaire, or double that amount for an accidental death. This insurance has been of inestimable assistance to families of deceased members. Bereavement Leave was introduced in 1995. These benefits were introduced slowly, as Commissionaires, previously consulted, preferred that additional costs not be charged to their pay accounts, nor our client competitive edge be disrupted.

The Gratuity Fund commenced in 1943 was dissolved in 1977 after paying out $220,500 during its tenure.

The following chart portrays salient statistics during 1975 to the present. Governors and Commandants, not too far into our past, would find the volume of business in these modern times difficult to comprehend. The figures in parentheses denote women which are included in the figure given.

Year	Basic Hourly Pay	Strength	Payroll (in millions)	Revenue (in millions)
1975	$3.00	274 (1)	1.7	1.9
1985	6.24	307 (8)	3.9	4.6
1992	7.50	498 (21)	6.4	8.0
1997	7.80	384 (22)	6.3	7.8

The column depicting our basic hourly wage over the years serves to back up the following declaration, usually pronounced by Division Operations & Training Officer Captain Gil Labine during our Basic Qualifying Course, "We are Commissionaires, not millionaires!"

During very early times, the Division was fortunate to share office space with the Department of Veterans Affairs in the Commercial Building, 169 Pioneer Avenue. This pleasant and very economical arrangement ended with the building being sold and later demolished. In 1985, the Division re-located to a nearby facility, which had previously housed an automobile dealership. We are now on our third five-year lease. The office overlooks the VIA Station, which appeals to Chief Warrant Officer Jack Rheaume and other railroad buffs. We can also observe the development of "The Forks," the historic confluence of the mighty and sometimes violent Red and Assiniboine Rivers.

The office is spacious and currently undergoing an expansion of computer capabilities.

In 1985, we laid down our quill pens and welcomed "Suzie," a microcomputer designed to absorb our general ledger and accounts receivable. Cost, $17,500. Our payroll was firstly handled by the Scotia Bank and later Comcheq.

In 1992, we welcomed our UNIX network with the wise counsel of Colonel Louis Joron and Major Christian Valet out of Montreal. Cost, $27,000. We were now capable of producing our payroll and invoices concurrently. This improved our cash flow immensely. The office is, at the time of writing, reconfiguring with more equipment. Cost, $17,000 in '97 dollars. These measures should take us into the new millennium.

A special occurrence must be recorded in our pages, and that is the unveiling of a national "Corps" film. In 1979, the lot fell to our Brigadier General Hugh Comack and his colleagues, Lieutenant General Gilles

Turcot of Montreal, and Colonel Marv Rich of Toronto, to produce this film. This was a task of mammoth proportions. The film was produced in the two official languages and became a valuable promotional tool for clients, potential clients, and Commissionaires. Many showings have been made since the preview at the Winter Club in Winnipeg in 1981. Hugh Comack's Manitoba colleagues were very appreciative of his efforts in bringing this project on line in record time and at reasonable cost. Brigadier General Comack was Chairman of our Division 1982-85, and National Chairman 1985-87.

Another Manitoba contribution to the national welfare was the Project 90 Committee. Struck in 1985 to ascertain where the Corps was going and what we would look like in the 1990s, this project was chaired by our own Lieutenant Colonel Bob Smellie and research was done at Brandon University by Dr. Tyler and associates. Their determinations were turned over to a National Planning Committee, which in turn assured all that the Corps was strong and would continue well into the next century. Lieutenant Colonel Bob Smellie was Chairman of Manitoba Division 1987-89, and National Chairman 1995-97.

Manitoba has always been a proponent of training, and from 1975 onward stressed this feature voluntarily until the Canadian General Standards Board (CGSB) made things mandatory. Our efforts started off slowly, with a four-hour training course in 1976. Attending Commissionaires received a $12 honorarium. By 1980, 93 percent of our force were trained. The course expanded to 8 hours in 1985 and 16 hours (two days) in 1986. The 40-hour (one week) CGSB course came on stream in 1987. The Division is 92 percent trained to the basic level, and has 56 qualified as Supervisors.

In 1982, a special group photograph was taken of our assembled Governors at the St. Charles Country Club during our Annual General Meeting. The corporal photographer made all the Generals and Colonels jump into line. The photo is shown, without names, but some readers may recognize more than a few faces.

It was at this meeting that a special resolution was sponsored by our Corps Solicitor, Lieutenant Colonel Lorne Campbell, that stipulated the disposal of our assets on dissolution and it is extracted as below:

Governors at 1982 Annual General Meeting.

Upon dissolution of the corporation and upon payment of all debts and liabilities, the remaining property of the corporation shall be distributed or disposed of to any organized or fully qualified registered charitable organization or organizations, the objects of which are beneficial to the Province of Manitoba, in such amounts as the Board of Directors shall recommend and the members approve.

In 1984 it was our privilege to hold our Annual Meeting and dinner at Government House, the residence of the Lieutenant Governor of Manitoba. It was at this event that our Chairman, Hugh Comack, presented a special Corps Long Service Medal to the Honourable Pearl McGonigal, who was attired in a knitted suit. Sensing some difficulties in "getting the thing pinned," the lady was heard to expound, "Get on with it, Hughie!"

In 1987 the Division hosted the National Annual General Meeting at the Westin Hotel (now The Lombard). Committees had been struck as early as 1984, so this event was most memorable, successful and well within budget. Numerous letters received by our Chairman, Lieutenant Colonel Jim Wilson, commented on the Memorial Service and the boat trip, including the programmed "late" transportation to dockside.

Earlier, we documented the need to enrol female Commissionaires for special duties at a munitions plant during the Second World War. When hostilities ceased, the women disappeared from the roster until the 1970s. Although eligible for enrolment through service credentials, times and circumstances were not conducive to permanent female representation in the Division. It was 1975 before the next female Commissionaire was enrolled and assigned to the radar station at Sioux Lookout, Ontario.

It was decided in 1991 to invite female representation on the heretofore all-male Board of Governors, as the significant contribution of women in uniform could no longer be discounted. Four women were elected to the Board that year – one each representing the Navy, Army, Air Force and Communications Branch. Two of these Governors now sit on the Executive Committee, and one occupies a Vice-Chair. The Division also has a former Lieutenant Governor of Manitoba as an elected Governor, Colonel the Honourable Pearl McGonigal. The "women of the 1990s" have arrived.

During the fiscal year 1996/97, we lost 24 positions as the Department of National

Chairman Hugh Cormack presenting Long Service Award to Lieutenant Governor of Manitoba, the Honourable Pearl McGonigal.

Defence, one of our largest, most valued clients, chose to remove Commissionaires from our four armouries and HMCS Chippawa. Electronic means and centralized response now replace our on-site human presence. On the winning side, we have participated in a major reorganization and subsequent increase in strength at our Winnipeg and Thunder Bay Airports. At CFB Shilo, we have gained a well-trained Emergency Services Dispatch Detachment and a Range Control Section. In Winnipeg, we now have a ten-member detachment at the new Federal Laboratory.

Highlighting the contributions of some special Commissionaires:

Chief Warrant Officer George Whitefield is our representative in Thunder Bay, Ontario and the only Commissionaire in this Division wearing the Corps Distinguished Service Medal. Manitoba Division was fortunate to obtain Mr Whitefield's services in December 1981. Up to that time, the Thunder Bay detachment was in a state of low morale and the image of the Corps was not impressive. George Whitefield rectified this situation with considerable enthusiasm and we now have well organized, credible representation in that region. Considerable personal sacrifice was made by this gentleman, above and beyond the faithful performance of duty. Truly, a Commissionaire Extraordinaire.

CWO George Whitefield.

Reporter Manfred Jager wrote a very special article for the *Winnipeg Free Press* in 1993. A photograph of three extraordinary Commissionaires accompanied the text. Left to right; Sergeant A. S. (Avion) Lelonde – This 12-year veteran of the Division is a well-recognized Commissionaire operating out of Kapyong Barracks on security patrol. He served with both the RCE and RCASC during 1940-45. Avion says, "Being part of the Corps has enriched my senior years beyond measure."

Sergeant A.J. (Jim) Hartle – Jim has been with the Division for 29 years, and during the last 16 years has overseen the main entrance to Kapyong Barracks, the home of the Second Battalion, Princess Patricia's Canadian Light Infantry. He has seen many Commanding Officers of the battalion pass through his portals over the years. Jim served as a gunner during the Second World War until his retirement in 1968, when he enrolled in the Corps.

Lelonde, Hartle and Hanna.

Corporal R.G. (Dick) Hanna – Dick joined the Corps in 1970 and was immediately placed at Winnipeg's airport. He was promoted to Corporal and appointed Detachment Commander from 1983-88. This gentleman was a gunner during the Second World War.

Captain F.S. (Fred) Dodd – was enrolled in 1978 and appointed Divisional Sergeant Major by the Commandant, Colonel Jock McManus. Mr Dodd had served with the 12th Manitoba Dragoons during the Second World War, and then with the Princess Patricia's Canadian Light Infantry. He attained the position of Regimental Sergeant Major of 1PPCLI, and finished his career as the Base Chief Warrant Officer at CFB Winnipeg. In 1987, Fred was promoted to Captain and appointed Division Operations and Training Officer. Captain Dodd left an indelible stamp on the performance and work ethic of this Division before his retirement in 1990.

Captain F.S. (Fred) Dodd.

Warrant Officer 1st Class K.J. (Ken) Poole – served 22 years with this Division, the last 15 years as Chief Dispatcher. He had been assigned to Revenue Canada (Taxation) before being selected for Divisional Staff. In 1987, he was appointed Senior Warrant Officer of the Division. Ken was very well known, and had the extraordinary talent of being able to recall the names and deployment of Commissionaires in Winnipeg, regardless of the hour.

The passage of the title Commandant has gone from Colonel J. (Jock) McManus, Royal Canadian Regiment, 1976-84, Colonel R.E. (Ron) Werry, a Queen's Own "Rifleman" 1980-97, and now to Colonel H.F. (Bert) Leggett on September 1, 1997. Manitoba Divisional Staff and Commissionaires, past, present or departed, must all be recognized for their contribution to the legacy which lives on today. The winds of change are in the air as the Manitoba Division seeks to meet the challenges and opportunities of the new millennia. Tremendous potential exists as more, younger, well-qualified former service personnel recognize the Corps of Commissionaires as a viable second career.

Colonel R.E. (Ron) Werry.

Chapter XI

HISTORY OF THE NOVA SCOTIA DIVISION

Commandant's Introduction – *Lionel Johns*

IT IS A GREAT pleasure and honour that I have been asked by the Chairman to write the introduction to the history of the Nova Scotia Division. Since the inception of the Division in 1937, the four previous Commandants contributed much to forming the operational visions and it is a difficult task to follow. Through their foresight and leadership the founding concepts of the Division were laid down which provide the guidance and philosophy that have led to the development of an outstanding Division.

For our organization to function effectively and efficiently, three critical elements are essential. The first is a viable and progressive Board of Governors who provide the policy and support so necessary for the Headquarters staff. The second is a cooperative and supportive Headquarters staff capable of implementing the policies of the Board of Governors, and the third is a group of well-trained motivated Commissionaires to perform the required duties. The Nova Scotia Division is blessed with these elements. We have a Board of Governors consisting of 16 distinguished and respected men and women who fully support the aims and objectives of the Division. They have the unique ability to assess the requirements of the Division and the Commissionaires throughout the province and implement policies affecting their needs. Our Headquarters staff are all experts in their own fields and they, too, are capable of implementing the Divisional policies in support of our personnel. We owe our history and our destiny to our past, present and future Commissionaires. They are the people who make our organization outstanding.

The Division has progressed in an above-average manner since its humble beginning in 1937 when we employed 20 Commissionaires to become the second largest Division in Canada with over 1,100 employees.

To quote from our Past Chairman, Colonel Malcolm Turner, CD, P.Eng., "The regard and esteem of the great body of the public for the Commissionaires has never fallen away; their name has become synonymous with honesty, sobriety, civility and good conduct. The Commissionaire is just that kind of reliable person that business houses require and ought to employ."

My sincere thanks go to all who helped compile this chapter. Sue Balint of Halifax deserves special recognition.

The Beginning

On instructions from the Veterans' Assistance Commission in Ottawa, the Montreal Veterans' Assistance Commission appointed a Committee to find a suitable person to act as President of the reorganized Canadian Corps of Commissionaires. They were fortunate in securing the services of Major General W.B.M. King, CMG, DSO, VD, a distinguished solider. In the summer of 1937, Major General King became aware of the necessity of establishing a Corps of Commissionaires in Halifax. Halifax had played a major role in the First World War and could expect to see even greater military activity with storm clouds brewing in Europe again. General King asked influential veterans in the city to form a new Division of the Corps.

Among the citizens who replied to General King's appeal was Lieutenant Colonel S.C. Oland, VD, CD, LLD, DEng, who served as Chairman of the meeting that led to the formation of the "H Division" of the Corps. At that meeting, a Board of Governors was elected. The members were Lieutenant Colonel T.E. Powers, DSO, VD, who agreed to act as Adjutant; Major W.C. Borrett, VD, appointed Assistant Adjutant and Secretary; Colonel A.N. Jones, VD, and Colonel L.M. MacKenzie, DSO, VD. Lieutenant Colonel S.C. Oland was the Division's first Commandant and first Chairman of the Board of Governors. The Division is indeed fortunate to have its original charter. It is included below in its original form.

An Act to Incorporate Nova Scotia Division of the Canadian Corps of Commissionaires
(Assented to the 7th day of April, A.D., 1955)

Be it enacted by the Governor and Assembly as follows:

1. *Sidney C. Oland, H.V. Darrett-Laing, William C. Borrett, L.H. MacKenzie, Alfred N. Jones and Victor deB. Oland all of Halifax, in the County of Halifax, Reginald E.G. Roome of Bedford, in the County of Halifax, A.L. Morfee of Granville Ferry, in the County of Annapolis, and Adrian Hope of Chester, in the County of Lunenburg, and such other persons as may from time to time become members of the corporation hereby incorporated, in accordance with its by-laws, are hereby created a body corporate under the name "Nova Scotia Division of the Canadian Corps of Commissionaires", hereinafter called "the corporation", having perpetual succession and the right to a common seal.*

2. The objects of the Corporation shall be to seek employment for worthy ex-servicemen and to create a genuine spirit of comradeship, mutual respect and assistance among them; to instill in the ex-servicemen for whom the Corporation may find employment the principles of service and efficiency and to perpetuate a wholehearted allegiance to Her Majesty the Queen and her successors: and generally to do all things necessary or convenient to the carrying out of the objects of the Corporation.

3. The Corporation shall not carry on for profit any trade, industry or business nor shall it be conducted for gain or profit but the Corporation shall be supported or maintained by such fees, assessments, contributions, benefactions and endorsements as its members shall determine to be necessary for its proper functioning.

4. The Corporation shall have power to:

   1. acquire all of the property, real or personal, now belonging to the Nova Scotia Division Of The Canadian Corps Of Commissionaires or now vested in Trustees for the benefit of the Nova Scotia Division Of The Canadian Corps Of Commissionaires;

   2. make, alter, amend or repeal by-laws, rules and regulations necessary or convenient to the carrying out o its objects, and for the conduct and management of its affairs and for any purpose incidental thereto;

   3. acquire and take by purchase, donation, devise, bequest or otherwise, real estate and personal property, and hold, enjoy, sell, exchange, lease, let, improve and develop the same, and erect and maintain buildings and structures;

   4. contract and be contracted with and sue or be sued in its corporate name;

   5. use of its funds and property for the attainment of its objects and purposes;

   6. borrow, raise and secure the payment of money in such manner as it thinks fit, and issue debentures or mortgage its real property to secure the payment of money borrowed by it;

   7. subject to its by-laws draw, make, accept, endorse, discount, execute and issue promissory notes, bills of exchange and other negotiable or transferrable instruments;

   8. do all such other acts and things as are incidental or conducive to or consequential upon the exercise of its powers or the attainment of its objects.

5. No member of the Corporation shall, in his individual capacity, be liable for any debt or liability of the Corporation unless he shall have made himself personally liable therefore.

The Halifax Division (which would become the Nova Scotia Division in 1952) officially opened for business on January 24, 1938 when Sergeant Major James Shiels, the Division's first Commissionaires, volunteered to assist Colonel Powers in operating the Division.

Twenty men, all of them former members of the permanent force, were enrolled as Commissionaires. They were told to report each morning

Col S.C. Oland, VD, CD.

Col W.C. Borrett, VD, CD.

LCol T.E. Powers, DSO, VD.

for available work. Initially, the Commissionaires of the Halifax Division received only odd assignments, averaging one or two days of work each week, to supplement their pensions. Gradually, more permanent positions were found for each man with local firms. The business community began to realize the pool of talented and disciplined men the Corps had to offer.

When the Division used to borrow the money required for the payroll of the Commissionaires, Lieutenant Colonel S.C. Oland guaranteed the loan with his own personal bank account.

The Division grew quickly in its early years. The progress, however, was interrupted by the outbreak of the Second World War. The demand for the services of the Corps slackened. Moreover, many veterans who were eligible to join the Corps found themselves again in a military uniform. Most became members of the Veterans Guard of Canada, although some who had been very young men during the First World War were accepted by the Army, Navy and Air Force.

Meanwhile, a small group of remaining Commissionaires carried on. During the Second World War, the opportunity was taken to show the Commissionaire's uniform by having them march, alongside many other patriotic organizations, whenever a public parade was organized.

After the cessation of hostilities in 1945, prospects for the Corps of Commissionaires were immeasurably enhanced when the federal govern-

Sgt Major Shiels – One of Nova Scotia's First Commissionaires.

ment authorized the formation of the War Assets Corporation. Especially in demand were security guards. This meant a tremendous boost in recruiting and many veterans of the armed forces enlisted in the Division.

Below is a summary of the Nova Scotia Division's strength since its inception.

Year	1937	1947	1957	1967	1977	1987	1997
Strength	20	416	435	735	803	1,011	1,112

In 1991, the Nova Scotia Division passed all expectations when its strength peaked at nearly 1,300 Commissionaires. The increase was due to the outbreak of hostilities in the Persian Gulf on January 16. There was a dramatic increase in security requirements primarily at federal government establishments and the Division provided 65 new positions within the first 28 days of conflict. With the conclusion of hostilities and an economic recession, the Division strength fell to 1,247 on 31 March, 1992.

Recent Years

The Division has introduced a number of modern advances that have made operations more efficient over the years. As early as 1969, the Division was looking into the purchase of computerized equipment. That year, an electronic payroll machine was installed to aid the finance staff in the increasing amount of work required of them. In the past decade, the Division introduced a computerized system to perform administrative tasks and the Finance Department upgraded its computer system with new state-of-the-art equipment. A picture identification card was also implemented so that Commissionaires could be easily identified by employers and customers.

Financially, the Division has encountered some obstacles in recent years. In 1992, the Maritime Premiers introduced a Maritime Procurement Agreement that required all services over $50,000 be tendered. The agreement had an impact on the operations of the Nova Scotia Division. It meant that contracts for security began to be awarded on the basis of cost rather than quality. The Division lost some provincial contracts which attributed to a decline in strength. The gross revenue of the Corps that year, however, continued to escalate and reach the 22 million dollar mark with over 21 million dollars being paid out in wages and benefits to the Commissionaires.

The Division has continued to prosper well into the 1990s and is earning employment at more private firms in order to compensate for government cutbacks. The Corps presently holds 59.6% of its contracts with private firms and 40.4% with government agencies. For the 1997 fiscal year, the Corps' gross revenue was $19,154,088, including wages and benefits.

Division Headquarters

Since its formation, the Nova Scotia Division has occupied a number of residences. In 1937, temporary offices were secured in Glacis Barracks, a collection of buildings that had been the home of Imperial Troops garrisoning the city in the previous century.

The first move of Headquarters was to Broadcasting House on Tobin Street. The old building had served many purposes over the years. Originally a church, it had also been occupied by several businesses, including radio station CHNS and a popular dance hall known as "The Bagdad."

The next move was to 310 Barrington Street, a three-storey brick and frame former dwelling that was purchased by the Division in 1949. The building's original state was maintained to preserve the cove and scrollwork plaster ceilings, walnut woodwork and four Italian marble fireplaces. The provincial government eventually took over the property and other properties in the area to make way for the expanding Nova Scotia Technical College. The building had served its purpose, but something more suitable was needed for the growing Division. A Halifax landmark would be the next Headquarters.

When the Commissionaires moved into Black-Binney House on Hollis Street in 1966, they acquired not only a national historic site, but in the opinion of many, the finest Headquarters of any Corps in Canada. After a fire in the building in 1965, the Corps recognized that it could be restored. Colonel S.C. Oland purchased the building and it was renovated to its original splendour with advice from the Department of Indian Affairs and Northern Development.

According to the North British Society, the three-storey Black-Binney House was built around 1819 by prominent Haligonian John Black, senior member of the shipping firm Black, Forsythe & Co. Black, being one of the most renowned Scottish merchants in the city, brought granite used in the construction from Aberdeen, Scotland.

Black's son-in-law, the Honourable James Boyle-Uniacke, Premier of Nova Scotia from 1848-54, lived in the house until about 1856. From then until 1887, the house was occupied by the Anglican Bishop of Nova Scotia, the Right Reverend Hibbert Binney.

On July 6, 1967, Doctor Stanley Haidasz,

Black Binney House.

then Parliamentary Secretary to the Minister of Indian Affairs and Northern Development, unveiled a plaque on the exterior of the house commemorating it as a National Historic Site. At the same time, a plaque was unveiled by Colonel S.C. Oland dedicating the house to the service of veterans.

On January 28, 1982, the Black-Binney House was registered as a city of Halifax historic property and was registered as a Municipal heritage property on 14 December, 1989. The "Historic Room" in Black-Binney House remains open to the public today.

Recreation

While records do not show an organized recreation association within the Nova Scotia Division, there are many accounts in the annual reports of money being put aside for movies and other forms of entertainment for Corps members. Throughout the years, money has also been budgeted to provide for gifts of magazines, candy and cigarettes to sick personnel. Wreaths and messages of condolences have also been sent to the families of deceased Corps members.

The Commissionaire

First published in January 1957, *The Commissionaire* is the official publication of the Nova Scotia Division. It aims to keep members and employers informed on events, appointments and other relevant news.

In the first edition of the newsletter, an editorial from the *Halifax Herald* entitled "Spit and Polish" was reproduced. The editorial emphasized how "spit and polish" parade smartness, as well as group and individual discipline, had played and continued to play an important role in the training of the British Army's famous Guards Brigade. In a footnote to the editorial, the editor of *The Commissionaire* wrote; "The Canadian Corps of Commissionaires is one unit which has greatly benefitted by the use of 'Spit and Polish.' No other organization has a better reputation for Cleanliness, Smartness and Discipline. That is why Government Departments, the Armed Services and many large firms are proud to employ their services. Reliability and Spit and Polish go together."

Annual Parades/Medals Presentation Ceremonies

The first annual parade of the Nova Scotia Division was held in 1939. The Inspecting Officer that year was Lieutenant Colonel T.E. Powers. Preceded by a church service, the parades were designed to provide an opportunity to show off the uniform of the Commissionaires and raise public awareness. Over the years, noteworthy officials of national and international prestige have served as Inspecting Officers including Lieutenant Governors, Premiers of Nova Scotia, city mayors and senior military officers.

During the Annual Parade in 1967 Colonel S.C. Oland presented the Nova Scotia Division Corps colours. It was decorated with the Corps badge and inscribed with the words "Nova Scotia Division, Canadian Corps of Commissionaires." Crowns represented the services in which members previously served and the fact that the Corps had the Vice-Regal Patronage of the Governor General and Lieutenant Governor. The flag was composed of the Corps' colours, with gold decoration. Lieutenant Colonel the Reverend Gordon Darragh (United Church) and Captain the Reverend George Hooper (Roman Catholic) were called upon to give the blessing of the Colours at the inspection. It was a proud day for Corps members who finally saw their flag flown.

Nova Scotia Corps Colours.

In 1993, after 54 years of tradition, the Corps' Annual Parade and Inspection was replaced by an Awards Dinner and Dance. The event exceeded all expectations and was attended by over 500 Governors, clients, Commissionaires and their spouses and friends. The event has since become an annual tradition and also provides a proper ceremony to present Long Service Medals and other awards.

Women in the Division

In October 1972, Colonel J.M. Kinnaird, OC, CD welcomed Mrs Elsie Herman, the first woman to be inducted into the Corps in Nova Scotia. By the spring of 1975, six women were working full time in the Corps and a seventh was employed part time. Their details were for work in the Pay Office and Orderly Room at Headquarters as well as at the Teacher's College in Truro and Dalhousie University's Killam Library.

In 1982, Commander Isabel Janet MacNeil, OC, OBE, LLD, was the first woman to be appointed to the Nova Scotia Division's Board of Governors. Commander MacNeil had previously served in the Women's Royal Canadian Navy Reserve during the Second World War and later commanded *HMCS Conestoga*, the training establishment for WRENS in Galt, Ontario. She also served as superintendent of the Prison for Women in Kingston, Ontario.

Commander (W) Isabel J. MacNeil.

Of the many women to join the Corps, several have followed in the footsteps of family members. Commissionaire Elsie Marie Alain's family has long been dedicated to service. In the December 1988 issue of *The Commissionaire* she was pictured alongside her proud father, Commissionaire A.D. Gabriel and husband, Sergeant J.F.J. Alain.

Currently, the longest serving female Commissionaire is MWO Mary M. Elias. Mary joined the Corps in March 1973 and has worked at various details including the Halifax International Airport where she walked to work from Dartmouth (a distance of 30 kilometres) on and off over 42 months for a salary of $1.85 per hour. She is presently the Orderly Room Clerk at Headquarters House.

Female strength has continued to grow in recent years. By 1997, 57 women were working as Commissionaires in the Nova Scotia Division.

The Alain's.

MWO Mary M. Ellias.

Training

During the early 1970s, the Department of Supply and Services determined that security standards must be upgraded. The September 1977 issue of *The Commissionaire* outlined new training standards for the Corps and by that time seven Basic Security Courses had already been held by the Nova Scotia Division. Running for four days each, the courses covered patrolling and surveillance, emergency measures, fire safety, crowd control and bomb threats among other topics. A course in first aid was also taught by the St. John Ambulance Brigade.

Effective April 1, 1988, there was a requirement to train all prospective Commissionaires in accordance with the Canadian General Standards Board. A new training plan was developed and the first course commenced on April 11 of that year.

Today, Corps members receive thorough training that is highly respected. As a commendation of this excellence, the First Nations chose the Division to train its security force at the Indian Brook Band Reserve in Shubenacadie in 1993. Eight students completed the two-week course.

On-the-job training is emphasized for the Division's Commissionaires. In addition to the training that the Corps offers, many members undergo additional training specific to the detail to which they have been assigned. Recent annual reports list training that is now provided by the Division. The list includes an array of skills from St. John Ambulance courses to training in note taking, traffic control, search techniques and induction training.

Uniforms/Quartermaster Operations

Originally, Commissionaires were required to purchase their own uniforms upon entering the Corps. In 1974, the uniforms became an allowable expense and were issued free of charge to members upon enrolment. They could be replaced after every two years of service. This system allowed Commissionaires to always look their best and smartest when on parade or at their detail. The uniform includes a tunic with belt and buckle, two pairs of trousers, one lanyard with whistle, one cap with braid and badge, one leather belt with buckle, one tie and one monsoon raincoat. In addition, the Division provides another uniform more in line with civilian dress. It consists of a blazer, grey flannels and a Corps tie.

In the past, the Quartermaster also supplied an alternate uniform to members serving at Citadel Hill in Halifax. The January 1964 issue of *The Commissionaire* pictured members of the Corps wearing special uniforms for tourists. During the daily firing of the noon day gun on Citadel Hill, Corps members dressed in the Victorian period uniform of the Corps, complete with feathered hats. The men became a landmark themselves for visitors to Halifax and contributed towards the respectability and good name of the Corps.

Commissionaires in Victorian age uniform firing Halifax Citadel noon-day gun.

Other Commissionaire Benefits

Life insurance has been in place for Division Commissionaires since 1948. The plan, however, only covered members under 65 years of age. In 1969, the plan was expanded to cover all members in the amounts of $3,000 for those under 65 and $1,500 for those 65 years of age and older. By 1997, coverage had grown to $5,000.

During the 1950s and 60s, there are also records of contributions being made toward accident and liability insurance, vacation pay and bonus awards for 10 and 15 Year Medals to members of the Corps.

In 1988, the Nova Scotia Division introduced Workers' Compensation benefits for its members. The purpose of obtaining this no-fault insurance was to provide income security for Commissionaires injured while on duty.

In the same year, the Division also became a volunteer member of the Federal Government Employment Equity Program, an affirmative action plan, which provided equal rights for women, aboriginal people, disabled persons and visible minorities. This was an obvious step to take considering that the original eight British Commissionaires in 1859 had all lost an arm in the Crimean War or the Indian Mutiny.

Strength

Strength of the Division has declined slightly since its peak in 1992. This is due in part to veteran strength which has obviously decreased to a very small number. As late as 1980, 75% of the entire Division had served in the Second World War and/or the Korean War, but by 1997, only 6.8% of the Division's members were veterans. To compensate, many Commissionaires have been taken on with a background of service in the United Nations or International Peacekeeping Commissions. In 1997, 25.6% of the Division's Commissionaires were veterans or had served in a peace organization.

ISO 9002

A recent accomplishment of the Division was recognition as the first security company in North America to achieve ISO 9002 registration from the International Standard Organization. The ISO was founded in Geneva, Switzerland in 1946. Its purpose is to promote the development of international standards and related activities, including conformity assessment to facilitate the exchange of goods and services within the European Union (EU).

In recent years, the United States entered into the ISO movement. Subsequently, Canada joined the ISO movement and in September 1996, the Division commenced the certification process. On May 27, 1997, the Division was audited and was granted registration as an ISO company with a quality management system meeting the requirements of ISO 9002.

Board of Governors – 1988.

Fiftieth Anniversary Celebrations

In 1988, the Division celebrated its fiftieth anniversary. The Lieutenant Governor, the Honourable Alan G. Abraham, CD, DEng, hosted a reception for the Board of Governors at Government House. The Commandant during the celebrations was Colonel A.E. MacAskill, CD. It was a year to celebrate. The Corps strength had reached 1,175 and was now the second largest in Canada.

Special Recognitions - Commissionaires Extraordinaire

Over the years, the Nova Scotia Division has distinguished itself for having a group of hardworking, dedicated members. The Corps' records are filled with accounts of awards and honours. In 1978, six members of the Corps were recipients of the Queen's Jubilee Medal on the occasion of the 25th Anniversary of the ascension of Her Majesty to the throne. Seven members of the Board of Governors have received the Order of Canada. They are Brigadier the Honourable Victor deB Oland, OC, ED, CD, DCL, LLD, DLITT; Commander Isabel J. MacNeil, OC, OBE, LLD; Colonel J.E.Harris Miller, CM, CD, MDCM, QHP; Flying Officer F.M. Covert, OC, OBE, DFC, QC; Colonel John M. Kinnaird, CM, CD; Rear Admiral D.W. Piers, DSC, CM, CD, RCN (Ret'd); and Lieutenant Colonel the Honourable Alan R. Abraham, CD, DEng.

Commissionaire Bernard N. Campbell also made the Nova Scotia Division proud by reaching a historic milestone on September 28, 1990. On that date he retired after serving with the Division for 44 years. At that time, he was the longest serving member of the Corps in Canada.

Many Commissionaires have received commendation during their details on the bridges linking Halifax and Dartmouth. The bridges have long been a site for suicide attempts in the area and many Corps members have been on the scene to intervene and save lives.

W.O. J. Campbell receiving his medal from Col. J.H. Turnbull.

In 1986, WO I Richard Hector Campbell, CD, Second in Command of the Halifax-Dartmouth Bridge Detail was called on for assistance when it was reported that a young man had climbed down to a bridge platform and was preparing to jump. Police lowered Campbell down alongside the would-be-jumper where he was able to persuade the young man to climb to safety. As a result of his exemplary action, WO I Campbell was presented with the Meritorious Service Award by Colonel J.H. Turnbull, OMM, CD, Second Vice Chairman of the National Board of Governors. This was only the second presentation of this award throughout the history of the Corps in Canada.

During the following years, many other Commissionaires were instrumental in convincing jumpers to cease their suicide attempts. They were Sergeant J.H.L. Carmen, CD; Staff Sergeant J.K. Johns; Sergeant L.E. Mayo, CD; and Sergeant J.J. Power. All were awarded the Meritorious Service Medal for their actions.

SSgt Johns and Sgt Carmen.   Sgt Mayo.   Sgt Power.

Sgt Rollings.

Sergeant J. Rollings was the most recent Corps member to receive a Meritorious Service Medal while on bridge detail. In November 1996, he responded to a report that a young woman was straddling the rail of the Angus L. MacDonald Bridge. With no hesitation toward risking his own life, Sergeant Rollings managed to edge up beside the woman while talking to her. When the woman made an attempt to jump over the rail, he was able to grab her around the waist and pull her to safety. He was aided in the rescue by Constable Gallant of the Halifax Regional Police.

Sergeant Robert R. Bennett, MB, CD, the NCO in charge of the Corps Detail at CFB Cornwallis was commended for saving the life of Arnold Andrews from the waters of Mulgrave Lake in the Cornwallis area. He was presented with the Medal of Bravery by our Patron-in-Chief, Her Excellency, The Right Honourable Jeanne Sauve, PC, CC, CMM, CD, at an Investiture Ceremony in Ottawa at Government House on November 10, 1989. Mr Andrews, an asthmatic bronchitis victim and sufferer of heart problems, was in a boat on September 16, 1988. Overcome by exertion, he slumped to the bottom of the boat which had a disabled motor. Sergeant Bennett was out jogging when he saw Mr Andrews was in serious trouble. He removed his outer garments and swam for 30 minutes to reach the boat. Using a broken oar, he then sculled the craft to shore. Carrying the weakened victim, he walked a distance of one and a half miles back to Mr Andrews' truck where medication and life-saving equipment was available. Sergeant Bennett brought credit to both himself and the Corps with his brave act. He was also awarded the Meritorious Service Medal by the Corps for his actions.

Sgt Robert Bennett, MB, CD, receiving the "Medal of Bravery" from Her Excellency The Right Honourable Jean Sauve, PC, CC, CCM, CD.

A Commissionaire Extraordinaire of another sort was recorded in the December 1974 issue of *The Commissionaire*. At the Bedford Institute of Oceanography, a German Shepherd wandered onto the grounds and formed a lasting relationship with the Commissionaires employed there. At first, "Lady" was near starvation, but the Commissionaires took good care of her and she returned their kindness by taking on their duties as her own. Lady learned to identify the Commissionaires by their uniforms and began conducting rounds alongside the members on duty. So seriously did she take her job that when Sergeant Merritt once deliberately missed one of his punching stations, Lady began barking and running back and forth until he retraced his steps and punched the missing station. Over her years of service, Lady made a lasting impression on every Corps member stationed at the Bedford Institute and typified the role of the Commissionaire Extraordinaire.

The Board Of Governors

In 1985, the Division mourned the passing of Brigadier General R.E.G. Roome, CBE, VD. He had been a member of the Board of

From Left to Right: BGen R.E.G. Roome, BGen V.deB. Oland, Col. L.H. MacKenzie and Col. S. Oland.

Governors since 1952. An Artillery Officer, he had served during the First World War in France and Mesopotamia, attached to the 14th Indian Division. In the Second World War, Lieutenant Colonel Roome took the 5th Field Regiment overseas. Promoted to Brigadier, he returned to Canada to command the 7th Division Field Artillery. Brigadier Roome was also part of one of the most interesting stories to come out of the Nova Scotia Division.

On Armistice Day, 1918, his unit, the 2nd Canadian Heavy Battery, was located in the Mons area. A member of the unit purchased a bottle of Veuve Clicquot Ponsardin champagne in Mons. The bottle was inscribed: "To The Last Man." The bottle passed into the custody of Brigadier Roome for safekeeping. In 1918, his unit had a strength of over 220, but in 1979, only 13 former members were alive. The bottle was placed in the Army Museum at Halifax waiting to be claimed by the last survivor of the 2nd Canadian Heavy Battery. The betting was that, when opened, the bottle would be found to contain vinegar instead of wine. When the company responsible for producing the champagne heard the story, Brigadier Roome, the last man, was sent a new bottle of the same brand so that the original bottle might be preserved.

Maj Thomas W, Bauld, National Chairman.

Other members of the Board of Governors have brought honour to the Division. A proud moment in Division history occurred in 1968, when the Prime Minister's Office in Ottawa announced that Brigadier Victor deB Oland would succeed the Honourable H.P. MacKeen as Lieutenant Governor of Nova Scotia. Brigadier Oland had been a member of the Board of Governors for 15 years.

Two other members of the Division's Board of Governors have served as Lieutenant Governor of Nova Scotia: Major E.C. General Plow, CBE, DSO, CD, DCL, DMS and Lieutenant Colonel Alan R. Abraham.

Another member of the Nova Scotia Board of Governors, Major Thomas W. Bauld, CD, FRAIC, was appointed National Chairman of the Canadian Corps of Commissionaires Board of Governors at the Annual General Meeting in Vancouver, June 19-21, 1997 and will serve for a two-year period. He is the first National Chairman from the Division since the Corps' inception. Major Bauld has contributed over 35 years as a member of the Nova Scotia Division Board of Governors.

The Board of Governors has been privileged to have three generations of the Oland family serve, beginning with Colonel S.C. Oland, VD, CD, LLD, DEng.; his two sons, Brigadier The Honourable Victor deB Oland, OC, ED, CD, DCL, LLD, DLITT and Commodore Bruce S. Oland, ED, CD, DCNL; and Bruce's son, Lieutenant Commander Richard H. Oland, CD. Sidney, Victor and Bruce all served a term as Chairman of the Board of Governors.

National Annual General Meeting

The Nova Scotia Division has hosted four National Annual General Meetings over the Corps history in Canada. The first event took place in 1953 at the Lord Nelson Hotel. The second General Meeting was in 1967 at the Citadel Inn. The annual report for that year records that the meeting was a notable success, garnering compliments and letters of gratitude from across the country.

In 1979, the Division once again hosted the General Meeting from June 21-23 at the Chateau Halifax under the Chairmanship of Brigadier the Honourable Victor deB Oland. The Chairman for the Planning Committee was Colonel J.E. Harris Miller. Some of those attending were Premier John Buchanan and Lieutenant Governor the Honourable John E. Shaffner.

Again in 1994, the Division, under the command of Colonel Malcolm Turner, hosted the National Annual General Meeting at the Halifax Sheraton Hotel from June 16-19. Commodore Bruce S. Oland was the Chairman of the Planning Committee that year. By all accounts, it was superb.

Community Involvement

Members of the Nova Scotia Division have always done their part to participate in volunteer community work during their spare time. The November 1975 issue of *The Commissionaire* reported on two such men; Lieutenant D.D. Harvey who volunteered as a member of the Big Brothers Association, and Colonel J.M. Kinnaird who volunteered at the Izaak Walton Killam Hospital for Children.

The November 1977 issue of *The Commissionaire* featured Commissionaire Dan McLeod and his wife, Peggy, who were awarded the Province of Nova Scotia Award for Exemplary Voluntary Work that year. The McLeods raised five foster children in addition to six children of their own. They also gave temporary homes to nearly 100 other youngsters during their years of community service. The McLeods did much for the good name of the Corps through their relentless dedication to the welfare of youth.

In the past few years, the Corps has continued its good work in the community. In 1995, Captain Harold (Sandy) Sanford distinguished himself as the first person in Nova Scotia to donate 300 pints of blood to the Red Cross, earning the nickname "The Lake." *The Commissionaire* for that year also records that many members of the Corps donated their time to the "jail and bail" fundraiser run by the Canadian Cancer Society.

Clients

As soon as the Nova Scotia Division was established, businesses began to hire members for their security needs. The Corps' discipline and devotion to duty made it a preferred provider of security services and many of the province's businesses would become long time supporters.

In 1991, the Division entered the top 150 employers in the Atlantic Provinces. Nova Scotia's universities, including Dalhousie, Mount Saint Vincent, St. Mary's, Acadia and University College of Cape Breton, all employ Commissionaires at various posts. The Halifax International Airport continues to hire Corps members for security work. Many of the Commissionaires posted there have been able to speak two, three or, in some cases, four languages. The Halifax Dockyard and bridges from Halifax to Dartmouth also hire many Corps members. Some of the larger corporations to use the Division's services are the Halifax International Airport, Kimberley Clark Nova Scotia Inc., and Maritime Tel & Tel. Corps members also provided security for the G-7 Conference when it was held in Halifax in 1995.

In addition to regular duties, the Commissionaires have also been called on for special details from time to time. One of the most memorable details was a 1967 request by MT&T, who needed a Santa Claus for their annual Christmas party. The Adjutant at the time was more than happy to play the role. Several relief Commissionaires were also hired for the party.

CHAIRMEN OF THE BOARD OF GOVERNORS
Nova Scotia Division

Colonel S.C. Oland, VD, CD, LLD, DEng	1937-1971
Major General The Hon. E.C. Plow, CBE, DSO, CD, DCL, DMS	1971-1974
Brigadier The Hon. V. deB Oland, OC, ED, CD, DCL, LLD, DLITT	1974-1982
Colonel J.E.H. Miller, CM, CD, MDCM, QHP	1982-1985
Major T.W Bauld, CD, FRAIC	1985-1988
Rear Admiral D.W. Piers, DSC, CM, CD, D.ScMil, RCN (Ret' d)	1988-1991
Colonel Malcolm Turner, CD, P.Eng	1991-1994
Group Captain E.L. Baudoux, DSO, DFC, CD	1994-1996
Commodore Bruce S. Oland, ED, CD, DCNL	1996-1997
Colonel J.E. Terry, CD, P.Eng	1997-

COMMANDANTS
Nova Scotia Division

Colonel S.C. Oland, VD, CD, LLD, DEng	1937-1955
Lieutenant Colonel T.E. Powers, DSO, VD, Vice-Commandant	1937-1952
Colonel W.C. Borrett, VD, JP	1955-1968
Colonel J.M. Kinnaird, CD	1968-1979
Colonel R.S. Scholey, MBE, CD	1979-1986
Colonel A.E. MacAskill, CD	1986-1990
Colonel L.R. Johns, CD	1991

Chapter XII

HISTORY OF THE NORTHERN ALBERTA DIVISION

Commandant's Introduction – *By Brian Craig*

IN SERVING this vast area, we provide services similar to those provided by other Divisions ranging from the one person security guard up to plant safety and security at large manufacturing complexes. Between these two extremes, one finds mobile and foot patrols for the city of Edmonton and base security at the growing Canadian Armed Forces base at Namao.

The challenge facing the Northern Alberta Division is to fully utilize its existing resources while continuing to operate under strict budgetary guidelines. Additional resources acquired must show either an immediate or long-time benefit. We must ensure that existing client needs are addressed while at the same time ensuring that new clients are added to our client base.

Our strength lies in the continued diversity of our personnel. The increasing level of technical abilities that newly acquired personnel often bring to the Corps gives us the ability to meet the demands of an expanding client base whose needs are, in some cases, becoming more and more sophisticated. Making this expanded level of expertise available to our existing clients, to those newly acquired and to those sought after, will allow us to continue to fulfill our mission statement.

Special thanks to Art Maskell and all others who worked so hard to produce this chapter.

Major S.C.S. Kerr, KC.

The Early Years

On September 5, 1939, the Canadian Corps of Commissionaires activated the

Col. L. Scott, DCM.

Left to Right: J.P. McCarthy, J.T. Ferguson and W.R. Blythman.

Edmonton Division. Major S.C.S. Kerr, KC who served with distinction during the First World War, became the first Chairman of the Board of Governors.

Another famous Edmonton soldier, Col L. Scott, DCM, who was one of the original members of the Princess Patricia's Canadian Light Infantry during the First World War, assumed the duties of the first Commandant. Other members of the first Board of Governors were: Vice Chairman, Major W.A. de Graves, DSO; Adjutant and Secretary, A. Menzies, and paymaster, Lt Col T.C. Simms, VD.

The first Commissionaires hired were J.P. McCarthy, J.T. Ferguson and W.R. Blythman, shown in this photograph.

Those involved with the Corps today may find it interesting to review the duties and services outlined in an article written in the *Edmonton Bulletin* in their issue dated August 26, 1939.

> *In smart blue uniforms with the badges of their Corps on cap and cross-belt, the first unit of the Canadian Corps of Commissionaires in Edmonton is now on duty, and shortly, a night patrol and property protection service will be at the disposal of Edmonton Citizens. The night patrol service, carried out under supervision by hand picked ex-servicemen with the best of records, will include an hourly visit from 6 p.m. to 6 a.m. In the case of business premises, the front and back doors are examined and a watch is kept on outside windows and transoms. The service in the residential sections includes patrolling front and back of homes, and where the subscribers leave the house vacant for even a short period, all doors, windows, etc., are carefully watched and checked. In addition, where a subscriber requests that a member of the family be escorted from the bus or streetcar lines at night, this service is also performed.*

Commissionaires will be available for the following positions:

messengers, bank guards, caretakers (house or works), club porters, club stewards, watchmen (day or night), elevator attendants, janitors, inquiry clerks, receptions clerks, turnstiles attendants, postal clerks, door attendants, telephone attendants, storekeepers, gate keepers, ticket takers, staff supervisors, time keepers, utility men, stokers (ex-Royal Navy) weighmen. Men are also available (in large or small numbers) at short notice, for duty at: conventions, theatres, weddings, dances, receptions, sports meetings, road controls, night patrols, agricultural shows, flower shows, board meetings, auction sales, tourists, guide, baseball matches, exhibitions, race meetings. There was no end to their talents!!

The first available record of any meeting of the Board of Governors was March 28, 1947, held at the MacDonald Hotel with his Honour Judge Kerr, Lt Col Strickland, Mr T. Anderson, Mr R. Steele and Col L. Scott in attendance. All Corps records prior to this date were lost, and only sketchy reports are available through archival material. For example, an article in the June 28, 1940 issue of the *Edmonton Journal* advised of a full dress inspection of the Canadian Corps of Commissionaires to be held that Saturday, and also included the Corps had agreed to provide nine men to guard the premises of the Air Observers' School that soon would be completed at the city airport. A reasonable assumption would be that Commissionaires fulfilled many duties of that nature during the war years.

Records of meetings in the 1940s indicated recurrent problems with finances and personnel. The following is an excerpt from a report written by Mr A.R. Gillies regarding personnel:

Our great difficulty is in securing the class of men our work requires – at one time men of 60 to 70 were acceptable but now younger men are required and older men must be withdrawn. The younger men today will not work for $1.00 per hour and older men cannot hold up their end to earn it.

In spite of such difficulties, manpower figures for the 1940s decade range from 60 men on June 28, 1940, to 166 men on June 4, 1947, then down again to 87 men on July 25, 1948.

Financial problems stemmed from the fact that, at the time, federal government projects were money losing efforts, while only a small margin of profit was being made on civilian contracts. As a result, the 1940s ended with a deficit, but with the exception of fiscal year 1991-92, the Northern Alberta Division has posted a surplus ever since.

Name and Numbers

The Edmonton Division of the Canadian Corps of Commissionaires retained that title until September, 1972, when it was re-designated the Northern Alberta Division. The number of personnel fluctuated considerably in the early years until 1965. At this time, a strength of 420 was reached, and that number has remained reasonably constant, from a low of 305 in March 1995 to a high of 452 in December 1988.

Accommodation

Over the years, the Edmonton/Northern Alberta Division has had several changes in location. The first office was situated in the Massey Harris building and after a stay of approximately nine years, the Department of Public Works requested that a move be made to the Department of Veterans' Affairs building. This move was effected in 1948, followed by a move to the Federal Building in 1958. These early accommodations were rent-free until the late '60s, at which time it was decided to rent privately owned accommodations in the Sprague Building on 109 Street. The continuous search for adequate office and training facilities prompted three further moves, until finally, in 1994, it was decided that it would be financially advisable to purchase accommodation. The present location at 10633-124 Street, is a two-storey building that provides finely appointed offices with the necessary training space, and some revenue from tenants who lease the top floor.

Headquarters Office 10633-124 Street, Northern Alberta Division.

First Ladies

In March 1973, five women entered the Division. The first one to go on duty was Mrs Iris Bilan who went to work at the Provincial Highways Building. The remainder would go to Armed Forces establishments and other points in Edmonton. Mrs Bilan, a widow with five children, held the rank of Aircrafts Woman in the Womens' Auxiliary Air Force in the Royal Air Force (WAAF) during the Second World War.

Mrs Iris Bilan.

Special People

Commissionaire Jim Olmstead joined the Corps in 1948 immediately after his discharge from the Army following the Second World War. He was a large man, nearly six feet in height and quite wide of girth. His manner was pleasant and because of all these factors he was placed on the parking meter patrol. Jim walked with a limp as a result of his war service but still walked the beat on the southside of Edmonton covering about 20 miles per day at a speed few people could match. Quite often the business people along Whyte Avenue and then north on 109 Street to the Garneau Theatre would see Jim having the company of his mother on the beat, maintaining the same speedy pace as her son. Jim retired in 1981.

Stanislaw Gorka was one of the many former members of the Polish Army who served with the British forces during the Second World War, and at the end of hostilities he took the opportunity to emigrate to Canada and joined the Corps. During the war, he had ben honoured by being given the Polish Cross of Valour, the Army Cross, the Monte Casino Cross, the 39/45 Star, the Italian Star and the Defence Medal. Stan was a hard worker for the Corps, which characterized his life.

Corps members have come from many countries as well as from many stations within military life. One outstanding person was Col Yu Fang Shih, the former head of the Taiwanese Airforce in the Government of Chiang Kai-shek. Col Shih was in every way a gentleman and greatly respected by all who came into contact with him. He never aspired to have rank in the Corps, but was quite content to work as a Commissionaire, always striving to please.

Alex Howie joined the Corps December 10, 1959 at the age of 60. He worked in many locations and continued providing above average service at the Jubilee Auditorium, working 40 hours per week until he retired June 10, 1985 at 86 years of age. Howie was always a stickler for performing to the letter of the law. One day the manager of the auditorium asked that a small sum of money be held by Mr Howie for someone that would pick it up later. Mr Howie refused because it said in his statement of duties he was not permitted to handle cash.

Col Yu Fang Shih.

Commissionaire Ernest Foster joined the Corps in the early 1970s upon retirement from the Edmonton Police Force where he had served 15 years. Prior to that he had served in the First World War as well as the Second World War. Ernie felt out of place if he was not wearing a uniform. In August 1986 his nephew Ernie joined the Corps and served until January 1995.

The Corps has on several occasions been a family employment service. This can be brought to mind when during the period July 5, 1983 and June 17, 1988, three members of one family were all employed full time at the same time. They were Ernest MacLean, his wife Pearl and their son David. Not being employed on the same post, and of course, being on shift work, it was very seldom that they could sit down to a family dinner.

In 1995, a book was published entitled "Find the Dragon – The Canadian Army in Korea 1950 - 1953." It was written by now-retired Edmonton Commissionaire Lewis Evans under the pen name Robert Hepenstall, and relates a soldier's view of the war, sometimes in stark contrast to official reports.

Tom West served in the Canadian Army for 25 years, including wartime before becoming an Edmonton Commissionaire. He became the first Corps member to be placed at Alberta Vocational College, and quickly became popular with everyone there, especially with the students and even more so with the small youngsters in the day-care centre. This came naturally, because Tom and his wife spent many years providing a foster home for children, and each was awarded a citation from the Alberta Government to commemorate service as foster parents.

Commissionaire Tom West.

Commissionaires Extraordinaire

Commissionaire Sgt Everett Johnson and Commissionaire Herb Buskowsky (no photo available) were on duty at the Alberta Legislature Building during the early hours of the morning on October 14, 1988. At 0705 hours, Buskowsky, who was attending the desk at the front entrance, heard a noise and investigated the source. He encountered a man who was standing at the top of the front steps holding a shotgun. To quote Buskowsky, *"I asked him if there was a problem and he said, several."* Herb immediately locked the front doors and called the

Sgt Everett Johnson.

city police. Meanwhile, Sgt Johnson alerted legislature security and ensured that all windows and exit doors were locked. Eventually the culprit was disabled and removed from the grounds by city police. Another notable occasion involving Sgt Johnson was that he received a merit certificate in recognition of his assistance to a youngster who suffered serious head injuries while riding his bicycle on the Legislature grounds.

Commissionaire Don Donaldson (second from left).

On June 10, 1995, while off duty, Commissionaire Don Donaldson helped a man subdue a robber in a grocery store parking lot. Donaldson witnessed the thief take money from a clerk, then hurried to the back of store and alerted the manager to call police. Meanwhile the bandit got into a car occupied by two small children and was about to effect his escape when the father and owner of the car threw him out of the car and jumped on him. Commissionaire Donaldson and a store employee helped hold the subject until the police arrived.

Sgt A.J. Day receiving a Corps Watch and Certificate from Col. Fred Davies in 1997.

At approximately 1000 hours at CFB Edmonton on July 29, 1996, a telephone call was received by the Military Police Dispatcher, Commissionaire Sgt A.J. Day, indicating that a serviceman had left his place of duty in a distraught state, and his current whereabouts was unknown. A rapid records check was made by Sergeant Day which enabled the Military Police to track the man to his home, where he was persuaded not to take life threatening action upon himself. Sergeant Day was commended for his ability to rapidly collate the necessary information to enable the M.P.s to divert a possibly tragic situation.

Commissionaire Tom Birrell receiving the Meritorious Service Medal & Certificate from Col Fred Davies.

On November 28, 1996, Commissionaire Thomas Birrell received an Edmonton Police Commission award for his role in wrestling a gun-toting bandit to the floor. It happened when he was on duty at the Canadian Imperial Bank of Commerce at 10102 Jasper Avenue. Birrell and another man overpowered the robber and held him until police arrived.

National Conventions

There have been three National Conventions held in Edmonton. The first was in September 1961. The second was in September 1973 and is listed as the thirty-eighth. After Friday's business meetings, on Saturday, delegates and guests boarded three buses set on a compass bearing of 270° – destination Jasper. The weather was perfect. Jasper Park Lodge was at its best and the accommodation and banquet were occasions to be remembered. Premier Manning was guest speaker and left no doubt in the minds of our guests that the Corps was indispensable. Sunday morning, the compass bearing was south on the Icefields Parkway to Banff. After a tour of Banff, dinner was held at the top of the new Calgary Husky Tower to conclude the event.

The third opportunity to host the National was in 1988. Alberta's first lady, Lieutenant Governor Helen Hunley gave a splendid address at the formal dinner held at the Edmonton Inn. She was a CWAC Captain during the Second World War. Saturday morning was Klondike Breakfast time. The wives of the Governors had spent weeks sewing and acquiring hats, vests, sashes, jewellery, and other adornments to suitably attire both men and women sourdoughs. A honky tonk band played for five hours or until the last dancer was exhausted. Klondike Kate "Yolanda Lee" belted out gay nineties songs, danced and flirted with the boys and wowed the ladies with her elaborate costumes. Breakfast was pancakes, scrambled eggs, sausage, bacon, and hash browns, washed down with "Sluice Juice." At noon, it was over, except to talk about it for years to come.

Lieutenant Governor Helen Hunley with RCMP aide.

Locations

The Northern Alberta Division have Commissionaires employed at Grande Prairie, Fort McMurray, Camrose, Wainwright, Wetaskiwin, Cold Lake, Redwater, Devon and Edmonton. Responsibilities for the Division began to expand in 1994 when administration control was assumed for the RCMP Guards and Matrons throughout northern Alberta, and further expansion occurred in September 1995 when the

Division posted Commissionaires at the Canadian Forces Northern Region Headquarters in Yellowknife, N.W.T. The latest additions included administrative responsibilities for the guards and matrons in the N.W.T, together with Commissionaire duties with the city of Yellowknife meter patrol in 1997.

New Business

On November 1, 1996, a Home Care and Security Patrol was instituted in the Edmonton area. This service provided a regularly scheduled home or office visitation while the property is vacant, and may include many extras such as plant maintenance, grass cutting, mail collection or snow removal. An additional package to this service is the provision of a colour VHS video tape of rooms and valuables. In the future, Northern Alberta Division will endeavour to increase the number of support services that we now provide, and is considering the possibility of conducting "fee for services" operations. This would involve such activities as alarm response, operating outlet for licences, or firearms registration, Neighbourhood Watch and Crimestoppers.

Training

In addition to Military/RCMP training received prior to joining the Corps, all Commissionaires receive additional training. The basic training is conducted by Northern Alberta in two ways: either by classroom instruction or home study with classroom testing. First-aid is provided by Corps Instructors. All Commissionaires are required to pass the Commissionaire Qualifying Course and First-Aid course. Further training may be required for various customer contracts. Some personnel currently operate numerous high tech systems. At many locations, Commissionaires operate closed circuit television systems, electronic card access systems and computers. In addition, there are clients who rely on our trained console operators to work their security monitoring and intrusion alarm system.

Benefits

In 1953, a newsletter to Commissionaires was established. This provides information regarding such matters such as personnel changes, awards that have been presented, graduates of recent training courses, recognition for outstanding service and other information of general interest.

Bonuses for long term service began in November 1980, and are as follows: 5 years - $100; 10 years – $200; 15 years – $300; 20 years – $400; 25 years – $500; and 30 years – $600.

A death benefit plan has been organized for all Commissionaires on full time service, together with Portal to Portal Accident Insurance, which covers members from the time they leave home until their return home. A uniform cleaning allowance, based on the number of hours worked by a member, is paid out each month. In 1979, Northern Alberta began having an Annual Awards Dinner, at which members are recognized for terms of service and are presented special awards. An RRSP was established in 1995 for full time members who have completed five years service.

Governance

The governance of the Northern Alberta Division has been unique in the length of the term that Chairmen and Commandants have been in office. Major S.C.S. Kerr was the Chairman from our start September 5, 1939 to June 2, 1947. The next long time Chairman was Capt F.U. Brown from November 5, 1951 to January 3, 1985, a total of 34 years.

The long term governance was an interesting management approach but was later considered not in the best interest of the Division and the By-laws were changed in 1986. All future Chairmen were to be limited to a three-year term. The Chairmen who served under the changed by-law are:

F/L J.K. McKenzie	3 Jan 1985 - 28 May 1986
G/C G.L. Wynn	28 May 1986 - 18 May 1989
Capt R. Reierson	18 May 1989 - 7 May 1991
Col D.V. Reynolds	7 May 1991 - 18 May 1994
Col F.C. Davies	18 May 1994 - 22 May 1997
LCol F.N. Pearce	22 May 1997 - Present

Our Commandants have also served for some long periods in office and there is no limitation on their management stay. Col L. Scott served from September 5, 1939 to July 4, 1950. Capt F.U. Brown was not only Chairman but was also Commandant, holding both positions from November 5, 1951 to April 1, 1969. Col F.N. Oslund held the Commandant's position from June 1, 1971 to March 31, 1992, a total of 20 years and 10 months. On April 1, 1992, Col R.J. Laing assumed the duties of Commandant and remained until February 1997. The present incumbent is Col B.J. Craig, who came on board May 5th, 1997.

Vignettes of Note

These snippets have been included for they are of value to the entire Corps.

Padre's Corner

A number who attended the Awards dinner at the Westin Hotel on 23 March 1995, have asked for a copy of the Grace our Padre, S/L Graham, used that evening. S/L Graham didn't keep his notes so the following is from his memory:

Bless our Corps O Lord we pray
And all who work by night and day

*Men and Women round the clock
They walk the walk and talk the talk*

*Commissionaires who serve our nation
We honor them for dedication*

*To the standards of our cause
And their respect for all the laws*

*We offer thanks for food and drink
It gives us time to stop and think*

*Of people up against the wall
While we are here to have a ball*

*So bless this banquet Lord tonight
Forgive the one who might get tight – Amen*

Padre Graham has also asked that I remind you he is available to members requiring the help of a chaplain. If you require his assistance please call the Corps Office and Headquarters Staff will arrange for Padre Graham to contact you.

This ode tells it as it is.

Ode to Commissionaire

Sir: Some comment, in poetry form:

*You say you would like to be a Commissionaire?
Well, come right in and pull up a chair.
I'll tell you a few stories, some of them fact.
It will depend on the bylaw or on the act.
Like the policeman, our lot is an unhappy one
We slosh around in the rain and sweat in the sun.*

*The grocer says the customer is always right,
But we think he stays awake day and night,
To figure out how they can stay
At a parking meter and not have to pay
We present them with a ticket and they get mad
Say the meter has a fast clock and they have been had.*

*The excuses we get are hard to believe
As each one has a different way to deceive
Of course, we listen to every word
To see if it's one we have not heard.
But we listen each time to guff and abuse
To a different version of the same old excuse.*

*I was only gone for a minute, said he.
How come you gave this ticket to me?
I didn't have any change in my purse.
I just came from the doctor. My heartburn is worse.
I just went for change at that store.
I was only gone ten minutes, no more.*

Now these are just a few excuses you will find
Are you sure a Commissionaire is what you had in mind?
You say you would still like to join the Corps?
Well let me tell you about some more.
Along comes a person with ticket in hand.
He waving it around like he's leading a band
I'm going to report this and have you fired.
There is just no way my meter was expired.

One lady said I was only gone a minute.
I'll admit to you, I forgot to put money in it
Now surely I'm allowed parking for such time.
Why should it cost me a nickle or dime?
I won't be coming back to this parking lot meter
I'm nobody's fool nor am I a repeater.

Others see us go by and pull into a stall
They don't put in any money at all.
They think their parking is free that day
But when they come back they have two dollars to pay.
Now these are just a few things people will do
To try to match wits with people like you.

Now wouldn't it be a grand sensation
If one day we didn't write even one citation?
If all the parking meters show they they had money,
If the day was dry but not too sunny,
We would know the people had been educated
To comply with the signs as indicated.

That's all there is. There is nothing more
Except to welcome you to the Corps.

N.Y. Johnson, 60th Street

NORTHERN ALBERTA CORPS ON PARADE

Participating in the 1996 "Edmonton Klondike Days Parade."

Chapter XIII

HISTORY OF THE OTTAWA DIVISION

Commandant's Introduction – *by Sam Houston*

IT IS DIFFICULT to know where to begin when trying to introduce the largest and perhaps most complex Division in the Canadian Corps of Commissionaires.

Many of our sister Divisions are no doubt envious of the Ottawa Division being able to serve the nation's capital. However, having the cornucopia of federal government business is indeed a mixed blessing. Being dependant on one client for over 90% of our business results in having to look at things such as marketing and future development in a somewhat different light than other Divisions. On the one hand we must do everything possible to maintain current relationships with the federal government, while on the other hand we must be prepared for the eventuality that our whole world could be changed by Treasury Board.

The geographic area served by the Ottawa Division also presents unique challenges. In addition to operating in two provinces, we have detachments in North Bay, Sudbury, Sault Ste Marie, Timmins and Kirkland Lake. To put the distances involved in dealing with our Northern locations into perspective, it is only eight kilometres further from Ottawa to Windsor than it is from Ottawa to Sault Ste Marie.

Like most other Divisions, we provide a variety of services to our clients. We do By-Law enforcement for the cities of North Bay, Sudbury, and Sault Ste Marie. We read water meters and manage landfill sites for the Regional Municipality of Sudbury. We provide guards in locations that range from freight loading docks to airports to Rideau Hall, the residence of the Governor General of Canada. While some Commissionaires operate some of the most modern and complex intrusion monitoring systems available, others provide the more simpler man-at-the-gate type of security.

One of our more interesting customers is the Department of Foreign

Affairs and International Trade. In addition to providing Commissionaires to provide security at their Ottawa locations, the Division has negotiated a separate contract to provide Commissionaires to act as replacement guards at missions abroad. Over the past few years, the Division has had members serve in such places as Washington, Paris, London, Mexico City, Havana, Hong Kong, and Amman, Jordan.

The Beginning

On September 30, 1937, Major-General W.B.M. King, CMG,DSO,VD, President of the Canadian Corps of Commissionaires Headquarters located in Montreal, appealed to a number of prominent citizens of the city of Ottawa in an attempt to establish a Board of Governors and form the Ottawa Division. A meeting was held on October 9, 1937 to complete the list of the Board of Governors, appoint an Executive Committee, Commandant and Adjutant, and to discuss general business.

There were delays however, and the Ottawa Division was not organized until 1939 with Brigadier General C.H. MacLaren, CMG, DSO, as Chairman of the Board of Governors, and Colonel C.M. Edwards, DSO, VD, as Commandant. Two Commissionaires, Logan and Burdett, were taken on strength on October 1, 1939. By the end of the year, there were 15 on strength. The Division owes a great debt of gratitude to the late Brigadier General C.H. MacLaren and the late Colonel C.M. Edwards who personally assumed financial responsibility for the Division until it was in a position to operate on its own resources.

Administration and expansion during the early years was slow and difficult. It was necessary to introduce the Corps to the public and to establish a reputation of "Service and Efficiency," to gain confidence of clients, and to convince them to employ Commissionaires.

Brigadier C.H. MacLaren, CMG, DSO, Chairman 1939-43, 1945-54.

Colonel C.M. Edwards, DSO, VD, CD, Chairman 1943-45, Commandant 1939, 1943-48.

Although detailed records are not available, the Division's strength has gone from 15 in 1939, to approximately 2,000 in 1997. Of this number, about 360 are employed in Hull, about 150 in Northern Ontario, and the remainder in Ottawa. Strength peaked in 1992 when the Ottawa Division had 2,230 Commissionaires. However, it should be noted that this number was not truly representational of actual strength, as it contained a large number of non-effective members who were not available for employment. Files were reviewed and many of these individuals were removed from Division strength.

The decrease in strength is due in part to cutbacks in federal government spending which has in turn, resulted in reductions to the number of Commissionaires being employed. A review of hours of business sold since 1990 shows the effect of cuts in federal government spending. FY 1990/1991 – 3,614,796 hours; FY 1994/1995 – 3,366,694 hours; and FY 1996/1997 – 3,097,643 hours.

The Recent Past

In 1955, the Division was incorporated as a non-profit company by Letters Patent under the Corporations Act, 1953, of the province of Ontario. Although the main centre of operations for the Division is in the Ottawa/Hull area, Commissionaires are also employed at detachments located in Petawawa, North Bay, Sudbury, Sault Ste Marie, Timmins, and Kirkland Lake.

Since the majority of federal government departments are located in the National Capital Region, approximately 93% of the Division's work is for the federal government. The remainder of the Division's contracts are with provincial and municipal governments and with commercial firms.

Location of Division Headquarters

The Division Headquarters was first set up in the old "Bank National" building on Rideau Street which has since been torn down. The Division had rented or been provided rent-free accommodation by the federal government, during the early years in the Laurentian Building, the Aylmer Building on Slater Street, and the Elgin Building at 70 Elgin Street. In 1957, property was purchased at 108 Lisgar Street at a cost of $28,000.

Architects were hired to design a three-storey building which became the current Division Headquarters on April 13, 1959. It was named the Edwards Building after Colonel C.M. Edwards, the first Commandant.

The new building housed the Headquarters staff of eight on the ground floor. The basement was used as caretaker's quarters and a recreation room for Commissionaires. The top floor was rented as an income producing unit. National Headquarters occupied space in this building when it moved from Montreal in April 1967 until December 1971 when it moved to 100 Gloucester Street. Over the years, the growth of the Division required more administrative, training and inspection personnel. Additional office and training space was required. Today, in addition to the building at 108 Lisgar Street, space has been rented at 116 Lisgar Street for training, security and some of the operations staff.

In 1993, three-by-five-foot crests of the Royal Canadian Navy, Canadian Army, Royal Canadian Air Force and the Royal Canadian Mounted Police were affixed to the exterior of the building as part the building refurbishment.

Recreation Association

On July 7, 1948 a meeting was held in the Daly Building for the purpose of organizing an Ottawa Division, Canadian Corps of Commissionaires Recreation Association. This meeting was open to all Commissionaires and was chaired by Commissionaire Roe. A deduction of $1 per month was authorized from the pay of interested members commencing July 15, 1948.

A dinner costing $1.40 was held at the Cartier Square Drill Hall, in the Cameron Highlanders of Ottawa Band Room, on November 26, 1948. It was attended by 90 individuals. A second dinner was held on January 12, 1949 for those unable to attend the first function. One hundred and twenty-five Commissionaires plus members of the Board of Governors and special guests attended.

The minutes of meetings of the Recreation Association show that it held raffles, visited and financially assisted sick members, organized blood donations, held annual dinners, held Christmas parties for children, organized dances and sent wreaths and messages of condolence to families of deceased members. The Recreation Association, as an active organization, appears to have faded away through lack of interest in 1965. Although cheques were given to sick personnel as late as 1967, no record of meetings of the Association were maintained after December 1965.

Annual Parades/Medals Presentation Ceremonies

There are records of annual parades being held as far back as June 1954. These parades seem to have been held primarily to receive publicity in the local media. VIP Inspecting Officers were invited to attend each year and have included the Governor-General in 1960 and 1980, and the

Minister of Veterans' Affairs in 1955, 1961, 1966 and 1976. The Chief of the Defence Staff of the Canadian Forces and other senior officers have also been the Inspecting Officer for this event.

No parades were held during 1970 to 1973 inclusive. In 1974, the parades were started once again. However, instead of requiring the attendance of all Commissionaires, which had always proven to be a big problem, only those eligible for long service awards were asked to be on parade. Interested Commissionaires were invited to attend as spectators. The Annual Medals Parade/Awards Ceremony has been held since 1974. In 1980, the parade was inspected by Governor-General Schreyer. This event was recorded on film produced for use by all Divisions in Canada for both publicity and training purposes.

In recent years, the retiring Chairman of the Ottawa Division Board of Governors has been the Inspecting Officer. In order to keep the time on parade to a minimum, other members of the Board of Governors have assisted in the presentation of medals and awards. In 1997, a convocation style ceremony similar to that used by Government House for presentation of medals and awards was adopted.

In 1976, Division Colours were purchased and, on September 30, 1976, they were blessed and dedicated by the Reverend Dr. E.G.B. Foote, OBE, CD. The Colours now rest in the Division Headquarters, and are present each year at the Annual Medals Presentation Ceremony.

Benefits and Awards

Over the years, the Ottawa Division has attempted to provide its members with the best employee benefits possible. At the same time, the Division has recognized that benefits add to the cost of operations and has had to try to balance benefits provided with the need to keep customer billing rates at a competitive level.

One key benefit provided to Commissionaires is life insurance coverage. Coverage started on July 1, 1976 in the amount of $3,000 for all Commissionaires under 70 years of age. The policy was increased to $5,000 in June 1979 and to $6,000 in 1980. In 1997 all members who have not attained their 72nd birthday are provided free life insurance coverage in the amount of $12,000. The Division also provides Portal-to-Portal disability insurance coverage to supplement coverage from provincial workers' compensation programs. This insurance covers members while travelling to and from their residence to their place of employment.

A performance gratuity was implemented in April 1962. Financial payments are made in conjunction with the award of long service honours and awards. These awards are paid after five years of exemplary service, and again at each subsequent five-year period. Since 1984, the basic award has been $40 for each year of service. An award of $200 is paid after five years, $400 after 10 years, $600 after 15 years and so on. In addition to

Commissionaire members of the Division being presented with the Commissionaire Long Service Medal, eligible Governors are presented with the medal at the Annual Meeting of the Ottawa Division Board of Governors in the spring of each year.

Women in the Division

The Ottawa Division began employing former-servicewomen in the Fall of 1973. As of 1997, 179 women are employed in the Division.

Training

Although training was carried out to some degree over the years, it was not until 1973 that concerted efforts were made to ensure everyone in the Division was trained to the highest standards possible. Today, new Commissionaires are provided a five-day course and are trained to meet the federal government standards for uniformed security guards. Supervisors are provided additional training which also meets federal government standards. In addition, Commissionaires are provided training in first aid which gives them a St. John Ambulance Emergency First Aid qualification. Special training is also provided to meet the requirements of individual customers. Commissionaires have been given training in such specialties as locksmithing, operation of X-ray sensing equipment, airport security operations, intrusion alarm systems and console operations.

In the five-year period from 1992 to 1996, approximately 2,000 Commissionaires of the Division were given the Basic Commissionaire and Emergency First Aid training. In addition, approximately 160 selected supervisors have been trained on the Corps Supervisor Course which is run by National Headquarters. The Ottawa Division has provided instructors for this course at every opportunity.

Commissionaires are provided refresher training every three years at which time they renew their first aid qualifications and upgrade the skills necessary for them to perform their duties.

Uniforms/Quartermaster Operations

Until 1974, uniforms were purchased by individual Commissionaires. After several years of lobbying by the Corps, it was agreed by the federal government that starting in 1974, uniforms could be considered an allowable expense and included in our billing rates for federal government contracts. The issue of free uniforms did a great deal to improve the image of the Division. Once Commissionaires were able to replace uniforms at no cost, the general appearance of our men and women was greatly enhanced.

The Division's Quartermaster Stores was established and maintains a supply of uniforms and accessories. Although most contracts require the wearing of the traditional uniform, blue blazers with grey flannel trousers or skirts were adopted for wear when the customer felt this image was required. A trial workdress uniform was introduced in 1996. The Division provides all items of uniform except footwear and replacement is done without cost to Commissionaires. The Quartermaster also stocks optional items of kit for sale to members.

Current Operations

As the strength of the Division increased over the years, the need to provide more and better services also increased. The Division Headquarters is currently manned on a 24-hour per day, seven-day per week basis. A dispatcher is available to receive and process calls from posts as required and an Inspector is available with a vehicle to monitor the operations during silent hours and to respond to any emergencies. This around-the-clock service provides the Division with the capability of immediately responding to any incidents as they arise. This provides both service to our customers and support to our personnel in the field.

Hull Operations

In 1982, in order to satisfy the requirement of having an office in the province of Quebec, accommodation was rented to set up a Hull Detachment. The Detachment, commanded by Lt A.W. Tremblay, was officially opened on April 1, 1983, with a staff of three. Although the numbers of Commissionaires employed in Quebec has varied, it has been in the 250 to 350 range for the past several years.

In 1996, the office functions being performed in Hull were integrated with the Headquarters in Ottawa. A smaller office was obtained in order to keep an office presence in the province of Quebec. The Operations Management Officer responsible for the operation of contracts in Hull occupies this new office.

In early 1995, Commissionaires employed in the province of Quebec voted to become members of The United Steelworkers of America, a union that represents most of the security guards in the province of Quebec. A collective agreement was negotiated with the union during the summer of 1995.

Fiftieth Anniversary Celebrations

In 1989, the Ottawa Division celebrated its fiftieth year as a Division. The celebrations included the Medals Parade on September 30 and October 1 was proclaimed "Commissionaires' Day" by the city of Ottawa. The Commandant at the time was BGen R.G. Heitshu, CD, and the Inspecting Officer was Captain (N) R.P. White, OBE, CM, VRD who had been the Chairman of the Ottawa Division from 1964 to 1967 and the National Chairman from 1972 until 1975. The Division conducted a Ceremonial Parade at the National War Memorial. In addition, a number of social events took place during the weeks of September 24 - October 10, 1989.

Commissionaires Extraordinaire

Many Commissionaires, who have been employed with the Ottawa Division over the years, deserve special recognition. Unfortunately, space does not permit us to acknowledge all of them. Those identified in the following paragraphs are but a representation of the many who performed their duties in an exceptional manner.

The Corps of Commissionaires awarded the "Meritorious Service Medal" to WO I E.J. Shouldice on March 27, 1987 for his role in the capture of a bank robbery suspect at the Bank of Nova Scotia, 303 Queen Street in the city of Ottawa. WO I Shouldice served with the Ottawa Division from May 1976 until his retirement in January 1989.

Commissionaire W.R. Hounsome of Petawawa received the "Meritorious Service Medal" for his rescue of a two-year-old child who had fallen into the backyard swimming pool. Hounsome's complete disregard for his own safety became more evident when it was established that he has a heart condition, and had to use nitroglycerine medication before he jumped into the pool. Commissionaire Hounsome was a member of the Division for about four years. He left the Division in 1991 when our contract at Canadian Forces Base Petawawa was reduced in size. He still resides in Petawawa.

Wayne Hounsome, snuggles with three-year-old Jessie Goodyear, as he reflects upon the day he dove into the Goodyear's pool and saved the life of the child.

WO II Keith Marks was awarded the St. John of Jerusalem "Meritorious Certificate" for saving the life of a man intent on ending his life on March 6, 1966. WO II Marks, an Inspector for the Ottawa Division, entered a building and found the man slumped over the driver's seat of a parked car with the engine running. After several attempts to arouse the individual in the locked vehicle, WO II Marks broke a window, shut off the engine and contacted an ambulance. He was commended for his emergency scene management and actions to make the area safe, thus saving the life of a man. Keith Marks joined the Ottawa Division in May 1992 and continues to be employed as one of our Inspectors.

MWO Keith Marks.

Commissionaire Gerard Seguin has served as a receptionist at the Government Conference Centre for over 23 of his 34 years with the Ottawa Division. During that time the Division has received over a dozen unsolicited letters from visitors and government staff commending him on

Commissionaire Seguin, Ottawa 1997.

his extraordinary kindness and hospitality. On May 27, 1997, the Association of Professional Executives of the Public Service of Canada (APEX) publicly acknowledged Commissionaire Seguin with a citation recognizing his contribution, as a non-public servant, in helping the public understand the public service. In presenting the citation, Ms Hélène Beauchemin, the Past President of APEX stated that Commissionaire Seguin "provides excellence in service and enforcement in a velvet glove."

WO2 Maurice Regimbal had a most unusual job before he retired in 1994. Maurice joined the Corps after serving in wartime and in peacetime from 1941 until 1971. He joined the Ottawa Division in 1972 and served at the Ottawa International Airport, the Canadian Mint, and in 1979 he became part of the security staff of Prime Minister Pierre Trudeau. In time he took over the security of the Cabinet Room. In his years with the Prime Minister's Office, Maurice met dignitaries from all over the world. He was part of the security staff when Cabinet went to Meach Lake and Quebec city. Maurice Regimbal's career with the Corps ended in 1994 when he was diagnosed with cancer. The cancer went into remission. Maurice served under five

Maurice Regimbal (left) with former Prime Minister Kim Campbell.

Prime Ministers and when he left, Jean Chretien wrote "You can be justly proud of your many years of service. You have always demonstrated a strong commitment to your work, and your dedicated efforts have long been appreciated by your colleagues." WO2 Maurice Regimbal was indeed a Commissionaire Extraordinaire. He passed away in November 1997.

The Board of Governors

On May 31, 1990, an amendment to the Ottawa Division By-Laws concerning the composition of the Board of Governors was passed. It appointed all Ordinary Members as Governors, thus deleting the category of "Ordinary Member." Prior to this time, there were 12 Governors and 24 Ordinary Members, with only the Governors having a vote on matters involved in the operation of the Division. The requirement for a quorum was also changed from five to 15 Governors.

Membership for Merchant Sailors

On May 31, 1991 the Annual General Meeting of the Board of Governors passed an amendment to the Ottawa Division By-Laws which permitted members with service with Canadian or British merchant navies, or the merchant navy of an allied nation during time of war, to become Commissionaires. At the time of writing, there are no members in the Division who served in the merchant navy.

Human Resources

In 1992 the Ottawa Division engaged the firm of William M. Mercer Ltd. to conduct a human resources study. The study was conducted to confirm the Division was operating in accordance with current labour practices. As a result of their report, the Ottawa Division prepared and issued a Division Policies and Procedures Manual. This Manual replaced the booklet "Rules and Regulations for Commissionaires" and put into writing the Division's policies and procedures for dealing with administrative and discipline matters. The report also resulted in the introduction of the Division "Performance Evaluation Appraisal" reporting system.

Continued emphasis on the importance of human resources matters led to a decision in 1997 to create a human resources Branch within the Headquarters with Major Donna Hansen as its leader.

National Annual General Meeting

In 1995, the Ottawa Division hosted the National Annual General Meeting of the Corps. Meetings and social functions were held at the Chateau Laurier Hotel in Ottawa and it was a tremendous success. The Ottawa Division had last hosted the event in 1977 as it is normally hosted by all Corps Divisions on a rotational basis.

Community Involvement

The Ottawa Division regularly contributes to the well-being of the local community. We participate in the annual United Way campaign and make an annual corporate donation that is in addition to the contributions made by our members.

In 1984, the Division participated in fundraising for the Children's Hospital and a cheque in the amount of $4,228.68 was presented at their annual telethon. The Division has been a strong supporter of the Federal District of St. John Ambulance. Contributions have been made on a number of occasions including $2,000 in 1989 towards the purchase of a vehicle, and $2,000 in 1993 towards the purchase of oxygen regulators. In addition, the Division has allowed St. John Ambulance to use our classroom free of charge on evenings and weekends.

In 1991, the Division supported the Dominion of Canada Rifle Association by donating $600 towards the cost of building a Headquarters for the Association at Connaught Ranges. When the Rideau Veterans joined with the Perley Hospital to form the Perley and Rideau Veterans' Health Centre in 1996, the Ottawa Division committed to contribute $15,000 over a five-year period. These contributions are representative of the many contributions the Division has made over the years to support the needs of our community.

Guard Quality Assurance Unit

Prior to 1972, the Division had provided guard services at all federal government buildings in the National Capital area except for those in possession of their own public service guard force. With many government departments expanding and decentralizing their resources into a number of newer and more modern office buildings, the Division could no longer provide sufficient bilingual manpower to meet the government's requirements. Commercial guards were contracted by the government to provide security in those areas not covered by the Corps. A number of problems were experienced with the quality of service provided by the commercial agencies and a Guard Quality Assurance (GQA) Unit was formed within the Security Branch of the Department of Supply and Services to deal with these problems and to ensure that guard services were provided at an acceptable standard. The Guard Quality Assurance Unit, which is staffed by members of the Ottawa Division, currently services approximately 50 separate guard sites where commercial (non-Commissionaire) guards provide service to the federal government.

Customers

The Ottawa Division has too many customers to permit our mentioning them all. However, the following will provide an overview of some of the customers served by the Division. National Defence Headquarters is our largest customer. Although not as large, the

Department of Foreign Affairs and International Trade (DFAIT) is another major customer. In addition to security services, we also provide DFAIT with assistance in the operation of its mailroom.

Some of the Division's many customers within the National Capital Region are Public Works and Government Services Canada, the Royal Canadian Mounted Police, Industry Canada, Health Canada, Natural Resources Canada, and Revenue Canada Taxation.

The Ottawa Division provides security services at airports in Ottawa, North Bay, Sudbury, Sault Ste Marie, and Timmins. It provides by-law enforcement to municipalities and provides guides for Laurier House, a museum in Ottawa. The Division is also proud to provide security services to the National Archives, Treasury Board, the residence of the Governor General at Rideau Hall, and to the Prime Minister's Office.

Among our commercial clients are Nav Canada, Computing Devices Canada and the Perley and Rideau Veterans' Health Centre.

Chairmen – Board of Governors

The following individuals served as Chairman of the Board of Governors during the period shown.

BGen G.H. Maclaren, CMG, DSO, CD	1939 - 1943
Col C.M. Edwards, DSO, VD, CD	1943 - 1945
BGen G.H. Maclaren, CMG, DSO, CD	1945 - 1954
MGen G.R. Turner, CB, MC, DCM, CD	1954 - 1958
Col J.D. Fraser, VD, CD	1958 - 1960
RAdm G.L. Stephens, CB, CBE, CD	1960 - 1964
Capt (N) R.P. White, OBE, CM, VRD	1964 - 1967
Capt J.C. Woodward, MC	1967 - 1969
LCol A.L. Fortey, ED, CD	1969 - 1971
LCol E.G. Simmons, MBE, CD	1971 - 1973
LCol C. Petch, OBE, ED	1973 - 1975
Capt (N) V.J. Wilgress, CD	1975 - 1977
Maj J.F. Maclaren, ED	1977 - 1980
BGen B.G. Aldous, MC, CD	1980 - 1980
Commissioner W.L. Higgitt	1980 - 1982
Lt Hilton B. Mersereau	1982 - 1984
VAdm R.L. Hennessy, DSC, CD	1984 - 1986
LGen W.A. Milroy, DSO, CD	1986 - 1988
LCol R.V. Inman, CD	1988 - 1990
LCol A.B.R. Lawrence, MC	1990 - 1992
LCol P.A. Labelle, CD	1992 - 1994
Col B. Shapiro, CD	1994 - 1996
LCol D. Digby, CD	1996 - 1998
MGen W.J. Grant, CD	1998 -

Commandants

The following individuals served as Commandant of the Ottawa Division during the periods shown:

Col C.M. Edwards, DSO, VD, CD	1939 - 1940
Col F.B. Inkster	1940 - 1943
Col C.M. Edwards, DSO, VD, CD	1943 - 1948
LCol R. Taylor, OBE, ED	1948 - 1962
Air Vice Marshall F.G. Wait, CBE, CD	1962 - 1973
Col M.H. Bateman, CD	1973 - 1986
LGen R. Gutknecht, CMM, CD	1986 - 1989
BGen R.G. Heitshu, CD	1989 - 1996
Col R.J. Houston, OMM, CD	1996 -

Conclusion

Like any dynamic organization, the Ottawa Division continues to change in order to fulfil its mandate. We recognize that there are many challenges to be met if the Corps is to remain a viable organization which will be able to survive in the future. Changes to our organizational structure, the training provided to our members, and to the way in which we manage the affairs of the Division, must keep pace with the needs of our clients and the changes taking place in society. We believe in our mandate; in the strength of our members, and believe we can meet the challenges that face us. We will be able to continue to serve those who have served their country.

Chapter XIV

NEW BRUNSWICK & PRINCE EDWARD ISLAND DIVISION

Commandant's Introduction – *By Clovis Everett*

*I*T IS AN honour to have been invited by the Board of Governors and the Chairman of the History Writing Committee to prepare this introduction to the history of the New Brunswick and Prince Edward Island Division.

I have filled the position of Commandant since 1983. The guidelines and standard operating procedures were already in place through the dedicated work of past Commandants.

With direction and advice from a cooperative Board of Governors and Executive Committee, a cross-trained HQ staff and all Commissionaires, this Division has made and continues to make a favourable impression on our many clients/customers.

It is worthy of mention that this Division is the only one in Canada to operate in three provinces, requiring our strict attention to three different Labour Standards, Human Rights, overtime rates and safety regulations.

The Commissionaires in the field are the true history – past, present and future.

The Early Years

There is written evidence which confirms that the formation of a New Brunswick Division of the Corps was considered in 1938. However, for reasons that are unclear, no further steps were taken at that time. The first positive action taken to organize the Division occurred in Saint John, N.B. in January 1945. Major A.R. Jones, the District Administrator, Department of Veterans Affairs, was anxious to appoint two Commissionaires to serve as watchmen at the Lancaster Veterans Hospital. At that time there was one Commissionaire (Dryden) employed at the Saint John Unemployment Insurance Commission office and several other

Commissionaires were employed in Moncton. Commissionaire Dryden was then employed through the Nova Scotia Division and those working in Moncton were employed through the Montreal Division.

When Major Jones approached the Nova Scotia Division regarding the need for two more men, he was advised that they could not supply any more Commissionaires. However, in March 1945, as a result of ongoing talks with the Nova Scotia officials, their Adjutant, Major William C. Borrett, offered to help in the organizing of a New Brunswick Division. He had stated that two things were necessary for success – reliable and interested gentlemen to act as Governors of the Corps and reliable ex-servicemen of good character, as Commissionaires.

Major Jones then discussed the possible organization with Major Brad Gilbert, former O.C. No. 7 Company, Veterans Guard of Canada, but no further action was taken when it was felt that there was not enough local interest at that time to proceed further. In the meantime, Lancaster Hospital hired the additional watchmen. The hope of forming a Division of the Corps was not allowed to die however, and Major Jones persisted. He visited Halifax and discussed organizational matters with Major Borrett. On his return to Saint John, he arranged for an organizational meeting on January 30, 1946 at the Lancaster Veterans Hospital. That gathering consisted of a few persons who had expressed an interest in the idea. Included were Major Brad Gilbert, Capt John McCoubrey and Capt R.M. MacFarlane. That small group agreed to form themselves into a provisional committee or Board of Governors to "organize a Branch of the Corps of Commissionaires." They decided to add other names to the committee, amongst those being Saint John veterans LCdr G.M. Butler and LCdr McAvity, Capt P. Caldwell, LCol G.A. Gamblin and Sgt Major Chambers. Several other names suggested included Lieutenant Governor, Honourable D.L. MacLaren, BGen G.G. Anglin and Col E. Ryder of Hampton, N.B.

They also considered the matter of finances and agreed that Capt McCoubrey would sound out two local Legion Branches regarding necessary start-up finances. In that regard, it was felt that an outright grant of $200 plus an additional loan of $300 would be sufficient to finance the Corps. Furthermore, they agreed that Major Jones would act as temporary Chairman, that a report would be sent to Major Borrett at Halifax and enquiries made regarding the eventual granting of a charter. Subsequent meetings of the provisional committee were held on March 21 and March 28, 1946. The minutes of those gatherings indicate that steady progress was made. Two local Legion Branches, Saint John #14 and Carleton #2, had agreed to make available the necessary start-up funds.

Commissionaire Dryden, who was the only member of the Corps employed in Saint John at the time, was introduced at one meeting and from an employee's point of view, offered details regarding uniform and salary. Letters of advice and encouragement had been received from Major

Borrett of the Nova Scotia Division and from Colonels Francis and Hanson of Montreal.

On March 28, 1946, Col Francis, Secretary Treasurer of the Canadian Corps of Commissionaires headquartered in Montreal, addressed the enlarged Provisional Committee meeting. He outlined the aims and objectives of the Corps. He referred to those few Commissionaires who were presently working at Moncton and at Renous, N.B. while attached to the Montreal office. They would be transferred to the New Brunswick Division as soon as it was operating. Branches of the New Brunswick Division could be formed in other centres of the province if and when conditions warranted. The New Brunswick Division would have the authority to draw up its own by-laws and operate independently, having regard to the purposes and aims of the Corps. The request for a Charter for the Division was granted and the Territorial limit at that time was the Province of New Brunswick. It was agreed that a New Brunswick Division of the Corps of Commissionaires be formed with Headquarters in Saint John and that BGen Anglin be the Chairman of the Board of Governors.

The first official meeting of the Board of Governors was held at 4:00 p.m. on April 15, 1946 in the board room, 56 Germain Street, Saint John, N.B. Chairman Anglin opened the meeting with a perusal of the Constitution which, after various amendments, was adopted. A nominating committee then proposed the following slate of officers:

Board of Governors:
    Chairman   BGen G.G. Anglin, CBE, MC & Bar, ED
    Vice Chairman   Major H.B. Gilbert
    Sec-Treasurer   Captain C.C. Crocker

Executive Committee:
    Chairman   Major A.R. Jones
    Vice Chairman   Captain P.W. Caldwell
    Member   B.A. McCarthy, Esq.
    Member   J.K. Kennedy, Esq.

    Commandant: LCol G.A. Gamblin, MC, VD
    Adjutant: Major W.S. Nelson, ED

That slate of officers plus the following additional members were then duly declared to be the charter members of the Board of Governors of this newly formed Division: BGen D.R. Agnew, CBE; Capt R.M. MacFarlane; BGen W.A.I. Anglin, OBE, MC; Lieutenant Governor D.L. MacLaren; LCdr G.M. Butler; G.H. Nichol, Esq.; Major J.B. Dever, N.C. Ralston, Esq.; J.V. Harquail, Esq.; S/L W.W. Rogers, MC; LCol R.A. McAvity, ED; E.B. Sweeney, Esq.; Capt J.L. MacCoubrey, DCM; Major S.C. Wright (Moncton).

Thereafter, action to organize was speeded up. Arrangements were made to open an office at 93 Germain Street in Saint John, A Constitution had been adopted, and both Standing Orders & Regulations were being printed. New Brunswick Division became operational effective Wednesday, May 1, 1946 on which date the Sergeant Major, Mr. Dyson Thomas, was to commence duty.

Col Francis, representative of the Dominion Headquarters of the Corps, presented the newly organized Division with a Charter with territorial limits within the Province of New Brunswick. He explained the by-laws and regulations regarding the operation of the Corps. The newly formed Division was granted its Charter from Dominion Headquarters of the Corps which was then located in the city of Montreal. It read as follows:

*TO ALL WHOM THESE PRESENTS MAY COME
OR IN ANY WISE CONCERN*

GREETINGS

WHEREAS The Canadian Corps of Commissionaires, a body corporate and politic without share capital, and incorporated by a Federal Charter on the 25th day of July, 1925, has been petitioned by certain gentlemen of the City and District of Saint John in the Province of New Brunswick for permission to form a branch or division with Headquarters in the City of Saint John, N.B.

Now be it known that the directors of The Canadian Corps of Commissionaires with Dominion Headquarters in the City of Montreal, in the Province of Quebec, do, by virtue of the powers invested in them, by the provisions of their By-laws, Article V, Para. 7, hereby grant to certain gentlemen to wit:

Brigadier G. Anglin; Major B. Gilbert; Captain R. MacFarlane; Captain John McCoubrey; Major A.R. Jones and such others as may be associated with them, as provisional governors pending confirmation by a general meeting of their members, power to organize a division with powers as set forth in the By-laws of The Canadian Corps of Commissionaires, adopted unanimously by the directors at a meeting called for the purpose of considering same and held in Montreal on Tuesday, 30th of November, 1937

That charter was signed on behalf of Dominion Headquarters by E. Gerald Hanson, President and G. LeB. Ross, Secretary Treasurer. It was sealed and dated at Montreal, P.Q. on 24 June 1946.

Eighty-five Commissionaires were on strength by mid-August 1946. The Hon. J.B. McNair, Premier of the Province of New Brunswick and BGen Milton F. Gregg, VC, had agreed to serve as members of the Board of Governors. By October 1946 the Division's strength had increased to 122 Commissionaires and because of distances between posts and

Divisional Headquarters, there was need to appoint the following Deputy Commandants and Officers to assist in administration and discipline: Major H.G. Crocker of Miramichi, W.A.D. Trent of Moncton, E.W. Allen of Fredericton and Col F.B. Conrad of Charlottetown.

At that time correspondence had been flowing back and forth between New Brunswick's Major Jones and Prince Edward Island's F.B. Conrad, MM, ED (both were senior employees with the Department of Veterans Affairs) indicated that they were giving serious consideration to establishing some presence of the Corps on Prince Edward Island. The advocates on the Island were not interested in forming a separate P.E.I. Division. On request, the New Brunswick Division agreed to administer the employment of Commissionaires on the Island. At that time two more Board Members from the Island were added: S/L R.E. Ellis of Summerside and Major Lowther of Charlottetown.

In March 1947, financial agreements were made with a selected bank. The Division was operating smoothly. Financial support was guaranteed to a maximum of $5,000 by Corps Headquarters. To the credit of the Division, within two years the Division had progressed to the point where the loan of $300 from the Legion Branches and the major loan of $5,000 plus interest from Corps Headquarters had been fully repaid.

At the commencement of the Division's operation, some New Brunswick Commissionaires had been originally employed through the Montreal Division but they were then taken on strength of the New Brunswick Division. During 1946 and 1947, there were several more Commissionaires employed in the province by War Assets Corporation. However, after an initial encouraging expansion, there followed a downward trend in the number of Commissionaires on strength. As War Assets were sold and warehouses closed, the strength of the Division dwindled to 65 employees. To offset that drastic drop in strength, a concentrated "selling" campaign was organized across Canada in early 1948. New Brunswick Division participated by forming a campaign committee. Considerable assistance was readily available during the campaign by Mr F.H. Horncastle and others from the Department of Veterans Affairs and from Canadian Legion officials throughout the province. New employers were found in both New Brunswick and Prince Edward Island. The Divisional strength had increased from the low point of 65 to 88 as a result of the campaign.

The Division's first "Annual" meeting was held on 16 April 1947, one full year after its first official Board of Governors meeting. From that date until the mid-1950s, the Board met on a quarterly basis – spring, summer, fall and winter. From the mid-1950s to 1968 they met tri-annually . Since 1968 they have met semi-annually – with one meeting in the late fall and the annual meeting in the spring of each year.

Soon after the Division was formed in 1946, the number of members on the Board of Governors was increased to 40 in accordance with the terms of the Constitution and for several years that figure was maintained. Then, over the years, the number of Governors was reduced somewhat and the actual number of Governors fluctuated as determined by the need for increased or decreased area representation. The number of elected Governors in 1997, including those members named by virtue of their office or appointment, stands at 30.

There was some further discussion in July and August 1948 about the Corps status on Prince Edward Island. By that time, the Division was operating as the **"New Brunswick and Prince Edward Island Division."** The matter was brought to the fore during a Board Meeting in August 1948 when senior Department of Veterans Affairs officials had expressed a preference to have the various Corps Divisions organized to correspond with the established DVA Districts. The veterans on Prince Edward Island were not serviced by the same DVA District as were the veterans in New Brunswick. Following some considerable discussion on the matter, Col. Conrad of Charlottetown expressed the firm opinion that on the Island they "were quite satisfied to be no more independent than at present." It was then suggested that no further action would be taken. Officials from the Island were advised that should they feel that a sub-Division was desired in the future, favourable consideration would be given to the matter.

Another rather significant change occurred in 1948 – the Divisional office was relocated from 56 Germain Street to 93 Prince William Street, in quarters provided by the Department of Veterans Affairs.

In January 1952, LCol G.A. Gamblin was appointed Honorary Life Member of the Board of Governors and he resigned his position as Commandant to accept the position of Comptroller on the full time staff, to be succeeded by MGen W.B. Anderson, CMG, DSO. He travelled extensively throughout the Division and on three occasions represented the Division at the Annual Meeting of the Corps Board of Directors.

In December 1952, employment opportunities were found for several Commissionaires with Enamel & Heating Products Limited in Amherst, Nova Scotia, located close to the New Brunswick border. Following negotiations with the Nova Scotia Division, it was agreed that these men should be taken on strength of the N.B. & P.E.I. Division for administration and discipline. This policy continues with the blessing of the Nova Scotia Division, making our Division unique – we have Commissionaires working in three different provinces – Prince Edward Island, Nova Scotia and New Brunswick.

In 1954, after serving as Chairman of the Board for nine outstanding years, BGen Anglin resigned due to pressure of other business and he was succeeded by Col. C.F. Leonard, DSO. However, Brigadier Anglin continued to serve as an active member of the Board for many years thereafter.

In May 1955, the first Divisional Parade was held in conjunction with the Annual Meeting of the Board of Governors. Commissionaires from outlying posts were subsidized and encouraged to attend. Some 60 uniformed Commissionaires paraded on King Street East under command of the Adjutant Major W.A. Schofield with the band of the 23rd Heavy Anti Aircraft Regiment in attendance. They were inspected by Lieutenant Governor MacLaren, who was most generous in his praise of the Parade's appearance and steadiness. The Commissionaires were entertained at dinner in the Armoury following the parade and the whole event was considered such a success that it was decided to make it an annual affair. During that same year, the opening of Camp Gagetown at Oromocto and the consequent construction activity in that district led to many new employment openings.

Officers and members of the Division were shocked and saddened to learn that Commissionaire Harry E. Knox of Saint John had died of injuries suffered while on duty at a pedestrian cross-walk on Rothesay Avenue during the afternoon of Saturday, December 8, 1956. Commissionaire Knox was directing pedestrian traffic at the time when he was struck by a car. He died of internal injuries on Sunday, December 10, 1956. He had served in Canada during both the South African War and the Second World War. Commissionaire Knox had served with the Corps for ten years and was widely known throughout the area. He has been chosen by this Division to be named a Commissionaire Extraordinaire.

Comm Harry E. Knox.

One of the highlights in the life of the Division occurred on September 13th and 14th of 1957 when the Board of Governors hosted the National Board of Governors and the Divisional Representatives from across Canada. In addition to the regular business meetings, many social events were enjoyed by the visiting delegates and their spouses. Corps Headquarters entertained the delegates at a luncheon and all visitors were received by Lieutenant Governor MacLaren at Government House in Saint John. The province of New Brunswick tendered a dinner under the Chairmanship of the Hon. A.E. Skaling, Minister of Labour. Following a meeting of Divisions on Saturday morning, the delegates were guests of the city of Saint John for lunch.

At 3 PM the Annual Parade was held in the Saint John Armoury where service decorations were presented to Commissionaires and members of the Board of Governors. Brigadier A.E.D. Tremain, CBE, ED, Chairman of the National Board of Governors, inspected the Commissionaires on parade and made the presentations. Later in the evening the Commissionaires had their Annual Dinner in the Armoury and the Governors of the Division entertained the visitors at a buffet supper in the Admiral Beatty Hotel. The whole event was an outstanding success and the Chairman of the Board expressed his appreciation to the sponsors of the various events, particularly Mr E.B. Sweeney, manager of the Admiral Beatty Hotel, and to others who had contributed so much.

In 1958, for the first time ever, the Divisional Board met at a centre other than Saint John. On November 5th that year, the meeting was held at Moncton. The event was complete with a full inspection and parade. In October 1959, the Board of Governors again held a meeting outside when they assembled in Fredericton.

By 1968 the Division's Corps strength had expanded to 970 ex-service men and women. An opportunity arose that permitted the Division to purchase one of Saint John's very historic and useful properties, widely known and identified as "Chubb's Corner." It has been indelibly linked with Saint John business life since Henry J. Chubb constructed the building in the mid 1840s. For many years it was undoubtedly the best known locality in the business section of the city. One writer referred to it as "the home of the curb-stone broker." It was the great centre of commercial speculation. Men came here to meet men who had money to lend, and those who had none came here to borrow it. Stocks and merchandise changed hands on this spot a dozen times a day. This solid building continues to serve the Division well, all the while drawing visitors from far and wide to marvel at the building's distinguishing features which include 16 stone heads, carved in the panels over the third floor. A sketch of the headquarters building appears at the start of this chapter.

There was a change in venue for the Division's Annual Meeting in 1973. For the first time, the decision was made to hold the Annual Board of Governors Meeting in Prince Edward Island rather than in New Brunswick. That historic meeting was held on May 12, 1973 . Headed by Joseph K. Kennedy, Esq., Chairman of the Board of Governors, the Board met at the Charlottetown Hotel. Following the historic business meeting, the members advanced to the Charlottetown Armouries at 1830 hours when Brig. M.F. Gregg, VC inspected a well turned-out detachment of Island Commissionaires. The parade was under the command of the Divisional Adjutant, Capt K.G.W. Doull. A march past followed after which well deserved awards were presented to several Commissionaires by Chairman Kennedy. The Board Members and Commissionaires then retired to a short stand-to followed by a banquet chaired by BGen K.M. Johnston, a member of the Board. BGen Johnston was the driving force in Corps activitiy in Prince Edward Island since 1960. In the meantime, arrangements had been made for visiting ladies to be conducted on a tour of historic sites, enjoy a dinner and attend a play at Confederation Centre.

In 1981, Commissionaire Arthur MacKinnon was honoured throughout the length and breadth of Prince Edward Island when he was chosen as the "1981 ISLANDER OF THE YEAR." Quite apart from serving the N.B. & P.E.I. Division well for many years at C.F.B.

Summerside, this retired school teacher spent countless hours of his time to aid or comfort Islanders less fortunate than himself. He was officially recognized on March 15 at the Charlottetown Rotary Club Luncheon and honoured by his fellow Islanders as the 22nd recipient of the Islander of The Year award. The Judges' citation read in part as follows:

Commissionaire Art MacKinnon.

Mr MacKinnon represents something very precious; the person who goes about quietly doing good through selfless acts to Islanders who are alone, sick and needing a helping hand. Although money seems to be the way society shows that it values the work of a person, that is not the case for Mr MacKinnon. For example, he spends countless hours providing transportation for the blind and other handicapped persons, even to the point of doing their shopping, all at his own expense in time and money. Most of Mr MacKinnon's acts are unknown; he spends many hours at the bedside of the sick and dying, easing the burden of their lonely hours. On his plot of land, Mr MacKinnon raises a garden and shares the bounty of nature with people no longer able to garden themselves. To quote a nominating letter – "We are proud to present this man who represents the highest example of integrity and selflessness. His continual contribution brings him no monetary reward other than the happiness of helping others who are in need."

There exists separate official records of two dogs which were singled out for commendations by clients. The dogs were named "Ranger" and "Bear." First, the story regarding Ranger:

The Department of Justice had decided to construct a modern prison in 1980 at Renous, N.B. Prior to the project startup, Commissionaires were engaged to patrol the fenced-in area. One day a dog arrived at the guardhouse and after being fed and shown affection by the Commissionaires, the dog decided to stay. He was part Doberman Pinscher and part "Heinz" – a good-looking dog. In no time, he was named Ranger and became noted for meeting and announcing the arrival of all visitors, day or night, and for escorting all departing vehicles off the premises. Soon the dog became a regular passenger, accompanying all Commissionaires on their mobile patrols of the area.

"Ranger" efficiently adhered to shift schedules, even after he had taken up residence with Sgt Routledge, NCO in charge of Detail. He doggedly made a round of the four miles of

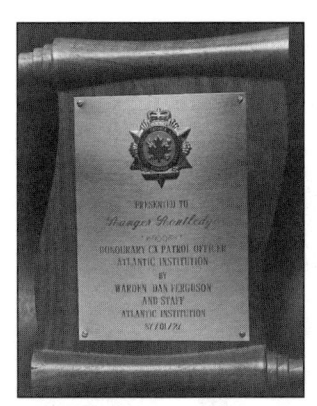

Plaque Dedicated to RANGER.

fencing areas letting all on the outside know that this was a restricted area. When the dog found a groundhog that had burrowed under the fence he returned the violating groundhog to the guardhouse.

After the new prison had been completed, Ranger was permitted to accompany Sgt Routledge on rounds within the prison, moving through closing security doors. His actions were written up in local newspapers and were mentioned on CBC programs. He was appreciated by both Commissionaires and by visiting correctional officials. When the Corps detail was phased out in 1987, all Commissionaires were invited to a luncheon by Warden Ferguson, Deputy Dawson and members of the correctional staff.

Although Ranger was unable to attend, a plaque was presented to him through Sgt Routledge. Note that Warden Ferguson designated Ranger Routledge as HONOURARY CX PATROL OFFICER, ATLANTIC INSTITUTE.

The second dog story developed in the 1990s. It involved "Bear", a large sleek German Shepherd. He was originally purchased by the RCMP and trained as a police service dog by "J" Division at the historic Old Government House in Fredericton, N.B.

When Bear was considered to be unsuitable for that service, he was left in the continuing care of the Corps Detail that was employed at the Headquarters. The RCMP later moved to a new Headquarters site but the Corps Detail and the dog continued to be stationed at the Old Government House now under renovations. All unannounced visitors are greeted by Bear who ensures that pedestrians remain outside the entrance or within their vehicles until such time as the duty Commissionaire identifies them. During silent hours Bear accompanies the Commissionaire on foot patrols and quickly responds to any strange noises within the building.

During a Royal visit, the advance protocol party believed it would be interesting to have Prince Charles throw Bear's rubber ball and then watch the dog retrieve it – an activity that he enjoys. The stage was set – the authorities obtained a new ball to replace the rather shabby old ball and Prince Charles happily agreed to participate. Unfortunately the matter had not been discussed with Bear. When the Prince threw the ball, the dog recognized that the ball was not his ball and quickly indicated by his looks and actions that if the Prince wanted that new ball, he could retrieve it himself. Bear is not easily fooled by anyone, regardless of rank or status.

Notwithstanding the dog's firm decision to remain aloof, his participation was later twice rewarded. He received a

Our other canine hero, Bear.

certificate which acknowledged that Bear had been a participant in the visit to Old Government House by HRH the Prince of Wales, Monday, April 29, 1996. Furthermore, Bear has also received an official letter of thanks from two Cabinet Ministers of the province of New Brunswick. His care continues to be provided for by Detail Corps members and he has already been assured of a good retirement home by Cpl Simard who is NCO in charge of the Detail.

In 1983, the Division again played host to the Corps' National Convention. It was a gala affair under the chairmanship of Col J.H. Turnbull, OMM, CD, then the presiding Chairman of the Division's Board of Governors.

On Thursday evening, June 23, a very successful Chairman's Reception was held when all delegates and spouses were able to meet others and renew acquaintances at the Reception or in the Hospitality Suite. Friday saw a swirl of activities — the Annual Meeting in the morning, the National Headquarters Reception and Luncheon at noon, separate gatherings in the afternoon for the Board of Governors and for the Commandants Meetings. Meanwhile, the ladies were treated to a scenic Bay of Fundy drive and luncheon at St. Andrews-by-the-Sea. Cocktails, dinner and a dance were enjoyed by all that evening when delegates and spouses from across the nation were treated to an Atlantic salmon and fiddlehead dinner with all the trimmings.

On Saturday morning, Canada's oldest incorporated city joined in on the festivities. A contingent of 60 Commissionaires, led by the band of the 3rd Field Artillery Regiment (The Loyal Company), paraded to city hall where her Worship Mayor Elsie Wayne granted the Key to the City to the Canadian Corps of Commissionaires. The actual presentation was made to national Chairman Brigadier General Raymond Normandeau, C.D. Her Worship then took pleasure in presenting individual scrolls to the Commandants of each of the Corps' 18 Divisions. That evening all present were treated to a bountiful lobster dinner at Market Square Trade and Convention Centre at 1900 hours. A "Bon Voyage" breakfast was made available for the departing delegates on Sunday, June 26.

Presentation of Key to the City.

Commissionaire Fred Walls was employed by the Corps on July 2, 1952 and after 35 years, 2 months and 22 days of exemplary service, he retired on October 5, 1987. During that period of service, Commissionaire Walls brought honour to the N.B. & P.E.I. Division when he was singled out for special recognition by Lieutenant General Paul Manson, then Commander of Air Command and former Base Commander of CFB Chatham. During a visit to Chatham, Lt Gen Manson presented Commissionaire Walls with an Air Command Commander's Commendation in recognition of Walls' outstanding service. The Commendation reads as follows:

Commanders Commendation presented to Commissionaire Fred Walls.

AIR COMMAND
COMMANDER'S COMMENDATION

In Recognition of Outstanding Service

TO

COMMISSIONAIRE FREDERICK WALLS

FOR

HIS PERSONAL CONTRIBUTION TO CANADIAN FORCES BASE CHATHAM. OVER A SPAN OF THIRTY-ONE YEARS, COMMISSIONAIRE WALLS HAS CONSISTENTLY GAINED THE RESPECT OF HIS SUPERIORS, PEERS AND EVERYONE IN THE LOCAL MILITARY AND CIVILIAN COMMUNITIES. BY HIS PERSONAL EFFORT AND EXAMPLE, COMMISSIONAIRE WALLS HAS BEEN A PERFECT AMBASSADOR FOR THE BASE. HE HAS SERVED WITH DISTINCTION, HONOUR, PRIDE AND TOTAL DEDICATION.

WINNIPEG, CANADA
15 MARCH 1984

(Signed) P.D. MANSON, LIEUTENANT-GENERAL
COMMANDER AIR COMMAND

It should be noted that, according to a 1984 letter received from National Chairman Major K.J. McRae, CD, the certificate presented to Commissionaire Walls was only the third such commendation to have been presented by the Canadian Armed Forces.

Available records below show the changes in strength over the years in this N.B. & P.E.I. Division:

YEAR		STRENGTH	HRS. INVOICED	REVENUE
MAY	1946	(Formation)		$ 500
AUG	1946	85		
JAN	1947	122	117,000	
	1958	268	508,000	
	1966	511	556,94	776,000
	1976	927	1,099,581	4,287,000
	1986	930	1,229,845	9,103,000
	1996	800	864,130	7,940,000

The Board is proud of the fact that, based on our last five years of operations, for each $1 invoiced to the customer, $95.74 is returned to the Commissionaire through wages and benefits. This has resulted in a less than 3% turnover rate of our Commissionaires. The Board of Governors ensures that the Division operates at maximum efficiency. Notwithstanding the inevitable turnover among the members of the Board due to death, transfers, etc., the Division has been fortunate in consistently being able to enlist prominent citizens who have held high positions in government, civil service and private business. It is felt that a prosperous future is assured as long as this interest can be maintained.

The Division's Board of Governors are indeed proud of Colonel Everett and his dedicated headquarters staff who are listed hereunder: Commandant - Col C,B, Everett, CD; Adjutant - Capt I.B. Vail; A/Adjutant - Capt D.W. Hunter CD; RSM - CWO J.A. Arseneault, CD; Secretary - C Hamilton; RQMS - CWO R.J. Clowater; Accounts Officer - S. Crawford; Pay Office - P. Iliffe and Sgt J. Smith CD.

Col Everett retired in the fall of 1997 after having served the Division for a period of 19 years, 3 months and 21 days. In recognition of his dedication to the Corps and to this Division he was recently awarded the Commissionaire Distinguished Service Medal. The Board of Governors are confident that Col Everett is handing over an efficient Division to Capt D.W. Hunter and that the Division will continue to meet the challenges of the future.

The members of the Board of Governors are: Dr. G.W. Bate; R.O. Bosence, Esq., CA; *Col P. E. Burden, DFC; Lt B. Cormier; G.T. Critch, Esq.; Capt J.S. Day; *Col. B.R. Doucet, CD; *Capt D.F. Filliter, CD, CMA; E.J. Gallant, Esq.; Major W.M. Harvey; *H.M. Heckbert, Esq., MM; Lt(N)

E.J. Kipping, CD, BA, Bed; F/L J.T. Logan, BA, Bed, MA; *Col The Hon. R.E. Logan, CD; Capt E. MacFarlane, CD; A.M. McLean, Esq.; LCdr J.A. McCrae, CD; *LCol R.S. McLeod, ED; C.J. Mew, Esq.; Capt(N) W.F. O'Connell, CD; Col B.A. Oulton, CD; Lt N/S N. Page, CD; *F/L J.A. Stewart, DFC, CA; *Col. J.H. Turnbull, OMM, CD.

Additional members by virtue of their office or appointment: Premier of New Brunswick; Premier of Prince Edward Island; Commander, Combat Training Center, CFB Gagetown; President, N.B. Command, Royal Canadian Legion; Commanding Officer "J" Division, RCMP, Fredericton, NB; Minister of Supply & Services, province of New Brunswick.

* = Served as Chairman, Board of Governors

The All Female Detail

On May 1, 1995, the Corps was awarded a contract by the city of Saint John, NB to provide female cell guards (matrons) to the Saint John police department. These Commissionaires provide 24-hour service to the Police Department on an "on-call" basis. They are administered by NCOs who liaise with the police, develop shift schedules, and look after discipline, dress and deportment. This detail is difficult in that most calls to the guards and NCO come in the night and on weekends. Some, over the years, obtained full time Corps jobs, but always make themselves available to help out on their off hours.

This has been a well run and successful detail and the contract has been renewed twice. It has recently been learned that this detail is the only one in the Corps that consists entirely of females both at the Commissionaires and NCO level.

ONE OF A KIND – ONLY ALL FEMALE UNIT IN CANADA
From left to right, Front Row: Comm Verch, Sgt Power, Capt Vail, and Cpl Power. Rear Row: Comm Katruk, Comm Ferguson, Comm Parker and Comm Payne.

Chapter XV

HISTORY OF THE QUEBEC DIVISION

Commandant's Introduction – *by Jean-Yves Lauzier*

WE OWE the Governors who created the Quebec Division a great deal of recognition and respect. They had a clear vision of the future mission of the Division and of the role which the Commissionaires would have to play in the security industry and the local community. These pioneers who created the Division, (the Governors as well as the Commissionaires) traced the path to excellence, laying the foundation of a legacy based on our culture and the Corps tradition.

The history of the Quebec Division highlights the high degree of professionalism of its members and the client's appreciation of the services rendered.

The Quebec Division history is dedicated to the women and men who picked up the torch, to those who carry it still and to those to whom they will pass it.

We also take this opportunity to underline the devotion with which the Directors have served, volunteering their time and sharing their knowledge in providing direction for the management and support of the Division. They have thus contributed to the success of the Division in a remarkable way.

The Early Years

After the Second World War, demobilization returned to civil life large numbers of veterans and finding civil employment for them became a problem.

The reorganization of wartime industries to peacetime ones and the geographic location of the Quebec District, indicated that the Montreal Branch of the Canadian Corps of Commissionaires could never succeed in finding employment for all veterans in spite of all its effort.

In 1946, Brigadier Georges Francoeur, OBE, VD, District Administrator of the Department of Veteran Affairs, realizing the difficulties met by the veterans to find suitable employment called upon a group of local citizens to organize a Division in the city of Quebec, with the help of Lieutenant General Sir Richard Turner, VC, KCB, CKMG, DSO, Major General Thomas Tremblay, CB, CMG, DSO, ED, Mr. J. Albert Towner, OBE, and Mr. Maurice Samson, OBE.

The Canadian Corps of Commissionaires was requested to send a representative to Quebec to explain the organization and the activities of the Corps.

Brigadier General G. Francoeur, OBE.

Subsequently, a group of prominent men selected among leaders in industry, finance, business and the armed forces, were recruited to form a provisional Board of Governors.

The first meeting of the provisional Board of Governors was held on October 4, 1946 in Quebec City. LCol Henri Desrosiers, CMG, DSO, VD, was elected Chairman and Major Maurice Painchaud, Supervisor Social Services DVA, acted as Secretary. The Chairman stated that the meeting had been called for the purpose of considering the formation of the Quebec Division of the Corps.

LCol Desrosiers explained the constitution, aim and object of the Canadian Corps of Commissionaires Inc. and LCol Gerald Hanson, DSO, ED, President of the Corps, outlined the organization and activities of the Corps in the various provinces of Canada.

LCol Henri Desrosiers.

It was then moved and unanimously resolved that the Canadian Corps of Commissionaires be petitioned for permission to form the Quebec Division with Headquarters in Quebec City. LCol Hanson informed the meeting that the Headquarters of the Corps would sponsor the creation of the Quebec Division and that its Board of Directors would grant and confirm the necessary authority in due course. He proposed that the organization of the Quebec Division be proceeded with.

The meeting moved and resolved that LCol Henri Desrosiers, Brigadier John H. Price, OBE, MC, and Mr. J.A. Towner be delegated and given authority to proceed with the organization and the establishment of the Quebec Division and to accept as of November 1, 1946 the handing over of operations and projects of the Corps in the territory of the province of Quebec extending from Trois-Rivières to the Lower St.

Lawrence and take any action deemed necessary in the dispatch of the business of the Quebec Division.

The Canadian Corps of Commissionaires Inc. at a meeting of its Board of Directors held in Montreal on December 13, 1946 granted power to the provisional Governors to organize the Division in Quebec City.

On January 16, 1947, a second meeting of the provisional Board of Governors was held under the chairmanship of LCol Desrosiers to read and approve the minutes of the first meeting and to ratify and confirm all its acts and proceedings.

The granting of the charter to the Quebec Division by the Canadian Corps of Commissionaires Inc. was read and entered in the minute book of the Division.

The meeting also approved the first By-Laws of the Division and after the provisional Board of Governors resigned to be replaced by a newly elected Board as provided by the By-Laws.

The first part-time Commandant was Brig Georges Francoeur of the Department of Veterans Affair. Brigadier Francoeur with the assistance of the officers of Veterans Affairs devoted considerable time and effort to the search for employment and security for the veterans possessing qualifications of honesty, sobriety and punctuality.

The first contract signed by the Quebec Division as such was for the security guard of the wartime surplus factories taken over by the city of Quebec.

Strength

From November 1, 1946 when it took over from the Montreal Division the responsibility for the operations in the territory from Trois-Rivières to the Lower St. Lawrence, the strength of the Commissionaires in the Quebec Division increased rapidly after a slow start as shown by the following summary: 1946 - 46, 1966 - 322, 1986 - 510 and in March 1997 the highest ever in the Division - 578.

Total hours worked by the Commissionaires during the last 30 years show the distribution between the federal government and the other customers.

Hours Worked

Years	Federal	Others	Total
1965 - 66	303,826	305,963	609,789
1975 - 76	474,334	401,493	875,827
1985 - 86	467,179	320,716	787,895
1995 - 96	370,354	210,253	580,607
1996 - 97	358,271	498,315	856,586

After 1976, the faster reduction in hours worked in the private than the government sector was due to increased competition from more security agencies entering the market and cuts in financial resources available for security.

The Recent Years

In 1955, on the recommendation of its legal advisor, the Board of Directors incorporated the Quebec Division as a non-profit corporation by Letters Patent under Part III of the Quebec Companies Act and new By-Laws were adopted.

On December 8, 1958, Col J.G. Charlesbois, CD, became the first full time employee of the Division as Adjutant paymaster and soon after, on April 4, 1959, Brigadier G.A.H. Trudeau, CBE, CD, resigned as Governor and was appointed the first full time Commandant, replacing Brig G. Francoeur.

From 1961 on, the Division as a security agency became bound by several Quebec Labour Acts: Construction Decree 1961, Workmen Compensation 1963, Minimum Wages 1970, *Loi des agences d'investigations et de sécurité Québec, Regulation no. 2, 1973.*

In 1971, Commissionaires replaced the *Sûreté du Quèbec* in St. Jean Vianney a few weeks after the tragic landslide.

The Division under its Commandant, Colonel A.C. Perron, ED, CD, developed classification standards for its Commissionaires. These standards were later accepted by the Security Advisory Committee for the Canadian Corps of Commissionaires in 1975.

Colonel J.G. Charlesbois.

Brigadier General G.A.H. Trudeau.

The Trois-Rivières region became part of the Division's territory in 1978 by decision of the Corps.

The Commissionaires voted in 1978 to become members of *"Union des Agents de sécurité"* and a collective agreement was signed on December 18, 1978. The *"Union des Agents de sécurité du Québec (Métalurgistes Unis d'Amérique) local 8922"* displaced the first union on May 4, 1984.

The Division joined the *Conseil des Agences de Sécurité et d'Investigation de l'Est du Québec (ASIEQ)* a security employers organization in 1983.

LCol Gérard R. Fortin, MBE, CD, CLJ, was appointed Padre and Governor of the Division in 1990.

The Corps authorized the employment as Commissionaires of non-eligible personnel with special qualifications if requested by customers in 1991.

Commissionaires replaced the RCMP in 1994 and took over baggage cart handling and taxi driver control in 1996 at the Quebec Airport. They also took over the security of a large group of Quebec region hospitals the same year.

Five ex-chairmen of the Division served the Corps at the National level on the Executive Committee: Mr K.R. Kane, 1959; LCol P.E. Defoy,

EM, CD, 1974; Brig R. Normandeau, CD, 1977, Col G. Dufresne, CM, ED, CD, 1993; and LCol J.C. Samson, CD, 1997. Brig Normandeau became National Chairman of the Corps in 1981.

During the last 20 years, the Division has been visited by four National Chairmen: Major A.F. Bruce, September 17, (1980); LCol J.C. Stewart, CD, June 13, (1988); LGen W.A. Milroy, DSO, CD, November 29, (1994); LCol R.G. Smellie, CD, QC, March 4-5, (1997).

Divisional Headquarters

The Division Headquarters was first set up in rent-free accommodation provided by the Department of Veterans Affairs in its district office, 51 des Capucins, Quebec City.

In 1953, new DVA regulations did not permit the Division to remain on DVA premises and it moved to the residence of the Commandant at 2250 Chemin St-Louis Sillery, until 1955 when temporary office space was rented in the Army and Navy Building, 13 St-Joachin, Quebec City.

The next move was to 144 Grande Allée on June 1, 1956 where it stayed for 20 years.

With the growth in personnel, equipment and quartermaster stores, more space was required and in 1976, accommodation was rented at 8 Jardins Mérici.

On October 1, 1981, Division Headquarters moved to its present location in Ste-Foy at 2323 Versant Nord.

Annual Parades and Medals Presentation

The first recorded parade is a guard of Honour inspected by the Governor General Lord Alexander when he visited the Veterans Hospital in 1947.

When the Deputy Minister of Veterans Affairs, Mr Walter Woods visited the Quebec District of DVA in 1948, the Commissionaires supplied a guard of honour and the Deputy Minister presented the Long Service Medal to Commissionaire Charles Levesque.

The Honourable Hughes Lapointe, KC, Minister of Veterans Affairs visited the Veterans Hospital in January 1951 and inspected a Commissionaire Guard of Honour.

The next year, the Commissionaires supplied a Guard of Honour with the R22^e Regiment Band in attendance at the Garrison Club for Governor General Vincent Massey who presented Long Service and Efficiency Medals to Sgt Major L. Dagenais, MBE, MM, Cpl J.P. St-Hilaire and Commissionaire Albert Lange.

At the official opening of the new Ste-Foy Veterans Hospital on May 16, 1954, the Honourable Louis St-Laurent, KC, CP, LLD inspected a detachment of Commissionaires.

On September 27, 1956, Governor General Vincent Massey inspected the last official parade, a detachment of 40 Commissionaires at the Citadel with the R22^e Regiment Band on parade.

After 1956, medals were presented before or after regular meetings of the Board of Directors at the Headquarters or on security posts during the Chairmen's or Commandant's inspection because the formation of the trade union made it difficult or expensive to hold parades in recent years.

Performance Gratuities

In 1948, a bonus of $25 per year was implemented for performance, payable at the rate of $10 for the first six months of service and $15 for the next six months.

This was changed to $1 per month of service, maximum $10 per year in 1952 and the next year the same amount was given in merchandise instead of money.

At the end of 1953, the scale became $3 plus $1 per month of service during the year with a maximum of $15 and a minimum of $4. The Board of Directors changed the gratuity scale in 1954 to $1 per month of service during the year plus $1 per year of service paid at Christmas.

1956 saw the end of the gratuities when cigarettes were added to the previous money bonus.

As from 1994, a wrist watch is presented after 15 years of exemplary service.

Women as Commissionaires

Two ex-servicewomen were first employed by the Division in 1980, one at Laval University and the other one at Revenue Canada. By the end of March 1981, this was increased to five as two more customers, Industries Valcartier and Hopital St-François d'Assise had openings for women.

In 1987, Laval University requested the replacement of some ex-servicemen by women without military service but in possession of a police technics certificate.

The Quebec Department of Supplies and Services advised the Division by letter on April 17, 1989 that firms with more than 100 employees must bind themselves to introduce the Quebec policy of Equity of Employment when submitting bids for contract.

As at March 31, 1997, there were 78 women employed as Commissionaires mostly at Laval University and in hospitals.

Training

Some training was carried out over the early years and in 1952 and 1953, 80 Commissionaires attended the St. John Ambulance Emergency First Aid course.

Four NCOs were qualified security agents at the Quebec Police Institute in 1972.

In 1973, a training officer was appointed, an audio-visual training film produced and a basic security agent course developed.

Starting in 1976, following these courses, Commissionaires were able to take an introduction course and a basic security agent course to meet federal government standards, as well as supervisor, patrolman, new elementary, cardio-pulmonary resuscitation, airport security, air passenger search, basic fire control and emergency first aid courses.

Special training to meet individual customer requirements has been given to Commissionaires such as radio operator, computer terminal operator, and hospital emergency procedures.

Since 1995, Quebec Act 90 "To promote the Development of manpower" compels employers to spend one percent of their yearly wage expenditure on employee training.

Uniforms

In 1948, a fur cap was adopted for winter wear by the Commissionaires and sold for $7. In 1955 the Division paid 25% of the cost of the uniforms.

The introduction of Bill 30 by the Quebec Legislature in 1963 made it compulsory for police forces to wear standard blue uniforms and for security agencies to adopt any other colour but blue. Consequently, Commissionaires serving in the province of Quebec wore steel grey uniforms instead of the blue and the Quebec Division changed the uniforms free of charge.

The law was changed in 1993 and the Commissionaires' uniforms reverted to the standard Corps blue colour.

Until 1975, Commissionaires purchased their uniforms. The federal government's agreement considered uniforms an allowable expense for government contracts, and made it imperative to issue uniforms free of charge to Commissionaires. Bilingual shoulder badges were issued in 1975.

For special jobs Commissionaires wore blue blazers, grey flannel trousers or skirts and Corps ties. The Quartermaster store carries a supply of uniforms, shirts, ties and winter wear.

Commissionaire Benefits

Until the Division became bound by different Quebec Labour Acts or collective agreements, it attempted to provide its members with as many monetary benefits as permitted by financial resources.

One week annual leave was paid in 1950, driver's insurance for Commissionaires driving a DND vehicle on duty and free telephone calls for isolated detachments were paid in 1952. A health insurance plan was added in 1959.

In 1976, an emergency fund was created to help Commissionaires in financial difficulties.

A collective retirement savings plan with a contribution of 7.5% of the cost paid by the Division was accepted by the Commissionaires in 1978.

Since the Commissionaires were covered by union collective agreement after 1978, only the office staff and non-union NCOs remained on Division benefit plan.

A termination indemnity of one week salary per year of service after a minimum of five-year service covered the office staff in 1979 and after.

In 1989, NCO's and detachment commanders accepted a collective group insurance plan with the Division agreeing to pay two thirds of the dues. The benefits of the office staff were increased to cover payments for annual sickness, social and statutory leaves.

The termination indemnity was limited to a maximum 60 days in 1993.

National Annual General Meeting

The Canadian Corps of Commissionaires held three National Annual General Meetings in Quebec City. The first one was on September 18, 1951 at the Chateau Frontenac when the Quebec Division gave a reception at the Garrison Club for the National Chairman, LCol Gerald Hanson, DSO, ED, and the delegates.

The Division hosted successfully the General Meeting at the Chateau Frontenac on September 12 - 14, 1974.

In 1990, the Quebec Division hosted the National Annual General Meeting at the Chateau Frontenac. Social functions were held at the Chateau and (a country dance and festivities) on a farm on the Island of Orleans. A boat trip on the St. Lawrence River and a tour of the Citadel were part of the outings. According to the letters of congratulations received, it was a tremendous success.

Community Involvement

From the beginning, the Division contributed to the well being of the Quebec community.

In the early days, Christmas baskets were distributed to needy veterans, monetary contributions given to the War Amputees of Canada and to the Christmas activities of the Ste-Foy Veterans Hospital.

In 1985, it participated in the organization of the 53rd Congress of the *Association canadienne française pour l'avancement des sciences* (ACFAS) and the next year to *Expo Habitat 1986* both held in Chicoutimi.

Again in 1990, in Chicoutimi, it participated in the Cerebral Palsy Telethon.

Security agents were supplied free of charge to the Red Cross for blood collection campaigns.

The Division hosted one teenager in 1992 for the "Star of the Day" program involving the exchange of duties with managers.

It contributed to the 50th Anniversary of D-Day celebrations in 1994 and the end of the Second World War in 1995 when Warrant Officer Denis Baillargeon helped organize the Canada Remembers exhibition at Revenue Canada.

The United Way Campaign is supported and Commissionaires, as part of the security service won the Gold Bucket at Laval University in 1995.

Special Recognition

The records of the Division contain many letters of congratulations and appreciation from customers for the work of the Commissionaires in Valcartier Camp at the ammunition dump, Laval University for an accident at the swimming pool, for the arrest of robbers, for the prevention of mischief and from the airport at Baie Comeau for emergency service during an accident.

LCdr S. Dery, a governor, was named "Transport man of the year" in 1982 and was presented with the prize by the Lieutenant Governor of British Columbia The Honourable Henry Bell-Irving.

Major Guy D'Artois, DSO, GM, CD, training officer of the Division was presented with the Flag of the Maquis de Sylla in 1984 for his service with the French resistance during the Second World War as a Special Service Officer.

On September 26, 1991, Commissionaire Leonard Gauvin saved the life of Mr. Yvon Roy, a construction worker on the work site of a building for CRDV in Valcartier Camp. Mr. Roy was working on a concrete base unaware that a paving roller left unattended with its engine running was moving towards him. Commissionaire Gauvin on duty at the site realizing that the worker would be crushed to death started immediately to shout warnings at the worker who realizing that something dangerous was happening and got away from his work place thus saving his life or serious injuries.

The Board of Governors

The Board of Governors is composed of 25 members selected from retired military officers and civilians.

Over the many years, many governors were or became well known citizens such as: LGen Sir Richard Turner and BGen Paul Triquet, both Victoria Cross winners; the Honourable Louis St. Laurent became Prime Minister of Canada; the Honourable Hughes Lapointe, CR, and Gilles Lamontagne, both Minister of the federal government (Veterans Affairs and National Defence respectively) who became Lieutenant Governors of the province of Quebec afterwards; Generals J.V. Allard, CB, CBE, DSO, ED, and J.A. Dextraze, CC, CBE, CMM, DSO, CD, became Chief of Defence Staff; Col Maurice

Major Rene Jalbert.

Roy, OBE, Archbishop of Quebec and Cardinal; and Major René Jalbert, CV, CD, calmed and led away the killer after the shooting in the National Assembly of the Quebec Parliament Building.

The first woman selected was Lieutenant Sonya D'Artois, MBE, a member of the British Special Service, who was parachuted into France during World War II to work with the French resistance.

Lieutenant Sonya D'Artois with husband Maj Guy D'Artois.

Three governors were decorated during their tenure of office. LCol Louis Taschereau, MBE, ED, CD, was awarded the French Legion d'Honneur in 1995; Col G. Coulombe, CM, CD, KCLJ, the Order of Canada in 1981; and LCol P.E. Defoy, EM, CD, OE, the *Ordre national du Mérite de France* in 1984.

Capt J.P. Savary, CD, ex-Commandant of the Division was awarded the Corps Distinguished Service Medal in 1993 for more than 20 years of meritorious service.

After long service, retiring Governors can be appointed Honorary Members without voting rights. Only Governors who have served on the Board of Directors are eligible for the Long Service Medal.

The Customers

The Quebec Division had a variety of customers during its 51 years of existence: the city of Quebec; the Federal Government Departments of National Defence, Immigration, Public Works, Revenue Canada, Transport and Unemployment Insurance; Defence Production; CMHC; War Assets; Canadian Armament Research Development Establishment; CBC; Airport; Park Canada; RCMP; and private enterprises such as Laval University; Bell Canada, Quebec Harbour, Post Canada, hospitals, school boards, St-Lawrence Cement, Davie Shipbuilding, Goodyear and construction companies, etc.

The trades covered by Commissionaires varied from security agents, boiler operators, cleaners, traffic controllers, investigators, parking lot attendants, to police work at airports, patrolmen, baggage cart handlers, console operators.

The largest customers are still the Federal Government, Laval University, and Partagec, an hospital service group. All the customers are mostly concentrated in the Quebec Region but as far as the Trois-Rivières, Chicoutimi, Lower St-Lawrence and North Shore Regions for smaller federal government contracts.

The Current Year (1997/98)

With the "Right of First Refusal" in doubt and the refusal of the provincial government to allow non-profit companies to bid for government contracts and the complaints of unfair competition from other agencies, the Directors and Governors decided after serious analysis of the problem and the advice of their lawyers to incorporate a company under the Quebec Companies Act.

The first step was to update the Letters Patent granted in 1955 and the By-Laws. This was done by a committee and after approval by the Directors and Governors at board meetings a request for supplementary Letters Patent and By-Laws was sent to the Inspector General of Financial Institutions. These were granted on April 15, 1997.

The second step was to request Letters Patent for the incorporation of a new company after approval by the Board of Directors and a meeting of governors. On May 28, 1997, the By-Laws and Letters Patent were granted by the government authority.

Chapter XVI

HISTORY OF THE SOUTH SASKATCHEWAN DIVISION

Commandant's Introduction – *By Elwood Byrnes*

The South Saskatchewan Division of The Canadian Corps of Commissionaires serves all of the southern half of the province of Saskatchewan, covering an area from the Manitoba border in the east to the Alberta border in the west; from the U.S. border in the south to approximately 300 kilometres north of the U.S. border. There are Commissionaire Detachments located in Swift Current, Moose Jaw and Yorkton, Saskatchewan. From Regina to Swift Current in the west is 245 kilometres and Yorkton to the northeast is 187 kilometres. Our geographic area is vast and we are presented with many challenges.

The business in the South Saskatchewan Division is diversified and is comprised of 38% federal and 62% commercial. Like most other Divisions, we guard in locations from the Regina Airport to the Provincial Legislative Building, to the Consumers Cooperative Refinery. We do by-law enforcement in the cities of Swift Current, Moose Jaw, Yorkton and Regina. We also have commissionaires manning the Regina City Police Equipment Room, and the Canadian Airport Security System monitor room at the Regina Airport, and we provide Identification Security Screening at 15 Wing CFB Moose Jaw.

We in the **South** Saskatchewan Division look forward to future challenges with great anticipation. We will remain a viable entity in the future of the Canadian Corps of Commissionaires.

Our Early Years

The South Saskatchewan Division of the Canadian Corps of Commissionaires began by failing. In 1947, the Manitoba Division attempted to start Corps activity in the Queen City when they dispatched Sergeant Thompson on loan to assist in the formation of the Regina Branch. The first contracts were with the Canadian Pacific Railway and the

War Assets Corporation. The initial five Commissionaires were to guard surplus stores for the War Assets Corporation. The new Commissionaires were poorly equipped as only three old used uniforms and two Corps caps had been provided from the Manitoba Division. As the future Corps RSM, Sgt G.C. Brooks, noted in his history of the Corps of August 1969, *"This was a very poor showing. I was sure it would not last long . . . it soon folded up."* It seems the first attempt only lasted a few weeks.

The collapse of the first attempt did not deter a group of interested officers who were determined to provide local veterans with meaningful employment. They submitted a proposal to the Headquarters in Montreal requesting authority to form a Corps in Regina. Headquarters dispatched Colonel Hanson from Montreal to assess the potential for employment, the administrative and management capability and the manpower resources available in the area. His report was obviously favourable as the necessary authorities were granted by Headquarters. This original group of "Founding Fathers" of the Regina Division included: LCol A.J. Hosie, Capt G.C. Gamey, Lt A.B.D. Campbell, Capt S.A. Gutheridge, F/O E. Dixon, Lt R.J. Hegan, Lt K.R. Miller, LCol, Fysh, Capt J.E. Haltonquist, F/O R.M. Bleakley, LCol M.A. Germaine, Maj T.P. Davidson, Petty Officer R.N. Keefer.

The leader of the group in 1947 that led to the formation of the first Corps of Commissionaires, South Saskatchewan in May 1948 was Col Hosie, a veteran of the First World War having served overseas with the rank of lieutenant. During the Second World War, Col Hosie commanded the Second Battalion, Regina Rifles from 1942 until June 1944. He served on the Board of Governors from 1948 until 1971. He was the Board Chairman and Commandant from 1961 to 1971.

The necessary authorities were granted by Headquarters. In the words of Commissionaire Brooks, *"So that was how the Division came into being. A Board of Governors was set up and Colonel Hosie was Commandant of the Division and Maj Little, Administrator of the Department of Veterans Affairs let two members of his staff assist in their spare time . . . So Captain R. Ledrew was made Chairman of the Board of Governors and Mr. R. Lamont was made Adjutant and I was made Divisional Sergeant Major. Major Little let Captain Ledrew and Mr. Lamont use their offices to do Corps work and interviews, etc."* Although we have no records available, we assume that both Capt Ledrew and Mr. Lamont were employees of DVA. The first Corps space in Regina was in the offices at DVA.

LCol Andrew J. Hosie, OBE.

The Division Sergeant Major and Adjutant immediately started recruiting and interviewing prospective Commissionaires. When the Department of National Defence requested Commissionaires for security

South Saskatchewan Division – 1 May 1948 – Inspection Day.
Back Row: Eight Original Uniformed Corps Members. Front Row:
Senior NCO Sgt G.C. Brooks, Capt R. Ledrew, Brigadier R. Morton,
LCol Hosie and Capt R.D. Lamont.

guard duties to begin at 0900 hours on May 1, 1948, the Regina Corps was ready with eight men fully outfitted in Corps uniforms. It was just as well as Brigadier General Morton, Officer Commanding, informed Sergeant Major Brooks that he would like to inspect the troops at 1600 hours that day. Brooks notes: *I started the men on 01 May. I was in charge of the guards. Brigadier Morton OC Military Headquarters there, called me in and said he wished to inspect the guard at 1600 hours that day so, I got Colonel Hosie, Captain Ledrew and the Adjutant and they came over at 1600 hours for the "Inspection." I have several photos of that inspection as the Adjutant had the Leader Post photographer come in and take photos. This inspection went over very good as the men looked very smart in their new uniforms.*

The original eight Commissionaires in the South Saskatchewan Division were Commissionaires W.S. Aitchinson, T.H. McCormick, E.R. Penman, E.H. Styles, J.R. Levers, C. Thompson, J.A. Stevenson and J. McPherson.

The publicity the Corps have gained from the press reports of the initial inspection must have had a very positive effect on local businessmen as our Commissionaire Extraordinaire Brooks goes on to state "... *the next job we got was for a man to run the elevator at the Drak Hotel. Then a man at Simpsons Store, one at the Army & Navy Store, one at CKCK Radio Station, one at CJME Radio Station, one at Rex Theatre on Hamilton Street . . . then we had three men at the Shell Oil Company."* The Corps in Regina was here to stay.

We owe our success today to the dedication of the initial Board of Governors and to Messers. Lamont and Brooks. Lamont retired from the DVA and became full-time Adjutant and set about establishing a Corps presence in Moose Jaw, Yorkton and Estevan. Commissionaires Brooks did an outstanding job as RSM. During a period when the Adjutant was hospitalized for two months, Brooks was not only the RSM but was required to . . . *make out the cheques, do the banking and send out the bills.* He was truly our first Commissionaire Extraordinaire.

Brooks was RSM from 1948 until his retirement in 1967. The Commissionaires' strength now numbered around 200 men and women. There were paid full time staff in addition to the RSM to help with the increased workload.

During the 1960s and 70s, the Corps continued to expand and diversify. The RCMP, in 1970, was finding it difficult to administrate the several custodians and matrons required at their many RCMP detachment jails throughout the province. These custodians and matrons were required to guard prisoners in jail awaiting trial or transfer to federal or provincial jails. On October 1, 1970, the Corps of Commissionaires in Saskatchewan assumed the responsibility for the pay of all RCMP Detachment custodians and matrons in the province. Most of these are casual help of whom the majority are civilians. A few are Commissionaires. The RCMP retained the authority for hiring and release. As far as it is known, the province of Saskatchewan is the only province in Canada where this unique system is in effect.

September 15, 1972

September 15, 1972 was a significant date in the history of the Regina Corps. It was on this date in 1972 that Regina became an independent Division in its own right, when Headquarters relinquished control and assigned all assets (in excess of $206,600) to the Canadian Corps of Commissionaires (South Saskatchewan).

Canadian Corps of Commissionaires
(South Saskatchewan)
Room 304 - 2024 - 21st Avenue
Regina, Saskatchewan

The Canadian Corps of Commissionaires – Le Corps Canadien des Commissionnaires, (hereinafter referred to as "Headquarters Corps") hereby releases and quits claim to and in favour of Canadian Corps of Commissionaires (South Saskatchewan) all right, title and interest which Headquarters Corps may have in and to those assets which are set out and referred to in the letter, dated June 1, 1972 from the Canadian Corps of Commissionaires (South Saskatchewan) to Headquarters Corps (a copy of which is hereto annexed).

Dated: September 15, 1972.

THE CANADIAN CORPS OF COMMISSIONAIRES -
LE CORPS CANADIEN DES COMMISSIONNAIRES

Signed By: R.P. White
Signed By: R. Balfour

The South Saskatchewan Division was in excellent shape to begin as an independent Division.

The Queen and Lieutenant Governors

During Her Majesty's first visit to Regina as our Queen, in 1959, the Corps played an important role in the overall security arrangements. RSM Brooks states in his history of the Corps,

> *I was called to the Legislative Building for a meeting with the Premier and the head of the RCMP. I was asked to supply 18 Commissionaires for duty the day the Queen was to visit the Legislative Building. I said I could, so myself and an RCMP Sergeant were in charge of security within the building. We placed a Commissionaire and an RCMP Constable at the entrance door, who checked the visitors before being allowed to enter the building as we had a list of all who had invitations. They were escorted by Commissionaires to the main foyer where we had eight Commissionaires at desks who checked their invitations against the seating list and if OK, the Commissionaires gave them a ticket with their seat numbers in the main Chamber. We had Commissionaires at the doors to the Chamber who checked the number of their seat and escorted the distinguished guests to their seats. This was a very important day for the Commissionaires.*

The whole exercise went without a hitch and the Corps was commended for its courteous and efficient performance. The exposure on this important day did much to promote the Corps image and led to increased requests for Commissionaire services and more jobs for deserving veterans. Because of the success of this operation, the Corps was requested to participate in the security arrangements for Her Majesty's visits to Regina in 1973 and 1978.

His Honour, The Lieutenant Governor of Saskatchewan (1970 - 1976) Dr. S. Worobetz, Patron of the South Saskatchewan Division, always attended the Annual Commissionaires Awards Dinner. As Guest of Honour, he spoke to the Commissionaires and presented the Long Service Awards. Among those receiving awards at the January 31, 1972 dinner, was Commissionaire Mike Symchyshen who joined the Corps in 1961 and served as a messenger at the Regina Police Service. He is seen here receiving his 10-Year Award from Dr. Worobetz.

Symchyshen was again presented with his 15-Year Award at a similar Awards Dinner in 1977. Here he is seen receiving his certificate and medal from His Honour, The Lieutenant Governor George Porteous (1976-1977). Commissionaire Symchyshen served with the Corps until March 1986, spending his entire service with the Regina Police Service. He died in July 1987.

Commissionaire Mike Symchyshen receiving Long Service Award from Dr. Worobetz.

The Lieutenant Governors continue to be Patrons of the South Saskatchewan Division. The current Lieutenant Governor is His Honour Jack Wiebe who began his appointment in 1994.

Our Growth and Strength

From a modest start in 1948 with eight Commissionaires, the Division had grown to 245 male and 16 female members by 1976, to our present strength of 326 male and 17 female Commissionaires in 1997. Our current Commissionaires include 106 who served outside Canada in the Second World War, 14 who served in Korea and 36 who served in United Nations Peacekeeping assignments throughout the world.

Commissionaire Mike Symchyshen receiving his 15-Year Certificate and Medal from His Honour Lieutenant Governor George Porteous (1976-1977).

In 1987, our Division began training all of our Commissionaires in the Basic Security Course and in Emergency First Aid. In addition, 68 members have attended the National Supervisors Course. Since training began over 979 members have been trained to Basic Security levels and 345 have Basic First Aid Certification. Each new member is now automatically scheduled for Basic and First Aid training upon enrolment.

Our Members are the Corps

While the majority of our members have made a significant contribution to our Division, there are a few we would like to single out for special recognition.

Commissionaire Muriel G. Kochanski served in the Canadian Army, CWAC for three years during the Second World War as a "medic." Muriel married in 1946 and has had a very active family and community life. She served with the Girl Guide Movement for 38 years and held various posts including District Commissioner, Division Commissioner and Camp Advisor. She was awarded Life Membership and the Medal of Merit for her contributions.

In 1972, "Mom" as her girls called her, started service with the Corps, providing Matron duty for the Royal Canadian Mounted Police. She continued this service until 1996 and is still available for duty on a part-time basis. The Corps

Muriel G. and husband Ed Kochanski.

and the RCMP Supervisors are most complimentary in their assessment of Cpl Kochanski's performance over the years. The Corps Long Service Medal, 20 Year Bar was awarded to Muriel in 1993.

Muriel is a Life Member of the Royal Canadian Legion Branch #001 and became the first female President. For her service, she has received the Meritorious Service Medal and is now President of the Ladies Auxiliary. She is considered a Commissionaire Extraordinaire.

The Love Story

Our records indicate that W.H. (Bill) and his wife Molly Love were the first husband and wife team employed by the Division

Bill Love joined the Corps on September 27, 1972 and retired March 12, 1980. Molly Love joined the Corps on September 7, 1973 and retired May 1, 1987. The Love's duties were with the Regina Police Service in the Traffic Division. This was mainly parking meter enforcement, issuing tickets for meter violations. Between them, Bill and Molly have heard every excuse imaginable. The most common excuse was *"I just ran into the store to get some change."* As Molly said, *"... that one is awfully hard to believe when the person comes out of the store holding a bag of groceries..."*

The couple enjoyed their careers with the Corps and had a very good working relationship with the Regina Police Service. Bill passed away in 1985 but Molly continues to reside in Regina.

W.H. (Bill) Love.   Molly Love.

The Corps has grown over the years and one of the many individuals who has dedicated himself to furthering the aims of our Division is Harold Hague, a member of our Board of Governors. Harold saw military service in the Regina Rifles Reserve prior to service in the RCNVR. His Naval service consisted of ocean convoy escort, corvettes, destroyer-minesweepers and the D-Day landing on Omaha Beach.

Harold Hague (Chairman) presenting CDSM to LCol W.M. (Bill) Terry.

Harold Hague joined the Board of Governors of South

Saskatchewan in 1972 and is still actively involved with the Corps. He has served on the Executive and was Chairman from 1989 to 1991. Harold has been an active member of the Royal Canadian Legion since 1947 and has been an active link between the Corps and the Legion.

The South Saskatchewan Division has had two Corps Distinguished Service Medals awarded. The first Commissionaire to receive this prestigious award was LCol W.M. (Bill) Terry, CD. Bill joined the Corps on April 1, 1978 after serving over 32 years in the Canadian Army. He spent one year as Corps Adjutant and was promoted to Commandant in 1979. Bill was an outstanding Commandant and was responsible for the complete modernization and restructuring of the Corps Division Headquarters. Bill retired from the Corps in 1996 and currently resides in Medicine Hat, Alberta.

The second CDSM was awarded in May 1997, to our current serving Commissionaire Extraordinaire, Captain W.D. (Wes) Kopp, CD, the Division Operations Officer. Wes joined the Corps in November 1980 after serving 25 years with the PPCLI. He initially worked with the Regina Police Service where he became Supervisor of By-law Traffic Enforcement. In 1987, he was promoted to Captain and appointed Operations and Training Officer. He was instrumental in establishing the Divisional Training Section which trained a large backlog of Commissionaires to the Basic Security Level. Among his many accomplishments as Operations Officer, Captain Kopp was given responsibility for the provision of security for the Premiers' Conference in 1985. This involved over 75 Commissionaires working seven days during the conference. The performance of the Corps received the praise of CSIS, RCMP and the Regina Police Service. He is highly respected by our Commissionaires and our clients and continues to provide the Division with outstanding leadership. Truly a Commissionaire Extraordinaire.

LCol K.C. Garbutt (Chairman) presents CDSM to Capt W.D. (Wess) Kopp.

Lt (N) John E. Sandison, CD, has been an active member of the South Saskatchewan Board of Governors since 1980. John joined the Navy in 1943 and served aboard *HMCS St. Hyacinthe* on convoy duty in the North Atlantic. He has been a member of the Naval Reserve until his retirement in 1986. John began a career in radio in 1953 and was a popular host of the "Morning Mayor" show on CKCK Radio. In 1962, he began as the TV weatherman at CKCK-TV.

During his career, John was heavily involved in volunteer work with the Saskatchewan Heart and Stroke Foundation, Regina Firefighters Burn Unit, Canadian Red Cross, CNIB, St. John Ambulance and Saskatchewan Diabetes Association. His outstanding contribution to his community was recognized in 1997 when he was appointed a Member of the Order of Canada.

Gallantry Awards

A number of Commissionaires who served in our Division were awarded gallantry medals during the Second World War. While our records are incomplete, we know of six current and former recipients.

LCol Melvin R. Douglas was awarded Croix de Guerre and mentioned in Dispatches. LCol Douglas was Chairman of the South Saskatchewan Board of Governors from 1971 until 1984 and was an Honorary Member until his death in 1994.

James Ellis of Regina was awarded the Military Medal. Commissionaire Ellis served in the Division from July 21, 1967 to April 11, 1992.

William Leonard Moore of Regina was awarded Member of the British Empire Medal. Commissionaire Len Moore began service in the Division on June 11, 1992 and is currently serving at the Royal Saskatchewan Museum.

Frederick George (Bud) McLean was awarded the Military Medal. Commissionaire Bud McLean served with the South Saskatchewan Division form October 9, 1988 until his retirement on November 20, 1996.

Walter Stewart Weaver was awarded the Croix de Guerre with Silver Star. Commissionaire Walter Weaver began service with the Corps September 2, 1978 to the present.

Lt William (Bill) D. Grayson (1918 - 1990). Awarded the Military Cross. Platoon Commander, Lt Bill Grayson became "A" Company Commander on D-Day, June 6, 1944.

The company had landed on Nan Green Beach at Courseulles sur Mer Normandy and was pinned down and taking casualties from heavy machine-gun fire and rounds from an 88mm gun from inside a nearby gun emplacement. Grayson worked his way through the heavy fire to the concrete bunker and tossed a grenade through the gun slit.

A gun crew threw a "potato masher" grenade at Grayson who picked it up and threw it back at the Germans. Grayson motioned with his pistol for the Germans to come out; 35 prisoners surrrendered to Grayson. With the 88mm gun out of action, "A" Company was able to reach their objective. Bill was awarded the Military Cross for galantry.

Bill Grayson joined the Board of Governors in 1967 and served until his death in 1990. He served as Board Chairman from 1984 until 1986.

The Future

1998 will mark the 50th Anniversary of the South Saskatchewan Division of The Canadian Corps of Commissionaires. We are extremely proud of what has been accomplished by our Commissionaires. Each has contributed to our past success, however, the dedication of our Governors who have contributed time and talent without fee must be acknowledged. Nine Chairmen have led the Division since 1948. They are: Capt R. Ledrew 1948 - 1961; Col A.J. Hosie 1961 - 1971; Maj M.R. Douglas 1971 - 1984; Honourary LCol W.D. Grayson 1984 - 1986; LCdr The Honourable R.A. Cruickshank, QC 1986 - 1989; Harold Hague 1989 - 1991; Honourary LCol J.F. MacKenzie 1991 - 1994; LCol K.C. Garbutt 1994 - 1997; and the current Chairman, LCol R.C. Cade.

We consider the South Saskatchewan Division to be a young, vibrant forward looking enterprise. While the perception may be that the Corps is aging, that is not the case in our Division. When we compare the ages of Commissionaires today with those of our Division in 1977, we find that we are indeed becoming younger. In 1977, only 39% of our Commissionaires were age 59 or younger while today, fully 50% of our Commissionaires are 59 or younger. In 1977, 61% of our Commissionaires were 60 years of age or older, today only 50% are in that age bracket. Our younger members bring a variety of skills to the Corps. Because of this, the South Saskatchewan Division looks forward to many more years of service to government and industry in the 21st century.

The Historical Committee was led by Chairman A/Comm E.L Martin, assisted by A/Comm R.J. Mills, Cpl M.B. Latreille and LCol T.A. Lyons.

Chapter XVII

HISTORY OF THE KINGSTON & REGION DIVISION
Five Decades of Service

Commandant's Introduction – *by Wally Zaharychuk*

WHEN THE Kingston Division was formed in 1947 little, if any, thought was given to organized record keeping with a view to an historical review 50 years later. Administration was much simpler, not just because of small numbers but because of the absence of red tape in the early years.

As the Division grew in size and scope it suffered the inevitable roller-coaster of fortune. Like most businesses in the '70s and '80s the Division experienced a period of strong and stable growth. However, the current economic climate of downsizing and use of high technology has resulted in greater competition for many Divisions. Some private security companies are taking advantage of the high unemployment rate by undercutting wages.

However, Kingston & Region Division maintains a fine reputation for quality service, integrity and customer satisfaction. Our history demonstrates the high calibre of our Commissionaires, past and present. The future will continue this proud tradition.

The First Decade - Birth of a Division 1947-1956

On August 7, 1946, at a Corps Board of Directors meeting in Montreal, a suggestion was made that a Division be formed in the city of Kingston. The village of Portsmouth had just joined the city bringing the population to over 40,000 inhabitants, the number required for a Division to be formed. Early in 1947, certain gentlemen of the City and District of Kingston petitioned the Canadian Corps of Commissionaires for permission to organize a Division in the city.

On March 26, 1947, a meeting of the Corps Board of Directors, held in Montreal, granted permission to Col E. Forde, Maj Gen C.F.

Constantine, G/C Captain H.L. Wright, LCol Courtland M. Strange, LCol de L. Panet, W.P. Black Esq., H.P. Swan Esq., and H.P. Robinson Esq. to form the Kingston Division.

Col E. Forde was elected as the first Chairman of the Board. He also became Commandant of the Division.

> *Colonel Forde was born in Dundas, Ontario, on September 16, 1885. He enlisted in the 77th Wentworth Regiment and after six years in the ranks was appointed a provisional Lieutenant. In 1909, he transferred to the newly organized Canadian Signal Corps. In January, 1931, he was appointed Director of Signals. Through the personal efforts of Colonel Forde, Kingston was chosen as the headquarters for RC Signals. Colonel Forde was instrumental in the building of Vimy Barracks. He became the first Commandant and Chairman of the Kingston Division on March 25, 1947, and served until April 25, 1950. He died in November 1953.*

Colonel Elroy Forde, First Commandant and Chairman (1948).

Division Boundaries

The original boundaries of the Division were set as that portion of the province of Ontario bounded on the west by a line running through and including Cobourg, Peterborough and Lindsay, and extending to the southwest corner of Algonquin Park. To the east and north it was bounded by a line running from and including Cornwall, Smith's Falls and Perth, and extending to the southwest corner of Algonquin Park.

KINGSTON DIVISION – 1948. Front Row, Left to Right: LCol Courtland, M. Strange, G\C H.L. Wright, MBE, MGen Constantine, CBE, Col Forde, LCol de L'Panet, Mr. W.P. Black and Mr. H.P. Robinson.

The First Commissionaires

Minutes from the Corps Board of Directors meeting held on March 26, 1947, indicate that authority was granted to transfer 16 Commissionaires from the Hamilton Division to the Kingston Division. Kingston Division records indicate the names of 22 Commissionaires known to have been enrolled by March 31, 1947. It is probable that some of these Commissionaires, listed below, were originally from the Hamilton Division:

Bovey, Brick, Buell, Burn's, Bycroft, Charles, Giles, Holder, Irwin, Jesse, Millard, McDemott, McLaughlin, Pugh, Robinson, Richardson, Smith, Snowdon, Stevenson, Trainor, Tyrell, and Wild.

The First Clients

It is known that, during 1947, one Commissionaire was employed at the Kingston Tax Office, six Commissionaires were at Queen's University and four were at Norman Rogers Airport. The Division still maintains detachments at the Tax Office (now Revenue Canada) and at Queen's University.

Overcoming Early Difficulties

Growth in the Division was slow. Early documents indicate that federal government departments were reluctant to contract Corps services and disputes over wages and billing required the intervention of the Board of Governors. These problems were eventually overcome. However, the financial position of the Division was precarious to say the least. Included in the Division's liabilities was a start-up loan of $1,000 from the National Headquarters. The Board made an unsuccessful attempt to have this loan written-off. However, National Headquarters did agree to carry the loan free of interest.

Growth continued to be slow, but through the efforts of the Board and the Commandant the Division slowly expanded and by June 30, 1955, the Division strength was 155. It is suspected that the Department of Labour radio programme, "Canada at Work," which featured the Corps of Commissionaires and was carried on 62 local radio stations across Canada, provided much needed publicity for the fledgling Division. The Canada-wide CBC audience was addressed by Col P.J. Philpott, OBE, MC, DCM, Department of Veterans Affairs. The programme was aired during the week of November 28 - December 3, 1955 and was heard over CKWS Kingston at 2000 hrs Tuesday, November 29, 1955.

The First Commendation

The first known letter of commendation was read to the Board of Governors at the July meeting of 1950. The letter was from the Administrative Officer, Fort Frontenac, commending Commissionaires Bycroft and McLaughlin for their excellent and courageous efforts during a fire at the Fort.

Early Working Conditions

In 1954, the Division Headquarters was located in a small room on the first floor of the Richardson Building located at the lower end of Princess Street and occupied by the Department of Veterans Affairs. It was formerly the old Kingston piano works. Mrs Joan McKnight, the first of a fine office staff, was hired as typist and Girl Friday on June 15, 1954. Joan quickly developed a feeling for the Corps and the Commissionaires, especially the First World War veterans. They were all "her boys" and she was constantly giving of her time in completing the many requests for help. Joan remained with the Division for the next 23 years. Fortunately, the Division records contain some of her early recollections. For example, how the Commandant carried the petty cash in his pants pocket and counted it each night before leaving the office. His thriftiness is illustrated in the following true anecdote. On Joan's first day at work she was shown the ladies washroom and informed that she was expected to provide her own toilet tissue. Joan further recalled that they were so poor in those early days that the office furniture was on loan from DVA. The Division purchased its first typewriter, a second hand model, on March 26, 1956. There was a Board stipulation that the local DVA staff test the machine first and find it acceptable and the cost was not to exceed $55.

Early Benefits

Division finances in the early days did not permit the introduction of benefits until 1955. The first known "benefit" was passed by the Board of Governors on December 17, 1956. A charge was made whereby all cheques to members of the Division outside the Kingston area be made payable at par and the mailing expense be charged as office expenses. Prior to this, the cost of mailing was deducted from the Commissionaires' pay cheques.

By December 11, 1956, the Board had authorized that the sum of $1.50 per month be paid from the newly established Division Gratuity Fund to Commissionaires who had retired due to ill health

Training

At the Annual Meeting in Ottawa on September 25, 1946, the National Board of Directors recognized the requirement for First Aid Training for Commissionaires. This initiative was followed up at a further meeting held on December 13, 1946, where it was decided that National Headquarters would make arrangements with the St. John Ambulance Brigade for the training of Commissionaires in all Divisions.

The Second Decade 1957 - 1966

The 1957 National Annual Meeting was held on September 14 in Saint John, New Brunswick. The chairman stated that invitations to host the 1958 Annual Meeting had been received from both Kingston and Quebec.

Two factors influenced the final choice: the Kingston correspondence was dated earlier than Quebec's and Quebec had already been the site of an Annual Meeting. Kingston was pleased to be accepted.

Division finances at this time were not strong. At a Board meeting on April 24, 1958, it was passed that the $225 per month which was paid into the Gratuity Fund be deferred for the period from April 1958 to September 1958. This amount was to be deposited into a special account to defray the expenses incurred by the Division for the Annual Meeting to be held on September 12 and 13, 1958. This proved a wise precaution as funds that had in the past been provided for certain National Annual Meeting events, by both the host city and provincial government, were not forthcoming. The Annual Meeting of 1958 was a great success and the Division had reason to be proud that such a small and relatively poor Division had organized and successfully carried out such a major event. Generally, the second decade was one of steady growth. Other than considerable correspondence concerning the Annual Meeting of 1958, the decade appears to have been relatively quiet. By December 2, 1967, the Division strength was 275.

Commissionaire Extraodinaire

On September 23, 1965, the following was included in Board Minutes. *That a letter of commendation be written by the Chairman to Commissionaire J. Ford for saving the lives of Mr. & Mrs Robertson of Rideau Street from drowning on September 8, 1965, while on duty at Kingston Mills Lock Station.*

Working Conditions

At the March 14, 1957, Board of Governors Meeting a motion was passed to accept the offer of the Department of Public Works for office space in the Richardson Building. The fourth floor was made available at $1.50 per square foot per annum. In conjunction with the move on May 1, 1957, a private telephone line was installed in the new office. It would seem that the Division had previously shared a line with the Department of Veterans Affairs.

In 1959, the Department of Veterans Affairs moved into what is now the federal building. Apparently, there was no room for the Division Headquarters and the Division found itself evicted. New accommodation was secured on the second floor above the Bank of Toronto at the corner of Brock and King Street. The rental charge was $100 per month. In 1963, the Bank of Toronto was demolished and the Headquarters moved to the second floor of 38 Clarence Street at a rent of $130 per month.

Death of Captain Jimmy Burns

In November, 1965, Jimmy Burns, Division Adjutant, passed away. He was one of the first enrolled Commissionaires and had also served as the first Division Sergeant Major from 1955-1958.

Benefits

At a meeting of the Board on October 24, 1957, it was decided that no action be taken to purchase a Group Insurance Plan as the cost was prohibitive.

At the same meeting, the Board approved the payment of a Christmas bonus of $25 to all Commissionaires, employed by the Division, who had at least one year of service. Commissionaires with less than one year were to be paid at the rate of $2 per month. By Christmas 1962, the bonus was increased to $2.50 for each month served.

At a Board Meeting in 1960, Efficiency Awards were instituted. These awards became effective in 1961 and were in the form of a monetary grant. The monetary value of the award was calculated on a per-month basis for each month the recipient was employed during the preceding twelve-month period. Exemplary service during this period was a contributing factor towards receipt of this award. The amount was set at $25 and increased to $30 in 1962.

Prior to joining the Workmen's Compensation Act, the Division was responsible for paying compensation to Commissionaires injured on the job. On April 1, 1964, the Division joined with the Toronto Division and signed-on with the WCB. The cost was $756 to cover the period April 1 - December 31, 1964.

Pay

By March 17, 1960, pay for Commissionaires employed in Parking By-Law Enforcement by the city of Kingston was $1.45 per hour for a Commissionaire and $1.55 for a Sergeant, plus a 10% Administration Fee.

Dress

On October 24, 1957, the Board of Directors resolved that the Division purchase a block of brass numerals from one to 400 and Star hat badges that would be issued to the Commissionaires, free of charge. It was decided that the Division should adopt the wearing of badges and numerals as soon as possible. The Star badge was taken out of service on December 1, 1965. At the same time, the brass numerals were taken out of service and replaced with plastic name tags.

Training

Prior to March 21, 1963, there is no record of training of any kind within the Division. Board minutes of this date indicate that the St. John Ambulance registration fee for seven Commissionaires who had attended first aid lectures in Smith's Falls, at a cost of $28, be paid.

The Third Decade 1967 - 1976

On May 15, 1969, Major F.J. Irwin retired after serving over 21 years as both Commissionaire and Commandant. Maj Irwin had been one of the original Commissionaires enrolled in 1947. He was replaced by Capt W.M. Hill. On July 4, 1973, Capt Hill resigned and was replaced by Capt J. Weir.

In June, 1975, a survey was completed to ascertain the average age of the Commissionaires employed in the Division: 14.8% were under 50 years of age; 21.2% were 50-54 years of age; 23.8% were 55-59 years of age; 18.7% were 60-64 years of age; 4.2% were 65-69 years of age, and 7.3% were 70 years of age or older.

In 1997, the average age was 59 years.

The summer of 1976 was an extra busy time for the Division. The Olympic Yachting Regatta was held in Kingston. The event prompted the Commandant to cancel all leave for this period. Even the office staff had to be available at all times. Also, the Division started a newsletter which was sent out to all Commissionaires three times per year. This proved to be a very popular endeavour and all Commissionaires were urged to participate. Many articles and stories came in from the detachments. Capt McGill, the training officer, served as the editor. The Division found that the newsletter maintained a high level of esprit de corps.

In March 31, 1976, the Division strength had reached 435. By the end of 1976, the Division was able to offer a wide variety of services to its clients. In addition to patrol and building security, the Division was employing Commissionaires as receptionists, identification processing at industrial plants and Canadian Forces Bases, translators, librarians, motor transport dispatchers and tour guides. It was becoming obvious that the reputation of the Corps had grown in stature and its ability to serve the customer efficiently was widely recognized.

Remembrance Day 1976

The civic services of remembrance held throughout the area on November 11, 1976, were well supported by representatives of the Corps. On behalf of the Division, a wreath was laid at the Cross of Sacrifice in Kingston by Comm J.H. McKinnon. The Commandant and Training Officer were deeply involved throughout the year as members of the Remembrance Day Committee. They each played important roles in the organization and in the ceremony itself.

A wreath was laid at the cenotaph in Cornwall by Comm William Jones. Thirteen Commissionaires, under Sgt Maj Henry McNamara, paraded as a body. This effort in support of the civic services of remembrance was much appreciated by the residents of the city of Cornwall. The Division continues to support Remembrance Day services in the city of Kingston.

Commendations

The Commissionaires excelled in carrying out their duties for the Olympic Committee. Wherever police or military were not available to provide security or other services the Commissionaires were able to step in and take over. One detachment in particular, consisting of female Commissionaires working a contract for the Canadian Broadcasting Corporation, was exceptional in the performance of its duties. The Commissionaires were later given a letter of commendation, a certificate of merit and a gold medallion attesting to the high standard of security and services they displayed in the performance of their duties.

Commissionaire Extraordinaire

The following extract is from the Division newsletter dated December 2, 1976. *Commissionaire Jim Marlow, who is employed at the Regional Headquarters, Penitentiary Services in Kingston, reported that Commissionaire Kenneth Spafford was on his rounds when he heard screams coming from the direction of Lake Ontario. Spafford immediately proceeded to the water's edge where he found a girl who appeared to be under the influence of narcotics. She was about to enter the water. He apprehended the girl, applied first aid and then called the police. The application of first aid, plus his quick reaction, probably saved the life of this young girl. Commissionaire Spafford was commended on the action he took in a situation that required a quick response.*

Benefits

Prior to May 18, 1967, the Gratuity Fund established on October 22, 1957, paid a retirement gratuity to the maximum of $300, regardless of

THE CANADIAN CORPS OF COMMISSIONAIRES SUPERVISORS' COURSE
CFB Kingston, Ontario, November 17-21 1975
4th Row: J. Brown, V.R.L. Bond, F. Kelly, S.R. Holtom, H.H. Casselman, H.B. Dixson, and S.W. McTitchell. 3rd Row: D. Crogie, J.A. Fraser, H. Newell, J.H. Johnston, R. Smith, G.E. Gauthier, P. Copeman, and R.F. Todd. 2nd Row: L.A. Bourque, P.E. Snow, W.B. Miller, D.J. Vuill, A.J. Boudreau, D.H.E. Reid, and W. Dafoe. 1st Row: SSgt L. Kennedy, SSgt A. Robb, WO11 J.A. Millington, Capt S.R. Moore, LCol J.E. deHart, SSgt F.E. Moss, SSgt W.L. Kingsbury and Sgt B.J. Reid.

service beyond 60 months. On May 18, 1967, gratuities were increased by an additional $25 per year for each year served after the first five years.

Training

The first National Supervisors' Course was hosted by the Division and held at Canadian Forces Base Kingston from November 17-25, 1975. At a National Executive Committee meeting on December 12, 1975, the Chairman stated that he had been to the Supervisors' Course in Kingston and was most impressed by the calibre of the students and the quality of the course.

On January 1, 1976, the Division hired its first, full-time Training Officer, Capt G.W. McGill. He planned and instituted a comprehensive training programme for the Division. During the year of 1976, three Basic Security Courses were held and a total of 101 Commissionaires qualified. In April, 1976, the Division sent the first Commissionaire to the Atomic Energy Control Board training school in Pinawa, Manitoba, where the school was conducting a Nuclear Protective Training Course. Throughout 1976, courses in first aid, fire fighting and industrial safety were continually being conducted in various centres within the Division. The success of these courses was due to the excellent relationship between Detachment Commanders, plant management personnel and local authorities, who, in most cases, provided the training equipment and the instructional expertise.

The Fourth Decade 1977-1986

The years 1977-1986 were a time of rapid growth in the Division under the leadership of the Commandant, Major Jack Weir.

In 1977, Stu Mulkerns became Divisional Sergeant Major with the rank of WO I. Capt McGill filled in for the retired Adjutant Capt Tugwood. Capt McGill died in 1983, shortly after Wally Zaharychuk (now Colonel and Commandant) became Adjutant. That same year saw Mulkerns promoted to Training Officer, and Ken Gourlay to Divisional Sergeant Major.

Upon WO I Bastien's retirement in 1984, Sgt Hayes took over as Quartermaster. Maj Weir retired as a LCol in 1986 and Wally Zaharychuk was appointed Commandant with the rank of Major. Jim Sauvageau (now LCol) became the Adjutant.

In January, 1979, the Kingston Division became a member of the Kingston Chamber of Commerce and was integrated into the Kingston business world.

Despite the turmoil that so many changes must have caused within the Division, there were some comical incidents reported. Commissionaire Russel Gruer declared that he was laid low by a golf ball even though no-one was nearby. An old-timer at the clubhouse said that it was attributed to the ghost of Brigadier Joshua Dinsmore-Jones, who still haunts the golf course. Anyway, believe it or not, Gruer had picked up the golf ball that hit him and it was clearly marked J.D.J.

Another humorous incident was at the expense of Sergeant Major Mulkerns the Division Sergeant Major. At quitting time he was all dressed to go home. He reached up to the rack to get his hat, which, by the way, was where the Quartermaster had his hats stored, and it was not there. It finally came out that the Quartermaster, thinking that the hat was part of his stock, had sold it.

Honesty Pays

A phone call was received by the Commandant from the manager of the Commodore Motor Hotel, Kingston, Ontario. He expressed his appreciation of Commissionaire Bill Baldwin for his honesty in returning $102. It had been inadvertently left behind by someone after closing hours on July 28, 1977. Bill turned the money in to a staff member who came on duty the next morning. The Commandant noted that the Commodore Motor Hotel renewed the contract.

Good Publicity

In a radio announcement on September 28, 1977, it was noted that many construction companies in the Kingston area were being plagued by acts of vandalism. There were both financial losses and increased insurance payments as a result. At Splinter's Construction, where Commissionaires were employed, no vandalism occurred. In the radio announcement, however, Mr Splinter gave full credit to the Corps of Commissionaires and the Division gained much free advertising.

Commendations

Numerous commendations appear in the files of the Division. This one is not unusual. The following letter of appreciation from the Ontario Provincial Police, Picton Detachment was directed to the Plant Manager, Lake Ontario Cement Ltd. It commended the action taken by Comm Clarence Yardley who was on duty at the time.

> *On February 14, 1981, Provincial Constable Goodkey of the Detachment responded to a call of a fire on Highway 49 in front of your company's business location. The call was received from Mr Clarence Yardley who was on duty at the Commissionaire's office that evening. Further investigation into this matter revealed that the persons responsible for setting this fire were also involved with setting fires in four other locations as well as breaking into an unoccupied residence and doing damage therein. I wish to bring to your attention that if it had not been for Mr Yardley's early call to the police, the above mentioned crimes might have gone unsolved. Mr Yardley not only called at his earliest opportunity but was able to provide our officer with a description of the vehicle involved. I wish to commend this citizen who is in your employ. It was his alertness and sense of duty which brought this investigation to a successful conclusion.*
>
> *On behalf of the officer involved in this investigation, I request that you convey my thanks to Mr Yardley.*

Commissionaire Extraordinaire

A Special Certificate of Commendation issued by the Ontario Council of St. John recognizes meritorious acts or achievements. In the case of Commissionaire Baldwin his associates presented submissions and documentary evidence of a specific act of valour which resulted in a citation being prepared and forwarded to the council of St. John in Toronto. According to the citation, Commissionaire Baldwin rescued an unconscious man from a burning vehicle, showing great bravery and disregard for his own safety. A letter dated October 30, 1979, from R.G. Loftus, HStJ, President of Ontario Council contained the following remark:

Commissionaire William H. Baldwin.

> *"Deeds of bravery are not soon forgotten and I take pleasure in enclosing a Special Certificate of Commendation for Mr Baldwin to be presented to him on an appropriate occasion and at the same time to pass on the congratulations of Ontario Council. It is obvious that Commissionaire Baldwin is a very courageous man."*

The award was presented to Commissionaire Baldwin by Mayor Ken Keyes at a ceremony held in Council Chambers on November 16, 1979, at 1200 hours.

Training

By 1977, the Division was heavily involved in training. Basic Security and Supervisor courses were carried out locally under the able direction of the Training Officer, Capt Gordon McGill. The Division provided its own instructors and training aids and received the kind assistance of the Base Commanders at both Canadian Forces Base Kingston and Trenton. These units never failed to supply accommodation to the Division and always bent over backwards to help whenever asked.

The Division sent candidates to the National Supervisors' Course and also supplied an instructor. Training in the art of fire fighting was carried out locally. Personnel were also sent to the Ansul Fire School in Marionette, Wisconsin. Contact was made with Canadian Forces Base, Borden, for the use of the facilities of the Fire Fighting Training Company. This request was approved by the Canadian Forces Fire Marshal, LCol L. MacLean, and the Commandant of the Fire Fighting Company, Maj R. Maxwell. The first course was scheduled for September 17 and 18, 1980.

Also, Defensive Driving Courses were held for Commissionaires who were required to drive while on duty.

During the fiscal year 1979-1980 the Board of Governors allotted $30,000 for training. In fiscal year 1980-1981 the Board allotted $35,000 for training.

Pay

By 1980, pay rates within the Division were being increased substantially. An example of this was the renewal of the Canadian General Electric Company Limited, Peterborough contract on January 1, 1980. The contract would be for two years with a substantial increase in pay for all Commissionaires employed at CGE. There were two other major changes in the contract that are worth noting. First, the company requested pre-billing every four weeks for the services of the Commissionaires. Secondly, the Detachment Commander was taken off the hourly rate and placed on salary. This position equated to middle management within the plant. It meant a considerable raise in pay and by 1981 the Detachment Commander's pay was $23,400 per year.

The Fifth Decade 1987-1997

The late 1980s and early 1990 were a time of active growth in the Division. By October 31, 1990, the Division had a reached a record strength of 801. However, the feelings of comfort and optimism were somewhat diminished by the recession of 1991. Although the Division managed to maintain the majority of its contracts, downsizing, or the threat of downsizing, was evident in nearly all contracts. Wage rates remained virtually stagnant. Some modest increases were negotiated by April, 1997.

Many challenges faced the Division and the Board of Governors during the fifth decade. Changes in WCB legislation, coupled with severe financial penalties to the Division, and the requirement to comply with Employment Equity provisions, demanded a great deal of time from both the Headquarters staff and the Board members. Increased emphasis on safety in the workplace, always a vital issue at any time, was inevitable after the WCB penalties. Concepts such as CORPS II, Auxiliary Commissionaires, the implications of Bill C40 and loss of the Right of First Refusal were all thoroughly discussed.

In 1989, the Kingston Division hosted the National Annual General Meeting of the Corps. The Division last hosted the meeting in 1972.

On March 26, 1997, the Kingston Division celebrated its fiftieth year as a Division. A number of social events were planned for July 26, 1997, in honour of this milestone.

The Corps in general, and this Division in particular, is actively pursuing ISO 9002 certification. Federal, provincial, municipal and private sector downsizing has had its effect on the Division and strength, as of March 1, 1997, was 581.

Equipment Purchase

The programme to install a new payroll computer system (UNIX), was carried out and became operational on April 1, 1990. The Division recently installed a new LAN integrated system in January, 1997, which is interfaced with UNIX and also utilizes the Windows 95 software package.

It is expected that Internet access will be available in the near future. It is further expected that the Kingston Division will be the model for other Divisions and that rapid, computer-generated desktop-to-desktop communications will be available across the country.

Benefits

Life insurance was offered to all Commissionaires up until age 72. No evidence of insurability was required. The Board carefully considered covering the cost. However, in 1987, the total liability to the Division would have been in excess of $75,000. Therefore, it was agreed that a payroll deduction be made. Coverage was, and still is, $10,000. The cost per pay to a non-smoking male Commissionaire at age 50 is $1.26. For non-smoking females the cost is $.60. Effective April 1, 1990, the Board authorized full pay to all Commissionaires during attendance at first aid training. On February 19, 1991, the Board approved one day's pay for bereavement leave and for jury duty selection.

Training

Since 1975, the Division has given Basic Security Course training to 1572 Commissionaires and First Aid training to 2,028 Commissionaires. The Division has also qualified a total of 304 Commissionaires on the Supervisors' Course.

Dress

On May 19, 1987, the board adopted the wearing of the wash and wear tunic for all Commissionaires employed at sites where the ability to maintain a clean dress uniform was in question. It is referred to as the Eisenhower jacket. The Division was also to purchase and distribute the new wash and wear dress tunic as soon as stocks of the older "dry clean only" uniforms were exhausted.

Commissionaires Extraordinaire

The following is quoted from the booklet, *Investiture Bravery Decorations*. On Friday, March 15, 1985, a presentation was made by the Governor General of Canada at Rideau Hall, Ottawa, to Comm J.V.L. Swann.

> *The gallant effort of a Korean War veteran, Joseph Swann of Peterborough, Ontario, saved a motorist from a fiery death on the afternoon of 11 September, 1983. After the driver had lost control of his vehicle, it bounced off a car parked in front of a convenience store, then hit another car a short distance away. The two cars burst into flames and the semi-conscious man, pinned behind the wheel, could not save himself. Many bystanders were gathered in small groups, but Mr Swann alone forced open the car door. Although well aware of the danger of an explosion, he reached inside and through intense heat and smoke released the safety belt and freed the driver. While carrying him, Mr Swann fell and aggravated injuries he had himself sustained during war service.*

On February 22, 1994, Sergeant Merilea Saucier was awarded the MSM for her actions on December 5, 1993. The following narrative details the incident and the recommendation to National Headquarters.

Since joining Kingston Corps in August 1988, Sergeant M.A. Saucier has been employed with the Security Detachment at Kingston General Hospital. During that period she has received five letters of commendation from her superiors and the hospital authorities. The latest incident exemplifies her Meritorious Service Above and Beyond the Faithful Performance of Duty. "On 5 December, 1993, at 1750 hrs I received a call from Security 7 stating that a patient wearing a robe of shimmering material was missing from Connell 4. Security 7 had seen the patient leaving the main entrance with the intention of going to the lakeshore. I asked for a name and more detailed description, then headed for the lake and saw a woman fitting the description standing at the water's edge. I approached, calling her name and warning her of the danger. She entered the water and ignored my pleas to stop. I immediately radioed for help and after removing my jacket I entered the lake. I was able to pull her from the water after she accidentally, or purposely, became submerged up to her neck. Wrapping her in my coat, I radioed that we were returning to the patient centre. A nurse met us and assisted me as the patient was resisting. The patient was speedily taken back to Connell 4 where nurses were waiting to help her."

Sgt Merilea Saucier being presented the MSM by Mr. Peter Glynn, CEO Kingston General Hospital.

Longest Serving Commissionaire

The distinction of being the longest serving Commissionaire belongs to CM07860 Charles Gray who was enrolled on June 15, 1962, and who retired December 5, 1994, after 32 1/2 years of dedicated service to the Corps.

Other Awards and Honours

The Royal Military College of Canada has granted two Commissionaires the degree of Honorary Cadet. In May, 1996, the graduating class of '96 conferred this degree on SSgt Barry Osborn, in recognition of his concern for the welfare of the Cadet Wing during his five years as Detachment

SSgt B.H. Osborn "Marching Off" with the Royal Military College of Canada Graduating Class of 1996.

Commander, Royal Military College. SSgt Osborn was given the honour of "Marching-Off" the parade square with the Class of '96. Osborn is now the Divisional Sergeant Major.

In May 1991, SSgt Lorne Richards was also granted the Degree of Honorary Cadet in recognition of his 25 years service to the Royal Military College, and the Cadet Wing in particular. SSgt Richards was paid this honour by the Class of '91.

Sports Hero

Jack Portland was a sports figure of some renown. He served at the Dupont Maitland Detachment for 24 years. A native of Collingwood, Jack taught himself the techniques of high jumping and went on to become Canadian School Boy Champion in 1930. He later set a Canadian record of 1.85 metres in 1932, which was the same year he represented Canada at the Los Angeles Olympics.

Oldtimers will remember Jack as an NHL defenceman with the Montreal Canadiens and the Boston Bruins. During his 10-year career,

Commissionaire Roy Chapman escorting The Honourable Flora MacDonald at Norman Rogers Airport, Kingston, Ontario 1985.

HANDS ACROSS THE SEA
Back Row: Nelson Kittner and Herb Sturgess. Front Row: Sharfundin, 14 yrs and Ahmadzai, 18 yrs. In centre: Prince Mohammed Mostapha. Afganistan Freedom Fighters during their stay at Hotel Dieu Hospital, Kingston, Ontario, 1987.

beginning in 1933, Jack shared the ice with such hockey legends as Howie Morenz, Rocket Richard, King Clancy and Charlie Conacher.

The highlight of Jack's hockey career was in 1938 when the Boston Bruins won the Stanley Cup.

Summary

In summary, the above represents the Division's first five decades of growth. Despite the many trials and tribulations encountered over the past 50 years, the Division has always met challenges head-on with perseverance and good humour. History is an ongoing record, whether verbal or written, of persons and events. It is the intention of this Division to continue to record events that mark our development. Most particularly, we shall honour the people who have and will continue to contribute so much to the character of Kingston & Region Division. The bond of comradeship that exists among ex-service personnel is unique. This bond will be recognized and service personnel supported by the Corps as long as the need exists. This chapter was written by CWO Barry Osborn of the Division.

Chapter XVIII

HISTORY OF THE NORTH SASKATCHEWAN DIVISION

Commandant's Introduction – *By Wally Turk*

NORTH SASKATCHEWAN DIVISION of the Corps of Commissionaires is one of the unique smaller Divisions. Our ingenuity and ambition have been paramount to our continued success. Previous management, under Col Lorne Stainger and Capt Adam Dielschneider was very innovative in the pursuit of new and unusual employment possibilities. The senior shuttle service, regional park policing, security course for the mining sector, security courses for Saskatchewan Indian Gaming Authority, and the initial operation in the Yukon are some examples of these initiatives.

An ambitious approach to business by our current staff continues. Pursuing employment opportunities that break away from stereotyped Commissionaire responsibilities have resulted in further continued success.

The financial management of the North Saskatchewan Division has been enhanced for the last 24 years by the financial wizardry of the comptroller, Ms. Florence Hedin. On April 1, 1973, Ms. Hedin was hired by Mr. Marvin Johnson (who insisted he had no military Army rank in the Commissionaires). Mr. Johnson, who for 27 years performed all office functions, employed Ms. Hedin. "A long time" is how Ms. Hedin describes the length of her career with the Corps. Ms. Hedin initially worked in a one-room office and has changed offices six times in her career; from the first one-room operation, to the entire eighth floor of the stately Bessborough Hotel and now our own office on Second Avenue in the heart of downtown Saskatoon.

North Saskatchewan Division of the Corps benefits from our seven detachments/branch offices located in Melfort, Prince Albert, North Battleford, Lloydminster, Meadow Lake, La Ronge and the vast Yukon.

North Saskatchewan Division is exceptionally proud of its relationship with the First Nations people of this province. The mutual respect experienced can be directly attributed to our dedicated and sincere Corps instructors and members. The information received on the successful First Nations youth who have graduated from our programs is very gratifying. Of particular pride is our security and supervisor training provided to all four First Nations casinos located in Saskatchewan at Prince Albert, North Battleford, Yorkton and White Bear First Nations, Carlyle District, Saskatchewan. It is hoped that our programs can be adopted by other Divisions and our successes shared. Special thanks are given to John Milani for all of his work on this chapter.

Division History

In the beginning there was ONE. In the summer of 1946 several Saskatoon gentlemen, mostly veterans of the Second World War, met informally to consider the future employment of veterans. A Corps of Commissionaires Division was already functioning with an office in Regina and employing personnel in the Saskatoon area. These "founding fathers" met from time to time in the offices of the Department of Veterans Affairs: one of them was the District Administrator and several were DVA staff members, including one Jim Baillie, a wartime bomber pilot, who, at the time of writing, is still serving on the Board of Governors. Another founder was Foster Matheson, who, as Commanding Officer of the Regina Rifle Regiment, waded ashore on the Normandy beaches on D-Day, June 6, 1944.

They hired the first Commissionaire, a Sgt Russell, who was employed as a security person at a hangar at the Royal Canadian Air Force Station in Saskatoon.

During the years 1940-48 several more veterans were employed in Saskatoon but accounted for through the Regina office because the Saskatoon operation had no official status. However, the original founders held the view that a Division in Northern Saskatchewan headquartered in Saskatoon, should be established. Accordingly, a committee was formed and met formally on May 14, 1948, and again only four days later. Extracts from the minutes of those historic meetings are shown below:

MINUTES OF MEETING OF THE CANADIAN CORPS OF COMMISSIONAIRES

COMMITTEE HELD MAY 14, 1948

Those present were:

Capt J.H. Erwin, Chairman, LCol. W.A. Cripps, LCol. W.W. Lambert, Major C.S.T. Tubb, F/L W.V. Agnew, Lt. A.J.E. Sumner, and BGen P.C. Klaehn

The meeting was opened with an introduction to all members, and the Chairman then described the general outline of the Canadian Corps of Commissionaires.

Mr. Tubb then explained the function of the Department of Veterans Affairs within this Committee and the fact that the department was willing to supply the services of a counsellor, and stenographic assistants, etc., until such time as the Corps was fully organized in this city.

The District Administrator, Mr. P.C. Klaehn, suggested that the members of the Committee give some thought to the creation of an independent division for Northern Saskatchewan.

It was considered that a great deal of support could be given the Corps if a luncheon was held to which would be invited prospective employers and businessmen with some influence in this community.

Signed: J. Baillie, Sec.
Signed: J.H. Erwin, Chairman

MINUTES OF MEETING OF THE CANADIAN CORPS OF COMMISSIONAIRES COMMITTEE HELD MAY 18, 1948

Those present were:

Capt J.H. Erwin, Chairman	F/L W.V. Agnew
LCol. W.W. Lambert	Lt A.J.E. Sumner
Maj C.S.T. Tubb	Maj K. Dickson

Considerable discussion re the individual functions of each member took place and it was finally decided that sub-committees be set up in the following manner:

Administration	Mr. Tubb, Mr. Agnew
Public Relations	Mr. Dickson, Mr. Boyce, Mr. Sumner
Selection	Mr. Erwin, Mr. Cripps, Mr. Lambert

Some discussion took place on the matter of enlarging the committee.

If the Corps is to function satisfactorily it was decided that financial assistance must be readily available to purchase uniforms, liability insurance, bonding of members, etc. It was agreed that the Military Institute should be asked to draft a letter for all their members, asking for financial assistance.

As there are now approximately 25 applicants for the Corps, screening and selection should take place immediately.

The matter of the correct method of approaching employers came in for considerable discussion and proposed selling plans were outlined.

Mr. Tubb then outlined some of the many administrative problems that will arise, such as relations with the Canadian Congress of Labour, etc., in order to acquaint the administrative committee with their type of work.

Signed: J. Baillie, Sec
Signed: J.H. Erwin, Chairman

Division Writer's Note: The approach to prospective employers, taken in 1948 is of special interest because 49 years later the Division is adopting a similar procedure to attract business.

The North Saskatchewan Division became a reality two months later. On 15 July, 1948 the National Board of Governors met, and the minutes reflect the following: *"The Charter for the formation of the North Saskatchewan Division is approved."*

The Division was activated in Saskatoon on July 15, 1948. The principals involved were: Captain J.H. Erwin, MC, DCM; Colonel F. Matheson, DSO, ED; and Captain J.S Woodward. The work of the committee during the summer of 1948 was accelerated. They considered ways of approaching local firms for work for the Commissionaires, developed administrative procedures for the operation of the northern Corps and sought additional members for their Board.

Minutes of an September 8, 1948 meeting reflect that Messrs Pinder, Pitts and Walker were appointed to the Board, and to its Executive Committee. At that meeting it was reported that at that date there were ten Commissionaires on fulltime employment, and since July 1948, the books of accounts reflected a $52 profit.

By the end of the year (1948) there were 19 Commissionaires on steady employment; the projection for the year was 15. By August 31, 1949 there were 22 on fulltime employment and the Division had an operating surplus of $813. A bonus of $12 per Commissionaire was approved.

The reports for the year ending December 31, 1951 reflected the following statistics: Strength 30 – a gain of 7 during the year; average age 61$^{1}/_{2}$, the oldest 74, the youngest 49; of the 30 Commissionaires, 29 were on full employment, with an average take home pay of $140 per month; about 80% of the Commissionaires were employed on federal government work; the demand for part time work for sports events, retail store sales, dances, and banquets exceeded the supply of staff available but it was difficult to keep men on strength unless they could be provided with fulltime employment; the gross earnings for the year 1951 were $46,042. By December 31, 1952 the operating surplus had reached $5,011.

The earliest financial records available indicate that in June 1948 there were five Commissionaires on the payroll. Pay cheques numbered one to four reflect an average pay of $120 for a full month's work. The fifth member was not issued a cheque – the item was posted to "suspense" in the ledger. Although there is no "paper trail" to confirm it, it seems likely that the member concerned had an application for financial assistance pending, and he didn't want to prejudice it by revealing that he was in receipt of pay for work being performed. Subsequent records reflect he was later issued a pay cheque. It seems probable that that was indeed the case because Florence Hedin said there were similar arrangements in later years. Those original five members provided security service for government offices and one commercial firm – Pinders Drugs. (A family member, Ross Pinder, has served as a Governor for 50 years). The contracts for service provided for a charge of 65 cents to 70 cents per hour: the Commissionaires were paid about 93 percent of the fee, the remaining seven percent was retained for administrative overhead costs. The ledger detail indicates that arrangements were made with the bankers of the day for a loan of $300 to cover the payroll costs. Authority to make the loan was approved at a meeting of the committee. The members of the Executive Committee were guarantors!!

The personnel records in those first days were maintained in an 8" x 13" hard-covered journal book, in almost "copperplate" quality handwriting by a very talented penman. The entries reflect the name and address of the Commissionaire, when he was taken on strength, where and what hours he worked, at what rate of pay, and details of days off and vacation time. The records also included an assessment of performance and troubles if any.

Comm Joe Brecknell.

The Governors and Administrative officers were very concerned in those early days, as they are today, of the Commissionaires' "image." They actively sought employment for these veterans by using their business connections. The Commissionaires were expected to maintain a high standard of dress and deportment and anything less was not tolerated. Indeed one of those original five was disciplined for being intoxicated on duty. He was suspended without pay for seven days.

Joe Brecknell a Second World War Navy veteran recalled recently that his father Tom, (a friend of Sgt. Russell, our first Commissionaire) worked for many years as a Commissionaire at city Hospital. Joe said his father, a veteran (from UK) of the Boer War and a Canadian Veteran of the First World War, turned out for work each day with shiny brass buttons, an immaculate uniform and glistening boots – just as he would for a formal parade and inspection.

The head office in Saskatoon had space in the DVA premises in the Federal Building. It was a convenient arrangement because several of the Board members were officers in the department. One paid, part time Corps Administrator was an employee of the Army Benevolent Fund.

In those early years the Board was dedicated to maintaining a lean operation: it was striving to provide maximum hours of employment at the best contract rates possible. Even in those days there was competition from others, and commercial clients, as expected, sought acceptable service at the lowest cost. At the end of each year's operation the financial statements were scrutinized carefully, and after providing for modest reserves, the operating surplus was paid out to Commissionaires as a bonus. Initially this was allocated on the basis of performance and hours of work and was rounded to even tens of dollars. Later on it was based on hours of work. The minutes of several Executive Committee and Annual General Meetings reflect the recurring matter of bonus payments. At one committee meeting held late in the calendar year, the financial report indicated a rather substantial surplus. Under current operating procedures bonus payments were approved at Annual General Meetings. As the next AGM was scheduled for several months in the future, one committee member insisted that a special meeting be called as quickly as possible so that bonus payments could be approved. The minutes of one meeting show that in another year rather innovative accounting was authorized in respect of bonus payments. It was classed as a clothing allowance and not reported as salary earned. There is no evidence available to indicate whether or not the matter was subject to an observation by our auditors of the day.

There was concern about overhead charges including the cost of providing uniforms. A cursory study quickly revealed that the uniforms of some Commissionaires were subjected to more wear and tear than others, and there appeared to be evidence that uniform items were being worn at times other than on duty. One Governor (non military) suggested that there should be "kit inspections." Fortunately the suggestion was never implemented, as it is highly likely that veterans who had been subjected to kit inspections during their service would have sought other employment rather than having that procedure inflicted upon them.

There were some lean times in the 1960s and 1970s when the Division was struggling to obtain contracts for veterans looking for employment, and administrative (overhead) costs were kept to the absolute minimum. While the Headquarters of the Division was located in the Federal Building there was limited storage space, and none for clothing stores. An unheated, unlighted room in a building about a block away was rented. If a Commissionaire needed clothing he was asked to meet a staff member there (usually Florence Hedin our current Controller) and to "please bring your own flashlight because the batteries in ours may be too weak to provide adequate lighting."

Our Headquarters Over the Years

Initially (1946) the Division offices were located in the Federal Building in space that had been assigned to the Department of Veterans Affairs (DVA). As several of the Board members were DVA employees it made for easy communication between Board members. The building was conveniently located downtown and although the records do not indicate exactly what administrative support was provided by DVA it is clear that much of it was by way of telephone and postage service, and that clerical/stenographic services were provided.

Over time, and with expanding service requirements, additional space was needed. As expansion in the DVA premises was not possible the Division arranged to rent space in the Central Chambers Building. This involved a move of one city block.

When the Division decided to undertake an expanded training program it was evident that additional classroom space was required. At that time a government agency (DREE) decided to vacate its premises on the top floor of the Bessborough Hotel. For many years (from 1935) the "castle" was the property of the CNR. It had been recently sold to a prominent Saskatoon family, which was well known to the Board Chairman of the day, Group Captain A.A. Myers. Arrangements were made to lease sufficient space for our administrative and training requirements.

The property owners were quite happy to have the Corps located in its premises. The sight of uniformed Commissionaires coming and going provided some measure of security, and later "paid service" was provided. It was officially opened by LCol J.C. Stewart, the National President, when he visited the Division. The hotel was home to the Division for seven years, from 1986 to 1993.

When it became apparent that the cost of renting space was an accelerating expense, the Board decided to investigate the possibility of purchasing a suitable building. In 1993 a separate (free standing) one-level structure came onto the market. It was ideal for our needs of the day and our bankers (Scotiabank) agreed to arrange financing. It seemed likely that this accommodation would serve us well for many years to come. However, four years later, the Division is considering the need for additional storage space.

A New Beginning

Our Annual General Meeting held on June 21, 1972 was a significant one, for it marked the beginning of a new era for the Division. The Chairman of the Board in his address to the meeting remarked, in welcoming the Governors, that *In a sense this is an historic meeting in the annals of the Division as it is the final one of our organization as at presently constituted. When we finally adjourn this afternoon we shall be a wholly autonomous body running our own show, so to speak, and only affiliated with the Dominion body.*

The Chairman briefly reviewed the highlights of the unit since it came into being some 26 years before. He suggested *being a member of the Corps is a fine aid to the longevity of our members as four of the five original founders were still in the land of the living – Stu Tubb, Drayton Walker, Guy Cole and Jim Baillie."* W/C Baillie is still serving as a Governor, and at the Annual General Meeting of the Corps, held in Vancouver on June 21, 1997, exactly 25 years later, it was announced that after 51 years of distinguished service to the North Saskatchewan Division he was being made an Honorary Life Governor.

The Chairman, at the 1972 meeting, remarked that the Division's first Commissionaire, Sgt. Russell, would be honoured that evening together with 28 members, for devotion to service of the Corps. In discussions with the Division Adjutant he said, *It was agreed that some 2500 men had seen service in the Division, and the Financial Statement, presented later at the meeting reflected a surplus of some $78,000. This of course would be turned over to the new body.*

Since its earlier days, the Division, because of its affiliation with the "Dominion body," had been subject to an annual assessment from the Head Office. There is evidence that this arrangement was not based on a formula that was firmly established. From time to time there were exchanges of correspondence regarding what the assessment should be and one year the discussion, by mail, dragged on for several months.

In the end however, the following exchange of letters, authorized the transfer to autonomous status:

6 June 1972

Major C.R. Balfour, Secretary
Canadian Corps of Commissionaires
Ottawa, Ontario

Dear Major Balfour:

re: **CORPS ORGANIZATION**

As requested, we are listing hereunder the Assets and Liabilities of the Canadian Corps of Commissionaires, North Saskatchewan Division, as of April 1st 1972.

ASSETS

Accounts Receivable Trade	$ 74,935
Employees Account	5,686
Clothing on Hand	2,837
Accrued Interest Receivable	757
Prepaid Expenses	3,063
Bonds:	
City of Saskatoon 1978	9,791
City of Saskatoon 1980	3,990
Metropolitan Toronto 1980	4,990
City of Saskatoon 1975	1,000
Province of Saskatchewan 1985	20,000
Canadian Utilities 1986	5,000
Bathurst Power and Paper Co Ltd 1984	2,040
Office Equipment	1,046
Pension Trust Fund Assets:	
Government of Canada Savings Bond 1978	5,000
Government of Canada Savings Bond 1981	10,000
Accrued Interest	1,915
Accrued Interest Due From Corps	**1,225**
TOTAL ASSETS	**$153,175**

LIABILITIES

Bank Overdraft	$ 34,368
Accounts Payable	2,215
Payment of Pension Trust Fund	1,225
Government Contract Equalization Reserve	381
Pension Trust Liability	18,140
Accrued Holiday Pay	18,284
Total Liabilities	74,613
TOTAL RETAINED EARNINGS	$ 78,562

(Signed) M.A. Johnson, Adjutant
Canadian Corps of Commissionaires
North Saskatchewan Division

The response:

**THE CANADIAN CORPS OF COMMISSIONAIRES
LE CORPS CANADIEN DES COMMISSIONAIRES
Suite 501, 100 Gloucester St, Ottawa, Ontario**

Canadian Corps of Commissionaires (North Saskatchewan)
Room 605 Federal Building
Saskatoon, Saskatchewan

The Canadian Corps of Commissionaires – Le Corps Canadien des Commissionaires (hereinafter referred to as "Headquarters Corps" hereby releases and quits claim to and in favour of Canadian Corps of Commissionaires (North Saskatchewan) all rights, title and interest which Headquarters Corps may have in and to those assets which are set out and referred to in the letter, dated June 6, 1972 from Canadian Corps of Commissionaires (North Saskatchewan) to Headquarters Corps (a copy of which is hereto annexed),

Dated September 15, 1972

THE CANADIAN CORPS OF COMMISSIONAIRES -
LE CORPS CANADIEN DES COMMISSIONAIRES

By R.P. White }
                                Signed
C.R. Balfour }

The final motion recorded in the minutes of the June 20, 1972 meeting, duly moved, seconded and carried provided "that the Canadian Corps of Commissionaires, North Saskatchewan Division, which existed and carried on business under the auspices of a Federal Charter held by the Canadian Corps of Commissionaires Inc. Ottawa, cease to exist as of June 1st 1972."

The minutes of that June 20, 1972 meeting reflect that in the preceding 17 years (since 1965) between eight and nine million dollars had been paid in wages to veterans. Although the Division had no difficulty in meeting personnel requirements for existing contracts, we had to pass up several possible contracts where younger men were required. In 1972 there were 275 Commissionaires on strength: of that number the majority were over 65 years of age, 30 percent were over 70, and some were 80. (We are faced with a similar image today. Too many prospective employers think the Corps is made up of "uniformed old men" and we continue to work at improving our image.)

At that June meeting the Governors attending paid special tribute to the Chairman, Capt. J.S. Woodward who had served in that office since the Division came into being. A presentation was made to him: the details are not recorded, but a long-time Governor, Ross Pinder, told this author that he understood it was in "bottled" form.

Training of First Nations Personnel

In 1989 the Division embarked on a new endeavour – the training of First Nations young men and women. At the request of the Prince Albert Development Corporation (the business arm of the Prince Albert District Chiefs (PADC)) who were looking for certified security guards, the Corps contracted to provide the four-month training course.

Many of the students had mixed emotions about finishing the course. For many, it meant being away from home for several weeks for the first time in their lives. Jennifer Stewart a 19-year-old from Cumberland House said she was ready to quit after the first few days but she was encouraged by her friends to stay on. She was one of the happy graduating students four months later.

The late Don McCullough, a Commissionaire with teaching experience at the high school and college level, was the Chief Instructor. He said the Corps considered this first course an outstanding success –

Law Enforcement Course (Dundurn) 1994-1995.

none of the candidates left the course of his or her volition. One was asked to leave.

The program covered a wide spectrum of classes from karate and first aid to math and geography. During training the students were housed in the Bessborough Hotel. The cost of the course to PADC was $115,000. Ray Sanderson of PADC (a former member of the Black Watch and Princess Patricia's Canadian Light Infantry) said "the Corporation got its money's worth and so did the 15 graduates." Other costs relating to the training were subsidized through the Manpower offices in La Ronge and Prince Albert, and Indian and Northern Affairs Canada. Sanderson said there were 70 applicants from 11 different Indian Bands and selection narrowed the candidates to 16. He said he was delighted with the results and expected employment for the graduating class through contracts with mining companies in the north.

The graduating exercises held on Friday, December 1, 1989 were held at the Reserve Naval Division – *HMCS Unicorn* and the class put on displays that delighted their friends and relatives who were invited to the ceremony. It is appropriate to record the names of the first class who were: Martin Bird, James Merasty, Byron Daniels, Alfred Naldzie, Donald Echodh, Jonas Roberts, Beatrice Ermine, Susan Roberts, James Fidler, Jennifer Stewart, Core Garvin, John Walker, Percy Hunt, Donald Whitecap, and Basil Lafond.

Subsequent courses were conducted at other centres including the Regular Force base at Camp Dundurn and at the former RADAR base at Dana. On those courses the students lived in a military environment and were subject to many of the rules and regulations that young military recruits could expect. They adapted extremely well.

The demand for training of First Nations men and women continued and courses have been conducted at Ile-a-la Crosse, North Battleford, Prince Albert, Yorkton and White Bear.

In preparation for the day when First Nations will be self-policing, the Peter Ballantyne Band sponsored a 16-week law enforcement course conducted by our Commissionaires. This course was one modified from the RCMP Depot course for police recruits, and introduced the trainees to most subjects in the RCMP standards except for driving skills, firearms and baton usage. The 21 graduates of the course are now working for band councils or police forces, and when native self-policing becomes a reality they are ready and prepared to take leadership roles.

Our Division developed a Casino Security Training course to meet the needs of First Nation-operated casinos in the province: it proved successful in training floor-security personnel. The Gold Eagle Casino in North Battleford, The Northern Lights Casino in Prince Albert, the Painted Hand Casino in Yorkton and the Bearclaw Casino at Whitebear now have efficient, professional security staff.

The training standards for this course are the only ones in Canada that are offered commercially. The trainees are taught how to deal with security problems in a manner that results in a comfortable, relaxed, enjoyable atmosphere for the patrons. The training program was later expanded to include a Supervisor's Course, the details of which are being considered by other Divisions.

Our training programs would not be efficient and effective without competent, dedicated staff. Their wide and varied training and experience, many with years of employment, fits them well for their employment in the Corps. Among them are:

Peter Cameron, BA, B.Ed, M.Sc. – Peter was the first long-service teacher to join the Corps. His professional qualifications were outstanding. He was an "accredited" teacher, a designation recognized by the Department of Education. He was authorized to set and mark the examinations of senior matriculation students. When the Division was once questioned about its instructor's ability to teach academic subjects the concern was withdrawn when Peter's name was mentioned. We were sorry to lose Peter when ill health forced him to retire, and saddened at his passing shortly thereafter.

Harry Pitzel, BA, B.Ed – was a school teacher for 30 years before joining the Commissionaires. His specialities were high school English, physical education and computer science.

Vernon Ash – a retired Captain from the Saskatoon Fire Department is Head Instructor in safety and first aid. He is a Level Two Advanced Emergency Medical Technician, a Certified Instructor for St. John Ambulance and Canadian Red Cross First Aid courses.

William (Bud) McAllister – After ten years in the Canadian Forces, Bud served as an Air Traffic Controller for the federal government. He is a qualified counsellor for chemical assistance programs and together with his knowledge of radio procedures and experience in stress management he has become a valuable member of our training staff.

Doug Wry – Before joining our Division Doug spent 28 years with the RCMP with nearly one-half of his service working with First Nations people. His training in the RCMP led to him being declared an Expert by the courts in the fields of Accident Reconstruction and Radar Operations. Doug has instructed on several of our courses for First Nations people, and is a member of the National Instructional team for the Commissionaires.

Norm Erickson BA, Bed – After 31 years as a school teacher Norm joined the Division. In addition to his professional teaching qualifications, he is a trained pilot and a certified radio operator examiner. He also holds a Red Cross First Aid Instructor's certificate and a Heart and Stroke Foundation Instructor's certificate. Norm has served as an Instructor and Supervisor on our Corps Basic Qualifying courses, Casino Security Courses and First Aid/CPR courses, and is also a member of the National Instructional Team.

Peter Tomkins – Peter served for 12 years with Canadian Forces – with the PPCLI and RCE He studied for one year at the Saskatchewan Urban Native Teacher's Education Program at the University of Regina. While in the forces he was employed as an instructor. Since joining the Division Peter has been employed as an instructor on the Casino Supervisor's Course and the Native Law Enforcement program.

Jim Busby – Jim, recently deceased, was for many years the only Security Staff member at a federal government building. He was well known and loved by the personnel who were employed by the many agencies located there. Although in later years it was apparent that his health was deteriorating, he never complained nor asked to be replaced on days when he was quite unwell. Only after his passing did we learn how much he was admired, respected and appreciated. On days when he wasn't able to make it to work some employee in one of the agencies would "cover" for him, and his absence was never ever reported to the Division office.

No history of this Division should exclude reference to the outstanding contribution of Mr Marvin Johnson, both as a staff employee and as a Member of the Board of Governors.

Marvin served with the Royal Regina Regiment during the North West European campaign. He waded ashore on D-Day and during the fierce fighting for Caen was wounded for the first time. A second very serious wound suffered in the water-logged terrain at the Leopold Canal resulted in his evacuation to U.K. and a six-month hospital stay there. He returned to Canada shortly before the battle in Europe was over.

Mr. Marvin Johnson.

Marvin was first employed in the Department of Veterans Affairs, then as the Executive Director of the Army Benevolent Fund. For a time he combined the latter duties with those of the Administration officer for the Corps of Commissionaires. However, he soon determined that it was impossible to do both, so accepted an offer of fulltime employment with the Division.

Full time employment meant more than a nine-to-five job at the office. Florence Hedin said that when she first went to work for the Division as a clerk/typist/bookkeeper, she found out that Mr Johnson had been "doing everything." He negotiated contracts for service, assigned Commissionaires to jobs, detailed their work shifts, days off and holidays, recorded their hours of employment, issued them their uniforms and signed their pay cheques. He maintained the financial ledger, raised invoices to clients and deposited their payments. In addition, he served as counsellor to the veteran commissionaires, many of whom were encountering difficulties adjusting to civvy street. After regular office hours, he was on-call to deal with emergency situations (requirements for service) and contacted prospective clients. It was indeed a seven-days-a-week, twenty-four-hours-a-day job. His concern was always for the welfare of veterans and particularly his Commissionaires. After years of fulltime service, the Board of Governors accepted with regret his decision to retire in December, 1981. He was immediately elected to the Board of Governors.

Florence Hedin recalls that for a long time after his formal retirement, he stopped in at the office regularly to counsel and help his successor who was new to the operation of the Division, having been recently retired from the Regular Force. His widow, Guy, living in Saskatoon told this writer that he was an accomplished saxophone player, a member of military orchestras overseas and after he returned home. He was particularly pleased, in later years, to play in a university orchestra with one of his sons who was also a talented musician. Guy said they both enjoyed immensely "their" time with the Commissionaires as she often accompanied Marvin when he travelled out of town on business, and to the National meetings of the Corps held in Newfoundland and Vancouver, and many places "in between."

After many years of operation under the late Marv Johnson, the Division was administered by retired "regulars" for 14 years. Ron Bobinski came to the Corps after 20 years of service in the RCN and was fortunate to have Marv teach him the ropes. Ron was the Commandant during those years when there was some questions as to whether or not the Corps would continue to survive into the '90s. Coming to the Division with Ron was a 33-year Navy veteran Adam Dielschneider who served as the "Second in Command" for 11 years. When Ron Bobinski left the Division on retirement he was succeeded by Lorne Stainger. After nearly 30 years of Air Force service and a couple in private business, Lorne joined the Corps and had served as an NCO Supervisor until succeeding Ron. His seven years of service as the Commandant were marked by a period of expansion that was due in the main to his aggressive salesmanship. From time to time he said the Division would eventually do $6 million in business volume. It reached the $6.5 million level just a year before he decided to take the retirement he had earned after ten years of dedicated service to the Division.

Camp Dundurn

The members of our Division are employed in a variety of jobs in the northern half of the province. (With another Division headquartered in Regina, the province has been divided into two jurisdictions.) One of the unique contracts for service is provided at the Military Ammunition Depot at the Camp Dundurn military base located about 25 miles south of the city. Heading the detachment is Commissionaire (Warrant Officer) Al Wilson, who joined the Division in 1988 after 29 years of service in the

Regular Force. He retired in the rank of Chief Warrant Officer. The detachment is armed–a unique requirement. Commissionaire service has been provided there since late in the '40s and initially consisted of two Commissionaires patrolling on foot to a detachment that travels in vehicles, monitors computer screens, provides overall surveillance at the camp and after normal hours provides "unofficial" telephone switchboard service. Al Wilson says they do other odd jobs when time permits–like painting fences and buildings and cutting grass–"anything to improve the quality of life." For several years, while serving in the Division, Al was very active in the Military Reserves, rising to be the District Chief Warrant Officer. In 1993 he was decorated by His Excellency, Governor General Hnatyshyn with the MMM for outstanding service.

Warrant Officer Al Wilson, MMM, being presented with the MMM by His Excellency, Governor General Ray Hnatyshyn.

City Staff on Strike

In 1994 the Commissionaires of the Division were involved in a very special operation, unlike anything they had experienced in the past. The city officials had been carrying on negotiations with representatives of its employees. Finally the workers exercised their right by beginning to withdraw their services.

The labour disputes began with a one-day walkout by city police on July 7. The Division was required on short notice to supply Matrons to guard female prisoners for the period of the 24-hour walkout of selected police services. This was followed by a general walkout (lockout?) of all members of the Police Association on July 15. It lasted until July 23. Once again, we were required to supply Matrons for city police cells for this period. We were also required to supply an additional three, then four, Commissionaires to provide additional security in the police station on a 24-hour basis during this general walkout. The labour dispute was settled on July 23 by appointment of a binding arbitrator. The Corps reverted to its pre-strike tasks on this date.

The main strike commenced on Tuesday, August 9, with a walkout and lockout of all unionized city employees. The main effects of the strike on the Corps–an overwhelming request for security guards–was not felt until the Tuesday evening when our Duty Officer received numerous requests after hours to provide security guards at various sites around the city. Within a matter of a few days, the Division was providing two, three and four Commissionaires on a 24-hour basis guarding 13 sites. The actual strike lasted from August 9 to October 18. By the end of the strike, we were guarding 21 sites either overnight or on a 24-hour basis. An additional 25 sites required partial coverage during this period.

These two strikes accounted for over 27,000 extra hours worked during this period. The personnel resources of the Saskatoon operations were used to the limit. Additional personnel were brought in from our North Battleford and Prince Albert Detachments. Fortunately, the Corps had just recently completed a Native Security Training Course at Isle a la Crosse. The Corps brought down eight of the graduates to Saskatoon and used them as security guards during the strike – additional "on the job" training. Their services were most satisfactory. A slight mix-up occurred with one of these trainees – a female – sent to guard a surface water line crossing a parking lot at a busy restaurant located at the edge of a certain part of the city that is noted for "problems." This was a night shift. When the Duty Officer learned of this, he immediately went to a four-man site, picked up a Commissionaire and proceeded to the parking lot site and switched the guard. When asked if she had had any problems at the site, she replied that there had been one young male in a "red sports car" who had been hassling her. As there was no red car in sight, she was asked how she handled the problem. She replied that, after several attempts to get the driver to move on failed to solve her problem, she just walked over to the side of the parking lot that fronts on a major thoroughfare and waved down the first police patrol car to pass by. The red car took off and was not seen again.

Although available documents reflect the details of work of the various work sites, there is no record or acknowledgment of the tremendous workload imposed on the administrative staff. Particular mention should be made of the long hours put in by the Duty Officers – 12- and 16-hour shifts on 24-hour work days became the norm for M. Cebryk, the Operations Officer; G. McLaughlin, the Administrative Officer and A. Peters. The accounting records reflect that, where applicable, the Commissionaires were paid at overtime rates but no special emolument was paid to the Commandant, the Duty Officers, accounting clerks and other administrative staff.

Throughout the years the Division continued to search for more work for its Commissionaires. Like all businesses, and despite our "right of first refusal" in respect of federal government contracts, the Division was subject to competition from other security service suppliers. Unfortunately, the Corps spent money on training programs for its Commissionaires while some competitors spend little if anything. While the cost of a local, one-week program was not excessive if the trainee could be immediately employed on a full time job, the cost of training one who might work only quarter-time for the next year was of some consequence.

Nor could the Division cater to the problem of the newly-trained Commissionaire who could leave immediately to take employment with some other security firm where full time work was available (and often in a supervisory capacity because of his training).

The provincial government recently introduced legislation to provide for the licensing of security service operators. While our officers were party to the discussions with government officials and had no particular quarrel with the legislation, they are concerned that the requirements for training will not be monitored. Our experience causes us to conclude that unless the regulations are strictly enforced the training requirements will not be adhered to by some operators. We believe self-policing will not be effective. The possibility (probability?) of our losing right of first refusal in respect of government contracts, (which provide about 50% of our revenue) compounds the problem because government agencies look for the best price notwithstanding they may not get the best service.

In spite of growing competition the Division continued to hold its own and increase its business volume. In the 18 years between 1977 and 1995 the Division's volume of business grew from $2.3 million to $6.5 million. In the earlier years federal contracts represented 57% of our business volume: by 1995 they had shrunk to 48%.

Vice-Regal Connections

For many years the Lieutenant Governor, the Honourable Colonel F.W. Johnson, was a Governor of our Division. He took great pleasure in meeting the people of the province when they came to see the recently refurbished Government House. He always had a special place in his heart for veterans and for members of the Corps. He had served with distinction in the Second World War. Once, when he was being briefed on the security arrangements for a Royal visit he was apprised of the function and duties of the Royal Canadian Mounted Police, particularly in respect of the arrival of the Royal visitors at Government House. He learned that the doors would be opened by a member of the force. He pointed out that the Commissionaire on duty opened the doors on a regular basis. When he was advised that in this case the RCMP officer would perform that duty he quietly said the Commissionaire ALWAYS opened the doors and no exception would be made for the Royal visitors. For long and distinguished service to the province as a barrister, a Queens Bench Justice, and Her Majesty's representative in the province of Saskatchewan, the Honourable Colonel Johnson was admitted to the Order of Canada and to the Saskatchewan Order of Merit.

The Division has another Vice Regal representative on its Board. Captain the Honourable S. Worobetz. Captain Worobetz served as a Medical Officer with the PPCLI in the Italian and European campaigns, and for gallant and distinguished service was awarded the Military Cross. Following the war, he resumed his practice and for contributions to his profession and the community at large, including a term as Her Majesty's representative in the province, he was admitted to the Order of Canada in 1996. At the 1997 Annual General Meeting of the Division Capt Worobetz was our first elected Honorary Life Governor.

Gallantry Awards

There probably have been a number of decorated Commissionaires who served in our Division at some time, but detail on them is not in our records: however, two whose records are known are:

Sgt Mahlon Westby: Mahlon served in the RCAF from 1941 to 1945 and trained as a Wireless Air Gunner. He completed two operational tours (50 missions) over Europe then served as an instructor for 10 months. In 1945 he was awarded the Distinguished Flying Cross for gallant and outstanding service. He retired in the rank of Flying Officer. Following 35 years of supervisory employment with the Wheat Pool he joined the Corps. Mahlon was first employed on security duties at several locations in the city, and for the last dozen years was the NCO in charge of the detail that served summons. For the past six years he has served, and continues to serve, on the Board of Directors of the Saskatchewan Branch of the Last Post Fund. The citation in connection with his decoration is reproduced below.

Flying Officer Westby.

> *During two successful tours of operational duty, Flying Officer Westby has participated in numerous sorties as wireless operator. He has consistently displayed courage and determination of a very high order which have set an excellent example to all members of his squadron. On many occasions, his skill and resolution have played a large part in the safe return of his aircraft. In December, 1944, his aircraft was detailed to attack Trier. Before the target was reached, serious damage was sustained from anti-aircraft fire. One engine was rendered unserviceable and another damaged. The controls were also affected and internal electrical damage combined with leaking petrol caused very great danger of fire. Through the coolness and determination of this officer the danger of fire was minimized under the most adverse conditions and the damaged aircraft was flown to England where a masterly emergency landing was executed.*

Commissionaire E.M. Keith MacGregor: Keith left university to join the army in 1942 after completing his first year at the University of Alberta. After being commissioned later that year he served in the Infantry for the next 35 years in a variety of regimental and staff appointments. He retired in 1977 in the rank of Brigadier General. He served with distinction in the

Loyal Edmonton Regiment in the Italian and European campaigns and was decorated with the Military Cross in 1945 for gallant service in the fighting in Italy. An extract from the citation relating to the award is as follows:

> On December 13, 1943 Lt MacGregor's battalion, The Loyal Edmonton Regiment, was involved in the vicious fighting in the advance from the Lamone to the Sanio rivers. Lt MacGregor was a platoon commander in the forward company. When its commander was wounded early in the attack, showing sterling qualities of initative and leadership, Lt MacGregor assumed command and pressed the attack to a successful conclusion. In the final assault on the enemy position Lt MacGregor dashed to the head of his men, exhorting them to follow him and personally lead a head-on charge across 400 yards of open ground. By his courage, coolness and magnificent leadership Lt MacGregor led his tired troops successfully. His gallant and unselfish conduct were of the highest order and in keeping with the best traditions of the British Army.

Keith served for only a short time in the Corps but was employed in a number of assignments, including one with one of the "big five" banks. Among his duties there was a requirement to unlock the doors at opening time. Keith was a stickler for being precise about everything including opening time. Unfortunately his watch (which he knew to be correct) didn't agree with the big bank clock that customers could see through the glass doors. It was several minutes fast. Some upset client waiting to get into the bank must have reported the matter to the manager because Keith was instructed to operate on "bank time" in the future.

Benevolent Fund

Throughout the more than 50 years of the Corps existence, the welfare of the Commissionaires has always been of paramount importance. From time to time emergency situations arose and these were dealt with on an "ad hoc" basis, usually by way of a salary advance, repayable over some agreed term. In 1991 the Division established an Emergency Aid Fund, and a Committee, headed by LCol R. Tinline (the current Chairman of the Division's Executive Committee), considers applications from Commissionaires in need of financial assistance. Funds are provided from operating revenue. Assistance is provided by way of outright grants, repayable non-interest loans, or a grant-loan combination. Although upper limits for grants and loans are dependant upon available funding, grants or loans usually do not exceed $1,500, and defaults on loans are minuscule.

Parking

Although the number of Commissionaires employed on parking enforcement duties is small, their projected public image is far-reaching. The stories these Commissionaires tell run the gamut from the sad to the ridiculous.

Once, at an Annual Dinner where a number of Commissionaires were being honoured and presented with medals for long and distinguished service, His Worship Mayor Cliff Wright was the guest speaker. He said that only one person got more abuse from citizens because of "unfair" parking tickets than Commissionaires and that was himself. There is no record of a driver ever complimenting a Commissionaire for getting a ticket but the excuses offered are legendary.

One of the excuses often used in the past was "I was held up in the doctor's office." Apparently, at one time, if it could be confirmed that that was in fact the case the ticket would be forgiven. Sometimes the cars were parked six blocks from the nearest doctor's office. However, that excuse (or reason) became so prevalent that it was no longer acceptable. There were instances when drivers rushed back to their cars just after they had been tagged to explain they had just gone to get change. Sometimes drivers left notes on their windshields saying they had just gone into a shop, and would be back in a few minutes. One driver stretched his luck a bit too far when he left a typewritten note under the windshield explaining he had gone to a nearby shop for change. The Commissionaire looked in the car, saw no evidence of a typewriter and issued the ticket.

While the parking ticket stories are legendary and the verbal abuse of Commissionaires was not considered incidental, there is no record of a Commissionaire being physically assaulted. However, there was an incident with a reverse twist.

A Commissionaire had issued a ticket and was about to get back into his vehicle when a car approached and ran through a water puddle beside him. He got a severe drenching. He was able to manoeuvre his car in front of the offender's, and a couple of blocks down the road was able to block the intersection preventing the offender driving by him. The driver got out of his vehicle and proceeded to verbally assault the Commissionaire and then make physical advances. He picked on the wrong man. The Commissionaire was a talented, experienced boxer. One punch and the offender was out cold, draped over the hood of his car. The Commissionaire stared at the driver's companions who witnessed the fracas and said, "get him out of here." The Commissionaire got back into his vehicle leaving the astonished group to deal with their own problem. Nothing more was ever heard of the incident.

One Commissionaire had just ticketed a luxury car when the driver arrived. She was a tiny elderly lady, fashionably dressed and elegantly coiffed. She started to berate the Commissionaire using language that cannot be printed. The Commissionaire said he had spent years in the Navy and never had heard some of the words she used.

The police and city officials always defended the work of the Commissionaires who were employed on ticketing duties and explained that it was much cheaper to employ Commissionaires than police officers whose salaries and fringe benefits cost in excess of $50,000 per year. Despite their good and necessary work they will never become popular.

Among the many "casual" security contracts was one associated with a road construction project in the Saskatoon area. The contractor was concerned about security during the hours when no work was in progress, and asked the Corps to provide service. By sheer coincidence a retired civil engineer (a veteran) had called at the office and asked if any casual short term work was available because he had some trouble "filling in time." He was delighted to accept the job at the work site. The engineer in charge of the project was a little miffed when the Commissionaire made some casual suggestions about improving the security of operations as a whole and pointed out some loopholes in other services being provided that were affecting the company's bottom line. When the Commissionaire's professional qualifications became known the company, of course, was delighted to have a security employee who provided "consultant service" at no charge.

Left: Randy Andrew; Right: Varn Ash (First Aid Instructor).

Commissionaire Randy Andrew has had a variety of experiences in his regular job as a cab driver and as a part time Commissionaire. He isn't easily surprised, shocked or dumbfounded, but was all three on an early Thursday morning.

An expectant mother was having pains about 5:00 a.m. and called her doctor. He advised her to get to the hospital at once. She called for a cab and Commissionaire Andrew was assigned the trip but when he got to the expectant mother's residence she was already in the late stages of labour. Andrew immediately called 911 and made the woman as comfortable as he could. The baby's head had already emerged by the time the paramedics arrived to complete the delivery. Everything turned out just fine. Although the First Aid training in the Corps program doesn't cover midwifery, the training Andrew did receive enabled him to act in a prompt, decisive fashion. The new mom was grateful and said to Andrew, "I couldn't have done it without you."

Our First Woman Commissionaire

After 30 years of operation the Division hired its first woman Commissionaire.

It was 1976 when Louise Gwin decided that with her children nearing self-sufficient age it was time for her to rejoin the work force she had left

25 years previously. She had been an "air force wife" for 25 years and joining the Commissionaires seemed to be a good idea.

Louise made application to join our Division on a Monday: on Tuesday she was called and told to report to the university. Her first job was as a Security Guard at an art gallery. She had no trouble doing the same job as male Commissionaires – she got "equal pay for equal work." She worked a six-day, 36-hour week and was pretty much in charge of the gallery. She wore a navy skirt with matching tunic with service ribbons denoting her two and one-half years service in the womens' division of the Royal Canadian Air Force (WDs). As she was a "first," visitors to the gallery had a little trouble trying to figure out just who and what she was. Louise said she was taken for everything from a member of St. John Ambulance to an airline pilot. Initially, even male members of the Corps were mystified. Early in her employment she was on the bus going to work when one of the Commissionaires said he was surprised to see women in the Corps. Her response was "there are and I'm it."

Louise Gwin.

Louise continued to serve in the Corps for the next ten years and after leaving the Corps enjoyed retirement life. Her lifetime partner Don, passed away in the summer of 1997.

* * * * * * *

Among the several courses conducted for our First Nations young men and women was one at the former R.C.A.F. Radar Base at Dana, (about 50 kilometres east of Saskatoon).

Occasionally some students visited the nearby town of Bruno and patronized the local restaurants and lounges. One evening five students were involved in an incident, precipitated by racist remarks made by some other lounge patrons. There was considerable damage to property and some cuts and bruises on both sides. The instructional staff held their collective breaths waiting for what might follow. They need not have worried. It turned out that the members of the other side (town bullies) were not at all popular with the citizens of the town and no charges were laid and no claim for damages was instituted. The whole matter was settled when His Worship the Mayor of Bruno declared our students involved with the fracas the "Citizens of the Year" at the Graduation banquet.

Jack Cote joined the Corps in Regina on May 14, 1986, and was employed at the RCMP Training Academy. A transfer to Saskatoon on August 30, 1987 resulted in Jack's posting to the Provincial Court House. Since October 1988, Jack has been the Exhibit Control Officer for the

Saskatoon Police Service and has been absolutely outstanding as the exhibit custodian. The significant aspect of Jack's position is that he must be scrupulous in being exact with all items controlled and documents completed. Any error controlling exhibits could result in the dismissal of a Court Case. With Jack's position, any excuse for a mistake is completely unacceptable. Jack will soon be tasked with responsibilities related to the DNA testing of evidence. The North Saskatchewan Division has its "Mr Perfect," CWO Jack Cote.

CWO Jacques (Jack) Cote.

* * * * * * *

The writer and Board members responsible were troubled over the selection of a Commissionaire to be designated our "Commissionaire Extraordinaire." While our records reflect that many are worthy of such recognition, a question always surfaced in our deliberations: What about those who were particularly deserving of consideration but who have been lost sight of in the passage of time? (And we were bound to go back 50 years.)

In the end we deemed it not inappropriate to go beyond our "uniformed" members and consider non-Commissionaire staff who have made outstanding contributions over the years. It was then not a difficult decision. Our Comptroller, Florence Hedin, was at the top of every list under any set of criteria we cared to develop.

Florence is reluctant to say much about herself. Her admission to our CEO/Commandant that "I have been here a long time" is about as far as she preferred to go. However, we do know that she trained as a Certified Nursing Assistant, and was employed in that field for several years. After completing training as a clerk/typist/accountant at a local business college she was offered an appointment as an instructor. When she came to the Division it was as an assistant to Marvin Johnson – Mr Everything. When Marvin retired she took on additional responsibilities, often acting for the Commandant in his absence. (She once substituted for him at an Annual Meeting of Commandants.) Although her "terms of reference" didn't provide for it she often acted as

Florence Hedin

a counsellor to Commissionaires. She was a willing listener and they impinged on her time at the office to the extent she worked many unpaid hours of overtime.

We are indeed fortunate to have such a dedicated staff member: we salute you, Florence, for your 25 years of outstanding service to the Division and the Corps.

The Future

As we embark on our second half-century we are proud of what has been accomplished by our Commissionaires. The dedication of the Governors, who have contributed time and talent without fee must be acknowledged. They have been led by five chairmen who have served us well; the first one for 30 years. It is appropriate to record their names in this history: Capt J.S. Woodward 1948 – 1978; W/C J. Baillie 1978 – 1981; LCdr C.F. Wentz 1981 – 1982; BGen J.A. Pringle 1982 – 1986; G/C A.A. Myers 1986 – 1996.

Under the leadership of the current chairman, LCol R.R. Buckley, we look forward to many more years of successful operation in service to the community in North Saskatchewan.

Chapter XIX

THE HISTORY OF THE NEWFOUNDLAND DIVISION

The Pitcher Plant

Commandant's Introduction – *By Brian Furlong*

THE NEWFOUNDLAND DIVISION has thrived since its inception in 1949. Given the marketplace in which it operates, and the recruiting base from which it draws, the Division has been operating close to capacity for a number of years.

As we approach our 50th anniversary of operations as a company (and we are a company), we are fully in the midst of using all of the modern business practices that should be used at the end of the millennium. As this text is being published, the Newfoundland Division will be registered under the ISO 9002 Quality Assurance Program–the Cadillac of Quality Assurance Programs. We are on the Internet. We have hired a marketing/development officer. We have established an investigations section, and continue to distinguish ourselves as the premiere security services company in the province. In 1993, the Newfoundland Division was awarded the first ever St. John's Board of Trade Business Achievement Award in the category of Customer Service and Reliability.

We have lovely new quarters overlooking the town's only public square (Churchill Square) and facing the beautiful treed region of a public golf course. We are in the midst of perhaps the best combination of commercial and residential real estate in the city of St. John's. At the risk of sounding immodest, we are very successful.

We are the first up in the morning, sometimes feeding the wild foxes that wander near our site at Cape Spear National Park, the most easterly point in North America. About three miles away, the Commissionaires (who are the second up) patrol Signal Hill National Historic Park where Marconi received the first transatlantic wireless message in 1901. The Corps may have started in England in 1859, but we were Britain's oldest colony, until we joined Confederation in 1949.

That the heritage of our traditions is often deeply rooted in the profession of arms is perhaps no more profoundly felt than in Newfoundland. Amidst the barbed wire and machine-guns of the first day of the Battle of the Somme, July 1, 1916, the Royal Newfoundland Regiment was nearly annihilated. Of the nearly 800 men who went over the top that day, only 68 answered the roll call the following morning. In Newfoundland's long history no other single event is as heart felt (or continues to be remembered as prominently) as the Battle of Beaumont Hamel. It remains the single most important testimony to remembrance in our culture. Our university is called Memorial University; our local stadium is called Memorial Stadium; a tribute to the youth of Newfoundland who died in battle.

We are a people bound together by tenacity in the face of poverty; hardship in the face of tough-luck geography; and a sense of belonging and togetherness that is found nowhere else (at least that's been the writer's experience). We are free spirited and good at everything. We are a family of salmon fishermen, moose hunters, accordion players, rum drinkers, poets, lovers, vegetable gardeners, actors, comedians, and social activists. We have the most outrageous sense of humour, and the kindest hearts of anybody in Canada.

We employ, full-time, approximately 230 Commissionaires in over 40 locations. We have a solid reputation for dependability and trust and are held in high regard by all of our customers. Our sense of togetherness and commonality are as deeply rooted today as they were when the Royal Newfoundland Regiment was all but slaughtered at Beaumont Hamel. To this day, the Board hosts the province's Premier and Lieutenant Governor at its Annual Luncheon; and our Annual Awards Ceremony is held at Government House. That we provide Commissionaires for security at the House of Assembly and at Government House is further testimony to the stature of the respect that the Corps has earned.

We are very proud to be Newfoundland and Labrador's Commissionaires and we are here to stay.

The Beginning

To the best of anyone's knowledge, the Newfoundland Division was the brainchild of Colonel G. LeB. Ross, Secretary Treasurer of the Corps. In 1949, accompanied by Colonel P.J. Philpott, Special Advisor, representing the Department of Veterans' Affairs, he visited St. John's to look into the startup of a Newfoundland Division of the Corps. They spoke with the local 'who's who' of the business and organizations community and concluded

Lieutenant Colonel G.C. Eaton, MC, CD.

that the Corps could and should have Newfoundland representation. Consequently, the first meeting of prospective governors for the Newfoundland Division was held at Government House through the kindness of the Lieutenant Governor, Colonel, the Honourable Sir Leonard Outerbridge, CBE, DSO. On that day (December 16th, 1949) Sir Leonard agreed to be the Patron, and the province's new Premier, The Honourable J.R. Smallwood had previously agreed to be Vice Patron. There is no record of exactly who attended that meeting, but Governor Cam Eaton, in a conversation that the author held with him about 10 years ago, remembered the meeting very well. He recalled being "frightened to death," because of the pre-eminent stature of the men in his company on that day. He talked about being just 26 years old and being in the company of men who were much older (some were decorated Veterans of the First World War) and were the upper crust of the St. John's Business Community. Lieutenant Colonel G. Campbell Eaton, MC, CD, was a founding Governor of the Newfoundland Division. He died as a serving Governor in 1992. He had a distinguished military career, serving overseas for the entire duration of the Second World War; earning the Military Cross in action in Italy in 1944. He went on to have a very distinguished business career and was an outstanding volunteer in many organizations. He was awarded the Order of Canada.

There were three other key players who helped shape the Division during its early days and went on to influence its progress for decades to come.

Sir Leonard Outerbridge, had a big influence in helping the Division get started. Sir Leonard's social, business, and ceremonial influences were always very prominent within Newfoundland and Labrador during his long distinguished life. He served with the Canadian Army in the First World War from 1914-1918 and was mentioned in dispatches. Sir Leonard went on to serve the Corps as Chairman from 1960-1964 and continued to serve as a Governor from 1964-1983. His heartfelt concern for the welfare of the veteran is still very evident today in the Newfoundland and Labrador Division; in the form of the Sir Leonard Outerbridge Trust Fund. In 1983 he donated a substantial sum of money which he requested be set up to help needy Commissionaires. Example: Four years ago a Commissionaire was burned out, losing every possession he had; and unfortunately had no insurance. The Trust Fund Committee wasted no time in approving a thousand dollars towards helping him get re-established.

The Division's first Chairman of the Board of Governor was Major F.W. Marshall, MBE, who was very active in the Great War Veteran's Association. Fred Marshall was Chairman from 1949 until his death on Christmas Day, 1959. He worked tirelessly during the first decade of the Division's history, never missing a meeting and personally lobbying everybody and anybody who could improve the well being of the veteran

Commissionaires. Fred Marshall personally intervened and looked after every detail when Commissionaires became bogged down in DVA bureaucracy, or if they were hospitalized. He was a caregiver extra ordinaire, helping commissionaires who were needy in any way. The virtue (at least to some extent) is perhaps best expressed in the story of Eleazor Brace. Eleazor Brace was born in Chance Cove, Trinity Bay, Newfoundland in 1895. He served in the Royal Navy from 1914-1918, and when discharged served as a policeman with the Royal Newfoundland Constabulary for over 20 years. Two of his sons served in the Second World War, one did not return. He was out of work for two years when he wrote Fred Marshall on December 19, 1949. The following verbatim excerpt is from his letter: *"I was employed at the National Convention for two years and after that I worked with the Economic Union for three months. Since that I have tried everywhere for work without success, I was told the reason I didn't get my job back at the Colonial Building was because I was not a Confederate."* Eleazor Brace was thrown out of work because he did not agree with Newfoundland's union with Canada. He could not get by on his small pension and Fred Marshall hired him as the very first Commissionaire of the Newfoundland Division. Nobody knows what Fred Marshall's political views were, but you can bet that if he was staunchly Pro Confederate he would still have hired Eleazor Brace.

"Leave me alone, I'll be allright; help others. There are many who are wounded worse than I am." It was the first day of the Battle of the Somme, July 1, 1916 and Captain Bert Dicks had gone over the top only minutes before. Now he lay wounded (in the leg) on the killing fields of the Somme. The 31-year-old officer and survivor of the Gallipoli Campaign would for the rest of his life exemplify the meaning of being his brother's keeper. Thirty-three years later, having been hand picked by Sir Leonard Outerbridge, Bert Dicks became the first Commandant of the Newfoundland Division.

Christopher Bertram Dicks, regimental number 33, Newfoundland Regiment (The word "Royal" was not prefixed to the title until after war) enlisted on September 1, 1914 and

Captain Bert Dicks.

served in the capacity of acting quartermaster. He continued to be promoted and in the process served with the British Mediterranean Expeditionary Force, enduring the disaster at Gallipoli. On May 29, 1916, he was promoted to the rank of Second Lieutenant and a few days later was wounded at Beaumont Hamel; the first day of the Battle of the Somme. He was invalided to England; and returned to the British Expeditionary Force on April 23, 1917. He was repatriated to Newfoundland on February 6, 1918 and became the Assistant Director, recruiting, for the British Army at St. John's. He became the Demobilization Officer on November 25, 1918 and retired March 31, 1919.

Bert Dicks was a handsome man and very much a gentleman. He was ever after referred to as Captain Dicks by everybody who knew him. His daughter, Elizabeth, described him as a no-nonsense businessman who very much believed in the proper conduct of every word and action in his dealings. Records show that Bert Dicks ran the Division by himself from 1950-1962. Correspondence (personnel files) shows that he personally paid attention to every detail concerning the Commissionaires. In its early days the Division perhaps did not employ very many people (there are no records to show the exact strength at any given period between 1950 and 1958). Nonetheless, it is testimony to his vigilance and hard work that he steered the Division from a day-to-day management point of view. His daughter Elizabeth told the author a fascinating story about his unselfishness and kindness. She remembers visiting him in hospital (he was hospitalized several times for his war wounds), and being told to cash his cheques (source unknown) and pay the Commissionaires because the receivables were often late coming in. It was later confirmed that he never collected back from the receivables; that the money was simply left in the coffers to assist the Corps' financial position.

By 1958, there had been approximately 100 veterans employed as Commissionaires. Amazingly, Bert Dicks carried on until 1968, and at age 85, with his health failing, he resigned his position as the first Commandant of the Division. Six years later in 1974 at the age of 91, he passed away. His "brothers keeper" legacy remains with us today.

In 1968, Bob Smith took over as Commandant. He was originally hired in 1966 to assist Bert Dicks. A veteran of the 166th Royal Artillery, Smith, although permanently scarred with his war wounds, earned himself a living as an accountant. His sister Margaret (who was later to become a key player in the management of the Corps) describes her brother: *"Bob was*

Bert Dicks
(as time progressed).

Bob Hillier.

A.G. (Tony) Ayre,
Board Chairman.

a very officious type of man, very serious. He growled a lot, but his bark was worse than his bite. He was a compassionate man who took his job very seriously." During most of Bob Smith's stewardship Bob Hillier was the Board Chairman. An interesting turn of events took place in 1977 when Bob Smith retired; he was replaced by Bob Hillier as Commandant.

An aggressive, no nonsense, "make it happen," type of man, Bob Hillier had everything to do with the Division's growth and expansion during the late '70s and early '80s. He travelled the province frequently and beat on many doors in order to get jobs for veterans. His efforts during his time as Commandant were complemented by the hard work of Lieutenant Commander A.G. (Tony) Ayre as Board Chairman. A hard working veteran of the Royal Navy, Ayre remained Chairman for the exact number of years that Hillier was Commandant, 1977-1984. Together, they doubled the strength of the Division.

All throughout the commands of both Smith and Hillier, Margaret Young took her place as a principal player in the expansion and development of the Corps. Bob Smith hired his sister in 1970 to assist with the payroll for a few weeks; she retired in 1987 after nearly 18 years of service. She had served with the CWAC from 1943-1946, and worked as a stenographer in the post-war years. She served the Division under the stewardships of five Chairmen and three Commandants in all of the functions of finance and administration. In between Commandants (two of whom died in office) she oversaw the administration of the affairs of the Division in a way which resulted in a minimum disruption of service.

Bob Hillier died suddenly in 1984 and was succeeded by Eric Harvey as Commandant. Also a veteran of the 166th Newfoundland Regiment, Eric Harvey came to the Corps as a Governor in 1978. A mild mannered, easy-going man, he was described by everybody who knew him as a real gentleman. Only two years into his office he was plagued by a series of illnesses that resulted in his death in the spring of 1987.

The Breadth and Depth of the Division

In the first 25 years of the Division's history, work for Commissionaires was confined to the St. John's area, and almost without exception was found in government contracts. The Division clung to its close ties with the RCMP, the Department of National Defence, the Department of Veteran's Affairs, and a myriad of gate keeping duties at provincial and municipal properties. Both the Division's business volume and the variety of tasks it contracted for were both expanded when Bob Hillier took over in the mid '70s. During the late '70s and early '80s the Corps began to find work for its Commissionaires in hospitals, post offices, labour strikes, and certain administrative and logistical jobs within both the public and private sectors. Despite the Division's expansion there was little or no attempt to find work in the private sector. Although the Division began to get away from purely federal government contracts, much of what was gained was in the provincial government, the municipal government and Crown Corporations area. Because of the province's long standing relationship with "uncle Ottawa," and the poverty of the province, both of which gave permanence to a handout syndrome, the Division rested on its laurels, and for a variety of reasons was not perceptive enough to realize the importance of sales, marketing and growth, particularly in the private sector. That being said, the Division bonded extremely well with all of the departments and agencies at all government levels where it provided services. The Division has cultivated a reputation for dependability and trust that is second to none. Given its restricted mandate and recruiting base from which it has to draw, coupled with a narrowly-based marketplace, and its reasonable expectations of market share, the Newfoundland Division has done very well. In 1991, it peaked with over 300 full time jobs. The Division continues to hold on to traditional jobs. In some instances however, it has strayed from the traditional "gate keeping" role into areas that are interesting and challenging. Within the last few years, the Division has provided security at several McDonald's restaurants in the St. John's area; enabling it to test and challenge its resolution abilities in dealing with youth. Another example is the provision of the monitoring of offenders' daily routine at correctional centers set up by the Correctional Services of Canada. Not to be dismissed is our role in providing support to activities that focus on our culture and tradition. The Corps is increasingly getting work providing security for folk festivals and concerts. A good example of this is the provision of security services for the ship, *The Matthew*, which toured the island in celebration of the 500th anniversary of John Cabot's discovery of Newfoundland.

For the first time ever, the Division has hired a Marketing/ Development Officer to enable it to aggressively compete in the marketplace and broaden its scope of work opportunities.

The Last Decade

The Division now administers its activities from space that is in stark contrast to the quarters that Bert Dicks had in the '50s. The Division originally had some space at what was known as Buckmaster's Field, which was an administrative and logistical support area for military training. The headquarters moved in the '60s to the Marshall building on Water Street. Rental cost increases sent the Headquarters to new facilities in the '70s in Pleasantville. This used to be Fort Pepperel, established by the American Forces in 1941 as an airbase as a defensive measure against enemy action. In 1942, at the expense of the American government, and employing thousands of Newfoundlanders, its construction and occupation was the biggest boost that the economy of St. John's (and Newfoundland) ever had. In the mid-'80s, because of Divisional growth and the requirement to expand the headquarter staff, the Division moved closer to its present location, into the Prudential Building on the east end of Elizabeth Avenue. It is a statement of the obvious that the province is closely tied to deeply rooted British traditions. This has been an incredible influence in the growth of organizations, and the social and geographic nomenclatures found within Canadian society. That the Division's previous location was on Elizabeth Avenue (named after her Majesty), and then moved about 600 yards away to a building on Churchill Square (Winston) provides ample testimony to the strength of our traditions within Great Britain.

In 1986, Squadron Leader Lamont (Lal) M. Parsons became the Division's Chairman. Throughout the period of Eric Harvey's illness (and death) Parsons had his hands full attending to the routine housekeeping issues of the Division. His biggest challenge was finding a Commandant to succeed Eric Harvey. The winds of change were blowing very strong indeed during this period (late '80s). Nationally, the Corps was taking stock of what it considered to be a somewhat precarious position. The veterans were aging. There was concern about the downsizing of the Canadian Forces and the consequential impact on recruiting. There was a lot of talk about the loss of the "right of first refusal" with the federal government. Other challenges came in the form of technology and marketplace competition. Locally, the old guard at the Division Headquarters was all but gone. After nearly two decades of service the ever-present Margaret Young decided to retire and was replaced by 28-year-old Anastasia Gibbons. This was a first sign that the management of the Corps was being tempered by a somewhat youthful influence. Gibbons had served as a technician in the Air Force and had worked as a Commissionaire in the field before joining the Headquarters staff in 1986. She remains there today as the Division's Comptroller and Office Manager. The reality of the challenges that all of these changes brought about was not lost on the Chairman. In consultation with the Executive Committee of the Board, Parsons decided that it would be in the Division's best interests to find a younger Chief Executive Officer to steer the Division towards the 21st century. In August of 1987, the Board hired Brian Furlong as Commandant; the fifth Commandant to command the Division. The next four years saw a lot of dramatic changes under the stewardship of Chairman Parsons and Commandant Furlong.

Squadron Leader Lamont (Lal) M. Parsons.

Squadron Leader Lal Parsons was a fighter pilot throughout the Second World War. A pillar of the community, having held high profile positions in several volunteer organizations, he went on to become a very successful businessman. He joined the Board in the mid-'70s and remains on the Executive Committee to this day. A kind and unassuming man, with impeccable manners that distinguish him as a real gentleman and a "class act," Parsons' strong sense of commitment to duty has made (and continues to make) a significant contribution to the business success of the Newfoundland Division.

Brian Furlong started his term of office implementing changes to the Headquarters infrastructure. He introduced computers, a new administration system, new communication tools, new orders of dress, new regulations, and overall a new sense of meaning. All of this brought the Division in line with the other 17 Divisions across Canada. In short order both Parsons and Furlong took up positions on National Canadian Corps of Commissionaires Committees concerned with marketing. This image gave the Newfoundland Division a higher profile on the national stage.

Today the Division is doing all it can from a purely astute business perspective to ensure that it carries on well into the 21st century. It has in place an outstanding system of quality control and communications that everybody has brought into. Although the Division's Operational Team has subscribed to the modern management styles of the 1990s; the traditional military system founded on discipline and obedience has not been lost. The Newfoundland Division was the first in the country, two years ago, to branch out into the area of insurance investigations and now has a full time Investigation Services Officer on staff. In 1990 Lal Parsons finished his chairmanship and was succeeded by Brigadier General Gordon C. Barnes. Barnes had a lifelong career with the militia, virtually all of it served with the Royal Newfoundland Regiment. He was the first Newfoundlander to command the Atlantic Region Reserves. A university teacher with a keen mind, Barnes took the torch from Lal Parsons and continued running with it in all the right directions. He continues to serve today as a member of the Newfoundland Division's Board Executive and as a member of the National Executive as one of the Atlantic Region Representatives. In 1994, he was succeeded by Lieutenant Colonel Harry G. Bown. A youthful chairman who is still raising his young sons, Bown fully supports the astute business practices that mark the Division's progress. He remains the Chairman as of the writing of this text.

Brigadier General Gordon C. Barnes.

The Men and Women in the Field

With the exception of a handful of the wisest converts, the Newfoundland Division consists of homegrown men and women. The ratio of men to women is still very excessive, but our few ladies do stand out for the quality persons that they are. Darlene St. George works for Revenue Canada and has been an employee of the Corps for a number of years. A few years back, before his death, she supervised her father Jack, a Korean War Veteran.

Newfoundlanders, while they are a transient lot, are perhaps noted for their homecomings more than any other provincial people. They eventually come home because of family ties, and are extremely tightly knit. This is perhaps to some extent rooted in our geography. We remain Canada's poorest province, and nothing generates a helping hand faster than being less fortunate while in the same boat with so many others. There is an out-stretched hand syndrome that permeates every place where Newfoundland Commissionaires serve. The natural extension of this characteristic is found in the Commissionaires care for all they come in contact with.

Darlene St. George, with her father Jack.

The following story titled "Deer Lake Airport Workers Display Newfoundland Hospitality" appeared in the *Humber Log*, the local newspaper of Corner Brook, Newfoundland.

> *DEER LAKE - When Andre Escaravage arrived at Deer Lake on the morning of December 25, 1987, he had no idea of the wonderful gift that awaited inside from total strangers.*
>
> *He had arrived early from Norris Point, attempting to avoid potential delays as a result of heavy snow along the Viking Trail, on his way home to Halifax.*
>
> *Dragging in his luggage, he felt tired and somewhat depressed having to travel during the Festive Season. Shortly afterwards, two officials from the Canadian Corps of Commissionaires, Corporal Ralph Rideout and Corporal Anne Gosse, approached him and asked him in the course of their conversation if he had had anything to eat.*
>
> *"No," he replied, and immediately attempted, unsuccessfully, to try and call local establishments to see if anyone in Deer Lake was opened on Christmas Day.*
>
> *As he sat down, wondering what he was going to do next, the two corporals came back with coffee and a small meal for him, which he*

later found out, came from their own lunches they had brought from home.

They sat with him for awhile as he ate and Escaravage was doubly appreciative; for the food and the company.

Later on, at about noon, Escaravage once again began to feel hungry and to his amazement, he was brought a complete hot turkey dinner in the terminal by the two corporals and their commanding officer, Sgt. Kevin LeRoux.

Apparently, LeRoux had gone to his home in Deer Lake and brought the dinner back with him. And not only did he bring turkey, but salt beef and rabbit too.

Escaravage offered money to the three, but they refused payment. He then realized that "it was a gift from them to a complete stranger."

In a letter to the airport manager, Escaravage said, "I cannot properly express the impact on me of that kind, thoughtful gesture. It restored my faith in humanity, and certainly personified what we once knew as Newfoundland hospitality, and the spirit of giving at Christmas."

"I must compliment Transport Canada on the calibre of these three employees and commend their professionalism, dedication and ability to deal with the general public. The fact that these three Newfoundlanders are employed at Deer Lake airport says a lot for Transport Canada.

I recently wrote in a Montreal newspaper on "The Real Christmas Spirit" and said, in part, that "Christmas is the personification of love. And love finds expression in giving, not material things, but the gift of yourself...Let that warmth spread to others in our community this Christmas."

Little did I know then that I would live to experience an example of this at Deer Lake airport, Newfoundland, on December 25, 1987."

Rideout, Gosse and LeRoux did nothing unusual; this story is told only to point out that anybody who has Christmas Dinner without rabbit and salt beef is a pagan.

There are no heroes, at least not in the romantic sense, that we know of, but there are lifesavers.

On November 21, 1990, at Deer Lake Airport in western Newfoundland, Mrs. Lilian Murrin began to show signs of weakness and distress. This progressed to a change in colour, sudden perspiration and the inability to breathe. By this time she had drawn a crowd and many people were doing all they could to try and make her comfortable. Her husband suddenly panicked and shouted, *"Please help, my wife is dying."* The shout was not lost on Commissionaire Corporal Tony Gillard who immediately ran to the scene. After quick examination he opened the

Commissionaire Corporal Tony Gillard.

Commissionaires Billard and Connolly.

woman's mouth to discover she was choking on her own tongue. He dislodged her tongue, immediately began to perform CPR and the end result was that he saved her life. Mrs. Murrin did in fact suffer a heat attack combined with a stroke but survived due to the training, quick thinking and competent actions of Tony Gillard.

On the of December 18, 1994, at Goose Bay Airport, Corporal Serge Thompson rushed to the side of Mr. Albert Bruce who had collapsed on the terminal floor. Unaided, he quickly put all of his First Aid Training to work; performing CPR on Mr. Bruce and continuing his life-saving

Corporal Serge Thompson.

activities until the ambulance arrived. Hospital authorities later recognized that had Corporal Thompson not acted as he did, Mr. Bruce certainly would have died. In February of 1995 Corporal Serge Thompson was invested with the order of the St. John's Ambulance Meritory Certificate by the Lieutenant Governor. The actions of both Gillard and Thompson are testimony to the value of sound training and quick thinking initiative that permeates the "uniformed way of life" of the Commissionaires. The Division is well suited to opportunities that are indeed somewhat different from the rest of Canada. The Commissionaires at Gander International Airport, over the last seven or eight years have had to deal with a lot of political refugees seeking asylum when they land here from Eastern European countries. The Commissionaires working at the Marine Atlantic Ferry Terminal at Port Aux Basques have staked out a reputation for courtesy and helpfulness that is legendary. The following story from a family of tourists illustrates very well the splendid professionalism and kindness of the Port Aux Basques crew in their letter to the Associate Terminal Manager.

Mr. Rod Keeping
Associate Terminal Manager
Marine Atlantic
P.O. Box 520
Port Aux Basques, NF
A0M 1C0

Dear Mr. Keeping:

In July of this year my family and I visited Newfoundland during our vacation. I would like to share with you an experience we encountered and ask you to share our thoughts with Mr. Billard and Mr. Connolly.

After we arrived at the Ferry Terminal in Port Aux Basques (departing to Nova Scotia) we went to the children's playground. Shortly after arriving there my three year old son fell from the top of the slide and hurt himself. Within seconds Mr. Billard and Mr. Connolly arrived to see if we needed help. My son passed out and we became very nervous. Mr. Billard immediately aided us into his vehicle and rushed us to the local hospital. Meanwhile Mr. Connolly cared for my mother, daughter, and niece who remained behind. My wife and I were both very nervous and Mr. Billard continued to reassure us and try to comfort our now crying son.

We are sharing this with you because we feel that the actions of Blandford and Leo as we soon came to know them, were over and above what their job required of them. Their caring manner and attitude towards us helped ease our minds and comfort us in the time when we were waiting to find out if our son was seriously injured or not. I am very happy to say that everything turned out fine and our son had only suffered a bruised stomach. Nonetheless we feel that Blandford and Leo should be commended on their behaviour and attitude towards total strangers.

To give examples of how these gentlemen cared for us is easy and I would like to mention some of them. After arriving at the hospital Blandford tried to calm my son and my wife who was becoming very panicked. He went to several stores to find my son's favourite ice cream in hope it may calm him down. He stayed with us until the doctor arrived and even then remained to see if everything would be OK. After learning that we would have to stay an additional night in Newfoundland, Blandford arranged to have our Ferry reservations changed and since we had nowhere to stay he contacted and made reservations at a local hotel for us. Before leaving his shift that evening Blandford again contacted us to see if our son was feeling any better. The next day we again saw Blandford when we got to the terminal and his obvious care for us was reassured.

Whilst Blandford helped my wife and I, Leo was trying to take the worry away from our mother and the two remaining children. He stayed with them and asked them questions to try to occupy their thoughts. When we returned my nine-year-old was very excited to tell us the stories and questions Leo had been asking. She was smiling and obviously comforted to have Leo around.

My family and I would greatly appreciate it if you would pass on our deepest appreciation to Blandford and Leo and also ask that you copy them on this letter. Having lived in the BIG CITY for many years it was extremely nice to see such unsolicited help from a total stranger. It gives one faith in humanity to know that such caring people as Blandford and Leo exist and it gives us pleasure to have been able to meet them.

Yours Truly:
Dorothy and Kevin Kendall, Trevor, Stephanie
Marie and Brigit Aquilina.

We have an incredibly good record for consistency on our work sites and many Commissionaires have served the same customers for ten years or longer.

The Division works hard at being who they are as Commissionaires. The Newfoundland Division has staked out its local image both inwardly and publicly. Two years ago a welfare committee was formed to help Commissionaires who occasionally may be "up against it" financially. This was started by Commissionaires and continues to be run by them; their fundraising and administration is strictly internal and continues to thrive without management influence. Two years ago an honour guard was formed to participate in the five or six major annual parades that take place in St. John's to honour the province's war dead. Cohesiveness, and the voluntary sense of unity, are trademarks of the Newfoundland tradition, and it lives on to this very day.

Besides working hard and projecting its professional pride, the Division remains a source of men and women who have a good understanding of each other, work well together, and love a good time. In 1964, a new detachment was created to serve the security needs of the Bavarian Brewery. The Division's enthusiasm for work in such a site resulted in over 200 commissionaires volunteering for the new place of work.

We regret (due to space and length of text) that we cannot do more kudos and forgive our errors of omission. Having said that; and strictly according to the current HQ staff, the following Governor and Commissionaires deserve special mention.

Governor Herb Morgan, Cyril Ryan (deceased), Austin Murphy (deceased), Charlie Noseworthy (deceased), Bill Follett, Chuck Hapgood, George King, Leo Stamp, Carl Park, Doug Parmiter, Ed James, Mike Walsh, Jim King and George Wheeler.

Final Word

The Newfoundland Division has established standards of excellence that are second to none. Its management structure, human resources practices, and strategies, marketing and sales initiatives, and its training and quality control, make it the leading, and best security services company in the province of Newfoundland. The operational and human resources management successes that the Division enjoy are due in large part to the exemplary commitment to duty shown by the Operations Officer, Tom Dodd, and the Divisions Sergeant Major, Tom Barrington; both 20-plus years career soldiers who have worked (and continue to work) tirelessly to ensure good welfare, outstanding career management, and excellent service. A willing partner and great supporter of its Member Divisions across the country, the Newfoundland Division remains a full time active member of the Canadian Corps of Commissionaires. In 1976, the Newfoundland Division hosted the Annual General Meeting. In 1999, the 50th anniversary of the Newfoundland Division and the 50th anniversary of Confederation with Canada, the Division will once again host the Annual General Meeting.

Steeped in history and tradition we are all very proud of the Newfoundland Division of the Canadian Corps of Commissionaires.

Cpl Dave Moore saluting Her Majesty at Bonavista, 500 years to the day John Cabot discovered Newfoundland.

Chapter XX

A Vision For The Future – *By Rene Gutknecht and Clive Addy*

WILL THE CORPS cease to exist when all the war veterans have retired, as was advocated many years ago, or will it continue to evolve and thrive into the new Millennium?

There was a time when the belief was held by some that, since the Corps had been founded for the purpose of helping returning war veterans to reintegrate into the work place and provide them with worthwhile employment, it should cease operation when there were no longer any of these individuals to be helped. Although this notion is still heard occasionally, the governors decided some years ago and reconfirmed more recently, that the Corps should continue to exist after this milestone is reached. Their conclusion was based on a number of considerations. Foremost, probably, was the opinion that society and the Corps owe a debt to those who serve their country in time of relative peace, particularly to the growing number of men and women who, as United Nations Peacekeepers, continue to face difficult or dangerous circumstances. The Governors also believed that, having to leave the forces early as a result of force reduction programs or to retire at a comparatively early age, these individuals deserve assistance similar to that given to their war veteran compatriots. It is believed that the Corps has a moral obligation to help servicemen and servicewomen to make the transition to civilian life. Not without significant impact, was the fact that the governors realized that Corps members were providing an array of worthwhile quality services to governments and private industry. Thus, the desire for the continued existence of the Corps was confirmed for the foreseeable future.

Nevertheless, this conclusion in itself is no guarantee of the extension into the future of the Corps.

The Corps now faces a number of internal and external challenges with which it will have to contend, if it is to exist as it has and still successfully accomplish its mission.

The mandate of the Corps has remained to help our compatriots who have served the country to find worthwhile and rewarding employment. Any fundamental change to this objective would alter the entire concept of the Corps. Nevertheless, certain aspects of the Corps mission are likely to evolve in the coming years.

There is a growing realization that the mission of the Corps must be expressed in terms more meaningful to clients and potential customers to assist in marketing Commissionaires' services.

The more difficult part of the mission to address is a question which might sound simple but is both complex and divisive: who is the Corps dedicated to help? Initially, the answer was simple, it was military veterans returning from the wars. Gradually, however, over the years, other eligible categories were added: allied veterans, former members of the Royal Canadian Mounted Police, merchant seamen, and reservists. Although the Governors recently refused to accept the Canadian citizens who had served in the United States forces during the Vietnam war, other changes were agreed without much controversy. An important step gaining acceptance within the Corps would include, as eligible for membership, individuals who have served as former police officers, coast guard members and correction officers.

This idea is rationalized on the same grounds of moral obligation in respect of service to society, but it probably has as much to do with the demands of the marketplace. Divisions are occasionally placed in the position of missing contract opportunities (employing only eligible members) because they lack the numbers or because of the demand from customers for special skills or requirements which are not available within the Corps. There is thus the pressure to broaden the eligibility criteria and provide more membership flexibility. Although steps have been taken and guidelines drawn to provide such flexibility in special circumstances, a consensus on these proposals to broaden membership eligibility must be developed in the future. The matter is complicated further by the legal implications such changes would have on the special status the corps enjoys with the federal government and upon the letters patent of certain Divisions.

The future will present challenges to the status of the Corps which will need to be addressed. Since 1945, the Corps has had a privileged position of being the security and security-related provider of choice to the federal government. This was first granted to assist the Corps in its work of helping war veterans. Over the years, this privileged situation has been challenged by commercial competitors and reviewed and maintained by the government. Its defence has been successful but it may be only a matter of time before this special consideration is lost. In such an event, the Corps will retain a good part of its federal employment because of the high quality of the services it provides to various departments. However, comprehensive contingencies will have to be developed to cater to this potential change.

Since its foundation in Canada, and in accordance with its original letters patent, the Corps has operated as a not-for-profit organization. Because the Corps operates in a business environment, this status has been occasionally called into question and could be challenged. Whether challenged or not, the Corps will examine the administrative advantages and disadvantages of such a status in order to determine our best future corporate posture. This status does limit the ability of some Divisions to bid on certain contracts or advise within their provinces. It should be noted that the United Kingdom counterpart of the Corps operates entirely as a commercial corporation.

Given the mandate and status of the Corps, a re-examination of its market niche is also likely to result in a number of changes. From its inception, physical security and related work has been the mainstay of Corps business. In the meantime, the security field has been evolving from a manpower intensive activity to a technologically oriented endeavour. The human being is being replaced by the magnetic card and the electronic surveillance camera. The Corps will have to contend with these changes and seek more and different opportunities to provide a broader spectrum of Commissionaire services. This evolution will be encouraged by the newer members of the Corps who possess more marketable skills and experience than their predecessors and who will demand more challenging and rewarding work.

A subject, which has caused many discussions and much ink to flow, has been the structure of the Corps. These discussions often and quaintly parallel the national debate between levels of government.

The present Corps grew from individual independent "Member Corps" which, under pressure from the federal government and business considerations, came together in the mid-seventies as a loose federation under the authority of a National Board of Governors. This management structure, a policy-making body, autonomously managing individual Corps or Divisions with minimal coordination from national office, worked well for many years. It permitted effective negotiations with the federal government and allowed the greatest flexibility for Divisions to operate within their local circumstances. The flaw in this structure was that it allowed the development of different standards and policies and made any national initiatives next to impossible in such fields as marketing, contracting, advertising, setting uniform standards, human resources management and quality assurance. The recent past has brought some recognition of these shortcomings and some agreement that something should be done.

At the time of writing, a number of promising ideas are being examined and forged into a management structure which will reflect our mission and status, and will produce a Corps capable of facing the business challenges of the twenty-first century.

If the original five gentlemen from Montreal had been asked to predict what their idea to form a Corps of Commissionaires in Canada would become 70-plus years later, it is doubtful they would have even come close to what we have at present. They would be pleased to see that the high ideals of service to others and the values of loyalty, honesty and devotion to duty upon which the Corps was founded, are still the cornerstones of the Corps' success.

Since predicting the future is a highly imperfect undertaking, it would be foolhardy to forecast the evolution of the Corps in the years to come. However, history, the leadership of its Governors and Commandants, the work of the staffs and the abilities of all Commissionaires auger well for continued success and even greater achievement. To the future! To the Corps!

Epilogue

Tom Bauld.

It is my great pleasure as the National Chairman of the Canadian Corps of Commissionaires to write this epilogue for our history.

Over the years, the Corps has attempted to record our past. This has now been done due to the collective efforts of the editor, staff at National Headquarters and all 18 divisions.

We soon learned that our historical records were not complete in many areas and that makes the finished product even more precious. Those who are serving today owe a great deal to those who have gone before. The 18 chapters on the Divisions all attest to the determination of the original Governors and the devotion to duty of the early Commissionaires. Those who kept the faith and made the Corps prosper are the true reason for our success.

The stories contained in this history truly reflect the zeal, which Commissionaires have always exhibited. Changes in Canadian society and in the work place have not daunted our Corps.

My personal gratitude to all those who worked so hard to record our long and eventful past. My personal thanks to our Patron, His Excellency Governor General Romeo Leblanc for his thoughtful FOREWORD. Finally, a thank you to John Gardam for putting a professional polish to our Corps history. My personal thanks to Fred Mifflin for agreeing to place the After Word in the Book. Without the help of Veterans Affairs, it is doubtful that the Corps would be "sea to sea."

People from all across Canada will now realize, most for the first time, what makes the Canadian Corps of Commissionaires such a unique provider of services. Our dedication in the business world is recognized and admired. Every woman and man who wears the uniform of the Corps has earned this well-deserved credit.

To all those serving now and to those who will serve in the future – you now know where we came from and it is you who will take the Corps into the next millennium. "Carry on the Corps."

After Word

by

THE HONOURABLE FRED MIFFLIN, CD
MINISTER OF VETERANS AFFAIRS

I am honoured to have been included in *"The Commissionaires."* The history included the many ways in which the Department of Veterans Affairs assisted in the formation of the Corps. Many departmental officials accepted double duty to enable the various Divisions to get started. Help was provided with the original formation of the Board of Governors in many cities.

Veterans Affairs Canada still provides help to Commissionaires when the traditional aid to veterans is required. John Gardam has provided a real sense of history to the Corps. At the Perley and Rideau Veterans Health Centre here in Ottawa, provision of care to more than a few veterans who have also served as Commissionaires is done in a world class facility.

My personal connections with the Corps have spanned my years as a post-war sailor plus I see the many Commissionaires, many of them shipmates from a few years ago, who serve today in airports, federal and provincial buildings. The Corps deserves a **Naval BRAVO ZULU** for a job well done.

The Honourable Fred Mifflin, CD.

The Last Word

by
JOHN GARDAM

THE COMMISSIONAIRES has not been an easy book to compile and get published, but despite difficulties we have succeeded in just 18 months.

The 18 divisions, members of the Headquarters staff and the publisher, General Store Publishing House, have all cooperated in a splendid fashion. The Chairman and Past Chairman have been most supportive as have the Executive Secretaries, past and present.

My very special thanks go to Commissionaire Fred Herman who worked tirelessly for over two months transposing everything into a "publisher ready" format; Craig McCarthy who assisted Fred in the intricate format details, and Sean Heatley has worked with me from the beginning. Fred also produced Brian Reid's handsome insert on the Corps' medals and cap badges assisted by photographer David Willard. Also, special thanks go to Solange Fortin, the translator, and all who helped to produce the French issue of the book. John Saunders was my link from home to Corps Headquarters. Dale Schott and Gilles Charest gave me advice when requested.

In all aspects it was a joint effort.

To order more copies of

The Commissionaires
An Organization with a Proud History

send $29.95 plus $5.05
to cover GST, shipping and handling to:

GENERAL STORE PUBLISHING HOUSE
1 Main Street, Burnstown, Ontario
K0J 1G0

Telephone 1-800-465-6072
or Fax 613-432-7184

VISA and MASTERCARD accepted